AN EXEGETICAL SUMMARY OF
1 & 2 THESSALONIANS

AN EXEGETICAL SUMMARY OF
1 & 2 THESSALONIANS

Second Edition

Richard C. Blight

SIL International

Second Edition
© 1989, 2008 by SIL International

Library of Congress Catalog Card Number: 2008923526
ISBN: 978-155671-200-5

Printed in the United States of America

All Rights Reserved
No part of this publication may be reproduced, stored in a retrieval system, or transmitted in any form or by any means without the express permission of SIL International. However, brief excerpts, generally understood to be within the limits of fair use, may be quoted without written permission.

Copies of this and other publications
of SIL International may be obtained from

International Academic Bookstore
SIL International
7500 West Camp Wisdom Road
Dallas, TX 75236-5699, USA

Voice: 972-708-7404
Fax: 972-708-7363
academic_books@sil.org
www.ethnologue.com

PREFACE

Exegesis is concerned with the interpretation of a text. Exegesis of the New Testament involves determining the meaning of the Greek text. Translators must be especially careful and thorough in their exegesis of the New Testament in order to accurately communicate its message in the vocabulary, grammar, and literary devices of another language. Questions occurring to translators as they study the Greek text are answered by summarizing how scholars have interpreted the text. This is information that should be considered by translators as they make their own exegetical decisions regarding the message they will communicate in their translations.

The Semi-Literal Translation

As a basis for discussion, a semi-literal translation of the Greek text is given so that the reasons for different interpretations can best be seen. When one Greek word is translated into English by several words, these words are joined by hyphens. There are a few times when clarity requires that a string of words joined by hyphens have a separate word, such as 'not' (μή) inserted in their midst. In this case, the separate word is surrounded by spaces between the hyphens. When alternate translations of a Greek word are given, these are separated by slashes.

The Text

Variations in the Greek text are noted under the heading TEXT. The base text for the summary is the text of the fourth revised edition of *The Greek New Testament,* published by the United Bible Societies, which has the same text as the twenty-sixth edition of the *Novum Testamentum Graece* (Nestle-Aland). The versions that follow different variations are listed without evaluating their choices.

The Lexicon

The meaning of a key word in context is the first question to be answered. Words marked with a raised letter in the semi-literal translation are treated separately under the heading LEXICON. First, the lexicon form of the Greek word is given. Within the parentheses following the Greek word is the location number where, in the author's judgment, this word is defined in the *Greek-English Lexicon of the New Testament Based on Semantic Domains* (Louw and Nida 1988). When a semantic domain includes a translation of the particular verse being treated, **LN** in bold type indicates that specific translation. If the specific reference for the verse is listed in *A Greek-English Lexicon of the New Testament and Other Early Christian Literature* (Bauer, Arndt, Gingrich, and Danker 1979), the outline location and page number is given. Then English equivalents of the Greek word are given to show how it is translated by commentators who offer their own translations of the whole text and, after a semicolon, all the versions in the list of abbreviations for translations. When reference is made to "all versions," it refers to only the versions in the list of translations. Sometimes further comments are made about the meaning of the word or the significance of a verb's tense, voice, or mood.

The Questions

Under the heading QUESTION, a question is asked that comes from examining the Greek text under consideration. Typical questions concern the identity of an implied actor or object of an event word, the antecedent of a pronominal reference, the connection indicated by a relational word, the meaning of a genitive construction, the meaning of figurative language, the function of a rhetorical question, the identification of an ambiguity, and the presence of implied information that is needed to understand the passage correctly. Background information is also considered for a proper understanding of a passage. Although not all implied information and background information is made explicit in a translation, it is important to consider it so that the translation will not be stated in such a way that prevents a reader from arriving at the proper interpretation. The question is answered with a summary of what commentators have said. If there are contrasting differences of opinion, the different interpretations are numbered and the commentaries that support each are listed. Differences that are not treated by many of the commentaries often are not numbered, but are introduced with a contrastive 'Or' at the beginning of the sentence. No attempt has been made to select which interpretation is best.

In listing support for various statements of interpretation, the author is often faced with the difficult task of matching the different terminologies used in commentaries with the terminology he has adopted. Sometimes he can only infer the position of a commentary from incidental remarks. This book, then, includes the author's interpretation of the views taken in the various commentaries. General statements are followed by specific statements, which indicate the author's understanding of the pertinent relationships, actors, events, and objects implied by that interpretation.

The Use of This Book

This book does not replace the commentaries that it summarizes. Commentaries contain much more information about the meaning of words and passages. They often contain arguments for the interpretations that are taken and they may have important discussions about the discourse features of the text. In addition, they have information about the historical, geographical, and cultural setting. Translators will want to refer to at least four commentaries as they exegete a passage. However, since no one commentary contains all the answers translators need, this book will be a valuable supplement. It makes more sources of exegetical help available than most translators have access to. Even if they had all the books available, few would have the time to search through all of them for the answers.

When many commentaries are studied, it soon becomes apparent that they frequently disagree in their interpretations. That is the reason why so many answers in this book are divided into two or more interpretations. The reader's initial reaction may be that all of these different interpretations complicate exegesis rather than help it. However, before translating a passage, a translator needs to know exactly where there is a problem of interpretation and what the exegetical options are.

Acknowledgments

This volume has been thoroughly reviewed by Robert E. Smith. He has studied the questions and answers and has made a significant contribution in determining their final forms. Dr. John R. Werner has also given valuable suggestions concerning the contents. Faith Blight edited and improved this book.

ABBREVIATIONS

COMMENTARIES AND REFERENCE BOOKS

Alf   Alford, Henry. *The Greek New Testament*, vol. 3. Reprint of 1857 edition with revision by E. F. Harrison. Chicago: Moody Press, 1968.

BAGD   Bauer, Walter. *A Greek-English Lexicon of the New Testament and Other Early Christian Literature*, translated and adapted from the 5th ed., 1958 by William F. Arndt and F. Wilbur Gingrich, 2d English ed. revised and augmented by F. Wilbur Gingrich and Frederick W. Danker. Chicago: University of Chicago Press, 1979.

Bul   Bullinger, E. W. *Figures of Speech Used in the Bible*. Reprint of 1898 edition. Grand Rapids: Baker, 1968.

Ea   Eadie, John. *Commentary on the Greek Text of the Epistles of Paul to the Thessalonians*. The John Eadie Greek Text Commentaries, vol. 5. Reprint of 1877 edition. Grand Rapids: Baker, 1979.

EBC   Thomas, Robert L. "1, 2 Thessalonians," in *The Expositor's Bible Commentary*, vol. 11. Grand Rapids: Zondervan, 1978.

EGT   Moffatt, James. *The First and Second Epistles to the Thessalonians*. The Expositor's Greek Testament. Reprint. Grand Rapids: Eerdmans, 1980.

El   Ellicott, Charles J. *St. Paul's Epistles to the Thessalonians*. London: Longman, Green, Longman, Roberts and Green, 1866.

Er   Erdman, Charles R. *The Epistles of Paul to the Thessalonians*. Philadelphia: Westminster Press, 1935.

Fn   Findlay, G. G. *The Epistles of Paul the Apostle to the Thessalonians*. Reprint of 1904 edition. Grand Rapids: Baker, 1982.

Hb   Hiebert, D. Edmond. *The Thessalonian Epistles*. Chicago: Moody Press. 1971.

Hn   Hendriksen, William. *Exposition of I and II Thessalonians*. New Testament Commentary. Grand Rapids: Baker, 1955.

HNTC   Best, Ernest. *A Commentary on the First and Second Epistles to the Thessalonians*. Harper's New Testament Commentary. San Francisco: Harper & Row, 1972.

ICC   Frame, James Everett. *A Critical and Exegetical Commentary on the Epistles of St. Paul to the Thessalonians*. The International Critical Commentary. Edinburgh: Clark, 1912.

LN   Louw, Johannes P. and Eugene A. Nida. *Greek-English Lexicon of the New Testament Based on Semantic Domains*. New York: United Bible Societies, 1988.

Lns   Lenski, R. C. H. *The Interpretation of St. Paul's Epistles to the Colossians, to the Thessalonians, to Timothy, to Titus and to Philemon*. Minneapolis: Augsburg, 1946.

Mn	Milligan, George. *St. Paul's Epistles to the Thessalonians*. Reprint of 1908 edition. Grand Rapids: Eerdmans, 1953.
Mou	Moule, C. F. D. *An Idiom Book of New Testament Greek*, 2d. ed. Cambridge: Cambridge University Press, 1959.
My	Lünemann, Gottlieb. *Critical and Exegetical Hand-Book to the Epistle to the Thessalonians*. Meyer's Commentary on the New Testament. New York: Funk & Wagnalls, 1885.
NCBC	Marshall, I. Howard. *1 and 2 Thessalonians*. New Century Bible Commentary. Grand Rapids: Eerdmans, 1983.
NIC	Morris, Leon. *The First and Second Epistles to the Thessalonians*. The New International Commentary on the New Testament. Grand Rapids: Eerdmans, 1959.
Rb	Robertson, Archibald Thomas. *The Epistles of Paul*. Word Pictures in the New Testament, vol. 4. Nashville: Broadman Press, 1931.
SSA	Callow, John. *A Semantic Structure Analysis of Second Thessalonians*. Dallas: Summer Institute of Linguistics, 1982.
TH	Ellingworth, Paul and Eugene A. Nida. *A Translator's Handbook on Paul's Letters to the Thessalonians*. New York: United Bible Societies, 1976.
WBC	Bruce, F. F. *1 and 2 Thessalonians*. Word Biblical Commentary, vol. 45. Waco, Texas: Word, 1982.
Wd	Ward, Ronald A. *Commentary on 1 & 2 Thessalonians*. Waco, Texas: Word, 1973.

GREEK TEXT AND TRANSLATIONS

GNT	Aland, Kurt, Matthew Black, Carlos Martini, Bruce Metzger, and Allen Wikgren. *The Greek New Testament*. 3d ed. (corrected). London, New York: United Bible Societies, 1983.
KJV	*The Holy Bible*. Authorized (or King James) Version. 1611.
NAB	*The New American Bible*. Camden, New Jersey: Thomas Nelson, 1971.
NASB	*The New American Standard Bible*. Nashville, Tennessee: Holman, 1977.
NEB	*The New English Bible*. 2d ed. (corrected) 1972. New York: Oxford University Press, 1970.
NIV	*The Holy Bible: New International Version*. Grand Rapids: Zondervan, 1978.
NJB	*The New Jerusalem Bible*. Garden City, New York: Doubleday, 1985.
RSV	*The Bible: Revised Standard Version*. 2d ed. New York: American Bible Society, 1971.
TEV	*Holy Bible: Today's English Version*. New York: American Bible Society, 1976.
TNT	*The Translator's New Testament*. London: British and Foreign Bible Society, 1973.

GRAMMATICAL TERMS

act.	active
fut.	future
impera.	imperative
indic.	indicative
infin.	infinitive
mid.	middle
opt.	optative
pass.	passive
perf.	perfect
pres.	present
subj.	subjunctive

EXEGETICAL SUMMARY OF 1 THESSALONIANS

DISCOURSE UNIT: 1:1 [Alf, EBC, EGT, Er, Fn, GNT, Hb, Hn, HNTC, ICC, Mn, My, NCBC, NIC, TH, WBC, Wd; NAB, NIV, NJB, TEV]. The formula, 'A to B: greetings', was the usual Greek way of beginning a letter [EBC, Er, Hb, Hn, HNTC, ICC, NCBC, NIC, TH, WBC]. The writer first identifies himself in the nominative case, then he identifies the recipients in the dative case, and gives them a word of greeting [ICC, Lns].

1:1 Paul and Silvanus[a] and Timothy

LEXICON—a. Σιλουανός (LN 93.340): 'Silvanus' [BAGD, Hn, HNTC, ICC, Lns, WBC; all versions except NIV, TEV]. Silvanus is a Latin name which, because of phonetic similarity, was sometimes used for the Aramaic name 'Saul' [Ea, EBC, Hn, HNTC, Lns, NCBC, Wd]. The Greek form is Σιλᾶς 'Silas' [EBC, Hn, HNTC, Lns, Wd] and many think that Silvanus is the same person as the Silas named in Acts 15:22–32, 40; 16:19–40; 17:1–16; 18:5 [BAGD, EBC, El, Er, Fn, Hb, Hn, HNTC, ICC, LN, Lns, Mn, NCBC, NIC, Rb, TH, WBC, Wd]. Some translate the name as 'Silas' here [NIV, TEV].

QUESTION—What part do Silvanus and Timothy have in writing the letter?

1. Paul alone is the author of the letter and Silvanus and Timothy are mentioned because they were friends of the Thessalonians [Ea, HNTC, My, Rb]. They had been with Paul when he visited Thessalonica (Acts 17:4, 14), and they were with him as he wrote the letter [Ea, El, HNTC, Rb]. Probably they wanted to be included in the greeting and if a verb needs to be supplied, it might be: Paul, Silvanus, and Timothy send this greeting to the church: grace and peace to you.
2. Paul is the primary author, but Silvanus and Timothy were also involved in writing the letter [Er, Fn, Hb, Hn, ICC, Lns, NCBC, NIC, TH, WBC]. Perhaps Paul consulted with them about the contents [NIC], or they read and approved of what he wrote [Hb, Hn, NIC], or Paul is expressing the feelings and beliefs of them all [Er, Hb]. If a verb needs to be supplied, it might be: Paul, Silvanus, and Timothy write to the church [TH].

to-the church[a] of-Thessalonians

LEXICON—a. ἐκκλησία (LN 11.32): 'church' [BAGD, Hn, LN, Lns, WBC; all versions except NEB, TEV], 'congregation' [BAGD, Hb, LN; NEB], 'assembly' [Hb, ICC], 'people of the church' [TEV], 'Christian community' [HNTC].

QUESTION—How are the two nouns related in the genitive construction τῇ ἐκκλησίᾳ Θεσσαλονικέων 'the church of Thessalonians'?

The church is composed of Thessalonians [Alf, Ea, Hb, NCBC, Wd] (that is, of people who live in the city of Thessalonica). Not all of the inhabitants of Thessalonica are meant, but only the believers [Hb, HNTC, Lns, TH].

QUESTION—Should Thessalonica be classified as a city or a town?
It was the largest city in Macedonia [Ea, Hb, Hn, NIC]. The population may have been as high as 200,000 at that time [EBC (p. 229), Hb (p. 12)].

in[a] God (the) Father and (the) Lord Jesus Christ:
LEXICON—a. ἐν (LN 89.119): 'in' [Hn, HNTC, ICC, WBC; KJV, NASB, NIV, NJB, RSV], '(which) belongs to' [NAB, NEB, TEV, TNT], 'in connection with' [Lns].
QUESTION—What relationship is indicated by ἐν 'in'?
  1. This indicates a close personal relationship [Alf, Ea, EBC, Hb, Hn, ICC, Mou (p. 80), NCBC, NIC, Rb, WBC, Wd]: the church which is spiritually joined to, or in union with, God and Jesus Christ.
  2. This indicates ownership [TH; NAB, NEB, TEV, TNT]: the church which belongs to God and Jesus Christ.
  3. This indicates the instrumental cause of the church's existence [Er, HNTC]: the church which was formed, or brought into being, by God and Jesus Christ.
  4. This specifies the type of congregation [Er, Fn, Lns]: the church which is connected with God and Jesus Christ. Since there were also civic and political assemblies, this identifies this assembly as Christian [Er, Fn].
QUESTION—Does πατρί 'Father' refer to God's relationship with believers, or to the special relationship God has with His Son within the Trinity?
  1. God is our Father [Hb, NCBC, TH, Wd; KJV]. The fuller phrase in the greeting in 2 Thess. 1:1 supports this: 'to the church of Thessalonians in God our Father and the Lord Jesus Christ' [NCBC].
  2. God is the Father in a comprehensive sense [HNTC, ICC, Lns]: he is the Father of the Son of God and also our Father.

grace[a] to-you and peace.[b]
TEXT—Some manuscripts add at the end, ἀπὸ θεοῦ πατρὸς ἡμῶν καὶ κυρίου Ἰησοῦ Χριστοῦ 'from God our Father and (the) Lord Jesus Christ'. GNT omits this phrase with a B rating, indicating some degree of doubt in omitting it. Only KJV includes it.
LEXICON—a. χάρις (LN 88.66): 'grace' [BAGD, Hn, HNTC, ICC, LN, Lns, WBC; all versions], 'favor' [BAGD], 'kindness' [LN].
  b. εἰρήνη (LN 22.42; 25.248): 'peace' [Hn, HNTC, ICC, LN, Lns, WBC; all versions].
QUESTION—What is the meaning of εἰρήνη 'peace' here?
  1. It indicates peace between the Thessalonians and God [HNTC, Mn].
  2. It indicates a sense of tranquility and spiritual well-being [Hb, Hn, ICC, NIC, Rb].
  3. It indicates both a state of peace with God and the resultant feeling of tranquility [EBC, Er, Fn, Lns, NCBC, TH].

QUESTION—Who is the actor of the implied event of giving grace and peace to the Thessalonians?
1. It is God [NCBC, NIC, TH]: may God be gracious to you and cause you to have peace.
2. Both God, the Father, and the Lord Jesus Christ are implied [Hn, ICC, WBC]. The parallel greeting in 2 Thessalonians mentions both as joint actors [WBC].

QUESTION—How does this prayer apply to people who are already believers?
Although grace and peace were already given to them at the time they believed, they could receive them in fuller measure, and in different aspects [EBC, Er, Hb, Hn, ICC, Wd].

DISCOURSE UNIT: 1:2–3:13 [Alf, Hb, ICC, Lns, Mn, My, Wd]. The topic is personal thoughts [Hb, Mn], the past response of the Thessalonians to the gospel [Alf], thanksgiving [ICC]. This section is one of two main parts of the letter, the second being the practical part with instructions and commands [Hb, My].

DISCOURSE UNIT: 1:2–10 [Alf, EBC, EGT, Er, Fn, GNT, Hb, Hn, HNTC, ICC, Lns, Mn, NCBC, TH, WBC, Wd; NAB, NIV, NJB, TEV]. The topic is thankfulness for the Thessalonians [EBC, EGT, Er, Fn, Hb, Hn, HNTC, Mn, NCBC, WBC, Wd; NASB, NIV, NJB]. A few commentators, however, focus on the specific causes for thankfulness and make the topic the lives and the faith of the Thessalonians [GNT, TH; NAB, TEV], the welcome they gave Paul [ICC]. This whole unit consists of a single Greek sentence. It is further divided by some into the following units: 1:2–3, 4–10 [Hn]; 1:2–4, 1:5–2:16 (1:5–10) [NIC]; 1:2, 3, 4–10 (4–5, 6–10) [EBC]; 1:2–3, 4–5, 6, 7–8, 9–10 [Wd]; 1:2, 3–10 (3, 4–7, 8–10) [Hb]; 1:2–5, 6–9, 10 [TH].

1:2 **We-thank**[a] **God always**[b] **concerning**[c] **all of-you,**
LEXICON—a. pres. act. indic. of εὐχαριστέω (LN 33.349; 25.100): 'to thank' [HNTC, ICC, LN, Lns; NAB, NEB, NIV, NJB, TEV, TNT], 'to give thanks' [Hn; KJV, NASB, RSV], 'to be thankful or grateful' [LN]. It can refer to an act of speaking to God [ICC], although perhaps it describes an attitude of 'thankfulness' or 'gratitude' [EBC, Wd]. The present tense of the verb is continuous and reinforces the use of 'always' [EBC, Hb; NAB].
b. πάντοτε (LN 67.88): 'always' [Hn, HNTC, ICC, LN, Lns; all versions except NAB], 'continually' [WBC]. This word has also been left implied and the present tense has been emphasized: 'to keep thanking' [NAB]. When taken as an act of speaking to God, it is explained as regularly thanking God [Hb, Hn], as a hyperbole [My, TH], or it is qualified in the following clause as meaning every time they pray [ICC].
c. περί (LN 89.6; 90.24): 'concerning' [Ea, Lns], 'for' [Hn, HNTC, ICC, WBC; all versions].

1 THESSALONIANS 1:2

QUESTION—To whom does 'we' refer?

'We' refers to Paul, Silvanus, and Timothy (1:1) [Alf, Ea, EBC, EGT, El, Hb, Hn, HNTC, ICC, Lns, My, NCBC, Rb, TH, WBC, Wd]. Although some mention the possibility of this being an editorial or literary plural referring only to Paul, none of the commentators have so taken it.

QUESTION—What is implied by thanking God for what the Thessalonians are doing?

This implies that God is responsible for what they are doing [Ea, EBC, Hb, Hn, HNTC, Lns, My, NCBC]: we thank God for what he has done in developing spiritual qualities in you. These qualities are specified in the following verse.

making mention[a] (of-you)[b] in[c] our prayers,[d]

LEXICON—a. μνεία (LN 29.18): 'mention' [BAGD, Hn, HNTC, ICC, LN, Lns; KJV, NASB]. The phrase μνείαν ποιούμενοι 'making mention' is also translated as a single verb: 'to mention' [NEB, NIV, NJB, RSV, TEV, TNT]. This area of meaning is also taken by most commentators [Ea, El, Fn, Hb, Hn, HNTC, ICC, Lns, Mn, My, NCBC, NIC, WBC]. Only NAB takes another area of meaning, 'to remember'. However, to remember someone in prayer implies that the person is also mentioned in prayer.

b. ὑμῶν 'of you' is added in some manuscripts, but GNT does not mention this. Although none state that this is the correct reading, it is implied by the context [Ea, Hn, HNTC, ICC, Lns, Mn, WBC; all versions].

c. ἐπί (LN 67.33; 90.9): 'in' [Hn, Lns, WBC; all versions]. Here it specifically means 'at the time of' [BAGD, Ea, EBC, Fn, HNTC, ICC, Mn, NIC, Rb]: we make mention of you when we pray.

d. προσευχή (LN 33.178): 'prayers' [BAGD, Hn, HNTC, ICC, LN, Lns, WBC; all versions]. The plural form suggests repeated occasions [HNTC].

QUESTION—What relationship is indicated by the participial phrase μνείαν ποιούμενοι 'making mention'?

1. It indicates the time of giving thanks [EGT, Fn, Hb, ICC, Lns, NIC]: we always thank God for you when we make mention of you in our prayers.
2. It indicates the means by which they gave thanks [Ea, EBC, El, Hn, Mn, My]: we always thank God for you by making mention of you in our prayers.
3. It is coordinate with the giving of thanks and makes another statement [NAB, NEB, TEV, TNT]: we always thank God for you and we make mention of you in our prayers. This could mean that they do two things: they thank God for some things about them and they also intercede for their needs.

unceasingly

LEXICON—ἀδιαλείπτως (LN 68.55): 'unceasingly' [BAGD, LN, Lns, WBC], 'constantly' [BAGD, HNTC; NAB, NASB, RSV, TNT], 'continually'

[Hn, ICC; NEB, NIV, NJB], 'continuously' [LN], 'without ceasing' [KJV], 'always' [TEV]. This is used hyperbolically [HNTC].

QUESTION—What does this word modify?
1. This modifies the preceding participle [Alf, BAGD, EGT, HNTC, Mn, NCBC, NIC, Wd; NEB, NJB, RSV, TEV]: unceasingly making mention of you.
2. This modifies the following participle [Ea, EBC, El, Fn, GNT, Hb, Hn, ICC, Lns, My, Rb, WBC; KJV, NAB, NASB, NIV, TNT]: unceasingly remembering.

1:3 remembering^a

LEXICON—a. pres. act. participle of μνημονεύω (LN **29.18**; 29.7; 29.16): 'to remember' [BAGD, HNTC, Lns; KJV, NIV, NJB, RSV, TEV, TNT], 'to remember and mention' [LN], 'to be mindful' [NAB], 'to bear in mind' [Hn, ICC; NASB], 'to call to mind' [WBC; NEB].

QUESTION—What relationship is indicated by this participial form?
1. This indicates the reason why they thank God (1:2) [Ea, Er, Fn, Hb, Hn, HNTC, ICC, Lns, NCBC, TH, Wd; NAB, TEV]: we thank God because we remember your work of faith, etc. It also implies that they thank God for what they remember [Hn, NCBC].
2. This indicates the time when they give thanks [EBC, El]: we thank God when we remember your work of faith, etc. This also implies that it is the reason why they thank God [El].

of-you the work^a of-faith^b

LEXICON—a. ἔργον (LN 42.11): 'work' [BAGD, Hn, ICC, Lns, WBC; KJV, NASB, NIV, RSV], 'action' [NEB, TNT], 'act, deed' [LN], 'achievement' [HNTC], 'manifestation' [BAGD]. This noun is also translated as a verbal phrase: 'to be active' [NJB], 'to put into practice' [TEV], 'to prove' [NAB].
b. πίστις (LN 31.85; 31.102): 'faith' [BAGD, Hn, HNTC, ICC, LN, Lns, WBC; all versions].

QUESTION—What does ὑμῶν 'of you' (= your) modify?
The word modifies all three nouns, work, labor, and steadfastness [Alf, Ea, EGT, El, Fn, Hb, Hn, HNTC, ICC, Lns, Mn, My, WBC]: I remember your work, your labor, and your steadfastness.

QUESTION—How are the two event nouns related in the genitive construction τοῦ ἔργου τῆς πίστεως 'the work of faith'?
1. Their work is the result of their faith [Alf, Bul (pp. 508, 993), EBC, EGT, Er, Fn, Hb, Hn, HNTC, ICC, Lns, Mn, NCBC, NIC, TH, Wd; NIV, TEV]: you work because you have faith.
2. Their work shows that they have faith [BAGD, Bul (p. 508), El, NCBC, WBC; NAB, NEB, TNT]: you work and in so doing it is evident that you have faith. Or their work is characteristic of faith [Ea, El, My, Rb]: you work and that work is the kind of work people do who have faith. This

also implies that the reason it is evident is that faith motivates such work [Ea, My, Rb].

QUESTION—Who or what was the object of their faith?

They believed in God (See 1:8) [Fn], in Christ [Lns, TH, Wd], in God and Christ [NCBC], in Christ as Savior [NIC], in the gospel [NCBC], or they believed that God had saved them by Christ [WBC].

QUESTION—What work did they do?

Their work consisted in helping needy people [EBC, Hn], instructing people [Hn], spreading the gospel [EBC, Hn], or, more generally, developing their spiritual lives [EGT, Mn], serving God and Christ [NCBC], being loyal to Christ [EBC, HNTC]. Some think that it should be kept general to cover everything they did [EBC, NIC].

and the labor[a] of-love[b]

LEXICON—a. κόπος (LN 42.47): 'labor' [BAGD, HNTC, WBC; KJV, NASB, NEB, NIV, RSV, TNT], 'activity' [ICC], 'work' [LN], 'toil' [Lns], 'exertion' [Hn]. This noun is also translated as a verb: 'to labor' [NAB], 'to work hard' [TEV], 'to be unsparing' [NJB]. There may be no significant difference between this word and ἔργον 'work' (in the preceding phrase) [WBC], but most comment that this word stresses the effort involved [Ea, EBC, Fn, Hb, HNTC, ICC, Lns, Mn, My, NCBC, NIC, TH, Wd]. Some make a distinction between the action involved, κόπος 'labor', and the result, ἔργον 'deed, work' [EBC, NIC, TH].

b. ἀγάπη (LN 25.43): 'love' [BAGD, Hn, HNTC, ICC, LN, Lns, WBC; all versions]. This means good will and a desire to help someone [Hb].

QUESTION—Who is the object of their love and how are the two event nouns related in the genitive construction τοῦ κόπου τῆς ἀγάπης 'the labor of love'?

1. They love other people and this love is the motive for their labor to help them [EBC, Fn, Hb, Hn, HNTC, ICC, Mn, NCBC, NIC, Rb]: you labor (for the benefit of people) because you love them. Some show this relationship but do not indicate the object of the love [NIV, TEV].
2. They love the Lord and this love is the motive for their labor [Lns, TH]: you labor (to do what the Lord wants you to do) because you love him. This may include labor for the benefit of other people since this is also what the Lord wants [Lns].
3. They love people and their labor shows that they love them [El]: you labor (for the benefit of people) and, in so doing, it is evident that you love them. Or the labor is characteristic of love [Ea, El, My]: you labor and that labor is the kind that people do who love others. Some show this relationship but do not indicate the object of this love [NEB, TNT]. This may also imply that the reason it is evident is that love causes such labor.

QUESTION—What labor did they do?

They helped needy people [Alf, EBC, El], they spread the gospel [Hn, HNTC, ICC], they did manual labor to support their ministry [ICC], or it should be kept general [Ea, EBC]. Some commentators think that this is a restatement of the work done in the previous phrase [Hn, Lns].

and the steadfastness[a] of-hope[b]

LEXICON—a. ὑπομονή (LN 25.174): 'steadfastness' [BAGD; NASB, RSV], 'endurance' [BAGD, Hn, HNTC, ICC, LN; NIV, TNT], 'constancy' [NAB], 'fortitude' [BAGD; NEB], 'patience' [BAGD, WBC; KJV], 'perseverance' [BAGD, Lns]. This noun is also translated as an adjective: 'firm' [TEV], 'persevering' [NJB].

b. ἐλπίς (LN 25.59): 'hope' [BAGD, Hn, HNTC, ICC, LN, Lns, WBC; all versions]. It is certainty about something in the future [Hb, NIC] and it is based on what God has said [Hb].

QUESTION—What remains steadfast and how is this attribute related to the event noun 'hope' in the genitive construction τῆς ὑπομονῆς τῆς ἐλπίδος 'the steadfastness of hope'?

1. The Thessalonians are themselves steadfast and this is caused by their hope in Christ [BAGD, Bul (p. 508), EBC, Er, Fn, Hb, Hn, HNTC, ICC, LN, NCBC, NIC, Rb, Wd; NIV]: you are steadfast because you hope. Here steadfastness means enduring troubles with courage [Hb], without self-pity [EBC] or discouragement [EBC]. It means to continue to labor in spite of difficulties [Wd]. The cause of the troubles are opposition and persecution from non-Christians [Fn, Hb, Hn, HNTC, My, Wd].
2. The Thessalonians are steadfast and this steadfastness is characteristic of hope [Alf, Ea, El, My, Rb; TNT]: you are steadfast and this steadfastness is characteristic of people who hope. This also may imply that the reason it is evident is that hope causes steadfastness.
3. Their hope was steadfast [Lns, TH, WBC; NAB, TEV]: you steadfastly hope. Here steadfastness means having a firm hope [TH], having a patient hope [WBC], or having a hope that perseveres no matter what happens [Lns].

of-the Lord of-us Jesus Christ

QUESTION—What is this genitive phrase connected with?

1. It is connected with ἐλπίδος 'hope' [Alf, Ea, EBC, El, Er, Fn, Hb, Hn, HNTC, ICC, Mn, My, NCBC, NIC, Rb, WBC, Wd; NAB, NEB, NIV, TEV, TNT]: your hope is in our Lord Jesus Christ.
2. It is connected with all three qualities [Lns]: your faith, love, and hope are all directed towards our Lord Jesus Christ.

QUESTION—What did they hope about Jesus Christ?

They confidently expected that he will come again [Alf, Ea, El, Er, Hb, Mn, My, Rb] with all the blessings that are involved with his appearance [EBC, NIC]. He will fulfill all the promises we await [Lns], he will complete all that pertains to our salvation [HNTC, ICC, WBC], he will save us from punishment at the final judgment [Hn], and he will cause us to enter the kingdom that he will establish [My].

before[a] the God and Father of-us,
LEXICON—a. ἔμπροσθεν (LN 83.33; 90.20): 'before' [BAGD, HNTC, LN, Lns; NAB, NEB, NIV, NJB, RSV, TEV], 'in the presence of' [BAGD, Hn, ICC, WBC; NASB, TNT], 'in the sight of' [KJV], 'in front of' [LN].
QUESTION—What is this phrase connected with?
  1. It is connected with μνημονεύοντες 'remembering' [Alf, Ea, EBC, EGT, El, Fn, HNTC, My, NCBC, TH, Wd; NAB, NEB, NIV, NJB, RSV, TEV, TNT]: remembering before God. This means that they remember the good qualities of the Thessalonians while they are in prayer [Ea, EBC, El, NCBC, TH], or that they are conscious of God's presence when they remember these things [HNTC, Wd], or that Paul expresses his sincerity by stating that he is conscious that God is a witness to what he says.
  2. It is connected with ἐλπίδος τοῦ κυρίου ἡμῶν Ἰησοῦ Χριστοῦ 'hope in our Lord Jesus Christ' [Er, Hn, ICC, Mn, NIC, Rb]: their hope is in Christ when they stand before their God and Father. This implies that God will be their judge [ICC].
  3. It is connected with all three genitive phrases [Hb, Lns, WBC]: they work, labor, and are steadfast with the awareness of being in God's presence [Hb, Lns, WBC], and being responsible to him [WBC], or under his care [Hb].
QUESTION—What is ἡμῶν 'of us' connected with?
  1. It goes with both 'God' and 'Father' [Hb, Hn, HNTC, ICC, Lns, Mn, NIC, Rb, WBC; NAB, NASB, NEB, NIV, NJB, RSV, TEV, TNT]: our God and Father.
  2. It goes with only 'Father' [Ea, El; KJV]: God, (who is) our Father.

1:4 knowing,[a]
LEXICON—a. perf. (used as pres.) act. participle of οἶδα (LN 28.1): 'to know' [Hn, HNTC, ICC, LN, Lns, WBC; all versions except NEB], 'to be certain' [NEB].
QUESTION—What relationship is indicated by this participial form?
This indicates a reason why they were thanking God (1:2) [Alf, Ea, EBC, El, Er, Fn, Hb, Hn, HNTC, ICC, My, NIC, WBC, Wd; NIV, RSV]: we thank God…because we know that he has chosen you. Some translations show this relationship by beginning the verse with 'for' [NIV, RSV]. Some take this as a second reason for giving thanks (we thank God…because we remember (1:3)…and because we know), and call this the ultimate or basic reason [Ea, Er, Fn, Hb, Hn, HNTC, ICC, Wd].

brothers[a] having-been-loved[b] by God,
LEXICON—a. ἀδελφός (LN 11.23): 'brothers' [BAGD, Hn, HNTC, ICC, LN, WBC; NAB, NEB, NIV, NJB, TEV, TNT], 'brethren' [Lns; KJV, NASB, RSV], 'fellow believer' [LN].
  b. perf. pass. participle of ἀγαπάω (LN 25.43): 'to be loved' [BAGD, ICC, LN; KJV, NAB, NASB, NEB, NIV, NJB, RSV]. Some translate this as an act. indic. verb: '(God) loves (you)' [TEV, TNT]. The perfect tense

indicates that his love for them began in the past and continues on through the present [EBC, Fn, Hb, Hn, HNTC, Lns, NIC, Wd].

QUESTION—What is indicated by addressing them as ἀδελφοί 'brothers'?

The term 'brothers' commonly refers to fellow Christians [HNTC] who are brothers in a spiritual sense [Lns]. It is an affectionate address, indicating the love Paul had for his converts [ICC]. This term occurs 18 times in this letter.

QUESTION—What is the participle ἠγαπημένοι 'having been loved' connected with?

It modifies ἀδελφοί 'brothers': [Ea, EBC, El, Fn, Hb, Hn, HNTC, ICC, Lns, Mn, My, NCBC, NIC, Rb, WBC, Wd; all versions except TEV]: brothers whom God loves. Although the participle is in the vocative case and is not the object of εἰδότες 'knowing', it is also translated as though it were the object [TH; TEV]: we know, brothers, that God loves you and chose you.

QUESTION—What is the phrase ὑπὸ τοῦ θεοῦ 'by God' connected with?

1. It is connected with ἠγαπημένοι 'having been loved' [Alf, Ea, EBC, El, Fn, Hb, Hn, HNTC, ICC, Lns, Mn, My, NCBC, NIC, Rb, TH, WBC, Wd; all versions except KJV]: having been loved by God.
2. It is connected with ἐκλογήν 'choice' [KJV]: chosen by God.

QUESTION—What is the purpose of mentioning that God loves them in this context?

This indicates that God's choice of them was brought about by his love for them [EBC, HNTC, ICC, NIC].

QUESTION—When did God begin to love them in this use of the perfect passive 'having been loved'?

There are different views about when God's love began. His love was from eternity [Hn], or this refers to the ultimate display of his love at the cross of Christ [Wd], or this is his fatherly love which began when they became his children [Lns].

the choice[a] of-you,

LEXICON—a. ἐκλογή (LN 30.92): 'choice' [LN; NASB], 'choosing' [BAGD], 'selection' [BAGD], 'election' [BAGD, Hn, HNTC, Lns, WBC; KJV]. This noun is also translated as a verb: 'to choose' [NEB, NIV, RSV, TEV, TNT], 'to be chosen' [ICC; NAB, NJB].

QUESTION—What did God choose them for?

God chose them to be his people [NCBC, TH; TEV], for salvation [Fn, Hb, Hn, ICC, NCBC, NIC], to receive eternal life [Alf, Ea], to be believers [My], to serve him [Hn], to be like Christ [WBC], to be in God's church [HNTC].

DISCOURSE UNIT: 1:5–2:16 [NIC]. This unit concern's Paul's recollections, specifically how the Thessalonians responded to the first preaching of the gospel (1:5–10), and an account of his preaching at Thessalonica (2:1–16).

1:5 because/that[a]

LEXICON—a. ὅτι (LN 89.33; 90.21; 91.15): 'because' [NIV, NJB, TNT], 'for' [KJV, NASB, RSV, TEV], 'seeing that' [Lns], 'from the fact that' [ICC], 'inasmuch as' [Hn], 'and that' [NEB], 'that' [HNTC], not explicit [WBC; NAB].

QUESTION—What relationship is indicated by this conjunction?
1. This indicates the grounds for 'knowing' (1:4): [Alf, Ea, EBC, El, Er, Fn, Hb, Hn, ICC, Lns, My, NIC, TH, Wd; probably KJV, NASB, NIV, NJB, RSV, TEV, TNT]: we know that God chose you since the gospel came with such effects.
2. This specifies or explains the occasion and means by which they were chosen [HNTC, Mn]: we know the way in which God chose you, specifically, we know that our gospel came, etc.
3. This indicates a second fact that they know [NEB]: we know that God chose you and that the gospel came, etc.

the gospel[a] of-us did not come[b] to you in word[c] only,

LEXICON—a. εὐαγγέλιον (LN 33.217): 'gospel' [BAGD, ICC, LN, Lns, WBC; KJV, NAB, NASB, NEB, NIV, NJB, RSV], 'Good News' [BAGD, LN; TEV, TNT].

b. aorist pass. (deponent = act.) indic. of γίνομαι (LN 15.1): 'to come' [Alf, Ea, Hn, HNTC, ICC, LN, Rb, WBC; KJV, NASB, NIV, NJB, RSV], 'to reach' [Fn], 'to get to be' [Lns]. This is the aorist tense of a verb which is usually translated 'to become, to occur, to happen'. It could be that this verb was used here for the verb εἶναι 'to be', since εἶναι has no aorist form [WBC]. Or it could be that it is referring to the gospel's development among them rather than its arrival [El], or that it was carried into effect among them [My]. It is an impersonal verb and therefore focuses on the gospel rather than on the missionaries [HNTC, ICC]. Yet some avoid the collocation of the gospel coming to them by stating the way it came: 'we brought (the gospel)' [NEB, TEV], 'we preached (the gospel)' [NAB, TNT].

c. λόγος (LN 33.98; 33.99): 'word' [BAGD, LN, Lns, WBC; KJV, NASB, RSV], 'words' [HNTC, ICC; NAB, NEB, NIV, NJB, TEV, TNT], 'speaking' [BAGD, LN].

QUESTION—How are the noun and pronoun related in the genitive construction τὸ εὐαγγέλιον ἡμῶν 'the gospel of us'?
1. This means the gospel which we brought to you [HNTC, TH; NEB, TEV], or more specifically, the gospel which we preached to you, or which we preach to everyone [Alf, BAGD, Ea, EBC, El, Fn, ICC, Lns, Mn, My, NCBC, Rb, WBC, Wd; NAB, TNT].
2. This means the gospel which was entrusted to us (2:4) for the purpose of proclaiming it [Hb, ICC, WBC].
3. This means the gospel which we believed and accepted [NIC, Wd].

but also in[a] power[b]

LEXICON—a. ἐν (LN 89.80; 90.10): 'in' [Hn, WBC; KJV, NASB, NEB, NJB, RSV], 'with' [HNTC, ICC; NIV, TEV], 'as' [NAB], 'in connection with' [Lns].

b. δύναμις (LN 76.1; 76.7): 'power' [BAGD, Hn, HNTC, ICC, LN, Lns, WBC; all versions].

QUESTION—How did the gospel come in power?

God used it to work powerfully in the Thessalonians' hearts [Fn, Lns, Mn, NIC]. It powerfully convicted the hearers [Hb, NCBC, Wd], converted them [Lns], saved them [HNTC, NIC, WBC, Wd], and developed their spiritual lives [Wd]. The missionaries dynamically preached the gospel [Alf, EBC, El, Er, Fn, HNTC] with eloquence and mental facility [Ea]. This could possibly refer to miracles [NCBC], or definitely does [TH], but most who mention this possibility reject it [Alf, Ea, EBC, EGT, El, Hb, HNTC, ICC, Lns, My].

and in (the) Holy Spirit

QUESTION—How is this phrase related to the other phrases?

1. This explains that the powerful effect of the gospel was produced by the Holy Spirit [Ea, Er, Fn, Hb, ICC, Lns, NCBC, NIC, TH, Wd; NEB, TNT]: the gospel came with power, and that power was produced by the Holy Spirit. The Holy Spirit empowered the preachers [Ea, Hb]. He applied the message to the listeners [Wd].

2. This explains that the assurance in the following phrase was produced by the Holy Spirit [Hb, Hn, ICC, NIC, Rb, WBC]: the gospel came with power, and it came with much assurance produced by the Holy Spirit. The absence in some manuscripts of the preposition ἐν 'in' in the phrase, 'and full assurance', is seen as linking these two phrases [EGT, Hb, Hn, NIC, Rb].

3. This is coordinate with the preceding clause [EBC, El, HNTC, My]: the gospel came with power, and it also came with all the influence of the Holy Spirit. The Holy Spirit enabled him to preach as he did [My] and gave the preacher wisdom [HNTC].

and in much[a] assurance/effect,[b]

TEXT—Some manuscripts do not have ἐν 'in'. GNT includes this word, but encloses it within brackets to indicate that its inclusion is doubtful. It is also included by Ea, El, HNTC, WBC, and KJV. It is omitted by EGT, Fn, Hb, Hn, HNTC, ICC, Lns, NIC, and Rb.

LEXICON—a. πολύς (LN 59.11; 78.3): 'much' [BAGD, HNTC, ICC, Lns; KJV], 'full' [Hn; NASB, RSV], 'fullest' [WBC], 'complete' [NAB, TEV], 'great' [BAGD; NJB], 'strong' [BAGD; NEB], 'deep' [BAGD; NIV], not explicit [TNT].

b. πληροφορία (LN **31.45**): 'assurance' [BAGD, Hn, Lns; KJV], 'conviction' [HNTC, ICC, WBC; NAB, NASB, NEB, NIV, RSV, TEV], 'certainty' [BAGD], 'complete certainty' [LN]; or 'effect' [NJB]. Those who translate it as 'conviction' and comment on the meaning do not mean conviction of wrong doing. Rather, they explain it as being persuaded of its truth [WBC; TEV, TNT], or having assurance about the Gospel [HNTC]. This noun is also translated as a verb: 'to be convinced' [TNT].

QUESTION—Who were assured?
1. The Thessalonians were assured [Lns, WBC]: and you were greatly assured. They were assured that the gospel they heard was true [WBC].
2. The three missionaries were assured [Alf, Ea, EBC, EGT, El, Er, Hb, Hn, HNTC, ICC, My, NCBC, NIC, TH, Wd; TNT]: and we were greatly assured. They were assured that the gospel they preached was true [Ea, EBC, Hb, TH], that it was from God [ICC, Wd], and that they were preaching as God willed [Ea]. They were assured that God was powerfully using the gospel as they preached it [Ea, EBC, Hb, NIC, Wd] and thus they were assured that he had selected those hearers [Ea].
3. Both the hearers and the preachers were assured [Fn].

as^a you-know^b what-kind^c we-were^d among you

LEXICON—a. καθώς (LN 64.14): 'as' [ICC; KJV, NEB], 'just as' [Hn; NASB], 'even as' [Lns], 'as well as' [NAB], not explicit [WBC; NIV, NJB, RSV, TEV, TNT].

b. perf. (used as pres.) act. indic. of οἶδα (LN 28.1): 'to know' [BAGD, HNTC, ICC, LN, Lns, WBC; KJV, NAB, NASB, NIV, RSV, TEV, TNT], 'to know well' [Hn; NEB], 'to observe' [NJB].

c. οἷος (LN 58.30): 'what kind' [Hn, LN, Lns, WBC; NASB, RSV], 'the kind' [Hn, HNTC, ICC; NEB], 'what manner (of men)' [KJV], 'what sort' [BAGD, LN; NJB], 'what (we proved to be) like' [NAB], 'how (we lived)' [NIV, TEV].

d. aorist pass. (deponent = act.) indic. of γίνομαι (LN 13.3): 'to be' [HNTC, LN, Lns, WBC; KJV, NEB, TNT], 'to become' [Hn, ICC], 'to prove to be' [NAB, NASB, RSV], 'to live' [NIV, NJB, TEV].

QUESTION—What relationship is indicated by καθώς 'as'?
1. When the assurance pertains to those who received the gospel, this compares the knowledge of the Thessalonians with that of the missionaries [Lns, WBC; NAB]: we know the kind of people you turned out to be (i.e., the gospel powerfully worked among you and gave full assurance) just as you know the kind of people we were when we brought the gospel to you. The power and conviction on the part of the Thessalonians matched the power and assurance of the missionaries [WBC]. The Thessalonians were assured because they knew the kind of men the missionaries were [Lns].
2. When the assurance pertains to those who brought the gospel, this indicates grounds for the preceding statement [Alf, Ea, EBC, El, Er, Fn, Hb, ICC, My, NCBC, NIC, Wd]: it is true that the word came just that way in our ministry, since you know how we were among you.

for-the-sake-of^a you.

LEXICON—a. διά (LN 90.38): 'for the sake of' [Hn, HNTC, ICC, LN, Lns, WBC; KJV, NASB, NEB, NIV, NJB, RSV], 'on behalf of' [LN; NAB], 'for the good of' [TEV], 'for the benefit of' [LN], 'in our attitude (to you)' [TNT].

QUESTION—How would they benefit the people?
If the missionaries did not live in accordance with their message, the people would reject the message [Lns, NIC, WBC]. They gave them a worthy example [Hb, WBC]. The benefit they had in mind was their salvation [Hn, NCBC] and bringing them into God's kingdom [My]. This implies the reciprocal fact, that they preached without self-interest [EBC, Hb, Hn, ICC, Lns, Wd].

1:6 And[a] you

LEXICON—a. καί (LN 89.92; 89.87): 'and' [Hn, HNTC, ICC, Lns; KJV, RSV], 'also' [NASB], 'and in turn' [NEB], 'in turn' [NAB, TNT], 'as for' [WBC], not explicit [NIV, NJB, TEV].

QUESTION—What relationship is indicated by καί 'and'?
This indicates another ground for knowing that God chose the Thessalonians [Alf, Ea, EBC, El, Er, Fn, Hb, HNTC, ICC, Mn, My, NCBC, NIC, Wd]: we know that God chose you, since the gospel came in a powerful way, and since you responded in the same manner that we missionaries and the Lord did. This connection with ὅτι 'since' (1:5a) makes the immediately preceding clause (1:5b) parenthetical [My].

QUESTION—Is ὑμεῖς 'you' emphatic?
It is emphatic [Ea, Hb, HNTC, Lns, Mn, NIC, TH, WBC]. It contrasts with 'our gospel' in verse 5 [Alf, Ea, Fn], and indicates a change of topic [EBC, Hb, TH].

became imitators[a] of-us and of-the Lord,

LEXICON—a. μιμητής (LN 41.45): 'imitators' [BAGD, Hn, HNTC, ICC, LN, Lns, WBC; NAB, NASB, NIV, RSV], 'followers' [KJV]. The phrase μιμηταὶ ἐγενήθητε 'became imitators' is translated 'to imitate' [TEV], 'to follow the example of' [NEB], 'to model oneself on' [TNT], 'to take as a model' [NJB].

having-received[a] the word[b] in much[c] affliction[d]

LEXICON—a. aorist mid. (deponent = act.) participle of δέχομαι (LN 31.51; 57.125): 'to receive' [HNTC, Lns; KJV, NAB, NASB, RSV, TEV], 'to receive readily' [LN], 'to welcome' [Hn, ICC; NEB, NIV, NJB, TNT], 'to accept' [BAGD, LN, WBC], 'to approve' [BAGD], 'to believe' [LN].

b. λόγος (LN 33.260): 'word' [BAGD, Hn, HNTC, ICC, Lns, WBC; KJV, NAB, NASB, NJB, RSV], 'message' [NEB, NIV, TEV, TNT], 'what is preached' [LN]. It is different from the meaning of λόγῳ 'word' in verse 5, having reference here specifically to the gospel [Alf, Ea, El, Hb, LN, TH].

c. πολύς (LN 59.11; 78.3): 'much' [HNTC, LN, Lns, WBC; KJV, NASB, RSV, TEV], 'great' [Hn, ICC, LN; NAB, NJB, TNT], 'grave' [NEB], 'severe' [NIV]. See this word at 1:5.

d. θλῖψις (LN 22.2): 'affliction' [BAGD, Lns; KJV, RSV], 'tribulation' [BAGD, Hn, HNTC, WBC; NASB], 'trouble' [LN; TNT], 'trials' [NAB], 'suffering' [LN; NEB, NIV], 'hardship' [NJB], 'persecution' [ICC, LN], 'oppression' [BAGD]. This noun is also translated as a verb: 'to suffer' [TEV].

QUESTION—What relationship is indicated by the participial form δεξάμενοι 'having received'?

    1. This specifies in what way they became imitators [Alf, Ea, Er, Hn, HNTC, ICC, Lns, Mn, My, NCBC, NIC, WBC, Wd]: you became imitators in that you joyfully suffered when you received the word. Some point out that the act of receiving the word could not be the point of imitation since the Lord gave the word rather than received it [Alf, Ea, Hb, My, NCBC, TH, Wd].

    2. This gives the time when they became imitators [EBC, Fn, Hb]: you became imitators after you accepted the word. In this case, the imitation can pertain to the whole way of life [EBC, Fn]. This also provides the grounds for the preceding statement [Fn, Hb]: it is true that you became imitators, since you received the word in much affliction with joy.

QUESTION—What affliction did they suffer?

They were opposed and persecuted by non-Christians because of their faith in Christ [EBC, Er, HNTC, ICC, NIC, TH, WBC] and because they witnessed for Christ [WBC].

with joy[a] of-(the) Holy Spirit,

LEXICON—a. χαρά (LN 25.123): 'joy' [BAGD, Hn, HNTC, ICC, LN, Lns, WBC; all versions except NEB], 'gladness' [LN]. This noun is also translated as a verb: 'to rejoice' [NEB].

QUESTION—How are the nouns related in the genitive construction χαρᾶς πνεύματος ἁγίου 'joy of the Holy Spirit'?

This means the joy that is caused by the Holy Spirit [Alf, Ea, EBC, El, Er, Fn, Hb, Hn, HNTC, ICC, Lns, Mn, My, NCBC, NIC, Rb, TH, WBC, Wd; NAB, NEB, NIV, RSV, TEV, TNT]. The verb 'to cause' can be more specific: 'joy inspired by the Holy Spirit' [El, Fn, HNTC, Wd; RSV], or a reciprocal verb can be given: 'joy that comes from the Holy Spirit' [NAB, TEV].

QUESTION—What did they rejoice about?

They rejoiced that they were saved [NCBC, NIC], that they were blessed [Ea], that they had the Christian hope [Ea, EGT], that they were related to Christ [Ea], that they suffered like Christ did [Lns], and that they were counted worthy to suffer for Christ [Hb, NIC].

1:7 so-that[a]

LEXICON—a. ὥστε (LN 89.52): 'so that' [BAGD, Hn, HNTC, ICC, Lns; KJV, NASB, RSV], 'so' [WBC; TEV], 'and so' [NIV, NJB, TNT], 'thus' [NAB, NEB].

QUESTION—What relationship is indicated by conjunction?

It indicates the result of 1:6 [BAGD, Fn, Hb, Hn, HNTC, ICC, Lns, Mn, NCBC, NIC, TH, WBC, Wd].

you became an-example^a to-all the (ones) believing in Macedonia and in Achaia.

TEXT—Instead of the singular form τύπον 'example', some manuscripts have the plural form τύπους 'examples'. GNT does not mention the plural form. The plural is selected by only KJV.

LEXICON—a. τύπος (LN 58.59): 'example' [BAGD, Hn, HNTC, Lns, WBC; NASB, NJB, RSV, TEV], 'ensamples' [KJV], 'model' [ICC; NAB, NEB, NIV], 'pattern' [BAGD; TNT].

QUESTION—In what respect had they become an example?

Since they were an example to believers, their example was not in receiving the word, but in how they joyfully suffered for it [Hb, Lns, NCBC, WBC, Wd], and how they proclaimed it in spite of suffering from opposition [WBC]. They were an example in respect to their imitation of the apostle and of the Lord [ICC]. They were an example in respect to their persistent faith and evangelism [Wd], or spiritual progress [El], or manner of life [TH].

QUESTION—What is the significance of the singular form τύπον 'example'?

The plural form, ὑμᾶς 'you', and the singular form, τύπον 'an example', means that the members of the church had, as a congregation, become a model church [Alf, Ea, El, Fn, Hb, HNTC, ICC, Lns, Mn, My, NIC, Rb, TH].

QUESTION—Where were these two places?

Greece was divided into two provinces: Macedonia, the northern province and Achaia, the southern one. Thessalonica was located in Macedonia and Paul was writing from Corinth, the principal city of Achaia [Hb, Hn, NCBC, WBC].

1:8 Because^a

LEXICON—a. γάρ (LN 89.23): 'because', 'for' [Hn, HNTC, ICC, Lns; KJV, NASB, RSV, TEV, TNT], 'since' [NJB], not explicit [WBC; NAB, NEB, NIV].

QUESTION—What relationship is indicated by this conjunction?

1. It indicates the grounds for saying that the church had become an example [Alf, Ea, EBC, El, Hb, Hn, HNTC, ICC, Mn, My; NJB]: it is true that you became an example, since from you God's word has sounded forth and all know about you. It also implies that this is another reason for thanking God (1:2) [Hb]. It also implies another grounds for saying that they were chosen [EBC].
2. It adds an explanation of how they came to be an example to others [Fn, Lns, NCBC, TH]: you became an example in that the Lord's word spread out from you and everyone talks about your conversion.

from you has-been-sounded-forth^a the word^b of-the Lord

LEXICON—a. perf. pass. indic. of ἐξηχέω (LN **33.222**): 'to be sounded forth', 'to be proclaimed' [LN]. The passive form is also translated actively: 'to sound forth' [BAGD, Lns; NASB, RSV], 'to sound out' [HNTC, ICC, WBC; KJV], 'to echo forth' [Hn], 'to echo forth resoundingly' [NAB], 'to ring out' [BAGD; NEB, NIV, NJB], 'to go out' [TEV], 'to be heard far and wide' [TNT]. The perfect tense indicates that it continues to sound forth [EBC, Hb, Lns, NCBC, NIC].

b. λόγος (LN 33.260): 'word' [BAGD, Hn, HNTC, ICC, Lns, WBC; KJV, NAB, NASB, NEB, NJB, RSV], 'message' [NIV, TEV, TNT]. It refers to the gospel [Alf, Ea, EBC, El, Hb, HNTC, LN, Lns, Mn, My, NCBC, NIC, Wd].

QUESTION—How are the nouns related in the genitive construction ὁ λόγος τοῦ κυρίου 'the word of the Lord'?

1. It means the word which is from the Lord [EBC, Fn, Hb, ICC, NIC, WBC, Wd; NIV]. More specifically, it is the word the Lord caused to be preached [My].
2. It means the word which is about the Lord [TH; TEV].
3. It means that the word is both from and about the Lord [Ea, Mn, Rb, Wd].

QUESTION—Who is the Lord?

'Lord' refers to Jesus Christ [Fn, Hb, ICC, TH, WBC, Wd].

QUESTION—What is meant by ἐξελήλυθεν 'has been sounded forth'?

1. This is a live metaphor [Ea, EBC, El, Er, Fn, Hb, Hn, HNTC, Lns, Mn, My, NCBC, NIC, Rb, TH, WBC, Wd; KJV, NAB, NEB, NIV, NJB]. The point of comparison is the act of spreading out in all directions from a source. There are different views about what sound is involved.
   1.1 (Like music) sounds forth (from a musical instrument, so) the word of the Lord (has spread out) from you. Suggestions for the musical instrument are a brass instrument [EBC], a trumpet [Ea, El, Er, Fn, Hb, Mn, NIC, Rb, WBC, Wd], a bell [NEB, NIV], any instrument in general [HNTC, My, NCBC, TH]. A few mention instruments with sounding boards to amplify the sound so it will be heard afar off [Hb, Hn, Lns].
   1.2 (Like thunder) sounds forth (from its source, so) the word of the Lord (has spread out) from you [NIC, Rb, Wd].
2. This is also translated as a dead metaphor without a comparison intended. It means that the word has spread out [NJB, TEV, TNT].

QUESTION—How did the word spread out from them?

This refers to location and means that, at the start, the word was with them and then it spread outward [Alf, Ea, EBC, El, HNTC, ICC, Mn, My, TH]. Their Christian lives and the gospel message that had changed them were the subject of reports by people who had passed through [Ea, Hb, My], and perhaps the Thessalonian believers or other townspeople told about what had happened as they traveled [Lns], or perhaps the Thessalonians sent missionaries to spread the word [NIC] and in other ways told others about it [NCBC, WBC].

not only in Macedonia and Achaia,

QUESTION—How is the syntax to be taken here?

1. Some consider the grammar to be irregular. The statement apparently starts out with the intention of ending after παντὶ τόπῳ 'every place', but

then 'every place' introduces a new subject and predicate [Alf, Ea, EBC, El, Fn, HNTC, Mn, Rb, Wd; probably ICC]: the word of the Lord sounded forth from you, not only in Macedonia and Achaia, but in every place (then instead of ending with a period, a new statement is made which ignores οὐ μόνον 'not only' and goes back to begin at ἀλλά 'but') your faith toward God has gone out.
2. A colon should be placed before οὐ μόνον 'not only' so that 'Macedonia, Achaia, and every place' are connected with the verb ἐξελήλυθεν 'has gone out' [My; NEB, TNT]: the word of the Lord sounded forth from you: not only in Macedonia and Achaia, but (also) in every place your faith toward God has gone out.
3. Οὐ μόνον 'not only' should be taken with the verb ἐξήχηται 'sounded forth' [RSV]: not only has the word of the Lord sounded forth from you in Macedonia and Achaia, but your faith toward God has gone out everywhere.

but in every place[a]
LEXICON—a. τόπος (LN 80.1): 'place' [BAGD, Hn, HNTC, ICC, LN, Lns, WBC; KJV, NASB], 'region' [BAGD; NAB]. The phrase ἐν παντὶ τόπῳ 'in every place' is translated 'everywhere' [NEB, NIV, NJB, RSV, TEV, TNT].
QUESTION—What is the meaning of παντί 'every' place?
It is a hyperbole for 'very many places' [Ea, EBC, EGT, El, Hb, HNTC, ICC, My, NCBC, Rb, TH, WBC, Wd]. It means every place Paul visits or hears about [Fn, NCBC].

your faith,[a] **the (faith) toward God, has-gone-out,**[b]
LEXICON—a. πίστις (LN 31.85): 'faith' [BAGD, Hn, HNTC, ICC, LN, Lns, WBC; all versions].
b. perf. act. indic. of ἐξέρχομαι (LN 15.40): 'to go out' [BAGD, ICC, LN; TNT], 'to go forth' [Hn, Lns, WBC; NASB, RSV], 'to go' [TEV], 'to spread' [NJB], 'to spread abroad' [KJV]. The direction is also reversed: 'to come into' [HNTC], 'to reach' [NEB]; or its reception is put in focus: 'to become known' [NIV], 'to be celebrated' [NAB].
QUESTION—In what respect can faith go out?
1. The report or news about their faith went out [EBC, El, Hn, HNTC, ICC, Lns, My, NCBC, TH, WBC; TEV, TNT]. ἡ πίστις ὑμῶν 'your faith' refers to the event of believing in God [EBC, My]. The perfect tense means that the news is still being discussed [Wd].
2. They propagated what they believed [Hn].

so-that we do not have need[a] **to-say anything;**
LEXICON—a. χρεία (LN 71.23): 'need' [BAGD, HNTC, LN, WBC; NASB, TNT], '(makes it) needless' [NAB]. This noun is also translated as a verb: 'to need to' [ICC, Lns; KJV, NIV, NJB, RSV, TEV], 'to be needed' [NEB], 'to be necessary' [Hn].

QUESTION—What relationship is indicated by ὥστε 'so that'?

It indicates the result of their faith going out [BAGD, Ea, Fn, Hb, Lns].

QUESTION—What does τι 'anything' refer to?

This means that he does not have to say anything about what has happened among the Thessalonians [Ea, Hb, Lns, NCBC], to tell about their faith [Alf, Ea, El, HNTC, Lns, My], or to praise them [Alf]. Some commentators think that this means that he would still have to preach [Lns, TH], however another thinks that it could be taken to mean that he does not even have to tell people about the word of the Lord [TH].

1:9 Because[a]

LEXICON—a. γάρ (LN 89.23): 'because', 'for' [Hn, HNTC, ICC, Lns; KJV, NASB, NEB, NIV, RSV], not explicit [WBC; NAB, NJB, TEV, TNT].

QUESTION—What relationship is indicated by this conjunction?

1. This indicates the grounds for the preceding statement [NCBC]: it is true that we do not have to say anything, since they themselves report about it.
2. This indicates the reason for the preceding statement [Ea, HNTC, ICC, Wd; NEB]: we do not have to say anything because they themselves report about it.
3. This explains further by indicating the extent that the news is being spread [Fn, Lns, My]: news of your faith has gone out, so much so that they themselves report about it.

they-themselves report[a] concerning us what-sort-of entrance/reception[b] we had to you

LEXICON—a. pres. act. indic. of ἀπαγγέλλω (LN 33.198): 'to report' [BAGD, Hn, HNTC, ICC, Lns, WBC; NAB, NASB, NIV, RSV], 'to tell' [BAGD, LN; NJB], 'to inform' [LN], 'to talk about' [TNT], 'to speak about' [TEV], 'to spread the news' [NEB], 'to show' [KJV]. The present tense indicates that reports are repeatedly being given [Hb, Hn, ICC, Lns, NIC, Rb, Wd].

b. εἴσοδος (LN 15.87; **34.56**): 'entrance' [BAGD, Fn, HNTC, WBC], 'entering in' [Hn, Lns; KJV], 'visit' [BAGD, ICC, NCBC, NIC; NEB, TNT], 'reception' [NAB, NASB, NIV], 'welcome' [BAGD; RSV]. This noun is also translated as a verb: '(you) welcomed (us)' [LN], '(you) received (us)' [TEV], '(we) started (a work)' [NJB].

QUESTION—To whom does αὐτοί 'they' refer?

The people referred to are the inhabitants of Macedonia, Achaia, and 'every place' (1:8) [Alf, El, Fn, HNTC, Lns, Mn, NCBC, TH, WBC, Wd]. This is in contrast to ἡμᾶς 'we' (1:8): we do not have to say anything, rather they themselves report it [Ea, El, ICC, My, NIC].

QUESTION—To whom did they report?

1. It is implied that they reported to 'us', i.e., Paul and his companions [EBC, Fn, Hb, ICC, NIC; NJB]. In this case, 'they' refers to those who met Paul [Hb, ICC].
2. They reported to people in general [Ea, El, Hn, Lns, WBC, Wd].

1 THESSALONIANS 1:9

QUESTION—To whom does περὶ ἡμῶν 'concerning us' refer?
1. It is an exclusive reference, referring to Paul, Silvanus, and Timothy but not to the Thessalonians [Alf, Ea, El, Hb, Hn].
2. It is an inclusive reference, referring to the three missionaries and also to the Thessalonians [My].

QUESTION—What is the focus of εἴσοδος 'entrance/reception'?
1. The focus is on the missionaries [Ea, EBC, EGT, El, Fn, Hb, Hn, HNTC, ICC, Lns, Mn, My, NCBC, NIC, TH, Wd; KJV, NEB, NJB, TNT]. It can mean the successful nature of their entrance [EGT, Fn, Mn], or it can include all that was accomplished while they were in Thessalonica [Hb, Hn, Lns, TH, Wd]. The kind of entrance would include the description of how the message came in 1:5 [Ea, EBC, El, My].
2. The focus is on the Thessalonians who received and welcomed the gospel [LN, WBC; NAB, NASB, NIV, RSV, TEV].

and how[a] you-turned[b] to God from the idols[c]

LEXICON—a. πῶς (LN 92.16): 'how' [BAGD, Hn, ICC, LN, Lns, WBC; all versions], 'that' [HNTC].
b. aorist act. indic. of ἐπιστρέφω (LN 31.60): 'to turn' [BAGD, Hn, HNTC, ICC, LN, Lns, WBC; all versions except NJB], 'to be converted' [NJB]. The active voice indicates that this is due to their own voluntary act [Hb]. This is not a physical turning, but it means changing whom they worshipped [TH].
c. εἴδωλον (LN 6.97; 12.23): 'idols' [BAGD, Hn, HNTC, ICC, LN, Lns, WBC; all versions except NJB], 'false gods' [BAGD], 'worship of false gods' [NJB]. The word refers both to the images and the gods they represent [Hn, HNTC, Lns, TH]. An idol is anything that substitutes for the true God [Wd].

QUESTION—How is this clause related to the previous one?
1. This gives the second object or topic of the reports [Ea, EBC, Hb, Hn, ICC, NCBC]: and they also report how you turned to God, etc.
2. This gives the specific point that is intended [NIC; NEB]: specifically, they report how you turned to God, etc.

QUESTION—What relationship is indicated by πῶς 'how/that'?
1. This indicates the manner in which they turned [Ea, Fn, My]: they report how you turned to God from idols.
2. This merely refers to the fact that they turned [Alf, El, HNTC, ICC, TH]: they report that you turned to God from idols.

to-be-a-slave-to[a] a-living[b] and true[c] God,

LEXICON—a. pres. act. infin. of δουλεύω (LN 35.27; 87.79): 'to be a slave to' [BAGD, LN, Lns], 'to serve' [BAGD, Hn, HNTC, ICC, LN, WBC; KJV, NAB, NASB, NIV, RSV, TEV, TNT], 'to be servants' [NEB, NJB].
b. pres. act. participle of ζάω (LN 23.88): 'to live' [BAGD, Hn, HNTC, ICC, LN, Lns, WBC; all versions], 'to be alive' [LN].

c. ἀληθινός (LN 70.3; 73.2): 'true' [WBC; all versions], 'real' [BAGD, Hn, HNTC, LN, Lns], 'genuine' [BAGD, Hn, ICC, LN, Lns].

QUESTION—What relationship is indicated by the use of the infinitive δουλεύειν 'to be a slave to'?

1. It is a restatement of the preceding clause [Lns]: you turned to God from idols, that is, you became slaves of the living and true God.
2. It gives their purpose for turning to God [Ea, EBC, El, Hb, ICC, My]: you turned to God from idols, in order to serve a living God, etc.
3. It gives the result of their turning [NCBC]: you turned to God from idols; as a result, you became slaves of the living and true God.

QUESTION—Is there any significance to the absence of an article before θεῷ 'God'?

The nature of God is emphasized rather than his person [Hb, Hn, Lns, Mn, NIC, Wd]. The specific characteristics in view are that he is living and real [Hb, Lns, Wd].

QUESTION—Why is the verb δουλεύειν 'to be a slave' used here?

1. It is a metaphor [EBC, Fn, Hb, Hn, ICC, Lns, NCBC, NIC]. The points of comparison are obedience [NCBC], complete subjection [EBC, Fn, Hb, Hn, Lns, NIC], and devotion [EBC]. This comparison might be stated: (Like a slave) obeys and serves (his master, so) you obey and serve God. This obedience is in the area of obedience to God's revealed will [NCBC, NIC], and worship [NCBC]. The negative aspects of slavery in respect to forced and unwilling obedience are not intended [Hn, TH].
2. Since God is actually our ruler, we literally obey and serve him. Many do not indicate that a comparison with a slave is intended [Er, WBC; all versions except perhaps NEB, NJB].

1:10 **and to-await[a] his Son from the heavens,[b]**

LEXICON—a. pres. act. infin. of ἀναμένω (LN **85.60**): 'to await' [Hn, ICC, Lns; NAB], 'to wait for' [BAGD, HNTC, LN, WBC; KJV, NASB, NIV, NJB, RSV, TEV, TNT], 'to expect' [BAGD], 'to wait expectantly for' [NEB]. The present tense indicates that this is a continuous attitude [Hb, Rb]. It is implied that he is expected [EBC, Mn], and it could be soon [Hb, NCBC, WBC]. It is also implied that they will welcome him when he comes [Hb]. They prepare for his coming by having their lives in order [Hn, Lns, NCBC, WBC]. Some see elements of eagerness and confidence implied by the verb [Hb, Hn; NEB]. This implies that they live holy lives so as to be ready for his coming [Hb, WBC].

b. οὐρανός (LN 1.11): The plural phrase, τῶν οὐρανῶν 'the heavens', follows Hebrew usage [Hb, HNTC, WBC] and means 'heaven' [BAGD, Hb, HNTC, LN, NIC, WBC; all versions]. Or, it may indicate a belief in multiple heavens [Fn, HNTC, ICC].

QUESTION—Why did they await God's Son?

They wanted to see him in all his glory [NCBC, WBC]. His coming will bring the present age to an end [Hb]. It will bring about their full deliverance [Ea, HNTC, ICC] and save them from the coming wrath [ICC].

whom he-raised[a] from the dead,[b]

LEXICON—a. aorist act. indic. of ἐγείρω (LN 23.94): 'to raise' [BAGD, Hn, HNTC, ICC, Lns, WBC; all versions], 'to raise to life' [LN], 'to make live again' [LN].

b. νεκρός (LN 23.121): 'dead' [LN]. This adjective is used substantively: 'the dead (people)' [BAGD, Hn, HNTC, ICC, Lns, WBC; KJV, NAB, NASB, NEB, NIV, NJB, RSV]. This is also translated as referring to the state of being dead rather than to being in the midst of dead people: 'death' [TEV, TNT].

QUESTION—Why is this clause mentioned here?

It gives a basis for waiting for him. He was raised to go to heaven and therefore he can return from heaven [EBC, Hb, NCBC, Wd]. It is an outstanding proof that he is God the Son [EBC, El, Er, Fn, Hb, My, Wd].

Jesus, the (one) delivering[a] us from the coming[b] wrath.[c]

LEXICON—a. pres. mid. (deponent = act.) participle of ῥύομαι (LN 21.23): 'to deliver' [BAGD, HNTC, ICC, LN; KJV, NAB, NASB, RSV], 'to rescue' [BAGD, Hn, LN, Lns; NIV, TEV], 'to save' [BAGD; NJB], 'to preserve' [BAGD]. This participle with an article is also translated as a substantive: 'deliverer' [WBC; NEB], 'rescuer' [TNT].

b. pres. mid. (deponent = act.) participle of ἔρχομαι (LN 15.81): 'to come' [BAGD, Hn, ICC, LN, Lns, WBC; all versions], 'to approach' [HNTC]. The present participle indicates that God's wrath is now coming, which emphasizes its certainty [El, Hb, Mn, NIC], or even its nearness [EBC, ICC, Mn, My].

c. ὀργή (LN 38.10; 88.173): 'wrath' [BAGD, Hn, Lns, WBC; KJV, NAB, NASB, NIV, RSV, TNT], 'anger' [BAGD, HNTC, LN; TEV], 'indignation' [BAGD]. To be saved from wrath implies that one is saved from the expression of that wrath: 'retribution' [NJB], 'judgment' [BAGD, Hb, ICC, My, WBC, Wd], 'punishment' [LN], 'terrors of judgment' [NEB].

QUESTION—What does the present tense of the participle ῥυόμενον 'delivering' indicate?

1. It is a timeless present tense [EBC, Fn, Hb, ICC, NIC, Wd; NEB, TNT] and denotes his character or office as being 'the deliverer' [Alf, EBC, El, Fn, Hb, Mn, NIC, WBC, Wd; NEB, TNT]. Not only is he our deliverer now, he will still be at the time when the coming wrath arrives [Wd].
2. It is a continuous present tense and indicates that there is a process of deliverance going on all the time [Ea, HNTC, My, TH]. He has begun the process but it must still be completed [TH]. He is presently delivering from the fear of being judged in the future [My].

QUESTION—Who are meant by ἡμᾶς 'us'?
   It is inclusive and refers to Paul, his companions, and the Thessalonians [Lns], and all believers [Hb, Hn].
QUESTION—Who has the wrath?
   It is God [EBC, El, Er, Fn, Hb, HNTC, Mn, NCBC, NIC, Rb, TH, WBC, Wd; TEV].
QUESTION—What is God angry about?
   He is angry at sin [El, Er, Fn, Hb, Mn, NCBC, NIC, Rb, Wd] and, since people commit sin, he is angry at sinners [Hb, NCBC].

DISCOURSE UNIT: 2:1–3:13 [EBC]. The topic is the vindication of the missionaries' characters and ministry. This can be further divided: 2:1–12, 2:13–16, 2:17–3:13 [EBC].

DISCOURSE UNIT: 2:1–16 [Alf, GNT, Hb, Hn, NIC, TH; NIV, TEV]. The topic is the missionaries' preaching [Alf, NIC], their ministry [GNT, TH; NIV, TEV], their relationship with the Thessalonians [Hb], their defense [Hn]. It is further divided into the following units: 2:1–12, 13–16 [Alf, Hb, Hn, TH]; 2:1–6a, 6b–9, 10–12, 13, 14–16 [NIC].

DISCOURSE UNIT: 2:1–13 [NAB]. The topic is the writer's sincerity.

DISCOURSE UNIT: 2:1–12 [Alf, EBC, EGT, Er, Fn, Hb, Hn, HNTC, ICC, Mn, NCBC, TH, WBC, Wd; NJB]. The topic is the missionaries' visit [ICC], their ministry [Er, Hb, Mn], their behavior [Fn, HNTC, NCBC, Wd], their example [NJB], their defense [EBC, WBC]. This is a defense against accusations of self-seeking made by opponents [EBC, EGT, Hb, ICC, Mn, NCBC, WBC]. It is further divided into the following units: 2:1–4, 5–8, 9–12 [WBC]; 2:1–2, 3–4, 5–12 [EBC, Hb, Mn].

2:1 Because[a]

LEXICON—a. γάρ (LN 89.23; 91.1): 'because', 'for' [HNTC, Lns; KJV, NASB, RSV], 'indeed' [Hn, ICC], not explicit [WBC; NAB, NEB, NIV, NJB, TEV, TNT].
QUESTION—What relationship is indicated by this conjunction?
   1. This indicates the grounds for what is said about their ministry [El, NIC, Wd]: what people report (1:9) is true, *since* you can bear witness to it [El, Wd], or what I say about our preaching is true, *since* you can bear witness to it [NIC].
   2. This indicates the grounds for the report of their work in Thessalonica, mentioned in 1:5 [HNTC]: it is true that our visit has been with power, the Holy Spirit, and much conviction, *since* you can bear witness that it was not empty or without result.
   3. This resumes the subject of their entrance in 1:5 and 9 [Ea, EBC, Fn, Hb, ICC, Lns, Mn, My, NCBC, NIC, Rb, TH] and elaborates on it [Ea, EBC, Fn, Hb, NCBC].

1 THESSALONIANS 2:1

you-yourselves know, brothers, our coming[a] to you,

LEXICON—a. εἴσοδος (LN 15.87): 'coming' [LN; NAB, NASB], 'coming in' [WBC], 'entrance' [BAGD, HNTC; KJV], 'entering in' [Hn, Lns], 'arrival' [LN], 'visit' [BAGD, ICC; NEB, NIV, NJB, RSV, TEV, TNT]. See this word at 1:9.

QUESTION—What is the significance of αὐτοί 'you yourselves'?

This is emphatic [Ea, EBC, Hb, Hn, HNTC, Lns, Mn, My, NIC, TH]. It is in contrast with 'for they themselves report concerning us' in 1:9 [Ea, EGT, Fn, Hb, Lns, Mn]. It contrasts their knowledge with the knowledge of those who give reports about them [Hb, Lns]. The people who talk about the visit have only heard about it, but the Thessalonians are the ones who know from experience [Lns]. It signals a change of subject [TH]. However, one commentator denies that this is emphatic and takes it to be a parenthetical comment [NCBC].

QUESTION—To whom does ἡμῶν 'our' refer?

It refers to Paul, Silvanus, and Timothy [Hb, Hn, ICC].

that it-has-been[a] not in-vain/empty,[b]

LEXICON—a. perf. act. indic. of γίνομαι (LN 13.3): 'to be' [Hn, LN, Lns; all versions], 'to prove (to be)' [HNTC, ICC, WBC]. The perfect tense indicates that the effects of their visit are continuing on [HNTC, Lns, Mn, TH], that the action is completed and all the facts are available [ICC, NCBC, NIC] and cannot be denied [Hb], and that like it was when they first came, it still continues to be [Alf, Ea, EBC].

b. κενός (LN **89.53**; 89.64; 57.42) 'in vain' [KJV, NASB, RSV], 'ineffectual' [WBC], 'without effect' [BAGD; NAB], 'without result' [BAGD, LN], 'fruitless' [HNTC; NEB], 'a failure' [NIV, TEV], 'a waste of time' [TNT], 'pointless' [NJB]; or 'empty' [Lns, NIC], 'empty-handed' [Hn], 'void of power' [ICC].

QUESTION—What is meant by κενός 'vain/empty'?

1. It refers to the effect of their visit on the Thessalonians [HNTC, Lns, Rb, TH, WBC; all versions]: our entrance was not without result. The result was that the Thessalonians accepted the gospel and spread it everywhere [WBC]. It can be considered a litotes: 'not without result' means that it had impressive results [Lns].
2. It refers to the character of their visit [Alf, Ea, EBC, Fn, Hb, Hn, ICC, Lns, Mn, My, NCBC, NIC, WBC, Wd]: our visit was not empty.
2.1 This refers to the description of the coming of the gospel in 1:5 [EBC, Fn, Hb, ICC, My]: we brought the gospel not in word only, but with power, the Holy Spirit, and conviction. Some commentators note that the effect on others is not taken up until 2:13 [Alf, Hb, ICC].
2.2 This refers to their motives [Hn, Wd]: we came not empty-handed, or greedy, in order to receive something from you, rather we brought you something, the gospel.

2.3 This refers to their purpose [NIC]: we did not come without any specific purpose.
2.4 This refers to all of the above [Ea, El]: we did not come without power, reality, or purpose.

2:2 but[a]

LEXICON—a. ἀλλά (LN 89.125): 'but' [HNTC; KJV, NASB, RSV], 'far from it' [NEB], 'on the contrary' [Hn, ICC, Lns], not explicit [WBC; NAB, NIV, NJB, TEV, TNT].

QUESTION—What relationship is indicated by this conjunction?

It indicates a strong positive contrast with the previous negative phrase; the visit was the opposite of 'empty' [Ea, EBC, El, Hb, ICC, Lns, Rb, TH], it was not empty of power, rather it was with courage to speak God's word [Hb, ICC]. It also introduces a definition of 'not empty' [ICC]. When 'empty' is interpreted to mean 'without results', the expected contrast, 'but with success' is missing, and this leads some to think that Paul changed his argument after he started to dictate the sentence [TH].

having-suffered-previously[a] **and having-been-shamefully-treated,**[b] **as you-know, in Philippi**

LEXICON—a. aorist act. participle of προπάσχω (LN 24.79): 'to suffer previously' [BAGD, Hn; NIV], 'to suffer before' [Lns; KJV], 'to suffer already' [BAGD, LN; NASB, RSV], 'to suffer earlier' [HNTC], 'to experience suffering previously' [TNT], 'to endure suffering previously' [WBC], 'to undergo suffering previously' [ICC], 'to suffer injury' [NEB], 'to receive rough treatment' [NJB]. The active voice is also translated in the passive: 'to be mistreated already' [TEV]. It is also conflated with the following participle: 'to suffer humiliation' [NAB]. This refers to physical suffering [Hb, HNTC, ICC, NIC]. It specifically refers to flogging and having their feet in stocks in Philippi (Acts 16:23–24) [Hb, NIC, TH, WBC]. One commentator says that what this means is defined in the following phrase, taking the καί 'even' to indicate an explanation of the preceding phrase [Lns]. The aorist tense indicates that this and the following aorist participle were antecedent to the leading verb 'we had courage' [Hb].

b. aorist pass. participle of ὑβρίζω (LN 88.130; 33.390): 'to be treated shamefully' [Hn, WBC; KJV, RSV], 'to be mistreated' [BAGD; NASB], 'to be mistreated with insolence' [LN], 'to be maltreated' [LN], 'to be insulted' [BAGD, ICC, LN; NIV, TEV], 'to be abused' [HNTC], 'to be outraged' [Lns]. The passive voice is also translated actively: 'to undergo insult' [ICC], 'to experience insult' [TNT], 'to receive insults' [NJB], 'to suffer outrage' [NEB], 'to suffer humiliation' [NAB]. This refers to being treated in an insulting way by others [Hb, Hn, ICC, NCBC, NIC, Wd]. It is being treated insolently [Ea, Hn, HNTC, Rb, TH] and being publicly humiliated [Hb, Wd]. Specifically, it refers to being arrested, slandered, stripped of their clothes, publicly beaten, imprisoned, put in stocks in

Philippi [Hb, Hn, WBC], or to having their Roman citizenship disregarded [EBC, Hn, HNTC, ICC, Mn, NCBC, NIC, WBC, Wd], enduring all that without the authorities making any effort to investigate the charges [WBC]. The agents of these actions are the authorities in Philippi [TH].

QUESTION—What relationship is indicated by the two participles?
1. They are concessive [EBC, EGT, Hb, Hn, ICC, Lns, My, TH, WBC, Wd; KJV, NIV, NJB, RSV, TEV, TNT]: *although* we suffered and were insulted, yet we were courageous.
2. They are temporal [Ea, El; KJV, NEB]: *after* we suffered and were insulted, we were courageous.

QUESTION—How did the Thessalonians come to know this?
Probably Paul himself told them while he was with them [ICC, WBC]. They saw the effects of the beating on the bodies of the missionaries [Ea, Hb, HNTC].

we-had-courage[a] in/by[b] our God to-speak[c] to you the gospel of-God
LEXICON—a. aorist mid. (deponent = active) indic. of παρρησιάζομαι (LN **25.159;** 33.90): 'to have courage' [BAGD, ICC; NJB, RSV, TEV, TNT], 'to be courageous' [HNTC], 'to draw courage' [NAB], 'to summon courage' [Hn], 'to dare' [NIV], 'to venture' [BAGD], 'to have boldness' [NASB], 'to be bold' [WBC; KJV], 'to be emboldened' [WBC], 'to be free and open' [Lns]. This is also conflated with the infinitive 'to speak': 'to declare frankly and fearlessly' [NEB]. Some commentators say that this verb includes the idea of speaking: 'to speak boldly' [El, Hb, HNTC, Mn, NCBC, TH], 'to be outspoken' [HNTC, Wd]. Then the following λαλῆσαι 'to speak' is an explanation giving a more specific reference [El, Hb, Mn]. Others say that this verb refers only to an attitude of confidence [Alf, Ea, Fn, ICC, My, NIC]. Then the following 'to speak' tells in what way they were confident or bold [Alf]. It indicates a confident manner in speaking [Hb, NIC], or to preach openly [Lns]. Some take the aorist to be inceptive [Fn, ICC, WBC]: we became bold. Others take it to be constative [Hb]: we were bold.
b. ἐν (LN 90.6; 89.119): 'in' [HNTC, Lns, WBC; KJV, NASB, RSV], 'by the help of' [Hn; NEB], 'with the help of' [NIV], 'in the power of' [ICC]. The phrase ἐπαρρησιασάμεθα ἐν τῷ θεῷ 'we had courage in God' is also conflated: 'God gave us courage' [NJB, TEV, TNT], 'we drew courage from God' [NAB].
c. aorist act. infin. of λαλέω (LN 33.70): 'to speak' [BAGD, HNTC, LN, Lns; KJV, NASB, NJB], 'to tell' [Hn, ICC, LN; NIV, TEV, TNT], 'to declare' [WBC; NEB, RSV], 'to preach' [NAB]. The aorist tense refers to all the speaking they did during their visit [Lns].

QUESTION—What is indicated by the aorist tense of ἐπαρρησιασάμεθα 'we had courage'?
1. It is a regular aorist [Hb, Lns; probably KJV, NASB, NIV, RSV]: we were courageous. It covers the whole time they were in Thessalonica [Hb, Lns].

It is not ingressive since that would imply that they had lost their courage but regained it when they arrived [Hb].
2. It is an ingressive or inceptive aorist [Fn, Hn, ICC, Mn, Rb, WBC, Wd; probably NAB]: we became courageous. They summoned up courage [Hn], they took courage [ICC, WBC]. This does not seem to imply that they had lost courage.

QUESTION—What relationship is indicated by ἐν 'in'?
1. It indicates that their courage was a result of being in fellowship with God [Hb, Hn, ICC, My, NIC, Wd]: we had courage because we were in fellowship/union with our God. Since they were close to God, they could receive the courage he gives [Hb]. The indwelling power of God empowered them to preach [ICC]. By being in union with God, God helped them to speak courageously [Hn].
2. It indicates that their courage was based on their trust in God [Ea, El, NCBC, Rb]: we had courage because we trusted in God (to protect us).
3. It is used instrumentally to indicate the means or cause of their courage [HNTC, Mn, TH, WBC; NJB, TEV, TNT]: we had courage by having God impart it to us.

QUESTION—How are the two nouns related in the genitive construction τὸ εὐαγγέλιον τοῦ θεοῦ 'the gospel of God'?
1. This means that the gospel came from God [Ea, El, Hb, Hn, HNTC, Lns, Mn, My, TH, WBC; TEV]. He was the author of the gospel [Hb, Lns, WBC], he sent it [Hb], and ordered it to be preached [Lns].
2. This means that the gospel came from God and also told about God [NIC, Wd].

in[a] much[b] opposition/struggle.[c]

LEXICON—a. ἐν (LN 89.80; 67.33; 67.136): 'in', 'in the face of' [NAB, RSV], 'amid' [WBC; NASB], 'amidst' [HNTC], 'in the midst of' [ICC], 'with' [Hn, Lns; KJV], 'even though there was' [TEV], 'though' [TNT], 'in spite of' [NIV, NJB].
b. πολύς (LN 59.11; 78.3): 'much' [BAGD, ICC, Lns; KJV, NASB, TEV], 'many' [TNT], 'great' [BAGD, HNTC, WBC; NAB, NJB, RSV], 'strong' [BAGD; NIV], 'hard' [BAGD; NEB], 'profound' [BAGD, Hn].
c. ἀγών (LN 39.29; 50.4): 'opposition' [BAGD, ICC; NAB, NASB, NIV, NJB, RSV, TEV], 'contention' [KJV], 'conflict' [WBC]; or 'agonizing' [Lns], 'struggle' [BAGD, LN; NEB]; or 'solicitude' [Hn]. This noun is also translated as a verb: 'to oppose' [TNT].

QUESTION—Is ἀγῶνι 'opposition/struggle' a live metaphor?
1. It is a live metaphor [EBC, Fn, Hb, HNTC, Lns, Mn, NCBC, NIC, Rb, TH, Wd]. It is from the athletic games [Hb, HNTC, Lns, NIC].
   1.1 The illustration concerns conflict with opponents in an athletic game [EBC, Fn, Hb, HNTC, Mn, NCBC, NIC, TH, Wd]. The topic is the conflict the missionaries had with opponents of the gospel [EBC, Hb, NCBC]. The point of comparison is conflict with opponents [Hb].

1 THESSALONIANS 2:2

Dropping the illustration, he is saying: in facing much opposition [EBC, Hb, NIC, WBC; all versions]. Opponents would be teachers of competing philosophies [Wd], jealous Jews [EBC, Wd], and rabble rousers [Wd]. Even though this is primary, it would include inner struggle and intense effort [Hb].

1.2 The illustration concerns the effort athletes make in order to win a prize. The topic is the effort made by the missionaries in order to persuade people to accept the gospel. The point of comparison is the strenuous effort involved. Dropping the illustration, he is saying that they worked hard to present the gospel [Lns]. This included fervent prayer and devotion to their work [Lns].

2. No comparison is in focus [probably all who do not discuss a comparison: Ea, El, Hn, ICC, My; probably NAB, NASB, NIV, NJB, RSV, TEV, TNT].

2.1 It refers to opposition [Ea, El, ICC; NAB, NASB, NIV, NJB, RSV, TEV, TNT]

2.2 It refers to their deep concern for the Thessalonians. They cared greatly for the people instead of being selfish [Hn].

2:3 Because[a]

LEXICON—a. γάρ (LN 89.23; 91.1): 'because', 'for' [Hn, HNTC, Lns; KJV, NASB, NIV, RSV]; or 'indeed' [ICC; NEB]; not explicit [WBC; NAB, NJB, TEV, TNT].

QUESTION—What relationship is indicated by this conjunction?

1. This indicates the reason they could preach with courage in spite of opposition [Alf, Ea, EBC, El, Wd]: we had courage to tell you the gospel *because* our appeal was not from error, etc. The reasons given are that his appeal was wholehearted [Alf, Ea], approved by God [EBC], and that it was because God's gospel was involved [Wd]. If they had had false motives, they would not have endured the opposition [Hb].

2. This is explanatory [El, Hb, HNTC, ICC, Lns, My, NCBC, TH]. Paul explains how they preach [Lns], what their motives were [HNTC], and how their preaching was not empty but based on confidence [NCBC]. This parallels the γάρ 'because' in 2:1 [ICC, TH] and continues Paul's self-defense with another explanation [ICC].

the appeal[a] of-us (is/was) not from[b] error/deceit[c]

LEXICON—a. παράκλησις (LN 33.168; 25.150): 'appeal' [Hn, HNTC, ICC, LN, WBC; NEB, NIV, RSV, TEV, TNT], 'exhortation' [BAGD; KJV, NAB, NASB], 'encouragement' [BAGD, LN; NJB], 'urging' [Lns].

b. ἐκ (LN 89.25; 90.12; 90.16): 'from' [Hn, HNTC, ICC, WBC; NAB, NASB, NEB, NIV, NJB, RSV], 'of' [KJV], 'out of' [Lns], '(to be based) on' [TEV], '(to rest) on' [TNT]. It indicates the source [Alf, Ea, El, Hb, HNTC, ICC, Lns, Mn, NCBC, NIC], or motives [WBC; NAB, NIV, TEV]. The source is indicated by supplying a verb: 'comes from' [ICC;

NASB], 'springs from' [Hn, HNTC; NAB, NEB, NIV, RSV], 'arises from' [WBC], 'rests on' [TNT], 'is based on' [TEV].

c. πλανή (LN 31.8; 31.10): 'error' [BAGD, HNTC, LN, Lns; NASB, NEB, NIV, RSV, TEV], 'mistaken view' [LN], 'delusion' [BAGD, Hn, ICC; NJB, TNT]; or 'deceit' [BAGD; KJV, NAB], 'deception' [LN].

QUESTION—How are the noun and pronoun related in the genitive construction ἡ παράκλησις ἡμῶν 'the appeal of us'?

This means the appeal that was given/made by us [ICC; NAB, NEB, NIV]: we appeal to people/you.

QUESTION—To whom is the appeal made?

1. It is made to people in general [Alf, Ea, El, Hb, HNTC, ICC, Lns, My, NCBC, Wd]. Some say that the implied verb is ἐστιν 'is' (in the present tense) [Alf, Ea, El, Hb, ICC, My]: the appeal we make to people (is) not from error, etc. The present tense would refer to their customary action, whenever and wherever they appeal to people [Ea, El, Hb, HNTC, ICC, My, NCBC, Wd]. He does not appeal to the Thessalonians' own knowledge in 2:3, 4 [ICC]. It includes the work done among the Thessalonians [Lns].
2. It is made specifically to the Thessalonians [TH, WBC; NJB, TEV; probably KJV]. The implied verb, then, is in the past tense [TH; KJV]: the appeal we made to you was not from error, etc.

QUESTION—What is meant by πλάνης 'error/deceit'?

1. It has a passive sense of being led astray [Alf, Ea, EBC, EGT, El, Er, Fn, Hb, Hn, HNTC, ICC, Lns, Mn, My, NCBC, NIC, Rb, TH, Wd; NASB, NEB, NIV, NJB, RSV, TEV, TNT]: our appeal is not from error. The missionaries were not deceived themselves, they were not in error. The missionaries were not mistaken in what they preached [Hb, NIC], because the gospel came from God [HNTC, ICC].
2. It has an active sense of leading astray [KJV, NAB]: our appeal is not from a motive to deceive people. The missionaries did not try to deceive others; they did not have deceit in mind as they appealed to people.
3. It means both of the above [WBC]. They were not deceived and did not deceive others.

QUESTION—What was the appeal or exhortation about?

They appealed to people to accept the Gospel [Ea, Fn, Hb, Lns, NCBC, NIC, TH], to turn from sin to God [Hn], to accept Jesus [Ea, Hn, HNTC, NCBC], and live for God [NCBC].

nor from uncleanness[a]

LEXICON—a. ἀκαθαρσία (LN 88.261): 'uncleanness' [Lns; KJV, RSV], 'impurity' [Hn, HNTC, ICC, LN, WBC; NASB], 'impure (motives)' [NAB, NIV, NJB, TEV], 'immorality' [BAGD, LN], 'base (motives)' [NEB], 'licentiousness' [TNT].

QUESTION—What is meant by ἀκαθαρσίας 'uncleanness'?
1. It refers to general moral impurity [Alf, Ea, EGT, El, Fn, Hn, HNTC, Lns, My, NCBC, TH]. Some of the wrong motives that are suggested are greed [Alf, Ea, EGT, El, Fn, Hn, HNTC, Lns, My], ambition [EGT, HNTC], vanity [My], pride [HNTC], and honor or popularity [EGT, Hn, HNTC, Lns]. This can include sexual immorality [NCBC].
2. It refers specifically to sexual impurity [EBC, Hb, ICC, Mn, NIC, WBC, Wd].

nor (is/was it) in[a] guile,[b]
LEXICON—a. ἐν (LN 89.80; 89.26): 'in' [KJV], 'in connection with' [Lns], 'by way of' [WBC; NASB], 'works through' [HNTC], 'with' [Hn, ICC; RSV], 'from' [NAB, NJB], not explicit [NEB, NIV, TEV, TNT]. This refers to the manner of giving their appeal [Hb, Lns, Mn, NCBC], or the sphere or atmosphere in which the appeal is given [Ea, El, Hb, ICC, NIC].
b. δόλος (LN 88.154): 'guile' [WBC; KJV, RSV], 'deceit' [BAGD, Hn; NASB], 'deception' [HNTC], 'trickery' [NAB, NJB], 'treachery' [LN], 'cunning' [BAGD, Lns]. This noun is also translated as a verb: 'to deceive' [ICC; NEB, TNT], 'to trick' [NIV, TEV]. Some translate the verb conatively: 'to try to deceive/trick' [NEB, NIV, TEV, TNT].
QUESTION—What verb is implied by the preposition ἐν 'in'?
This implies the verb 'to be made (with)' [WBC; RSV], 'to come (with)' [Hn], 'to work (through)' [HNTC], 'to use' [NIC], or the phrase is rendered as a verb: 'to deceive/trick' [NEB, NIV, TEV, TNT].
QUESTION—What is the significance of the change of prepositions from ἐκ 'from' to ἐν 'in'?
1. There is a difference of meaning [Ea, Fn, Hb, Hn, HNTC, ICC, Lns, Mn, My, NCBC, NIC, WBC; NASB, NEB, NIV, RSV, TEV]. The focus changes from the source of the appeal (ἐκ) to the atmosphere in which it was made (ἐν) [Ea, Fn, Hb, Hn, ICC, NIC; RSV], or to the means by which it was made [HNTC, Lns, Mn]. This means that there was no intention to deceive [ICC; NEB, NIV, TEV].
2. There is no significant difference. Some translations do not indicate any change of meaning: 'from...from' [NAB, NJB].
QUESTION—What would be the purpose of using guile?
The purpose of the preacher would be to win the attention of people [ICC], to impress them [Hn], to attract them [NIC], to trick them into believing the message [NCBC], and becoming his converts [Hb, HNTC] so that he could get money [ICC].

2:4 but[a]
LEXICON—a. ἀλλά (LN 89.125): 'but' [HNTC; KJV, NASB, NEB, RSV], 'rather' [NAB], 'on the contrary' [Hn, ICC, Lns; NIV], 'instead' [TEV], 'no' [WBC; NJB, TNT].

QUESTION—What relationship is indicated by this conjunction?
This contrasts the negative statements in 2:3 with the positive statements in this verse [Hb, ICC].

as[a] we-have-been-approved[b] by God to-be-entrusted-with[c] the gospel

LEXICON—a. καθώς (LN 78.53; 64.14): This is paired with οὕτως 'so' to make a comparison. The pairs are: 'as...so' [Hn, ICC, WBC], 'just as...so' [NASB, RSV], 'even as...so' [HNTC], 'as...even so' [KJV], 'just as...just so' [Lns]. The other translations rearrange the clauses and avoid using these words.

b. perf. pass. indic. of δοκιμάζω (LN 27.45; 30.114): 'to be approved' [BAGD, Hn, HNTC, ICC, WBC; NASB, NIV, RSV], 'to be judged worthy' [TEV], 'to be tested' [LN, Lns], 'to be examined' [BAGD, LN], 'to be allowed' [KJV], 'to be thought fit' [Alf, Ea]. The passive voice is also translated actively: '(God) has approved (us)' [NJB], '(God) has approved (us) as fit' [NEB], 'to have met the test imposed on one' [NAB]. This is also translated as a prepositional phrase: 'with his approval' [TNT]. The perfect tense indicates that they are in a state of continued approvedness after being tested [EBC, Fn, Hb, Hn, HNTC, ICC, Lns, NIC, Rb, Wd], or that the testing and the approving both continue [TH].

c. aorist pass. infin. of πιστεύω (LN 35.50): 'to be entrusted' [BAGD, Hn, HNTC, ICC, LN, Lns, WBC; all versions except KJV, TNT], 'to be put in trust' [KJV]. The passive voice is also translated actively: '(God) decided that he could trust (us)' [TNT]. The infinitive indicates that this is the result of being tested and approved [Ea, Hb, Hn, Lns], or this is an explanation of what the testing was for [El].

QUESTION—How were they tested?
Their previous work in local areas won God's approval for missionary service [EBC, Hb, NCBC]. Or, this simply refers to God's knowledge of them [My] and means that he judged that he could entrust them with the gospel [HNTC, My, TH, Wd].

QUESTION—Who entrusted them with the gospel?
The passive voice implies that God entrusted it to them [Hb, HNTC, TH; TNT].

QUESTION—What is meant by being entrusted with the gospel?
This refers to their assignment or commission from God to preach the gospel [Hb, HNTC, NCBC]. They had the responsibility to preach it [TH]. They were to maintain its content [HNTC]. This ministry was to the Gentiles [EBC].

so[a] we-speak,[b]

LEXICON—a. οὕτως (LN 78.4): This is paired with καθώς 'as', above, to make a comparison.

b. pres. act. indic. of λαλέω (LN 33.70): 'to speak' [BAGD, HNTC, LN, Lns, WBC; all versions except NJB], 'to tell' [Hn, ICC, LN], 'to preach'

[NJB]. The present tense indicates customary or habitual action [Hb, Hn, HNTC, ICC, Lns, NIC, TH, Wd].

QUESTION—What is being compared?
Their practice corresponded exactly with their commission [Ea, El, Hb, My, WBC, Wd].

not as[a] pleasing[b] men,[c]

LEXICON—a. ὡς (LN 64.12; 89.61): 'as' [Hn, HNTC, Lns; KJV, NASB], 'like' [NAB], not explicit [ICC, WBC; NEB, NIV, NJB, RSV, TEV, TNT]. It marks the quality or condition of the people [My]: not as people who…but as people who, etc. Or, it implies manner [Fn]: not as though we were pleasing men.
  b. pres. act. participle of ἀρέσκω (LN 25.90): 'to please' [BAGD, Hn, HNTC, ICC, LN, Lns, WBC; all versions except NEB], 'to curry favor' [NEB]. The present tense is continuous [Alf, El]. Some commentators take the present tense to be conative: 'to strive/try/aim to please' [Alf, El, Lns, My, WBC; NAB, NIV, NJB, TEV, TNT]. Others think that this actually states the fact that they did not please men and that they did please God [HNTC, Mn, TH]. An example of pleasing men is to flatter them [NCBC]. To please God would be to serve him [Ea, NCBC] and do what he wants.
  c. ἄνθρωπος (LN 9.1): 'men' [BAGD, Hn, HNTC, ICC, Lns; all versions except NJB], 'people' [LN], 'human beings' [BAGD, WBC; NJB], 'mankind' [LN].

QUESTION—How literally is this to be understood?
Their basic aim is to please God, not men [WBC]. They were also trying to please men in accordance with God's will for their benefit [WBC]. They did not deliberately aim to displease men [Wd]. This was their ruling aim and if any conflict between pleasing God or men should occur, they would always choose to please God [Hb].

but (as pleasing) God, the (one) testing[a] our hearts.[b]

LEXICON—a. pres. act. participle of δοκιμάζω (LN 27.45): 'to test' [BAGD, Hn, ICC, LN, Lns, WBC; all versions except KJV, NASB], 'to try' [KJV], 'to examine' [BAGD, LN; NASB], 'to scrutinize' [HNTC]. The present tense indicates that the testing was continuous [Fn, Hb, HNTC, Lns, NCBC, TH, Wd; NEB], or it characterizes God as 'the Tester' [NAB].
  b. καρδία (LN 26.3): 'hearts' [BAGD, Hn, HNTC, ICC, LN, Lns, WBC; all versions except TEV, TNT], 'inner selves' [LN], 'minds' [LN], 'motives' [TEV, TNT]. 'Heart' stands for thoughts and motives [HNTC, NCBC] and for the whole inner life [Fn, Hb, HNTC, Mn, NIC, TH, Wd]. The heart is the source of their motives [WBC].

QUESTION—What is the purpose of adding that God tests their hearts?
  1. This implies that this is the reason Paul is concerned about pleasing God [Hb, HNTC, NIC, Rb; TNT].

2. This implies that Paul is calling God to be the witness of the truth of his statement about their motives [Ea, EBC, Hn, WBC].

QUESTION—To whom does ἡμῶν 'our' refer?

It is used exclusively, referring to Paul, Silvanus, and Timothy [Alf, Ea, El, Hb, ICC, Mn, My, TH]. It is the same reference as λαλοῦμεν 'we speak' above [Ea].

2:5 Because/Indeed[a]

LEXICON—a. γάρ (LN 89.23; 91.1): 'because', 'for' [HNTC, Lns; KJV, NASB, RSV]; or 'indeed' [Hn, ICC; NJB]; not explicit [WBC; NAB, NEB, NIV, TEV, TNT].

QUESTION—What relationship is indicated by this conjunction?

1. It indicates the grounds for the statements made in 2:3–4 [Alf, El, Hb, Hn, HNTC, My, Wd]: it is true that we do not speak to please men but God, *since* we proved this in your case. The general statements are thus supported by the facts known by the readers [Hb, Hn, Wd].
2. It is explanatory [Ea, EBC, ICC, Lns, NCBC, NIC, TH]. It elaborates on the general principles (2:3–4) by specifying how these were applied in their behavior in Thessalonica [Ea, Hb, ICC, NCBC, NIC, TH], or it explains the words 'not in guile' (2:3) [Ea], or it resumes the γάρ 'because' of 2:3 [ICC, NIC].

neither at-any-time[a] we-were[b] with[c] word[d] of-flattery,[e]

LEXICON—a. ποτέ (LN 67.9): 'at any time' [LN, Lns; KJV], not explicit [HNTC; NAB, TEV]. This word is also conflated with the negative idea in οὔτε 'neither': 'never' [Hn, WBC; NASB, NEB, NIV, NJB, RSV, TNT], 'never once' [ICC].

b. aorist pass. (deponent = active) indic. of γίνομαι (LN 13.3; 41.1): 'to be' [LN, Lns; NEB], 'to come' [Hn, ICC; NASB, TEV], 'to behave' [HNTC, LN], 'to conduct oneself' [LN], 'to act' [NJB]. This verb is also conflated with the preposition ἐν 'with': 'to use' [KJV, NIV, RSV, TNT], 'to be guilty of' [NAB], 'to have recourse to' [WBC], 'to come to share in' [El]. Here the verb with ἐν 'in' means to enter a state where they used flattery [Fn, Hb, Mn, NIC, TH] and to remain in it [Mn, NIC, TH].

c. ἐν (LN 89.80): 'with' [Hn, HNTC, ICC; NASB, NJB, TEV], 'in connection with' [Lns].

d. λόγος (LN 33.99): 'words' [BAGD; KJV, NAB, NEB, RSV, TNT], 'speech' [BAGD, Hn, HNTC, LN, Lns; NASB], 'talk' [WBC; TEV], 'address' [ICC]. This noun is also left implied in the following noun 'flattery' [NIV], or the verb 'to flatter' [NJB].

e. κολακεία (LN **33.367**): 'flattery', 'flattering' [BAGD, Hn, HNTC, LN, Lns, WBC; all versions], 'cajoling' [ICC].

QUESTION—How are the two nouns related in the genitive construction λόγῳ κολακείας 'word of flattery'?
1. The words are used in a flattering way [Alf, Ea, El, Fn, Hb, Hn, HNTC, ICC, Lns, My, WBC; KJV, NAB, NASB, NEB, TEV, TNT]: we did not use flattering words.
2. The words were motivated by flattery [EBC]: we did not use words that came from a desire to flatter you. This interpretation is mentioned as equally possible by HNTC.

as you-know,
QUESTION—How did they know?
They could remember Paul's visit with them [Hb, Hn]. They had heard him [ICC] and they knew that he did not flatter them [HNTC, Lns, NCBC].

nor with a-pretext[a] of-greed,[b]
LEXICON—a. πρόφασις (LN 88.230; 33.437): 'pretext' [BAGD, Hn, ICC, Lns, WBC; NAB, NASB], 'pretense' [LN], 'excuse' [BAGD, LN; NJB], 'cloak' [KJV, NEB, RSV], 'veiled desire' [HNTC]. This noun is also translated as a verb: 'to cover up' [TEV], 'to hide' [TNT], or as a phrase: 'to put on a mask to cover up' [NIV]. Something that appears good is used to conceal the real purpose [Ea, Hb]. A pretext may be plausible in itself, but it is used to conceal the real motive [NIC]. An example is to preach the gospel in order to obtain money [My, NCBC, NIC]. Those who translate with 'cloak' introduce a metaphor that is not in the Greek [Lns].
b. πλεονεξία (LN 25.22; 88.144): 'greed' [BAGD, Hn, ICC, LN; all versions except KJV], 'covetousness' [BAGD, Lns, WBC; KJV], 'avarice' [BAGD], 'exploitation' [LN]. This noun is also translated as a phrase: 'to desire to exploit' [HNTC].
QUESTION—How are the two nouns related in the genitive construction προφάσει πλεονεξίας 'pretext of greed'?
1. The pretext hides greed [Alf, Ea, El, Fn, Hn, Lns, My, NCBC, NIC, TH, WBC, Wd]: we did not use a pretext to conceal greedy plans. This should not imply that they actually were greedy and simply did not try to hide it [TH].
2. The pretext is caused or inspired by greed [EBC, HNTC, ICC, Mn]: what we did was not a pretext inspired by greed. There seems to be little difference in what is meant by the two interpretations [Hb, Hn].

God (is) witness,[a]
LEXICON—a. μάρτυς (LN 33.270): 'witness' [BAGD, Hn, HNTC, ICC, LN, Lns, WBC; all versions], 'one who testifies' [LN].
QUESTION—Why is this stated here?
The Thessalonians observed that they had not been flattered [Ea, Lns], but only God knew the motives behind the missionaries' conduct [Ea, EBC, El, Hb, HNTC, Lns, Mn, My, Wd]. This is a solemn affirmation of his statement

2:6 nor seeking[a] praise[b] from men,

LEXICON—a. pres. act. participle of ζητέω (LN 25.9; 57.59): 'to seek' [BAGD, Hn, HNTC, LN, Lns, WBC; KJV, NAB, NASB, NEB, RSV, TNT], 'to look for' [BAGD; NIV, NJB], 'to try to get' [BAGD, LN; TEV], 'to require' [ICC]. This does not imply that they did not receive unsought praise, but states that they did not seek it [EBC, Hb, ICC, NCBC, NIC]. The present tense indicates that it was their practice not to seek such praise [Hb].

b. δόξα (LN 33.357; 87.4): 'praise' [LN; NIV, TEV, TNT], 'honor' [BAGD, Hn, HNTC, ICC, LN; NEB, NJB], 'respect' [LN], 'glory' [Lns; KJV, NAB, NASB, RSV], 'fame' [BAGD], 'applause' [WBC].

QUESTION—What relationship is indicated by the participial form ζητοῦντες 'seeking'?

It indicates the manner in which they lived among them (2:5) [EBC, El, ICC], and it is the third negative statement 'we were neither...nor...nor...' [Hb, ICC, TH].

neither from you nor from others,

QUESTION—Is there any significance in the change of prepositions: not seeking praise *from* (ἐκ) men..., neither *from* (ἀπό) you nor *from* (ἀπό) others?

1. There is no significant difference [El, HNTC, Lns, WBC].
2. There is a difference [Alf, Ea, Mn, My, NIC]. This is explained in two ways: ἐκ refers to the ultimate source, while ἀπό refers to the immediate agents [Mn, NIC], or ἐκ is used with the general source, while ἀπό is used with the special and specific sources [Alf, Ea, My].

QUESTION—Who are the ἄλλων 'others'?

They are people other than the Thessalonians, either other Christians [Hb], or other people in general, whether Christians or not [HNTC, Rb].

2:7 being-able[a] to be with weight[b]

LEXICON—a. pres. mid. (deponent = active) participle of δύναμαι (LN 74.5): 'to be able' [HNTC, ICC, LN, Lns; all versions], 'to be in a position to' [Hn], 'we might have' [WBC].

b. βάρος (LN 22.4; **65.56**): 'weight' [BAGD, Lns; NEB], 'full weight' [NJB], 'importance' [HNTC, LN; NAB], 'honor' [ICC], 'authority' [NASB], 'burden' [NIV], 'demands' [RSV, TEV], 'heavy demands' [TNT]. This noun is also translated as an adjective: 'burdensome' [KJV], 'formidable' [Hn]. The phrase ἐν βάρει εἶναι 'to be with weight' is translated as an idiom by most: 'to appear with weight' [Lns], 'to impose oneself on another with full weight' [NJB], 'to make one's weight felt' [NEB], 'to have a position of importance' [HNTC], 'to be in a position of honor' [ICC], 'to insist on one's own importance' [BAGD, LN; NAB], 'to assert one's authority' [NASB], 'to make oneself formidable' [Hn], 'to be a burden' [KJV, NIV], 'to make demands' [RSV, TEV, TNT], 'to require a person to support someone' [WBC].

QUESTION—What relationship is indicated by the participial form δυνάμενοι 'being able'?

1. It is concessive and is related to what precedes [Alf, Ea, EBC, El, Hb, Hn, HNTC, ICC, Mn, My, NCBC, Rb; NAB, NASB, NEB, RSV, TEV, TNT]: we did not seek praise, *although* we could have made demands. Some who label this as concessive translate with *when* [Alf, Ea, Mn]. Others do not state the connection but translate with *when* [KJV, NJB].
2. It is concessive and is related to what follows: [WBC; NIV]: *although* we could have made demands, yet we were gentle.

QUESTION—What is meant by βάρει 'weight'?

1. It means being a financial burden to the congregation [NIC, TH, WBC; KJV, NIV; probably RSV, TEV, TNT]: we had the right to have you provide what we wanted. It is a demand that the congregation maintain them [NIC, WBC]. It concerns pay (Luke 10:7) and food (Matt. 10:10) [WBC].
2. It means importance [Alf, Ea, EBC, El, Fn, Hn, HNTC, ICC, Lns, My, NCBC; NAB, NASB]: we had the right to wield authority and demand respect.
3. It means both of the above [EGT, Fn, Hb, Mn, Wd]: they were men of importance who could put a burden on the congregation's funds.

as[a] apostles[b] of-Christ;

LEXICON—a. ὡς (LN 64.12; 89.37): 'as' [BAGD, Hn, HNTC, ICC, Lns, WBC; all versions].

b. ἀπόστολος (LN 53.74): 'apostles' [BAGD, Hn, HNTC, ICC, LN, Lns, WBC; all versions except NEB], 'envoys' [BAGD; NEB], 'special messengers' [LN].

QUESTION—Who are the apostles?

They are the three men, Paul, Silvanus, and Timothy [Alf, Ea, EBC, El, Fn, Hb, HNTC, ICC, Lns, Mn, Rb, TH, WBC, Wd]. This is a broader use of the term than the technical term for the twelve plus Paul [Alf, EBC, Fn, Hb, HNTC, Lns, NCBC, WBC, Wd]. This refers to them as being missionaries [Hb, Mn, NCBC, Rb, Wd]. Their function was to found churches [NCBC].

but[a]

LEXICON—a. ἀλλά (LN 89.125): 'but' [BAGD, Hn, HNTC, WBC; KJV, NASB, NEB, NIV, RSV, TEV, TNT], 'instead' [NJB], 'on the contrary' [ICC, Lns; NAB].

QUESTION—What relationship is indicated by this conjunction?

This gives the positive side in contrast to the negatives in 2:5–7a [Alf, Ea, EBC, El, Hb, ICC, Lns, Mn, My].

we-were gentle^a in (the) midst^b of-you,

TEXT—Instead of ἤπιοι 'gentle', some manuscripts have νήπιοι 'babies'. GNT selects the reading 'babies' with a C rating, indicating a considerable degree of doubt in doing so. The reading 'babies' is also taken by ICC, Mn, NIC, and Rb. Some commentators grant that manuscript evidence favors the use of 'babies', but feel that the context forces them to accept the reading 'gentle' [Alf, Ea, EBC, El, Hb, Hn, HNTC, Lns, My, NCBC, TH, WBC, Wd].

LEXICON—a. ἤπιος (LN 88.61): 'gentle' [BAGD, Hn, HNTC, LN, Lns, WBC; all versions except NJB], 'kind' [LN]. This adjective is also translated as an adverb: '(to live) unassumingly' [NJB].

b. μέσος (LN 83.9): 'midst' [Hn, ICC, LN, Lns], 'middle' [BAGD]. Many conflate the phrase ἐν μέσῳ 'in the midst': 'among' [BAGD, HNTC, WBC; KJV, NAB, NASB, NIV, NJB, RSV], 'with' [NEB, TEV, TNT].

as if a nurse^a should-care-for^b her-own children;

LEXICON—a. τροφός (LN 35.52): 'nurse' [BAGD, Hn, ICC, LN, Lns, WBC; KJV, NEB, RSV, TNT]; or 'mother' [BAGD; NIV, NJB, TEV], 'nursing mother' [HNTC; NAB, NASB].

b. pres. act. subj. of θάλπω (LN 35.36): 'to care for' [NIV, TNT], 'to take care of' [LN; RSV, TEV], 'to tenderly care for' [NASB], 'to fondly care for' [NEB], 'to cherish' [BAGD, Hn, HNTC, ICC, WBC; KJV], 'to feed and look after' [NJB], 'to fondle' [NAB], 'to warm' [Lns], 'to comfort' [BAGD].

QUESTION—What is this phrase connected with and what is being compared?

1. It is connected with what precedes [EBC, Hb, Hn, Lns, NIC, WBC, Wd; KJV, NAB, NASB, NEB, NIV, RSV, TEV, TNT]: we were gentle among you, like a nurse (is gentle while) taking care of her children.
2. It is connected with what follows [HNTC, ICC, My, NCBC; NJB]: like a nurse (loves and) cares for her children, so we shared ourselves with you. When the preceding phrase is taken to refer to babies rather than gentleness, this is the best division [ICC]: although we were entitled to demand honor as Christ's apostles, yet we came as babies among you. As a nurse cares for her children, so we shared ourselves with you.
3. It serves double duty. It illustrates the preceding clause and serves as the protasis of the following clause [Ea, El].

QUESTION—Is the nurse the mother of the children?

1. The nurse is the mother [Alf, Ea, EBC, EGT, El, Fn, Hb, Hn, HNTC, ICC, Mn, My, NCBC, NIC, Rb, TH, WBC]. She is a nursing mother [Alf, Ea, EGT, El, Hb, HNTC, Mn, My, Rb, TH, WBC], or she nurses her own children by holding them and caring for them [EBC, Hn, NCBC, NIC].
2. The nurse is not the mother. The phrase τὰ ἑαυτῆς τέκνα 'her own children' would then mean the children put in her care [Lns].

2:8 so[a] loving[b] you

LEXICON—a. οὕτως (LN 61.9; 78.4): 'so' [BAGD, Hn, HNTC, ICC; KJV, RSV], 'thus' [BAGD, Lns; NASB], 'indeed' [TNT], not explicit [TEV]. This is also used to intensify the verb: 'so (much)' [BAGD; NAB, NIV, NJB], 'such' [WBC; NEB].
- b. pres. mid. (deponent = active) participle of ὁμείρομαι (LN **25.47**): 'to love' [NIV, TNT], '(to have) love for' [TEV], 'to be well disposed to' [NAB], 'to feel devoted to' [NJB], 'to have affection for' [WBC], 'to have a fond affection for' [NASB], 'to have kindly feeling' [BAGD], '(to have) great affection for' [LN], 'to be affectionately desirous of' [Hn; KJV, RSV], 'to be affectionately anxious about' [Lns], '(to have) yearning love' [NEB], 'to yearn after' [ICC], '(to have) great care for' [HNTC]. The present tense marks the continuous state of this affection [Hb].

QUESTION—What relationship is indicated by οὕτως 'so'?
1. It functions as a relational word [Alf, Ea, El, Hb, Hn, HNTC, ICC, Lns, My; KJV, RSV].
1.1 It summarizes 2:7 by dropping the figure and stating the thought literally [Hb, Lns; RSV]: so, in summary, we were pleased to share our souls with you.
1.2 It indicates the application of the preceding comparison [Alf, El, HNTC, ICC, My]: as a nurse cares for her children so we, etc.
2. It indicates degree [My, WBC; NAB, NEB, NIV]: so intensely did we love you (that) we were pleased to share our souls with you.

we-were-pleased/we-determined[a] to-share[b] with-you not only the gospel of-God

LEXICON—a. imperf. act. indic. of εὐδοκέω (LN 25.113; 30.97): 'to be pleased' [Lns], 'to be well pleased' [NASB], 'to be delighted' [NIV], 'to be glad' [Hn, ICC], 'to be happy' [NJB], 'to enjoy' [LN], 'to consider good' [BAGD]; or 'to be ready' [RSV, TEV], 'to be willing' [KJV], 'to consent' [BAGD], 'to want' [NAB], 'to choose' [WBC; NEB, TNT]; or 'to determine, to resolve' [BAGD], 'to prefer' [LN], 'to choose as better' [LN], 'to gladly determine' [HNTC]. This is not only what was intended, but what was accomplished [NIC]. The imperfect tense is a continuous tense [EBC, Hb, Lns] and indicates their habitual practice [NIC], while they were in Thessalonica [Rb].
- b. aorist act. infin. of μεταδίδωμι (LN 57.96): 'to share' [BAGD, Hn, HNTC, ICC, LN, WBC; NAB, NIV, NJB, RSV, TEV, TNT], 'to give' [LN], 'to impart' [BAGD, Lns; KJV, NASB, NEB]. 'To share' does not mean to get a share, but to give a share [Wd]. The aorist tense summarizes their work in Thessalonica [Hb], and states it as a fact [Lns].

QUESTION—What is meant by εὐδοκοῦμεν 'we were pleased/we determined'?
1. It emphasizes the delight it gave the missionaries to do so [Alf, EBC, Hn, ICC, Lns, Mn, NIC; NASB, NIV, NJB]: we were pleased to share with you.
2. It emphasizes the act of will in doing so [WBC; KJV, NAB, NEB, RSV, TEV, TNT]: we determined to share with you.
3. It means both of the above, a delighted resolve [Ea, Hb, HNTC, Wd].

QUESTION—In what way did they share the gospel?
They shared it by imparting the news of salvation [NIC].

QUESTION—How are the two nouns related in the genitive construction τὸ εὐαγγέλιον τοῦ θεοῦ 'the gospel of God'?
The gospel came from God [Hb, Lns; TEV]. See this phrase at 2:2.

but also our-own souls,[a]
LEXICON—a. ψυχή (LN 9.20): 'souls' [BAGD, Hn, Lns; KJV], 'selves' [ICC, WBC; NEB, RSV, TNT], 'lives' [NAB, NASB, NIV, NJB, TEV], 'persons' [LN], 'being' [HNTC]. This means the whole personality [Hb, HNTC, Mn, NIC] and includes the inmost being of a person [EBC, Hb, NCBC, NIC].

QUESTION—How does one share one's soul?
This does not merely mean to be ready to die for them [HNTC, WBC], it means to put one's self at another's disposal [WBC], to give one's time and energy to help others [Ea, Hn].

because[a] you-became[b] dear[c] to-us.
LEXICON—a. διότι (LN 89.26): 'because' [BAGD, Hn, HNTC, Lns; KJV, NASB, NIV, RSV], 'for' [ICC], not explicit [WBC; NAB, NEB, NJB, TEV]. The order of the clauses is also reversed and the relational word then occurs with the result clause 'that' [TNT].
  b. aorist pass. (deponent = active) indic. of γίνομαι (LN **13.3**; 13.48): 'to become' [Hn, HNTC, ICC, WBC; NAB, NASB, NEB, NIV, NJB, RSV], 'to be' [BAGD, LN, Lns; KJV, TEV]. The aorist tense states the fact [Lns]. This attitude has been developed once for all [Mn]. They came into this relationship when the missionaries began to preach to them [HNTC] and they accepted the gospel [El, Hb]. This also can indicate a development of affection [Ea, Hb].
  c. ἀγαπητός (LN 25.45): 'dear' [BAGD, ICC; KJV], 'very dear' [Hn, LN; NASB, RSV], 'so dear' [WBC; NAB, NEB, NIV, NJB, TEV], 'beloved' [BAGD, HNTC, LN, Lns]. This adjective is also translated as a verb: 'to dearly care for' [TNT].

QUESTION—What relationship is indicated by διότι 'because'?
This indicates the reason for the preceding clause [Ea, Hb, Hn, HNTC, Lns, My]: we were pleased to share our own souls with you *because* you became so dear to us. This repeats with other words the reason at the beginning of the verse, ὁμειρόμενοι 'because we loved you' [WBC].

1 THESSALONIANS 2:9

2:9 Because[a]

LEXICON—a. γάρ (LN 89.23; 91.1): 'because', 'for' [Hn, Lns; KJV, NASB, RSV], 'surely' [NIV, TEV], 'of course' [ICC], 'and' [HNTC], not explicit [WBC; NAB, NEB, NJB, TNT].

QUESTION—What relationship is indicated by this conjunction?
1. This indicates the grounds for the statement that the Thessalonians were dear to the missionaries (2:8) [Alf, My, NIC]. Here the proof is that he didn't want to burden them [Alf].
2. This indicates the grounds for the statement that the missionaries were imparting their very selves (2:8) [Ea, EBC, El]. The proof is the hard work they underwent on behalf of the Thessalonians [Ea, EBC, El].
3. This indicates the grounds for the statement that they were not using a pretext of greed (2:5) [Hn].
4. This indicates the grounds for the statements about their conduct in 2:5–8 [Hb, NCBC, Wd]. It includes their statements of loving concern and absence of greed [NCBC, Wd].
5. This explains what is involved in taking care of them (2:7) [HNTC, Lns].
6. This explains 2:7 and also illustrates what is meant by not seeking praise (2:6) [ICC].
7. This simply introduces a related topic [TH].

you-remember,[a] **brothers, the labor**[b] **of-us and the toil;**[c]

LEXICON—a. pres. act. indic./impera. of μνημονεύω (LN **29.7**): 'to remember' [BAGD, Hn, HNTC, ICC, LN, Lns, WBC; KJV, NEB, NIV, NJB, RSV, TEV, TNT], 'to recall' [NAB, NASB].

b. κόπος (LN 42.47): 'labor' [BAGD, WBC; KJV, NASB, RSV], 'toil' [BAGD, Hn, ICC, LN, Lns; NIV], 'work' [BAGD], 'efforts' [NAB], 'hard work' [LN], 'hard labor' [HNTC]. This noun is also translated as a verb: 'to toil' [NEB, TNT], 'to work' [TEV], 'to work with unsparing energy' [NJB]. See this word at 1:3.

c. μόχθος (LN 42.48): 'toil' [HNTC, LN, WBC; NAB, RSV], 'labor' [BAGD], 'hard labor' [LN], 'hardship' [Hn, ICC, Lns; NASB, NIV], 'exertion' [BAGD], 'travail' [KJV]. This noun is also translated as a verb: 'to drudge' [NEB], 'to toil' [TEV], 'to labor' [TNT].

QUESTION—What mood is μνημονεύετε 'you remember'?
1. It is indicative [Alf, Ea, Hn, HNTC, ICC, Lns, My, TH, WBC, Wd; KJV, NASB, NIV, NJB, RSV, TEV]: (I know that) you remember. This is a variation of the expression οἴδατε 'you know' (1:5; 2:1, 11) [Lns, TH].
2. It is imperative [NAB, NEB, TNT]: (you should) remember.

QUESTION—What is the purpose of using the two nouns κόπον 'toil' and μόχθον 'labor'?

This combination emphasizes the real and exhausting work they did [Alf, Ea, Hb, HNTC, TH, Wd]. Some commentators say that 'toil' stresses the activity involved and 'labor' stresses the exhaustion involved [Hb]. Others say that they mean, respectively, tiring work and painfulness [NCBC], or the fatigue they felt and the difficulties they encountered [EBC, Fn, Hb, Mn, TH], or suffering and hardships [El]. Others say that there is no significant difference between the two words [Alf, Ea, HNTC, Lns].

working[a] night and day

LEXICON—a. pres. mid. (deponent = active) participle of ἐργάζομαι (LN 42.41): 'to work' [BAGD, HNTC, LN, Lns, WBC; NAB, NASB, NIV, RSV, TEV], 'to labor' [LN; KJV], 'to slave' [NJB], 'to work for a living' [ICC; NEB], 'to work at a trade' [Hn; TNT]. The present tense indicates that this is their regular practice [Hb].

QUESTION—What kind of work is implied?

It implies working for wages [Hb, ICC, My]. In the case of Paul, it would probably be tentmaking (Acts 18:3) [Alf, EBC, Er, Hb, My, NCBC, WBC]. The other two did some sort of manual work [Alf, Hb, WBC], perhaps also tentmaking [NCBC].

QUESTION—What relationship is indicated by the participial form ἐργαζόμενοι 'working'?

1. This indicates an attendant circumstance to proclaiming the gospel [El, Hb, ICC]: we proclaimed the gospel *as* we worked night and day.
2. This explains what is involved in the previous clause 'our labor and toil' [My]: you remember our labor and toil, *that is*, we worked night and day.

QUESTION—How continuously did they work?

They did not work all night and all day, but part of the night and part of the day [Hb, Hn, ICC, Lns, NCBC, Wd]. Presumably, Paul preached when he was not working at a trade [Hb, Hn], although he might have preached as he worked [Wd].

QUESTION—What is implied by placing night before day?

The sequence with night preceding day emphasizes the noteworthy point that he even worked at night [Alf, Hb]. Perhaps it means that he started to work before dawn and on into the day so that part of the day could be used for preaching [EGT, Hb, Hn, Rb]. However, others say that the sequence 'night and day' is the normal order for Greek and Hebrew idioms [El, Fn, HNTC, Mn, TH] and could be rendered 'day and night' in English [HNTC, TH].

in-order-to[a] not to-burden[b] any of-you,

LEXICON—a. πρός (LN 89.60): 'in order to' [Hn; NAB, NIV], 'so as' [HNTC, Lns, WBC; NASB, NJB], 'so that' [TEV, TNT], 'that' [RSV], 'because' [KJV]. Some conflate this with the negative: 'rather than' [ICC; NEB].

b. aorist act. infin. of ἐπιβαρέω (LN **57.224**): 'to burden' [BAGD; RSV], 'to put a burden on' [ICC], 'to become burdensome' [WBC], 'to be a burden' [BAGD, Hn, LN, Lns; NASB, NEB, NIV, NJB, TNT], 'to impose on' [NAB], 'to be trouble' [TEV], 'to be a charge' [HNTC], 'to be chargeable' [KJV].

QUESTION—What relationship is indicated by πρός 'in order to'?

It indicates the purpose for working so hard [Hb, Hn, HNTC, Lns, NCBC, NIC, WBC; NAB, NASB, NIV, NJB].

QUESTION—What kind of a burden did he avoid putting on them?

The burden would have been a financial one [Hb, ICC, LN, TH, WBC, Wd], to look after the missionaries [NCBC] and maintain them [Alf, My].

we-proclaimed[a] to you the gospel of-God.
LEXICON—a. aorist act. indic. of κηρύσσω (LN 33.206; 33.207; 33.256): 'to proclaim' [BAGD, Hn, LN; NASB, NEB, NJB], 'to announce' [LN], 'to preach' [HNTC, ICC, LN, Lns, WBC; KJV, NAB, NIV, RSV, TEV, TNT], 'to tell' [LN]. The aorist tense summarizes the proclaiming they did the whole time they were in Thessalonica [Hb].

QUESTION—How are the nouns related in the genitive construction τὸ εὐαγγέλιον τοῦ θεοῦ 'the gospel of God'?

See this construction at 2:2, 8. Here, only NIC mentions God to be the source of the gospel.

2:10 You (are) witnesses[a] and God,
LEXICON—a. μάρτυς (LN 33.270): 'witnesses' [BAGD, Hn, HNTC, ICC, LN, Lns, WBC; all versions except NEB, TNT], 'ones who testify' [LN]. This noun is also translated as a verb: 'to testify' [TNT], 'to be called to witness' [NEB]. See this word at 2:5.

QUESTION—Why is God also called to witness?

The Thessalonians can bear witness to what they have seen, but only God knows the heart and motives [Alf, Ea, EBC, El, Hb, Hn, Lns, My, Wd]. God would know if there were any deception in the outward acts [HNTC, NCBC]. This implies that he is confident that their knowledge will bear out his statements [Ea].

how[a] holily[b] and righteously[c] and blamelessly[d] we-behaved[e]
LEXICON—a. ὡς (LN 89.86; 90.21; 78.13): 'how' [BAGD, Hn, HNTC, ICC, Lns, WBC; all versions except NJB, TEV], 'that' [BAGD; NJB, TEV]. This word indicates the degree in which they showed these qualities [Hb, Lns]. It implies a high degree of these qualities [Hb, My].
b. ὁσίως (LN **88.24**): 'holily' [Lns; KJV], 'devoutly' [BAGD; NASB], 'piously' [Hn, ICC]. This adverb is also translated as an adjective: 'holy' [HNTC, LN; NIV, RSV], 'devout' [WBC; NEB], 'upright' [NAB, NJB], 'pure' [TEV, TNT].
c. δικαίως (LN 88.15): 'righteously' [Hn, ICC, LN, Lns], 'justly' [LN; KJV], 'uprightly' [BAGD; NASB]. This adverb is also translated as an adjective: 'righteous' [NIV, RSV], 'just' [HNTC, WBC; NAB, NEB, TNT], 'right' [TEV], 'fair' [NJB].
d. ἀμέμπτως (LN **88.317**): 'blamelessly' [BAGD, Hn, ICC, Lns; NASB], 'unblameably' [KJV]. This adverb is also translated as an adjective: 'blameless' [WBC; NEB, NIV, RSV, TNT], 'without blame' [LN], 'irreproachable' [NAB], 'faultless' [HNTC], 'without fault' [TEV]. It is also translated as an adverb which modifies the other two words: 'impeccably' [NJB].

e. aorist passive (deponent = active) indic. of γίνομαι (LN 13.3; **41.1**): 'to behave' [HNTC, ICC; KJV, NASB], 'to be' [NIV], 'to conduct oneself' [Hn], 'to show oneself' [Lns], 'to prove oneself' [BAGD]. This verb is also translated as a phrase: 'our conduct was' [LN; NAB, TEV, TNT], 'our behavior was' [WBC; NEB, RSV], 'our treatment (of you) has been' [NJB]. The aorist tense considers the whole time of their visit as a unit [Hb], it is a past fact [Lns].

QUESTION—What is indicated by the combination of these three adverbs?

They are similar in meaning, and emphasize their right behavior [Ea, Hb, NCBC, NIC, TH, Wd]. The use of adverbs instead of adjectives focuses on the way they behaved rather than on their character [Ea, El, Hb, HNTC, Mn]. The first two are positive qualities, and the last is the negative result of doing the positive ones [Ea, EBC, El, Hb, HNTC, ICC, Mn, My, NIC].

to-you the (ones) believing,

QUESTION—What relationship is indicated by the use of the dative case ὑμῖν 'to you'?

1. This means 'in relation to you', 'towards you' [Hb, HNTC, Rb, WBC; all versions except KJV, NIV].
2. This means 'in your sight or opinion' [Alf, Ea, ICC, Lns, My]. The specification that they are believers is important, because the judgment of unbelievers is of no value [Lns], only believers are qualified to judge in these matters [Ea], and the outsiders were opposed to them [My].
3. This means 'among you' [NCBC; KJV, NIV].
4. This means 'for your benefit', 'for your sake' [EBC, El, HNTC].

2:11 just-as[a] you-know how[b] each one of-you,

LEXICON—a. καθάπερ (LN 64.15): 'just as' [Hn, Lns; NASB], 'as' [HNTC, ICC, WBC; KJV, NEB, NJB], 'likewise' [NAB], 'for' [NIV, RSV], not explicit [TEV, TNT].

b. ὡς (LN 89.86; 90.21): 'how' [Hn, Lns, WBC; KJV, NAB, NASB, RSV, TNT], 'that' [NIV, TEV], not explicit [HNTC, ICC; NEB, NJB].

QUESTION—What is the function of καθάπερ 'just as'?

Their knowledge confirms his statement in 2:10 [Alf, El, Hb, My, NCBC]: what we said about our conduct is true, because you know we urged you to live good lives. The argument assumes that what someone earnestly desires others to do is what he himself wants to do [My].

like[a] a-father (with) his children,

LEXICON—a. ὡς (LN 64.12): 'like' [Hn; RSV], 'as' [HNTC, ICC, Lns, WBC; all versions except RSV, TEV], 'just as' [TEV].

QUESTION—What are the comparisons involved in this simile?

The nonfigurative statement is: (we) (verb) each one of you. The comparison is: like a father (verb) his children. There are various ways of filling in the implied verbs according to how the point of comparison is taken.

1. The point of comparison is the common responsibility or right of the missionaries and a father in training [Hb], or in instructing [EBC, El, Hb, HNTC, Mn, My, NCBC, TH, WBC] those who are in their charge and need to be trained. The point of comparison can be indicated by making explicit the similar actions of the missionaries and a father. Suggested verbs are 'we treated' [WBC; NJB, TEV, TNT], 'we dealt with' [Hn, NIC; NEB, NIV], 'we counseled' [HNTC]. The comparison then is: we treated/dealt/dealt with you like a father treats/counsels/deals with his children. Specifically, we exhorted, encouraged, and charged you. Instead of a generic word, some want to supply the specific verbs in the comparison: like a father exhorts, encourages, and charges his children [Bul (p. 89)]. In such a case, the different categories of address are the points of comparison, but the actual words would be different, i.e., the missionaries would be concerned about their spiritual conduct and a father would be concerned about all aspects of child training.
2. The point of comparison is the manner in which both missionaries and a father exhort, encourage, and charge the people and children. It is suggested that this refers to their earnest concern for the believers'/children's welfare [Ea, Hb, NCBC], and also to their love [NCBC].
3. There are secondary points of similarity. 'We' is compared to 'a father' and 'you' is compared with 'children'. The points of comparison for these are probably (1) the begetting relationship [Hb, Lns, NCBC]: we brought you to spiritual life, like a father brings his children to physical life; (2) the affection involved [Hb, Hn, Lns, NCBC]: we love you, like a father loves his children; (3) the immaturity of those being trained [Hb, Hn, Lns]: you were spiritually immature, like children are mentally, emotionally, and physically immature.

QUESTION—What is the significance of the phrase ἕνα ἕκαστον ὑμῶν 'each one of you'?

Each believer had his own needs to be dealt with [Hb, HNTC, ICC], thus requiring one or the other of the participles in 2:12 [ICC]. This may indicate that they spoke to people individually [Hb, Hn], or that they gave attention to special needs in the course of public preaching [NIC].

2:12 exhorting[a] you and encouraging/comforting[b] and charging[c]

TEXT—Instead of beginning 2:12 with this phrase, some begin it after the first participle παρακαλοῦντες 'exhorting' [NAB], or after the second participle παραμυθούμενοι 'encouraging' [ICC], or after the third participle μαρτυρόμενοι 'charging' [Hb, Lns; KJV, NASB, NEB, RSV].

LEXICON—a. pres. act. participle of παρακαλέω (LN 25.150; 33.168): 'to exhort' [BAGD, HNTC, WBC; KJV, NAB, NASB, RSV], 'to encourage' [BAGD, LN; NIV, TEV], 'to appeal' [BAGD, LN; NEB], 'to admonish' [Hn, Lns], 'to urge' [BAGD, ICC; NJB, TNT].

b. pres. mid. (deponent = act.) participle of παραμυθέομαι (LN 25.153): 'to encourage' [BAGD, Hn, HNTC, LN, Lns, WBC; NAB, NASB, NJB,

RSV, TNT], 'to comfort' [LN; KJV, NIV, TEV], 'to console' [LN]. This participle is also translated as a noun: 'encouragement' [ICC; NEB]. The difference between encouraging and comforting is whether the affliction is still to come or has already happened [Lns].
  c. pres. mid. (deponent = act.) participle of μαρτύρομαι (LN **33.319**; 33.223): 'to charge' [WBC; KJV, RSV], 'to urge' [NIV, TEV], 'to appeal to' [NJB], 'to plead with' [NAB], 'to implore' [BAGD; NASB, TNT], 'to insist' [BAGD, HNTC, LN], 'to testify' [Hn, Lns]. This participle is also translated as a noun: 'solemn appeal' [ICC], '(to appeal with) solemn injunctions' [NEB]. This differs from the other two participles by implying that they have authority to make demands on them [HNTC].

QUESTION—What is indicated by the use of the present tense for the three participles?

This indicates their continual practice [Hb, TH]. The present participles can be combined with an implied repetition of ἐγενήθημεν 'we were', in the imperfect tense, to form an imperfect periphrastic [Alf, Ea, EBC, Hn, Lns]: we were exhorting, encouraging, and charging you.

QUESTION—What is the difference between the first two participles παρακαλοῦντες 'exhorting' and παραμυθούμενοι 'encouraging'?
  1. They are almost synonymous [HNTC, TH, WBC]. Both words contain the elements of admonishing and consoling, and they reinforce each other [HNTC].
  2. There is a difference intended: 'exhorting' refers to a strong appeal to do something while 'encouraging' focuses on inspiring them to continue in what they are doing [Hb]. The first emphasizes the command to do something, the second the assurance that they can do what is commanded [NCBC].
  3. The first is generic, the second and third are specific applications according to the need [ICC].

that/in-order-that[a] you walk[b] worthily[c] of-God

LEXICON—a. εἰς τό (LN 90.23; 89.57) with infinitive: 'that' [Hn, HNTC; KJV]; or 'so that' [NASB]. Some do not translate this word, but merely have the infinitive 'to walk', indicating that it is the content of the charge [ICC, WBC; NAB, NEB, NIV, NJB, RSV, TEV, TNT].
  b. pres. act. infin. of περιπατέω (LN 41.11): 'to walk' [HNTC, ICC, Lns; KJV, NASB], 'to live' [LN], 'to behave' [LN], 'to live a life' [Hn; NEB, NIV, NJB, TEV, TNT], 'to lead a life' [RSV], 'to make a life' [NAB], 'to conduct oneself' [BAGD, WBC]. The present tense indicates habitual conduct [Hb].
  c. ἀξίως (LN 65.17): 'worthily, worthy' [BAGD, Hn, HNTC, ICC, LN, Lns, WBC; all versions except TEV]. This is also translated as a phrase: 'the kind that pleases (God)' [TEV].

QUESTION—What relationship is indicated by εἰς 'that/in order that'?
1. This indicates the content of the exhorting, encouraging, and charging [Hn, HNTC, ICC, Lns, Mn, WBC; KJV, NAB, NEB, NIV, NJB, RSV, TEV, TNT]: that.
2. This indicates their purpose in doing these actions [Alf, Ea, EBC, El, My, NIC, Rb; NASB]: in order that.
3. This indicates both the purpose and the content [Hb, NCBC].

QUESTION—What is meant by walking worthily of God?
Although some commentators refer to this as a metaphor to describe one's conduct [HNTC, Mn, NCBC, TH, Wd], many do not mention the figure and seem to treat it as an idiom [ICC], or dead metaphor, with no comparison with walking intended. It means to live in a manner worthy of the relationship they have with God [Hn, HNTC, ICC], to live as the gospel teaches [Hb], to live in a way that will honor God and agree with God's character [NCBC], to live like God lives [Lns], to live in accordance with God's standards [EBC], to live as is appropriate for one who is in God's kingdom [HNTC], or to live as is appropriate for the relationship they have with God [TH].

the (one) calling[a] you to his-own kingdom[b] and glory.[c]
LEXICON—a. pres. act. participle of καλέω (LN 33.312): 'to call' [BAGD, Hn, HNTC, ICC, LN, Lns, WBC; all versions].
b. βασιλεία (LN 37.64): 'kingdom' [BAGD, Hn, HNTC, ICC, Lns, WBC; all versions except NAB], 'kingship' [NAB], 'rule' [LN], 'reign' [LN].
c. δόξα (LN 79.18; 1.15): 'glory' [Hn, HNTC, ICC, LN, Lns, WBC; all versions except TNT], 'splendor' [LN]. This noun is also translated as an adjective modifying βασιλείαν 'kingdom': 'glorious' [TNT].

QUESTION—What is the significance of the present tense of the participle καλοῦντος 'calling'?
1. The present tense is used in a timeless sense and characterizes God as the one who calls: 'the Caller' [EBC, Fn, ICC, Lns, WBC]. It does not focus on any particular call or time [Lns]. Believers were individually called to salvation in the past [EBC, WBC]. With this interpretation, 'the caller' keeps on calling new people to be his people [HNTC].
2. The present tense is continuous [Alf, Ea, El, Hb, HNTC, Mn, My, NCBC, NIC, Rb, Wd]: God is continually calling you. They were initially called in the past to salvation [Fn, Hb], but there is also a continuing call concerning the future which is directed to them until the manifestation of the kingdom and glory [El, Hb, HNTC, NCBC, NIC].

QUESTION—How does God call them?
He calls them by means of men preaching and teaching the gospel to them [Hn, ICC]. The gospel message is God's call [NCBC].

QUESTION—What is the relationship between the nouns in the phrase τὴν βασιλείαν καὶ δόξαν 'the kingdom and glory'?
1. They are two objects of the call [Alf, El, Mn, My, NIC, WBC]: he calls you to his kingdom and also to his glory. The kingdom will be manifested at the same time God's glory will be manifested [NIC, WBC].
2. This is a hendiadys in which the second noun is emphatic and modifies the first [Bul (p. 668); TNT]: he calls you to his glorious kingdom.
3. 'And glory' explains 'his own kingdom' [Lns]: he calls you to his kingdom, specifically to the form of the kingdom that will exist when we shall share in God's glory.

QUESTION—Why is this descriptive phrase added here?
The future kingdom and glory are an incentive for living a life worthy of God now [EBC, NCBC, NIC].

DISCOURSE UNIT: 2:13–16 [EBC, EGT, El, Fn, Hb, Hn, HNTC, ICC, Mn, My, NCBC, NIC, TH, WBC, Wd; NJB]. The topic is thanksgiving [EBC, EGT, Hb, HNTC, Mn, WBC], the missionaries' message [NIC], the reception of the message [ICC, NCBC], the Thessalonians' faith and patience [NJB], persecution [Fn, Wd]. It is further divided into the following units: 2:13, 14–16 [EBC, NIC]; 2:13, 14, 15–16 [Wd].

2:13 And[a]
TEXT—This word is omitted in some manuscripts. It is included in GNT without an indication that some omit it. It is omitted by KJV. Some do not translate it [NAB, NEB, NJB, TNT], probably more for literary style than for textual reasons.
LEXICON—a. καί (LN 89.92): 'and' [Hn, HNTC, ICC, Lns, WBC; NASB, NIV, RSV, TEV], not explicit [KJV, NAB, NEB, NJB, TNT].
QUESTION—What relationship is indicated by this conjunction?
It indicates a close relationship with the preceding paragraph [Hb, My, TH], but a new development [TH]. The preceding paragraph was about the way the gospel was delivered in Thessalonica; this paragraph is about the way it was received [Hb, HNTC, Lns, My, NCBC].

because-of[a] this also[b] we thank[c] God unceasingly,[d]
LEXICON—a. διά (LN 89.26): 'because'. The phrase διὰ τοῦτο is translated 'because of this' [HNTC], 'for this' [Lns; RSV], 'for this reason' [Hn, ICC, WBC; NASB], 'for this cause' [KJV], 'the reason why is that' [NJB], 'that is why' [NAB], 'this is why' [NEB], 'there is a reason why' [TEV], 'there is something (else)' [TNT]. This phrase is also conflated with ὅτι 'because' in the following clause: 'because' [NIV].
b. καί (LN 89.93): 'also' [Hn, WBC; KJV, NASB, NIV, RSV], 'too' [ICC, Lns], 'another (reason)' [NJB, TEV], '(something) else' [TNT], not explicit [HNTC; NAB, NEB].
c. pres. act. indic. of εὐχαριστέω (LN 33.349; 25.100): 'to thank' [Hn, HNTC, ICC, LN; all versions except TEV], 'to give thanks' [BAGD,

WBC; TEV], 'to be thankful' [LN, Lns], 'to be grateful' [LN]. The present tense indicates that they continue to be thankful [Hb]. This may not refer to words spoken to God, but to a constant feeling of gratitude [Lns]. See this word at 1:2.
- d. ἀδιαλείπτως (LN **68.55**): 'unceasingly' [BAGD, HNTC, LN, WBC], 'constantly' [BAGD, Hn; NAB, NASB, RSV, TNT], 'continually' [ICC; NEB, NIV, NJB], 'without ceasing' [Lns; KJV], 'always' [TEV]. See this word at 1:2.

QUESTION—What does διὰ τοῦτο 'because of this' refer to, and how is it connected with the following ὅτι 'that/because'?
1. 'Because of this' refers forward and indicates that the reason for giving thanks is that the Thessalonians accepted God's word [EGT, Hn, Lns, NCBC, TH, WBC, Wd; NEB, NIV, NJB, RSV, TEV, TNT]: we thank God because of this, namely, because/that you accepted his word.
2. 'Because of this' refers backward and indicates that the reason for giving thanks is something that has already been stated and ὅτι 'that' introduces the content of the thanksgiving [Alf, Ea, EBC, El, Fn, Hb, HNTC, Mn, My; NAB]: because of that which has been stated, we thank God that you accepted his word. It is because their visit was not empty (2:1) that they still thank God [HNTC], or it is because God is calling the Thessalonians (2:12) that they thank God that the Thessalonians accepted the word [Alf, My], or it is because of the missionaries' earnest work to deliver the gospel (2:1–12), that they thank God that the Thessalonians responded to it [EBC, El, Mn].
3. The reference is both backward and forward [ICC, NCBC]: because of the preceding, we thank God and specifically because of this, namely, that you accepted his word.

QUESTION—What is meant by καί 'also'?
1. This implies that others are also giving thanks [Alf, Ea, El, Hb, Hn, ICC, Lns, My, Rb, WBC].
    1.1 The other people are the Thessalonians [Ea, El, Hb, Hn, ICC, Lns, Rb, WBC]: (along with you Thessalonians) we also give thanks.
    1.2 The other people are all the believers in Macedonia and Achaia (1:7) [Alf] and everywhere (1:8) [My]: (along with all the other believers who have heard about you) we also give thanks.
2. This implies that the missionaries have already given one reason for giving thanks [KJV, NJB, TEV, TNT]: (besides the previously mentioned reason or reasons) we give thanks also because, etc.
3. The word merely emphasizes 'we thank' without pointing to something else [EBC, EGT, HNTC, Mn, Mou (p. 167), NIC, TH]: we, on our part, thank God, or this is in fact why we thank God. This gives the missionaries' response to the news that they had received [Mn].

QUESTION—What is implied by thanking God for the way the Thessalonians received the gospel?

This implies that they recognize that God worked in the hearts of the Thessalonians to make it possible for them to accept the message as they did [Hb].

that/because^a having-received^b (the) word^c of-hearing/message^d from us, the (word) of-God

LEXICON—a. ὅτι (LN 90.21; 89.33): 'that' [Hn, HNTC, Lns, WBC; NAB, NASB, NJB, RSV, TNT]; or 'because' [ICC; KJV, NEB, NIV]; not explicit [TEV].

b. aorist act. participle of παραλαμβάνω (LN 27.13; 33.238): 'to receive' [BAGD, Hn, HNTC, ICC, Lns, WBC; KJV, NAB, NASB, NIV, RSV], 'to learn from someone' [LN], 'to learn by tradition' [LN], 'to receive instruction from' [LN], 'to be taught by' [LN]. This is also translated by using the reciprocal verb: 'to bring (to you)' [NJB, TEV], 'to hand on (to you)' [NEB], 'to pass on (to you)' [TNT].

c. λόγος (LN 33.260; 33.98): 'word' [BAGD, Hn, HNTC, ICC, LN, Lns, WBC; KJV, NASB, NIV, NJB, RSV], 'message' [BAGD, Hb, LN; NAB, NEB, TEV, TNT], 'gospel' [LN].

d. ἀκοή (LN 24.57; 24.52): in the active sense, 'hearing' [LN, Lns, Wd], or in the passive sense, 'what is heard' [LN], 'message' [Hb, HNTC, LN, Mn, My, Rb; NASB], 'report' [BAGD], 'preaching' [BAGD, Ea, My]. This noun is also translated as a verb in the active sense: 'to hear' [Hn, ICC, WBC; KJV, NIV, NJB, RSV, TEV, TNT].

QUESTION—What relationship is indicated by the participial form παραλαμβόντες 'having received'?

It is temporal: *when* [Hb, Hn, HNTC, ICC, WBC; KJV, NASB, NEB, NIV, RSV, TEV, TNT], or *immediately after* [El], or *as soon as* [NJB], you received the word, you accepted it.

QUESTION—How are the words to be related in the double genitive construction, λόγον ἀκοῆς παρ' ἡμῶν τοῦ θεοῦ 'word of hearing/message from us the (word) of God'?

1. 'Word' goes with of 'hearing/message' [Ea, El, Hb, Hn, ICC, Mn, NIC, Rb].
    1.1 'From us' goes with 'receiving' [El, Fn, Hn, ICC, Mn, NIC]: having received from us the word which you heard, which word is the word from God.
    1.2 'From us' goes with 'hearing' [NJB]: having received the word which you heard from us, which word is the word from God.
2. 'Word' goes with 'of God' [Bul (p. 414), Lns, My, WBC; KJV, NIV, RSV]: having received the word of God, which you heard from us. The genitive phrase λόγον τοῦ θεοῦ 'word of God' means the word which is from God [Lns, My].

you-accepted[a] (it) not (as) a-word of-men

LEXICON—a. aorist mid. (deponent = active) indic. of δέχομαι (LN 31.51; 57.125): 'to accept' [BAGD, Hn, HNTC, LN, WBC; NASB, NIV, RSV, TEV], 'to receive' [LN; KJV, NEB, TNT], 'to receive readily' [LN], 'to take' [NAB], 'to welcome' [ICC; NJB], 'to obtain' [Lns]. See this word at 1:6.

QUESTION—What is the difference between παραλαμβάνω 'to receive' and δέχομαι 'to accept'?

1. There is a difference: the first is an external, outward hearing while the second is an internal reaction of approval [Ea, Hb, Hn, ICC, Mn, NIC], and the first is objective and the second is subjective [Alf, Ea, EBC, Fn, My, NIC, WBC].
2. There is no significant difference between the two verbs [Lns, NCBC].

QUESTION—What is the object of ἐδέξασθε 'you accepted'?

1. They accepted *it* (the word they heard) in a certain way, with 'as' implied [Hn, ICC, NCBC, NIC, Rb, TH, WBC, Wd; all versions except NJB]: you accepted it not as the word of man but as the word of God.
2. They accepted the word, without 'as' implied, thus stressing the character of the word itself [Alf, Ea, EBC, El, Fn, Hb, HNTC, Lns, Mn, My; NJB]: you accepted not the word of man, but the word of God.

QUESTION—What is implied in this clause?

Since it was actually spoken by men (Paul, Silvanus, and Timothy [HNTC]), it is implied that they did not accept it *merely* as the word of men [Ea, NCBC, TH, WBC], and that they recognized that it did not originate from man's ideas [Alf, El, Hb, HNTC, NIC, TH].

but as truly[a] it-is a-word of-God,

LEXICON—a. ἀληθῶς (LN 70.3): 'truly' [BAGD, LN, Lns, WBC; NAB, NEB], 'in truth' [BAGD; KJV], 'really' [BAGD, Hn, HNTC, ICC, LN; NASB, NJB, RSV], 'actually' [BAGD; NIV], 'indeed' [TEV, TNT].

QUESTION—Why isn't the article with λόγον 'word'?

No one discusses this matter. Some translate this with the article [WBC; KJV, NAB, NASB, NEB, NIV, RSV]: the word of God. Other translate with an indefinite article [Hn, HNTC, ICC; TNT]: a word of God.

which/who also[a] works[b] in[c] you

LEXICON—a. καί (LN 89.93): 'also' [Hn, ICC, Lns; KJV, NASB], not explicit [HNTC, WBC; NAB, NEB, NIV, NJB, RSV, TEV, TNT].
  b. pres. mid. indic. of ἐνεργέω (LN 42.3): 'to work' [BAGD, HNTC, LN; NJB], 'to be at work' [BAGD, Hn, LN; NAB, NEB, NIV, RSV, TEV, TNT], 'to effectually work' [WBC; KJV], 'to perform work' [NASB], 'to be operative' [ICC], 'to be effective' [BAGD, Lns]. The present tense indicates a continuous working [Hb; NJB].
  c. ἐν (LN 83.13; 83.9): 'in' [Hn, HNTC, ICC, Lns, WBC; KJV, NASB, NEB, NIV, RSV, TEV], 'within' [NAB], 'among' [NJB, TNT].

QUESTION—What is the significance of καί 'also'?
The message is not only from God, it also works in them [Alf, Ea, El, Hb], or the message is not only heard by them, it also works in them [ICC, NCBC]. Many do not explicitly translate this word [HNTC, WBC; NAB, NEB, NIV, NJB, RSV, TEV, TNT].

QUESTION—What or who is working in the people?
1. The word is working in them [Ea, EBC, El, Fn, Hb, Hn, HNTC, ICC, Lns, My, WBC, Wd; all versions except TEV, TNT]: the word *which* works in you. It is implied that God works through his word [Hn, HNTC].
2. God is working in them [NIC, TH; TEV, TNT]: *who* works in you.

QUESTION—What work is done?
The word (or God) affects the lives of the believers [EBC, Hb, Hn, Lns]. It changes their thoughts and actions [TH]. As a result of this work, they turned from idols to God [Hn, Lns] and joyfully witness in the midst of persecution [Hn].

the (ones) believing.
QUESTION—Why is this phrase included here?
It identifies ὑμῖν 'you' [Hb, My]. It indicates that the condition for being worked upon is that the people believe [Ea, Hb, HNTC, Lns, Mn, My, NCBC, NIC].

QUESTION—What is the significance of the present tense of the participle πιστεύουσιν 'believing'?
It indicates a present characteristic of the people [Ea, El, Hb, Mn, NIC]. Some have shown this by translating with the substantive 'believers' [Hb, Lns, WBC; RSV]. The present tense indicates that they must continue to believe to continue to benefit from the work [Mn, NIC].

QUESTION—What or who is the object of the event *to believe?*
They believe in Jesus Christ. This is probably implied by those who translate with the noun *believers* [Hb, Lns, WBC; NJB, RSV].

DISCOURSE UNIT: 2:14–20 [NAB]. The topic is the suffering they share in common.

2:14 Because[a]
LEXICON—a. γάρ (LN 89.23): 'because', 'for' [Hn, HNTC, ICC, Lns, WBC; KJV, NASB, NIV, NJB, RSV], not explicit [NAB, NEB, TEV, TNT].
QUESTION—What relationship is indicated by this conjunction?
1. This indicates the grounds for the statement that they received the word of God (2:13a) [EBC, HNTC, NCBC, WBC]: it is true that you received the word of God, *since* you became imitators of the churches in Judea. Receiving the word usually resulted in suffering for it [EBC, WBC]. Being willing to suffer for the word showed that they had really accepted it [NCBC].
2. This indicates the grounds for the statement that the word was working in them (2:13b) [Alf, Ea, EGT, El, Hb, Hn, Mn, My, NIC, Wd]: it is true that

the word works in you, *since* you became imitators of the churches in Judea. Its work was shown by the strength it gave them to endure persecution [Alf, Ea, NIC], or by their willingness to endure suffering [Hn, My].

you became imitators,[a] brothers, of-the churches[b] of-God the (ones) being in Judea

LEXICON—a. μιμητής (LN 41.45): 'imitators' [BAGD, Hn, HNTC, ICC, LN, Lns, WBC; NASB, NIV, RSV], 'followers' [KJV], 'one who does what others do' [LN]. This noun is also combined with the verb: 'to be made like' [NAB], 'to fare like' [NEB], 'your experience has been just like' [TNT], 'the same things happened' [TEV], 'to model oneself' [NJB].

b. ἐκκλησία (LN 11.32): 'churches' [BAGD, Hn, LN, Lns, WBC; all versions except NEB], 'congregations' [BAGD, LN; NEB], 'assemblies' [ICC], 'Christian communities' [HNTC]. See this word at 1:1.

QUESTION—What is meant by calling them μιμηταί 'imitators'?

The imitation was not a conscious act of theirs [Alf, Ea, HNTC, My, TH, WBC, Wd]. The kind of thing that happened to the Judean churches later happened to them [NCBC, TH, WBC; NEB, TEV, TNT].

QUESTION—How are the two nouns related in the genitive construction τῶν ἐκκλησιῶν τοῦ θεοῦ 'the churches of God'?

The churches belong to God [Hb, TH].

QUESTION—What area is included in Ἰουδαίᾳ 'Judea'?

1. This word refers only to the province of Judea, in distinction from the rest of Palestine [Rb, WBC]. Then Ἰουδαίων 'Jews' probably refers specifically to those Jews living in Judea [WBC].
2. This word is used in the wider sense to refer to all of Palestine, that is, it includes the provinces of Judea, Samaria, and Galilee [Hb, HNTC, Mn, NIC, TH].

in[a] Christ Jesus,

LEXICON—a. ἐν (LN 89.119): 'in' [Hn, HNTC, ICC, Lns, WBC; all versions except TEV, TNT], 'belong to' [TEV, TNT]. See this word at 1:1.

QUESTION—What relationship is indicated by ἐν 'in'?

1. This indicates a close personal relationship [Ea, El, Hb, Hn, NIC, WBC]: the churches which are in union with Christ Jesus, or the churches which are in fellowship with Christ Jesus.
2. This indicates ownership [TH; TEV]: the churches which belong to Christ Jesus.
3. This indicates a general relationship [Lns; TNT]: the churches which are connected with Christ Jesus.

QUESTION—What is the function of this phrase?

It identifies the church as Christian [Rb], in distinction from Jewish synagogues [EBC, Hb, HNTC, Lns, NCBC, NIC, TH], and from Greek assemblies [NIC]. It indicates the fellowship with unites the Christian churches [El, Hb, Mn, WBC].

because^a the same-things^b you also^c suffered^d from^e your-own countrymen^f

LEXICON—a. ὅτι (LN 89.33; 91.15): 'because' [HNTC, Lns], 'for' [Hn; KJV, NASB, RSV], 'in that' [ICC, WBC; NJB], not explicit [NAB, NEB, NIV, TEV, TNT].

  b. αὐτός (LN 58.31): 'same things' [Hn, LN, Lns, WBC; NIV, RSV], 'like things' [KJV], 'same treatment' [NAB, NJB], 'same' [HNTC, ICC; NASB], 'same persecutions' [TEV], not explicit [NEB]. It is also indicated by the relationship 'as...so did' [TNT].

  c. καί (LN 89.93): 'also' [Lns; KJV, NASB], 'in turn' [WBC], not explicit [Hn, HNTC, ICC; NAB, NEB, NIV, NJB, RSV, TEV, TNT].

  d. aorist act. indic. of πάσχω (LN 24.78): 'to suffer' [Hn, LN, Lns, WBC; all versions except NASB, NEB], 'to endure sufferings' [NASB], 'to endure afflictions' [HNTC], 'to undergo sufferings' [ICC], 'to be treated' [NEB]. The aorist tense could refer to a series of suffering considered collectively [Hb], but probably it refers to some single event in the past after Paul had left them [Hb, Hn].

  e. ὑπό (LN 90.1; 89.26): 'from' [Hn, HNTC; NAB, NIV, NJB, RSV, TEV, TNT], 'of' [KJV], 'at the hands of' [ICC, Lns, WBC; NASB], 'by' [NEB].

  f. συμφυλέτης (LN **11.57**): 'countrymen' [Hn, ICC, LN, Lns; all versions except NAB], 'fellow countrymen' [BAGD, HNTC, WBC; NAB].

QUESTION—What relationship is indicated by ὅτι 'because'?

  1. This indicates the grounds for the statement that they became imitators of the churches in Judea [Hb, Lns]: it is true that you became imitators *since* you suffered the same things from your countrymen. The proof is that they suffered in the same way [Hb, Hn, Lns, NIC, TH] and that, in both instances, it was caused by the people in their area [Hb, TH]. Some commentators add that the imitation also included their being steadfast in enduring the suffering [Hn, ICC, NIC].

  2. This explains in what respect they imitated the churches [Fn]: you became imitators *in that* you suffered the same things from your countrymen.

QUESTION—What are the same things that both suffered?

  They were persecuted for being Christians [EBC, EGT, Hb, Hn, Lns, NIC, TH, WBC]. Their own countrymen persecuted them [Hb].

QUESTION—What is meant by καί 'also'?

  They experienced suffering for their faith like the churches in Judea [Hb, Lns], or this can be taken with the following καί 'also' to bring out the comparison [My].

as^a also^b they from the Jews,

LEXICON—a. καθώς (LN 64.14): 'as' [Hn, HNTC, ICC, Lns, WBC; all versions except NIV, TEV], not explicit [NIV, TEV].

  b. καί (LN 89.93): 'also' [Lns]; or 'even' [KJV, NASB], 'themselves' [ICC], 'for their part' [WBC], not explicit [Hn, HNTC; NAB, NEB, NIV, NJB, RSV, TEV, TNT].

QUESTION—What is meant by καί 'also'?

It strengthens the comparison [EGT, El, Mn, My].

QUESTION—What is the significance of αὐτοί 'they' being in the masculine gender rather than agreeing with ἐκκλησιῶν 'churches' which is in the feminine gender?

It refers to the individual members, men or women, of the Judean churches [Alf, Ea, El, Hb, Mn, My].

2:15 **the (ones) both[a] the Lord having-killed[b] Jesus, and the prophets,[c] and us having-driven-out,[d]**

TEXT—Some manuscripts add ἰδίους 'their own' before προφήτας 'prophets'. GNT omits this with an A rating, indicating virtual certainty. Only KJV includes this word.

LEXICON—a. καί (LN 89.93): 'both' [Hn, HNTC, ICC, Lns; KJV, NASB, RSV, TNT], 'too' [NJB], not explicit [WBC; NAB, NEB, NIV, TEV].
  b. aorist act. participle of ἀποκτείνω (LN 20.61): 'to kill' [Hn, HNTC, ICC, LN, WBC; all versions except NJB], 'to put to death' [NJB], 'to kill off' [Lns].
  c. προφήτης (LN 53.79): 'prophets' [Hn, HNTC, ICC, LN, Lns, WBC; all versions].
  d. aorist act. participle of ἐκδιώκω (LN **15.159; 39.45**): 'to drive out' [Hn, LN, Lns, WBC; NASB, NEB, NIV, RSV, TNT], 'to persecute' [HNTC, ICC, LN; KJV, NAB, NJB, TEV], 'to persecute severely' [BAGD]. The aorist tense refers to the one time this happened in Thessalonica [Alf, Hb, Hn, HNTC, NCBC, Rb], or to repeated times in various places viewed collectively [Hb, ICC].

QUESTION—What is indicated by separating the words 'Lord' and 'Jesus'?

English does not have provision for separating the words and the separation is not indicated by any of the translations. They simply translate the names together, 'the Lord Jesus'.
  1. This separation emphasizes 'Lord' and points out the enormity of the sin of killing Jesus [Alf, Ea, EBC, El, Hn, Lns, My, Wd].
  2. This separation does not stress one name more than the other, but stresses both his exalted character as Lord and his human character as the man Jesus [Fn, Hb, HNTC, Mn].

QUESTION—How does the statement that the Jews killed the Lord agree with the fact that Pilate's soldiers killed Jesus?

The Jews were responsible for the execution which was carried out by the soldiers [Ea, EBC, Hb, Hn, HNTC, Lns, Mn, TH, Wd].

QUESTION—Of which participle is προφήτας 'prophet' the object?
  1. It is the object of ἀποκτεινάντων 'killing' [Alf, Ea, El, Er, Hb, Hn, HNTC, ICC, LN, Lns, My, NCBC, NIC, Rb, WBC, Wd; all versions]: the ones who killed the Lord Jesus and the prophets.
  2. It is the object of ἐκδιωξάντων 'driving out' [EBC, Fn, Mn]; the ones who killed the Lord Jesus, and who drove out the prophets and us.

QUESTION—Does the word προφήτας 'prophets' refer to the Old Testament prophets or to the Christian prophets of the early church?

It refers to the Old Testament prophets [EBC, Hb, Hn, HNTC, ICC, Lns, NCBC, NIC, Rb, WBC, Wd].

QUESTION—To whom does ἡμᾶς 'us' refer?
1. It refers to Paul and Silas (Acts 17:4, 10) [Alf, Lns].
2. It refers to Paul and his companions [Ea, El, Hb, HNTC, ICC, TH, WBC], specifically, Silas and Timothy (Acts 17:14) [Ea, ICC]. It could even include all the apostles in general [El, My], or all Christian missionaries [Hb].

and God not pleasing,[a]

LEXICON—a. pres. act. participle of ἀρέσκω (LN 25.90): 'to please' [BAGD, Hn, HNTC, ICC, LN, Lns, WBC; KJV, NASB, NJB, TNT]. Some conflate this with the negative: 'to displease' [NAB, NIV, RSV, TEV], 'to be heedless of (God's will)' [NEB]. The present tense here and in the following verb indicates that this is an habitual relationship [Alf, Ea, El, Hb, HNTC, ICC, NIC, TH, Wd].

QUESTION—What is meant by μὴ ἀρεσκόντων 'not pleasing'?

This is a litotes in which a fact is emphatically affirmed by denying its opposite, and it is of the type that makes a deliberate understatement [EBC, Fn, Hb, Hn, Lns, Mn]: they very much displease God, or they are hateful to him. This does not refer to a conscious attempt to displease God, but to how God looked on what they do [Hb, NCBC].

QUESTION—How do they displease God?
1. This is the result of what they did in killing the Lord and the prophets and driving out the missionaries [Ea, Hb, My, NCBC].
2. This is what they constantly do. The way they live displeases God [El, NIC] and they act contrary to his will [HNTC]. They oppose God in his desire to save the Gentiles [ICC].

and to-all men (being) opposed,[a]

LEXICON—a. ἐναντίος (LN 39.6): 'opposed' [BAGD, HNTC, WBC], 'hostile' [BAGD, LN; NAB, NASB, NIV, TEV], 'contrary' [BAGD, Hn, Lns; KJV], 'against' [ICC]. This adjective is also translated as a verb: 'to oppose' [RSV], 'to be enemies' [NEB, NJB, TNT].

QUESTION—How did they oppose all people?

The following verse explains this. They were against offering salvation to the Gentiles [Ea, Hb, Hn, ICC, Lns, Mn].

2:16 hindering[a] **us to-speak**[b] **to-the Gentiles**[c]

LEXICON—a. pres. act. participle of κωλύω (LN 13.146): 'to hinder' [BAGD, HNTC, ICC, LN; NASB, NEB, NJB, RSV], 'to prevent' [LN], 'to try to keep from' [NAB, NIV], 'to try to stop' [TEV], 'to try to prevent' [BAGD, Hn, Lns, WBC; TNT], 'to forbid' [BAGD; KJV]. The present tense indicates that they were constantly doing this [El, Hn, ICC, TH].

1 THESSALONIANS 2:16   65

   b. aorist act. infin. of λαλέω (LN 33.70): 'to speak' [BAGD, Hn, LN, Lns, WBC; KJV, NASB, NEB, NIV, RSV], 'to tell' [LN; TNT], 'to preach' [HNTC; NAB, NJB, TEV], 'to talk' [ICC, LN].
   c. ἔθνος (LN 11.55; 11.37): 'Gentiles' [BAGD, Hn, HNTC, ICC, Lns, WBC; all versions], 'nations or peoples' [LN], 'heathen or pagans' [LN].
QUESTION—What relationship is indicated by the participial form κωλυόντων 'hindering'?
   1. It indicates the grounds of the preceding statement [EBC, El, My; NJB, TNT]: it is true that they are opposing all people *since* they are hindering us from speaking and thus hindering people from being saved.
   2. It indicates the manner of the preceding statement [Hb, Lns, NCBC, Wd; RSV]: they are opposing all people *by* hindering us, etc.
   3. It explains the preceding statement by indicating the specific act intended [Alf, Ea, EGT, Fn, Hn, HNTC, ICC, Mn, Rb]: they are opposing all people, *that is*, they hinder us, etc.
   4. It indicates an example of the preceding statement [TEV]: they are opposing all people, *for example*, they are hindering us, etc.

in-order-that they-might-be-saved,[a]
LEXICON—a. aorist pass. subj. of σῴζω (LN 21.27): 'to be saved' [BAGD, Hn, HNTC, LN, Lns; KJV, NASB, NIV, RSV, TNT]. The passive voice is also translated actively: 'to save' [NJB], 'to bring salvation' [TEV], 'to lead (them) to salvation' [NEB]. It is also translated as a noun: 'salvation' [NAB], '(with a view to their) salvation' [ICC, WBC].
QUESTION—What is the relationship indicated by ἵνα 'in order that'?
   This indicates the purpose of the missionaries in speaking to the Gentiles [Ea, EBC, Hb, Hn, HNTC, ICC, Lns, NCBC, NIC, WBC]. At the same time, it was the result of their speaking [Ea, HNTC].
QUESTION—Who is the implied actor in the passive σωθῶσιν 'they might be saved'?
   God is the one who saves [Hb].

in-order-to/so-that[a] **to-fill-up**[b] **their sins**[c] **always.**[d]
LEXICON—a. εἰς (LN 89.57; 89.48): 'in order that' [ICC], 'so that' [Lns], 'their aim was' [WBC], 'to' [KJV]; or 'with the result that' [NASB], 'in this way' [NIV, TEV], 'so as' [Hn, HNTC; RSV], 'thus' [NJB, TNT]; not explicit [NAB, NEB].
   b. aorist act. infin. of ἀναπληρόω (LN **59.33; 68.27**): 'to fill up' [Lns; KJV], 'to fill up one's quota' [NAB], 'to fill up the measure' [BAGD, Hn, ICC; NASB, RSV], 'to fill to the full' [HNTC], 'to fill full the measure' [WBC], 'to reach the full extent' [NJB], 'to make up the full measure' [NEB], 'to complete the (full) total' [LN; TEV], 'to ensure that the list is complete' [TNT], 'to make complete' [BAGD, LN], 'to heap up to the limit' [NIV]. The aorist tense looks forward to the time when the filling is finished [Hb].

c. ἁμαρτία (LN 88.289): 'sins' [BAGD, Hn, HNTC, ICC, LN, Lns, WBC; all versions except NEB, NJB], 'guilt' [NEB]. 'iniquity' [NJB].

d. πάντοτε (LN 67.88): 'always' [BAGD, Hn, HNTC, ICC, LN, Lns; KJV, NASB, NIV, RSV, TEV], 'continuous' [WBC], 'all this/the time' [NAB, NEB, NJB], not explicit [TNT].

QUESTION—What relationship is indicated by εἰς 'in order to/so that'?
1. This indicates God's purpose [Alf, Ea, EBC, El, ICC, Mn, My, NCBC, Wd]: all that the Jews are doing is in God's plans, so that God's purpose of filling up their sins will be accomplished.
2. This indicates the Jews' purpose [NIC].
3. This indicates the result of all that the Jews are doing [HNTC, Lns; NASB, NIV, NJB, TEV, TNT]: all that the Jews have done results in the filling up of their sins. The use of 'always' is easier to understand with a continuous result rather than with continuously forming a purpose [HNTC].

QUESTION—What is meant by ἀναπληρῶσαι αὐτῶν τὰς ἁμαρτίας 'to fill up their sins'?

This is a metaphor. The comparison is: (like) (a person) fills up (a cup) (with a liquid). The point of comparison is the reaching of an imposed limit (by the volume of a cup or by God's plan). The nonfigurative statement is: (the Jews) (complete the limit set by God) of the number of sins they commit.
1. Each time the Jews sin they come closer to completing the total number of sins that God has allotted them before he will bring them to judgment and punish them [Alf, EBC, Hb, HNTC, ICC, My, NCBC]. Πάντοτε 'always' indicates that they are constantly in the process of reaching this point [Alf, Hb, ICC, NCBC]. They are completing what their ancestors started [Mn].
2. The Jews have sinned in the past, and now with their latest sins have finally reached their limit [Ea, El, TH].
3. The Jews are going to leave nothing out of their list of sins [NIC]. They are finishing up the course of action begun with killing the Lord and the prophets [WBC].
4. Each time the Jews sinned in the ways described, they filled up their sins [Lns].

But/And[a] the wrath[b] has-come[c] on[d] them to (the) end.[e]

LEXICON—a. δέ (LN 89.124; 89.94): 'but' [Hn, ICC, WBC; NAB, NASB, NJB, RSV, TNT]; or 'and now' [NEB, TEV], 'moreover' [Lns], 'and' [HNTC]; or 'for' [KJV]; not explicit [NIV].

b. ὀργή (LN 88.173; 38.10): 'wrath' [BAGD, Hn, ICC, Lns, WBC; KJV, NAB, NASB, NIV, RSV, TNT], 'anger' [BAGD, HNTC, LN; TEV]; or 'retribution' [NEB, NJB], 'punishment' [LN]. See this word at 1:10.

c. aorist act. indic. of φθάνω (LN 13.123): 'to come' [BAGD, Hn, ICC, Lns; KJV, NASB, NIV, RSV], 'to come down' [TEV], 'to come upon' [LN], 'to descend' [NAB], 'to come down' [TEV]. This is conflated with

ἐπί 'on': 'to overtake' [WBC; NEB, NJB, TNT], 'to catch up with' [HNTC].
d. ἐπί (LN 90.57): 'on' [LN; TEV], 'upon' [Hn, ICC, Lns; KJV, NAB, NASB, NIV, RSV], 'to' [LN].
e. τέλος (LN **67.66; 78.47**): 'end' [BAGD], 'uttermost' [Hn, Lns; KJV], 'utmost' [NASB]. The phrase εἰς τέλος 'to the end' is translated 'at last' [ICC, LN; NAB, NIV, RSV, TEV, TNT], 'finally' [HNTC; NJB], 'for good and all' [WBC; NEB], 'completely' [LN, Mou (p. 70)].

QUESTION—What relationship is indicated by δέ 'but/and'?
1. It indicates a contrast [Alf, Ea, El, Hn, ICC, My, WBC; NAB, NASB, NJB, RSV, TNT]: they have always sinned, *but* God's wrath finally has come [Ea], or they oppose God, *but* (it will not be successful, because) the wrath of God has come [Alf].
2. It introduces another result [HNTC, Lns; NEB, TEV]: all that the Jews have done results in the filling up of their sins *and also* in wrath coming on them.

QUESTION—What is indicated by the article in ἡ ὀργή 'the wrath'?
This means the well-known wrath of God, which he will show when sin is committed [El, Hb, Hn, ICC], or it means the wrath that has been prophesied [Alf, Ea, El, My], or the wrath that they deserve [Alf, Ea, El, My].

QUESTION—What is meant by ὀργή 'wrath'?
1. This refers to God's reaction to sin and can be considered separately from judgment and punishment [Ea, El, Hb, Hn, My].
2. This is a metonymy: wrath stands for the punishment resulting from God's wrath [ICC, Lns, NCBC, NIC, TH; NEB, NJB].

QUESTION—What is indicated by the aorist tense, ἔφθασεν '(the wrath) came'?
1. When 'wrath' refers to the final judgment.
1.1 It indicates the certainty of the future day of judgment by speaking of it as having already come [Fn, NIC, Wd]: wrath will certainly come on them. It does not indicate how near it is [NIC].
1.2 It indicates the nearness of the future day of judgment by speaking of it as having already come [HNTC, ICC, NCBC]: wrath will soon come on them. God's judgment has been pronounced [HNTC].
2. When 'wrath' refers to judgments in history. The Jews were always filling up their sins and God was continually punishing them [Lns], or it has just happened that God has stopped dealing with them as his special nation [Mn].
3. When 'wrath' refers to God's attitude. It indicates that God no longer tolerates their sins and has in the past reached the point that he became so angry with them that they will not escape a future punishment [Ea, El, Hb, Hn, My]. He has now rejected Israel [Hn].

QUESTION—What is the meaning of the phrase εἰς τέλος 'to the end'?
1. It is temporal [HNTC, ICC, Rb, TH; NAB, NIV, NJB, RSV, TEV, TNT]: at last.

68   1 THESSALONIANS 2:16

2. It is intensive [Alf, Ea, EBC, El, Hb, Hn, Lns, Mou (p. 70), My, NIC, WBC; KJV, NASB, NEB]: completely, utterly, or to its full extent. The wrath reached its limit so that punishment must follow [Alf, Ea, My].

DISCOURSE UNIT: 2:17–3:13 [Alf, EBC, EGT, GNT, Hb, HNTC, NCBC, NIC, TH, WBC; TEV]. The topic is the planned visit [GNT, WBC; TEV], Paul's relationship to the Thessalonians [Hb, HNTC, NIC, TH], concern for the Thessalonians [NCBC], vindication [EBC, EGT].

DISCOURSE UNIT: 2:17–3:10 [Mn, Wd]. The topic is Paul's relationship to the Thessalonians [Mn], relief from the good report [Wd].

DISCOURSE UNIT: 2:17–3:5 [Er, Fn, TH; NIV]. The topic is Paul's separation from the Thessalonians [Fn], Paul's desire to see them [NIV], Timothy's mission [Er].

DISCOURSE UNIT: 2:17–20 [EBC, Hb, Hn, HNTC, ICC, Mn, NCBC, WBC, Wd; NJB]. The topic is the planned visit [ICC, Mn], the hindered visit [Hb, HNTC, Wd], Paul's concern for them [NJB]. It is further divided into the following units: 2:17–18, 19–20 [Hb].

2:17 But/Now[a] we, brothers,
LEXICON—a. δέ (LN 89.124; 89.94): 'but' [KJV, NASB, NIV, RSV]; or 'now' [Hn, HNTC, ICC, Lns]; not explicit [WBC; NAB, NEB, NJB, TEV, TNT].
QUESTION—What relationship is indicated by δέ 'but/now'?
1. It indicates a contrast [Alf, Ea, EBC, El, Fn, ICC, Mn, NIC, Wd; KJV, NASB, NIV, RSV]: but. The Jews do what is described in 2:15–16, but we do the following [Alf, Ea, EBC, El, Mn, NIC]. Or, you have become imitators (2:14), but we, etc. [Fn].
2. It indicates transition and is continuative [Ea, Hb, Hn, HNTC, ICC, Lns, My, NCBC, WBC]: and, now. This introduces a new point and continues his defense [Hn], or it resumes the main theme of their relationship [NCBC], or it introduces a new stage of thanksgiving [HNTC]. The emphatic ἡμεῖς 'we' contrasts with the Jewish opponents [Hb].

being-made-orphans/being-separated[a] from you for a-time[b] of-an-hour[c]
LEXICON—a. aorist pass. participle of ἀπορφανίζω (LN **85.17**): 'to be made orphans' [BAGD, HNTC], 'to be orphaned' [Lns; NAB], 'to be bereft' [WBC; NASB, RSV], 'to be bereaved' [ICC], 'to be taken' [KJV], 'to be lost to' [NEB], 'to be torn away from' [Hn; NIV], 'to be deprived of' [LN; NJB], or 'to be separated' [LN; TEV], 'to leave' [TNT]. The aorist tense indicates a single event [HNTC, TH], that moment of separation [TH]. The passive indicates that the separation was forced upon them [Hb, Lns].
b. καιρός (LN 67.78; **67.109**): 'time' [BAGD, Hn, ICC, Lns, WBC; KJV, NAB, NIV, NJB, RSV], 'a while' [NASB, TEV, TNT], 'a little while' [LN], 'spell' [NEB], 'period' [BAGD, HNTC, Lns].

c. ὥρα (LN 67.148): 'hour' [BAGD], 'time' [Lns], 'a while' [LN], not explicit [NAB]. This second noun emphasizes the shortness of the time [Hb, ICC], and is translated by some as an adjective: 'short' [Hn, HNTC, ICC; KJV, NASB, NEB, NIV, NJB, RSV], 'little' [TEV, TNT].

QUESTION—What relationship is indicated by the participial form ἀπορφανισθέντες 'being made orphans'?
1. It is temporal: *when* [Ea, Hb, HNTC, ICC, Mn, WBC; NAB, NEB, NIV, TEV] or *after* [My; TNT] we were separated from you for a time, we were eager to see you.
2. It is causal [RSV]: *because* we were separated from you, we were eager to see you.
3. It is concessive [NJB]: *although* we were separated for only a short time, yet we were eager to see you.

QUESTION—Is the verb ἀπορφανίζω 'to be orphaned' a live or dead metaphor?
1. It is a live metaphor [Alf, EBC, El, Hb, Hn, HNTC, ICC, Lns, Mn, My, NCBC, NIC, Rb, TH, WBC, Wd; KJV, NAB, NASB, NEB, NIV, RSV].
   1.1 The comparison is with children who are orphaned [Alf, EBC, Hb, HNTC, ICC, NIC, Rb, Wd; NAB]. The comparison is: (like) (children) are orphaned (by the death of their parents). The point of comparison is separation from loved ones [EBC, Hb, Hn, HNTC, NIC, Rb; NAB], perhaps with the idea of it being a forced separation [Hb, Hn, HNTC, Lns, My, Rb], or being accompanied with a feeling of bereavement [EBC, ICC, My, NIC, Wd]. The nonfigurative statement is: we were separated from you.
   1.2 The comparison is with fathers whose children have died [Fn, Lns, NCBC, WBC]. Unlike English, the Greek word ἀπορφανίζω 'to be orphaned' can refer to parents also [HNTC, Lns, NCBC, Wd]. The comparison is: (like) (fathers or parents) are 'orphaned' (by the death of their children). The point of comparison is separation from loved ones [Lns, NCBC], perhaps with the resultant feeling of loss [NCBC]. The nonfigurative statement is: we were separated from you.
   1.3 Others have kept a metaphor by using a more general term which still focuses on separation from loved ones by death, perhaps with the addition of grief over that separation: 'to be bereft' [TH, WBC; NASB, RSV], 'to be bereaved' [El, Mn]. Keeping close to the basic meaning of being orphaned, the picture is: (like) children are bereaved (by the death of their parents), or it can be taken to mean: (like) (parents) are bereaved (by the death of their children) [WBC].
   1.4 Others keep a metaphor, but focus on the separation without necessarily implying a death: be taken [KJV], be lost to [NEB], be torn away [Hn; NIV].
2. Some translate this as a dead metaphor without any indication of a comparison [Ea; NJB, TEV, TNT]: being separated.

in-face[a] not in-heart,[b]

LEXICON—a. πρόσωπον (LN 8.18; 9.9; 85.26): 'face' [BAGD, LN, Lns], 'body' [NJB, TEV], 'presence' [LN, WBC; KJV], 'person' [LN; NASB, NIV, RSV], 'sight' [Hn, ICC; NAB, NEB, TNT], 'physically' [HNTC].

b. καρδία (LN 26.3): 'heart' [BAGD, Hn, LN, Lns, WBC; KJV, NEB, RSV], 'thought' [NIV, TEV], 'mind' [ICC, LN; NAB, TNT], 'spirit' [NASB], 'spiritually' [HNTC], 'affection' [NJB].

much-more/very-much[a] we-endeavored/were-eager[b] to-see[c] your face with[d] great[e] desire.[f]

LEXICON—a. περισσοτέρως (LN 78.31): 'more abundantly' [WBC; KJV], 'more diligent' [Lns], 'more eagerly' [RSV], 'all the more' [BAGD, Hn, HNTC; NASB], 'excessively' [ICC, LN], 'how hard' [TEV], 'especially' [NJB], 'every' [NIV], 'exceedingly' [NEB].

b. aorist act. indic. of σπουδάζω (LN 68.63; 25.74): 'to endeavor' [HNTC, LN; KJV, RSV], 'to try' [TEV], 'to make an effort' [BAGD, Lns; NIV], 'to bestir oneself' [WBC], 'to endeavor eagerly' [Hn; RSV], 'to do one's best' [LN]; or 'to be eager' [BAGD, LN, NASB], 'to have a desire' [NJB], 'to be anxious' [ICC; NEB], 'to be seized with' [NAB].

c. aorist act. infin. of ὁράω (LN 24.1; 34.50): 'to see' [Hn, HNTC, ICC, LN, Lns, WBC; all versions], 'to go to see' [LN], 'to visit' [LN].

d. ἐν (LN 89.80; 89.84): 'with' [Hn, HNTC, ICC, WBC; KJV, NAB, NASB, RSV], 'out of' [NIV], 'in' [Lns].

e. πολύς (LN 59.11; 78.3): 'great' [HNTC, ICC, Lns, WBC; KJV, NASB, RSV, TNT], 'intense' [Hn; NIV], 'greatest' [NAB], 'strong' [NJB].

f. ἐπιθυμία (LN 25.12): 'desire' [BAGD, HNTC, ICC, LN, Lns; KJV, NASB, RSV], 'longing' [BAGD, Hn, WBC; NAB, NIV, NJB, TNT].

QUESTION—Is the comparative sense retained in the use of περισσοτέρως 'much more/very much'?

1. It is comparative [Alf, Ea, El, Fn, Hb, Hn, HNTC, Lns, Mn, My, Rb; KJV, NASB, RSV]: much more/all the more we endeavored. He made more than an ordinary effort [Fn, Hb, HNTC], more than if he had not been forced to leave [Lns, Rb], more than if he had not been hindered [Hn, Mn], more than if the time of separation had been longer [Alf, My], more than if they were separated in heart as well as face [Ea, El].

2. It is not comparative [ICC, NIC, TH; NJB, TEV]: we very much/diligently endeavored.

QUESTION—What area of meaning is intended in the verb σπουδάζω 'to endeavor/to be eager'?

1. It focuses on the effort they made [Alf, Ea, Hb, Hn, Lns, My, NCBC, NIC, WBC, Wd; KJV, NIV, RSV, TEV]: we endeavored to see you. It also indicates haste [Hb, NIC, Wd], or eagerness [Wd].

2. It focuses on the desire they felt [ICC, Mn; NAB, NASB, NEB, NJB, TNT]: we were eager to see you.

2:18 because/therefore[a] we-wanted/resolved[b] to-come to you,

LEXICON—a. διότι (LN 89.26): 'because' [BAGD; RSV], 'for' [Hn, HNTC, ICC, Lns; NASB, NIV]; or 'wherefore' [KJV], 'for that reason' [TNT], 'so' [NAB, NEB], 'in fact' [WBC], 'and' [NJB]; not explicit [TEV].

b. aorist act. indic. of θέλω (LN 25.1; 30.58): 'to want' [LN; NASB, NIV, RSV, TEV, TNT], 'to wish' [BAGD, Hn, ICC, LN], 'to will' [KJV]; or 'to resolve' [HNTC, Lns], 'to purpose' [LN], 'to propose' [NEB], 'to try' [NAB, NJB], 'to make up one's mind' [WBC].

QUESTION—What relationship is indicated by διότι 'because/therefore'?
  1. This indicates the grounds for the preceding statement in 2:17 [EBC, EGT, Hb, Hn, HNTC, ICC, Lns, Mn, NCBC, WBC, Wd; NASB, NIV, RSV]: it is true that we desired [EBC, WBC] or endeavored [Hn, Lns] to see you, *since* we wanted to (and tried to) several times.
  2. This indicates the result of the preceding verse [Alf, Ea, El, My; KJV, NAB, NEB, TNT]: we desired to see you, *therefore* we wanted (and tried) to come to you.

QUESTION—What is meant by θέλω 'to want/to resolve'?
  1. It refers to a general wish [EBC, El, Hb, Hn, ICC, NIC, Rb; KJV, NASB, NIV, RSV, TEV, TNT]: we wanted to come.
  2. It refers to a resolve with a definite plan [Alf, Fn, HNTC, Lns, Mn, My, NCBC, WBC, Wd; NEB]: we resolved to come.

indeed I Paul both once and twice,

QUESTION—How many times did Paul want, and try, to go see them?
  1. This means once and again a second time, that is, two times [Alf, Ea, El, Fn, Lns, Mn, My; KJV].
  2. This means an inexact number, more than two, but less than 'repeatedly' [EBC, HNTC, NIC, WBC; NAB, NASB, NEB, NJB, TEV]: he tried more than once [NIC, WBC; NAB, NASB, NEB, NJB, TEV], or several times [EBC, HNTC].
  3. This means a large, indefinite number [Hn, ICC, NCBC, TH; NIV, RSV, TNT]: he tried repeatedly [Hn, ICC, TH], or again and again [TH; NIV, RSV].

QUESTION—Why doesn't Paul include Silvanus and Timothy here as he does in the preceding and following clauses?

Paul refers to special efforts he alone made (Silvanus and Timothy were included in other efforts) [Hb, Hn, Lns, WBC], or Timothy and Silvanus may have been elsewhere when he made these attempts [Ea]. Paul adds a parenthesis because he was especially criticized by opponents [Hb, ICC, Wd]. Timothy, and maybe Silvanus, had been able to return to Thessalonica [EBC, Hb, TH]. Or this is merely for sake of emphasis and it is implied that the others were also included [El]. Or, the plural references are literary plurals, referring only to Paul [Rb].

and/but^a Satan broke-up/hindered^b us.

LEXICON—a. καί (LN 89.92; 91.12): 'and' [Lns]; or 'but' [Hn, HNTC, WBC; all versions except NASB], 'and yet' [ICC; NASB].

b. aorist act. indic. of ἐγκόπτω (LN 13.147): 'to hinder' [BAGD, LN, WBC; KJV, RSV], 'to thwart' [BAGD; NASB, NEB], 'to prevent' [HNTC, LN; NJB, TNT], 'to stop' [Hn, ICC; NIV], 'to block the way' [NAB], 'to not let' [TEV], 'to cut off' [Lns].

QUESTION—What relationship is indicated by καί 'and/but'?
1. This is coordinate and adds another statement [Alf, El, Fn, Hb, Lns]: we wanted to come *and* Satan hindered us.
2. This indicates a contrast [Hn, HNTC, ICC, Rb, WBC; all versions]: we wanted to come, *but* (we couldn't come because) Satan hindered us.
3. This indicates the outcome of their desire [Ea, My]: we wanted to come to you, *the result was* that Satan hindered us.

QUESTION—Is a metaphor intended by the use of the verb ἐγκόπτω 'to break up/hinder' here?
1. This is a live metaphor [El, Fn, Hn, ICC, NIC, Rb, WBC, Wd]. The comparison is: (like) (an army) breaks up (a road the enemy will come over). The point of comparison is the action of hindering [El, Rb] an enemy from moving or doing something. The nonfigurative statement is: Satan hindered us.
2. This is a dead metaphor [Mn]. Greek-English lexicons, the rest of the commentaries, and all of the versions do not indicate any reference to a comparison and apparently treat it as a dead metaphor.

QUESTION—How did Satan hinder them?
Satan inspired the authorities in Thessalonica to have Jason give a bond to insure that Paul would remain out of the city [EGT, Fn, Hn, WBC, Wd], he produced trouble locally that prevented him from going [EGT, Hn, NCBC, Wd], or he caused illness [EBC, EGT, NCBC].

2:19 Because^a

LEXICON—a. γάρ (LN 89.23): 'because', 'for' [Hn, HNTC, ICC, Lns, WBC; KJV, NASB, NIV, RSV, TNT], 'for after all' [NEB], 'after all' [NAB, TEV], not explicit [NJB].

QUESTION—What relationship is indicated by this conjunction?
It indicates the reason for wanting to see them [Alf, Ea, EGT, El, Fn, Hb, Hn, HNTC, ICC, My, NCBC, TH, WBC, Wd]: we want to see you *because* you are our hope, etc.

what/who^a (is/will be) our hope^b or joy^c

LEXICON—a. τίς (LN 92.14): 'what' [WBC; KJV, NEB, NIV, NJB, RSV], 'who' [Hn, HNTC, ICC, Lns; NAB, NASB, TEV, TNT]. The three following nouns are impersonal words, favoring the use of 'what', but people are the ones who are the basis of these three nouns, favoring the use of 'who' [Hb].

b. ἐλπίς (LN **25.62**): 'hope' [BAGD, Hn, HNTC, ICC, Lns, WBC; all versions], 'the basis for hope' [LN].

c. χαρά (LN **25.124**): 'joy' [BAGD, Hn, HNTC, ICC, Lns, WBC; all versions], 'the reason for joy' [LN].

QUESTION—How are the Thessalonians related to the missionaries' hopes?

The Thessalonians are the cause of their hope [NCBC, TH]. Specifically, the missionaries are confident that the Thessalonians will not disappoint them [Hb], they are confident that the Thessalonians will be able to stand before the Lord at his return [Alf, Ea], they are confident that they will be able to present them to the Lord as their converts [Lns], they are confident that God will continue to work in the Thessalonians' hearts and bring them to spiritual maturity [WBC], they are confident that at the final judgment the Thessalonians would serve as proof that they had fulfilled their ministry [NCBC].

QUESTION—How are the Thessalonians related to the missionaries' joy?

The Thessalonians are the cause of their joy [EBC, NCBC, TH]. Specifically, the missionaries rejoice because they have converted the Thessalonians [Ea, My], because the Thessalonians truly believe [HNTC, WBC] and live as Christians [My], because the Thessalonians will be able to stand before the Lord [Alf, EBC]. They will rejoice because their hopes about the Thessalonians will be realized [Hb], because they will stand before the Lord with them [Hn], because the conversion of the Thessalonians will enable them to rejoice about the Lord's approval [NCBC].

QUESTION—Does ἤ 'or' mean that the Thessalonians might be only one or two of the three things Paul lists?

The rhetorical questions separated by 'or' mean that the Thessalonian believers are all three things—they are his hope, his joy, and his crown of boasting [HNTC, ICC, Lns; TEV].

or crown[a] of-boasting[b]

LEXICON—a. στέφανος (LN 6.192; 57.121; 42.19): 'crown' [BAGD, HNTC, LN, Lns, WBC; KJV, NAB, NASB, NEB, NIV, NJB, RSV], 'wreath' [BAGD, Hn, LN], 'chaplet' [ICC], 'prize or reward' [LN], 'symbol of success' [LN]. This is also translated in a nonfigurative sense: 'victory' [TEV], 'evidence of achievement' [TNT], 'prize' [BAGD]. This refers to a victor's wreath of leaves awarded at athletic games [Ea, EBC, El, Hb, Hn, ICC, Mn, NCBC, NIC, WBC, Wd].

b. καύχησις (LN 33.368; 25.204): 'boasting' [BAGD, HNTC, LN, Lns; RSV], 'pride' [BAGD, LN; NEB], 'exultation' [WBC; NASB], 'rejoicing' [KJV], 'glory' [Hn], 'honor' [NJB]. This noun is also translated as a verb: 'to exalt' [NAB], 'to glory' [NIV], 'to boast' [ICC; TEV]; or as an adjective: 'proud' [TNT].

QUESTION—How are the two nouns related in the genitive construction στέφανος καυχήσεως 'crown of boasting'?

It is a crown that they will boast about [Ea, EBC, El, Hb, HNTC, My, NCBC, TH, WBC, Wd; NAB, NIV]. The missionaries will boast about the victory that won their crown [EBC, Hb, HNTC, NCBC, TH, WBC, Wd], or about what their victory involves (the presence of the converts) [Hb].

QUESTION—What metaphor is involved in the use of στέφανος 'crown' and how is this related to the Thessalonians?

1. The Thessalonians are the reason that they will receive the crown [Hb]. The comparison is: (like) (the winning of a contest is the reason a contestant) (is awarded with) a crown (by the judge). The point of comparison is the reward or prize given for the successful completion of some endeavor. The nonfigurative statement is: our successful evangelization of you is the reason we will be rewarded by the Lord.
2. The Thessalonians are the crown [EBC, EGT, El, Mn, My, NCBC, WBC, Wd].
2.1 The comparison is: (like) a crown (is a symbol and proof of victory in an athletic contest). The point of comparison is that of a symbol representing a successful achievement of some event. The nonfigurative statement is: you are the symbol and proof of our successful evangelistic work [My, NCBC, WBC].
2.2 The comparison is: (like) a crown (is something to be proud about). The point of comparison is the object that is worthy of being proud about. The nonfigurative statement is: you are what I am proud about [EGT, Wd].

—or[a] not also/even[b] you?—

LEXICON—a. ἤ (LN 89.139): 'or' [Hn, Lns], not explicit [HNTC, ICC, WBC; all versions].

b. καί (LN 89.93): 'also' [Hn, Lns], 'too' [ICC], 'no less than (others)' [TEV], 'with (others)' [HNTC]; or 'even' [KJV, NASB], 'indeed' [WBC; NEB], not explicit [NAB, NIV, NJB, RSV, TNT].

QUESTION—How is this phrase connected with its context?

1. This is a parenthetical addition in the midst of one long rhetorical question [EBC, Fn, GNT, Hn, HNTC, ICC, Mn, NCBC, NIC, TH, WBC, Wd; NAB, NIV, RSV, TNT]: what is our hope, joy, and crown before our Lord at his coming? (Isn't it you?). This parenthetical addition is sometimes put at the end of the longer question [WBC; NIV, RSV, TNT], or at the beginning ('Who, if not you, will be our hope, etc.') [NAB].
2. This begins a second question which includes the following phrase [Hb, Lns; KJV, NASB]: what is our hope, joy, and crown? Isn't it you who are before the Lord at his coming?

QUESTION—What relationship is indicated by ἤ 'or'?

1. This indicates an alternative [Ea, El, Hb, Lns]: or, to state it in another way, is it not you who will be before the Lord, etc. [Hb], or to refer

specifically to you [Lns]. It states a second, and negative, question [Alf, Ea, El, My].
2. This should be accented differently, with a circumflex accent, to indicate that this is a question introducer [WBC].

QUESTION—What is meant by καί 'also/even'?
1. It means 'also' [Alf, Ea, El, Hn, HNTC, ICC, Lns, My, TH; TEV]. It means you, as well as others of my converts [Alf, Ea, El, Hn, HNTC, ICC, Lns, My, TH; TEV].
2. It means 'indeed, even' [EBC, WBC; KJV, NASB, NEB; probably NAB, NIV, RSV, TNT which do not translate the word]: is it not even you?

before[a] our Lord Jesus at[b] his coming?[c]

TEXT—Some manuscripts add Χριστοῦ 'Christ' after 'Lord Jesus'. GNT does not mention this alternate text. Only KJV includes the word.

LEXICON—a. ἔμπροσθεν (LN 83.33): 'before' [BAGD, HNTC, LN; NAB, RSV], 'in the presence of' [BAGD, Hn, ICC, Lns, WBC; KJV, NASB, NIV, NJB, TEV, TNT], 'in front of' [LN]. This is also translated as a phrase: 'to stand before' [NEB]. See this word at 1:3.

b. ἐν (LN 67.33): 'at' [Hn, WBC; KJV, NAB, NASB, NEB, RSV], 'in connection with' [Lns], 'when' [ICC; NIV, NJB, TEV, TNT] 'in' [HNTC].

c. παρουσία (LN 85.25; 15.86): 'the coming' [BAGD, Hn, LN; KJV, NAB, NASB, NEB, RSV], 'advent' [BAGD, WBC], 'Parousia' [HNTC, Lns], 'presence' [LN]. This noun is translated as a verb: 'to come' [ICC; NIV, NJB, TEV, TNT].

QUESTION—How are the two phrases related?
'In his coming' indicates the time when they will stand before the Lord Jesus [Ea, Hn, ICC, Lns, WBC; KJV, NAB, NASB, NEB, NIV, NJB, RSV, TEV, TNT]. This refers to the Lord's second coming [Alf, Ea, EBC, El, Hb, Hn, ICC, Lns, Mn, My, NCBC, NIC, Rb, TH, WBC]. It is the time when the Lord returns and makes his final review and gives rewards [EBC, El, WBC].

2:20 Because[a]

LEXICON—a. γάρ (LN 89.23; 91.1): 'because', 'for' [KJV, NASB, NJB, RSV]; or 'indeed' [Hn, ICC, Lns; NIV, TEV], 'yes, indeed' [HNTC, NEB], 'yes' [WBC]; not explicit [NAB, TNT].

QUESTION—What relationship is indicated by this conjunction?
1. It indicates the grounds for an implied affirmation of the previous rhetorical question [Alf, Hb, NCBC, WBC, Wd; KJV, NJB, RSV]: (Yes, it is you), *since* you are, etc. It confirms his statement about future joy by pointing out that they are so at the present time and always [Alf].
2. It emphasizes the previous verse [El, Hn, HNTC, ICC, Lns, Mn, My, TH, WBC; NEB, NIV, TEV]: yes, indeed.

you are[a] **the glory**[b] **of-us and the joy.**[c]

LEXICON—a. pres. act. indic. of εἰμί (LN 13.1): 'to be' [all versions]. The present tense indicates that this is Paul's present attitude [EBC, Hb, My, NCBC, NIC].
  b. δόξα (LN **25.205**): 'glory' [Hn, HNTC, ICC, Lns, WBC; KJV, NASB, NEB, NIV, RSV, TNT], 'pride' [LN; NJB, TEV], 'boast' [NAB], 'renown' [BAGD].
  c. χαρά (LN 25.124): 'joy' [BAGD, Hn, HNTC, ICC, Lns, WBC; all versions except NAB], 'delight' [NAB], 'cause of joy or gladness' [LN]. See this word at 2:19.

QUESTION—How are the Thessalonians related to the missionaries' glory?
  1. 'Glory' means what one takes pride in [WBC]: the missionaries are proud of them.
  2. 'Glory' means praise [NCBC, Wd]: the Thessalonians are the cause of any praise given to the missionaries.

QUESTION—How are the Thessalonians related to the missionaries' joy?
  The Thessalonians are the cause of the joy the missionaries feel about their work [NCBC].
  1. 'Glory' means what one takes pride in [WBC]: the missionaries are proud of them.
  2. 'Glory' means praise [NCBC, Wd]: the Thessalonians are the cause of any praise given to the missionaries.

QUESTION—How are the Thessalonians related to the missionaries' joy?
  The Thessalonians are the cause of the joy the missionaries feel about their work [NCBC].

DISCOURSE UNIT: 3:1–13 [NASB]. The topic is the encouragement brought about by Timothy's report.

DISCOURSE UNIT: 3:1–10 [Mn]. The topic is the sending of Timothy and his return.

DISCOURSE UNIT: 3:1–8 [NAB]. The topic is Timothy's mission.

DISCOURSE UNIT: 3:1–5 [EBC, Hb, Hn, HNTC, ICC, NIC, TH, WBC, Wd; NJB]. The topic is Timothy's mission [NIC, WBC, Wd; NJB], the sending of Timothy to the Thessalonians [EBC, Hb, HNTC, ICC, TH], Paul's motivation for sending Timothy [Hn].

3:1 Therefore[a]

LEXICON—a. διό (LN 89.47): 'therefore' [BAGD, Hn; NASB, RSV], 'wherefore' [ICC, Lns; KJV], 'so' [NEB, NIV, TNT], 'and so' [HNTC], 'that is why' [NAB], 'for this reason' [BAGD, WBC], 'finally' [TEV], not explicit [NJB].

1 THESSALONIANS 3:1

QUESTION—What relationship is indicated by this conjunction?
1. This indicates the result of their desire to see the Thessalonians (2:17, 18) [Ea, El, ICC, Mn, WBC] and also of being hindered from returning there [Ea, ICC].
2. This indicates the result of their being hindered from going to see the Thessalonians [Hn, HNTC, Lns, Mn, NCBC].
3. This indicates the result of their affection (which is implied in the preceding paragraph) [Alf].
4. This indicates the result of the Thessalonians being their glory and joy (2:20) [My].

no–longer[a] enduring[b]

LEXICON—a. μηκέτι (LN 67.130): 'no longer' [BAGD, HNTC, ICC, LN, Lns, WBC; all versions except NJB, TEV], 'not any longer' [Hn; NJB, TEV].
  b. pres. act. participle of στέγω (LN 25.176): 'to endure' [BAGD, HNTC, ICC, LN; NAB, NASB], 'to bear' [BAGD; NEB, NJB, RSV, TEV, TNT], 'to put up with' [LN], 'to forbear' [KJV], 'to stand (it)' [BAGD, Hn, Lns; NIV], 'to hold out' [WBC]. The present tense indicates that they could not continue to endure it [Hb].

QUESTION—What relationship is indicated by the participial form στέγοντες 'enduring'?
1. This indicates the reason for the following clause [EBC, Er, Fn, HNTC, ICC, NCBC, TH, WBC; TEV]: because we could not endure it, therefore we decided, etc.
2. This indicates the time (or circumstance [Hb]) of the following clause [Ea, Hb, Hn; KJV, NAB, NASB, NEB, NIV, NJB, RSV, TNT]: when we could not endure it, we decided, etc. This also implies that this is the reason for the following clause [Ea, Hn].

QUESTION—What could they no longer endure?
They could not endure the lack of information about the condition of the believers in Thessalonica (3:5–6) [Ea, El, Hb], they could not endure the separation [Alf, Ea, Er, Fn, Hn, ICC, TH], they could no longer endure their anxiety [Bul (p. 14)].

we-decided[a] to-remain[b] in Athens alone,[c]

LEXICON—a. aorist act. indic. of εὐδοκέω (LN 30.97): 'to decide' [NAB, NEB, TEV, TNT], 'to decide it to be best' [NJB], 'to choose as better' [LN], 'to think it best' [Hn, Lns; NASB, NIV], 'to think it good' [KJV], 'to seem good' [LN], 'to be willing' [RSV], 'to resolve' [ICC, WBC], 'to willingly resolve' [HNTC]. See this word at 2:8.
  b. aorist pass. infin. of καταλείπω (LN 85.65): 'to remain' [NAB, NEB], 'to remain behind' [HNTC], 'to stay behind' [TNT], 'to stay on' [TEV], 'to be left' [LN, Lns; KJV, NIV, NJB], 'to be left behind' [BAGD, Hn, ICC, LN, WBC; NASB, RSV].

c. μόνος (LN 58.51): 'alone' [BAGD, Hn, HNTC, ICC, LN, Lns, WBC; all versions except NIV, NJB], 'by oneself' [NIV], 'without a companion' [NJB].

QUESTION—When was Paul in Athens?
He was not now in Athens. He probably wrote this letter from Corinth and had stopped over at Athens on his way there [Lns, WBC].

QUESTION—To whom does 'we' refer and how does this relate to the account in Acts 17?

1. It is a literary plural and refers only to Paul [Alf, Ea, EBC, El, Mou (p. 118), My, NIC]: when/because I could no longer endure it, I decided to remain alone and I sent Timothy. Paul arrived at Athens without the other two. Then, although not made explicit in Acts, Timothy arrived. There is no indication whether Silvanus came with him. Paul then sent Timothy back to Thessalonica, and Paul was alone in Acts 17:16–34 [Ea, El, My, NIC].
2. It refers to Paul and Silvanus and excludes Timothy since he was sent away [Hn, ICC, Mn, Rb, WBC]: when/because we, Paul and Silvanus, could no longer endure it, we two decided to remain alone and we two sent Timothy. Paul was escorted by Christians to Athens without the other two. The escort left him. Then Silvanus and Timothy arrived. Paul and Silvanus sent Timothy back to Thessalonica, then Silvanus was sent somewhere else before Paul was alone in Acts 17:16–34 [ICC].
3. It refers to Paul, Silvanus, Timothy in varying combinations [Hb, Lns, NCBC, TH, Wd]. The movements are similar to those in interpretation 2. It is also possible that Silvanus was not there at all [NCBC].
    3.1 When/because we, Paul, Silvanus, and Timothy, could no longer endure it, we three decided that we, Paul and Silvanus, would remain alone and we two sent Timothy [Lns, TH].
    3.2 When/because we, Paul, Silvanus, and Timothy, could no longer endure it, we three decided that I, Paul, would remain alone and we, Paul and Silvanus, sent Timothy [Hb, NCBC].
    3.3 When/because we, Paul, Silvanus, decided that we, Paul and Silvanus, would remain alone and we two sent Timothy [Wd].

3:2 and we-sent[a] Timothy,
LEXICON—a. aorist act. indic. of πέμπω (LN 15.66): 'to send' [BAGD, Hn, HNTC, ICC, LN, Lns, WBC; all versions].

the brother of-us and fellow-worker[a]/minister[b] of-God in[c] the gospel of-Christ,
TEXT—Instead of συνεργόν 'fellow worker', some manuscripts have διάκονον 'minister'. GNT chooses 'fellow worker' with a B rating, indicating some degree of doubt. Also choosing 'fellow worker' are Alf, Ea, El, HNTC, ICC, My, NCBC, TH, WBC, Wd, NAB, NASB, NEB, NIV, TEV, and TNT. 'Minister' is chosen by EBC, Er, Fn, Hb, Hn, Lns, Mn, NIC,

Rb, NJB, and RSV. Some manuscripts have both 'minister' and 'fellow worker', and read 'our brother, and minister of God, and our fellow worker'. Only KJV follows this reading.

LEXICON—a. συνεργός (LN 42.44): 'fellow worker' [BAGD, HNTC, LN, WBC; NAB, NASB, NEB, NIV, TNT], 'fellow laborer' [KJV], 'coworker' [ICC]. This noun is also translated as a phrase: 'to work with us' [TEV].
   b. Following another text, διάκονος (LN 35.20): 'minister' [Hn, Lns; KJV], 'helper' [BAGD; NJB], 'servant' [BAGD, LN; RSV].
   c. ἐν (LN 89.5): 'in' [Hn, HNTC, ICC, Lns, WBC; KJV, NASB, RSV]. This means 'in connection with' or 'in the interest of' [Hb]. Some include an implied activity: 'in preaching' [NAB, TEV], 'in the service of' [NEB], 'in spreading' [NIV, NJB, TNT].

QUESTION—How are the two nouns related in the genitive construction συνεργὸν τοῦ θεοῦ 'fellow worker of God'?
   1. When the text with 'fellow worker' is followed.
   1.1 Timothy is a fellow worker with God in that he and God work together [Alf, Ea, El, ICC, My, NCBC, TH, WBC, Wd]. The work is God's work [WBC] and the exact work is specified in the following clause [ICC, TH, Wd].
   1.2 Timothy is a fellow worker with Paul and Silvanus and all three work together for God [HNTC; TEV, TNT].
   2. When the text with 'minister' is followed: Timothy serves God [Hb] by helping believers [Hb]; or he serves both God and people [NIC]; or God has appointed him to serve people [Lns]. He ministers in the sphere of the gospel [Hn, Mn].

QUESTION—How are the two nouns related in the genitive construction τῷ εὐαγγελίῳ τοῦ Χριστοῦ 'the gospel of Christ'?
   1. The gospel is about Christ [Fn, Hb, Mn, NIC, TH, WBC] and what Christ has done for people [Hn, Mn, NIC].
   2. The gospel is inspired by Christ [ICC], or the gospel is what Christ ordered to be preached [Lns].
   3. The gospel is both from Christ and about him [HNTC, NCBC].

in-order[a] to-establish[b] you and to-encourage/comfort[c] for-the-sake-of/concerning[d] your faith,[e]

LEXICON—a. εἰς (LN 89.57): 'in order to' [Hn], 'to' [HNTC, ICC, Lns, WBC; all versions].
   b. aorist act. infin. of στηρίζω (LN 74.19): 'to establish' [BAGD; KJV, RSV], 'to establish firmly' [WBC], 'to strengthen' [BAGD, Hn, HNTC, ICC, LN; NAB, NASB, NIV, TEV], 'to keep firm' [NJB], 'to make more firm' [LN], 'to make solid' [Lns]. This is also made the object of the following verb with a change of subject to 'you': '(to encourage you) to stand firm' [NEB], '(to encourage you) to stand fast' [TNT].

c. aorist act. infin. of παρακαλέω (LN 25.150): 'to encourage' [BAGD, Hn, HNTC, ICC, LN, Lns, WBC; NAB, NASB, NEB, NIV, NJB, TNT], 'to exhort' [RSV], 'to help' [TEV]; or 'to comfort' [BAGD; KJV], 'to console' [LN]. See this word at 2:12.
d. ὑπέρ (LN 90.36; 90.24): 'for the sake of' [WBC], 'in behalf of' [Lns], 'for' [NEB]; or 'in regard to' [NAB], 'in respect to' [Hn], 'in respect of' [HNTC], 'in reference to' [ICC], 'in' [NIV, RSV, TNT], 'concerning' [KJV], 'as to' [NASB], 'about' [ICC; NJB]; not explicit [TEV].
e. πίστις (LN 31.85; 31.88): 'faith' [BAGD, Hn, HNTC, ICC, LN, Lns, WBC; all versions], 'trustworthiness' [LN], 'faithfulness' [LN].

QUESTION—How are the two verbs related?

Most translations and commentaries make these two separate acts. However, it is noted that the two acts overlap [Hn], and a few say that the second verb is the means of accomplishing the first: their purpose was to establish them by encouraging them [Hb, Lns, Wd; NEB, TNT].

QUESTION—What area of meaning is intended by ὑπέρ 'for the sake of/concerning'?

1. It means 'for the sake of' [Alf, Ea, El, Fn, Hb, HNTC, Mn, My, NIC, WBC, Wd; perhaps NEB, TEV]: to establish and encourage you for the sake of your faith. Instead of merely indicating the subject matter, this implies that it is to reinforce or increase their faith [Alf, Ea, El, Fn, Hb, Mn, WBC] or their faithful works [HNTC]. It is done for the advantage of their faith [Hb, NIC].
2. It means 'concerning' [Hn, HNTC, ICC, Lns, Mou (p. 65), TH; all versions except NEB, TEV]: to establish and encourage you concerning your faith. There is no significant difference between this word and περί 'concerning' [ICC, Lns].

QUESTION—What aspect of faith is meant here?

Most commentators do not discuss this, but the following suggestions are made: this is their personal trust in Christ [Hb, TH], this is their trust in God to supply strength to face persecution [EBC], this is their faithfulness in living out their belief in God [HNTC], this is their continuing trust and loyalty [NCBC], this is their Christian faith [ICC], faith is both the content of what they believed and the activity of believing it [Lns].

3:3 the no-one to-be-disturbed/deceived[a] in/by[b] these afflictions.[c]

LEXICON—a. pres. pass. infin. of σαίνω (LN **31.66**): 'to be disturbed' [BAGD, HNTC; NASB], 'to be perturbed' [WBC], 'to be moved' [BAGD; KJV, RSV], 'to be shaken' [NAB, NEB, TNT], 'to be unsettled' [NIV, NJB], 'to turn back' [LN; TEV]; or 'to be deceived' [Hn], 'to be beguiled' [ICC], 'to let oneself be fooled' [Lns]. The present passive is permissive [Hb, Lns]: do not let any one disturb you.
b. ἐν (LN 89.26; 89.76): 'in' [Lns], 'in the midst of' [Hn, ICC, WBC], 'under' [NEB]; or 'by' [HNTC; KJV, NAB, NASB, NIV, NJB, RSV, TNT], 'because of' [TEV].

c. θλῖψις (LN 22.2): 'afflictions' [Hn, ICC, Lns, WBC; KJV, NASB, RSV], 'hardships' [NEB, NJB], 'sufferings' [LN], 'trials' [NAB, NIV], 'troubles' [LN; TNT], 'tribulations' [HNTC], 'persecutions' [LN; TEV]. See this word at 1:6.

QUESTION—What relationship is indicated by the infinitive σαίνεσθαι 'to be disturbed/deceived'?

    1. It indicates the purpose of the preceding verse [Hb, Hn, HNTC, ICC, Lns, NCBC, WBC; KJV, NAB, NASB, NEB, NIV, RSV, TEV, TNT]: we sent Timothy to establish and exhort you so that no one will be disturbed/deceived. Some refer this purpose to the verb ἐπέμψαμεν 'we sent' [Hn; NAB, NEB, NJB, TEV, TNT], and probably this view includes the two following verbs στηρίξαι 'to establish' and παρακαλέσαι 'to exhort'; others refer the purpose to the two verbs 'to establish' and 'to exhort' [Lns]; others narrow the purpose to the verb 'to exhort' [HNTC]. Some join this to the preceding purposes with the conjunction 'and' [NEB]. Some supply a conjunction to introduce this clause: 'that' [Lns; KJV, RSV], 'so that' [HNTC, WBC; NASB, NIV, TEV], 'lest' [NAB]. Others supply a verb that indicates another purpose: 'and to prevent' [Hn, ICC; NJB], 'and to see to it that' [TNT]. Some refer to it as a secondary, negative, purpose [Hb, ICC, NCBC] that will be realized by accomplishing the primary positive purposes of establishing and exhorting them [ICC]. It is also referred to as a contemplated result of the preceding two verbs [Hn, Lns, NCBC, WBC; probably NASB, NIV, TEV].

    2. This clause is in apposition to the preceding one [Alf, Fn, Mn, My, NIC]. It explains in what sense they need to be established and exhorted [Alf, Fn, My].

    3. It indicates the object of the verb παρακαλέω, taking the meaning to be 'to exhort' [Ea, El]: to exhort you, on behalf of your faith, that you should not be disturbed/deceived [Ea, El].

QUESTION—What area of meaning is intended by the verb?

    1. It refers to a state of mind, 'to be disturbed' [Alf, Ea, EBC, El, HNTC, My, NCBC, TH, WBC; NASB, NEB, NIV, NJB]. It is in connection with their faith that they are disturbed [Hb, My].

    2. It refers to being deceived by others [Fn, Hn, ICC, Lns, Mn, NIC; TEV]. Some focus on the result of the deceit and refer to their being drawn away or led astray from their faith [NIC; TEV].

QUESTION—What relationship is indicated by ἐν 'in/by'?

    1. This indicates the circumstances under which one might be disturbed/deceived [Alf, Ea, El, Fn, Hb, Hn, ICC, Lns, Mn, NIC, WBC; NEB]: in the midst of these afflictions. It probably implies that the afflictions are the reason they would become disturbed/deceived.

    2. This indicates the means by which they would become disturbed/deceived [HNTC, NCBC; KJV, NAB, NASB, NIV, NJB, RSV, TEV, TNT]: by these afflictions.

QUESTION—What afflictions are referred to?
They are the afflictions which come to the Thessalonians [Alf, Ea, El, Hb, Hn, HNTC, ICC, Lns, Mn, My, NCBC, NIC, TH, WBC] and also to Paul [Alf, Ea, El, Hn, HNTC, Lns, My, NCBC], or to all Christians generally [Hb, Hn]. They have just experienced them [My, TH], Paul has referred to them in 2:14 [TH, WBC], or they are occurring then [Mn], or he is referring to whatever afflictions come at any time [El, My, NCBC]. It refers to persecution [ICC].

Because[a] you (your)selves know that to[b] this we-are-appointed;[c]
LEXICON—a. γάρ (LN 89.23; 91.1): 'because', 'for' [Hn, HNTC, ICC, Lns; KJV, NASB, NEB], not explicit [WBC; NAB, NIV, NJB, RSV, TEV, TNT].
  b. εἰς (LN 90.23): 'to' [ICC], 'unto' [KJV], 'for' [Hn, HNTC, Lns, WBC; NASB, NIV], not explicit [NAB, NEB, RSV, TEV, TNT].
  c. pres. mid. (deponent = active) indic. of κεῖμαι (LN 13.73): 'to be appointed' [BAGD, Hn, Lns, WBC; KJV], 'to be destined' [BAGD, HNTC, ICC; NASB, NIV], 'to be one's lot' [NAB, RSV], 'to be one's appointed lot' [NEB, TNT], 'to be bound to come' [NJB], 'to be God's will' [TEV], 'to exist for' [LN], 'to be set' [LN].
QUESTION—What relationship is indicated by γάρ 'for'?
  1. This indicates the grounds for mentioning their afflictions [ICC, My]. He talked about afflictions since they know that they are destined to have afflictions [ICC].
  2. This indicates the reason for the preceding clause [Alf, Ea, El, Hb]. They should not be disturbed because they know that they are destined to have these afflictions [Alf, Ea].
  3. This introduces an explanatory statement [Lns].
QUESTION—What is the significance of the fronted αὐτοί 'yourselves'?
It is emphasized [Hb, NIC, TH].
QUESTION—What does τοῦτο 'this' refer to?
This singular form summarizes the plural form ταῖς θλίψεσιν ταύταις 'these afflictions' in the preceding clause [Hb, Lns]. It refers to the event of being afflicted, implied by the noun 'afflictions' [Alf, Wd].
QUESTION—To whom does the 'we' in the verb refer?
It is inclusive and refers to the three missionaries and the Thessalonians [Ea, Fn, Hb, Hn, HNTC, Lns, Mn, My, TH], and even to all Christians in general [Alf, Ea, Fn, Hb, Hn, HNTC, ICC, Lns, Mn, My, Rb, Wd].
QUESTION—Who appointed them to this?
God appointed them [Ea, Hb, HNTC, Lns, NIC, TH, WBC, Wd].

3:4 because[a] indeed[b]
LEXICON—a. γάρ (LN 89.23; 91.1): 'because', 'for' [Hn, HNTC, ICC, Lns; KJV, NASB, RSV, TEV], not explicit [WBC; NAB, NEB, NIV, NJB, TNT].

b. καί (LN 89.93; 91.12): 'indeed' [HNTC, WBC; NASB, NJB], 'verily' [KJV], 'also' [Lns], 'in fact' [NIV], not explicit [Hn, ICC; NAB, NEB, RSV, TEV, TNT].

QUESTION—What relationship is indicated by γάρ 'for'?

This indicates the reason or grounds for the Thessalonians' knowledge (3:3) [Alf, BAGD, Ea, El, Hb, HNTC, Mn, My]: you know because we told you beforehand.

when we-were with you, we-were-telling-beforehand/warning[a] you that we-were-going[b] to-be-afflicted,[c]

LEXICON—a. imperf. act. indic. of προλέγω (LN **33.281**): 'to tell beforehand' [BAGD, ICC; RSV], 'to tell before' [KJV], 'to tell in advance' [BAGD, Hn, Lns; NASB], 'to tell ahead of time' [LN; TEV], 'to foretell' [HNTC], 'to tell' [NIV]; or 'to warn' [WBC; NAB, NEB, NJB, TNT]. The imperfect tense indicates repeated occasions [Fn, Hb, Hn, HNTC, ICC, Lns, NCBC, NIC, Rb, Wd; NAB, NASB, NIV].

b. pres. act. indic. of μέλλω (LN 71.36; 67.62): 'to be going to' [NASB, TEV], 'to be bound to' [WBC; NEB], 'to be certain to' [ICC; NJB, TNT], 'to be about to' [BAGD, Hn, Lns]. This is also indicated in the following ways: 'we should' [KJV], 'we would' [NAB, NIV], 'we were to' [HNTC; RSV].

c. pres. pass. infin. of θλίβω (LN 22.21): 'to be afflicted' [BAGD, Hn, Lns], 'to suffer affliction' [WBC; NASB, RSV], 'to suffer tribulation' [KJV], 'to suffer hardship' [LN; NEB], 'to suffer persecution' [TNT], 'to undergo trial' [NAB], 'to be persecuted' [LN; NIV, TEV], 'to have hardships to bear' [NJB], 'to experience tribulation' [HNTC], 'to experience affliction' [ICC]. The present tense indicates that this will be continuous or repeated [Hb]. The passive voice indicates an outside source [Hb].

QUESTION—To whom does 'we' refer in the verb μέλλω 'we were going (to be afflicted)'?

This is inclusive and refers to Paul, his companions, the Thessalonians [Fn, TH], and all Christians [Alf, BAGD, Hb, HNTC, ICC, My].

QUESTION—What is indicated by the verb μέλλω 'to be going to'?

This indicates an inevitable experience [Ea, El, Hb, HNTC, ICC, My, NIC, TH, WBC; NEB, NJB, TNT]. It implies that God destined them to experience this [Ea, El, Hb, Mn, My, NIC, TH, Wd]. It may also imply that this will soon take place [Ea, Hn, Lns].

as[a] indeed[b] it-happened[c]

LEXICON—a. καθώς (LN 64.14): 'as' [HNTC, ICC, Lns, WBC; KJV, NASB, NEB, NJB, TEV], 'just as' [Hn, LN; RSV], not explicit [NAB]. It is also translated as a phrase: 'that way' [NIV]. Some rearrange the syntax so that this word occurs with the following phrase [Hn; NASB, NEB, NJB, TEV].

b. καί (LN 91.12; 89.92; 89.93): 'indeed' [ICC], 'even' [HNTC, WBC; KJV], 'exactly' [TEV]; or 'and' [NASB, NEB, NIV]; or 'now' [NAB], 'and now' [NJB], 'even also' [Lns]; not explicit [Hn; RSV, TNT].
c. aorist mid. (deponent = active) indic. of γίνομαι (LN 13.107): 'to happen' [Hn, HNTC, LN; NAB, NJB, TEV], 'to come to pass' [KJV, NASB, RSV], 'to come to be' [LN], 'to turn out' [ICC, WBC; NEB, NIV, TNT], 'to occur' [LN, Lns].

QUESTION—What is the function of this clause?
This confirms his prediction [Hb, ICC]. This proof of the truth of his prediction results in strengthening their faith [Hb, Hn].

and you know.

QUESTION—What did they know?
From their own experience, they know that it happened [Alf, Ea, El, HNTC, My; NJB]. Some seem to consider this phrase to be coordinate with the preceding one [Ea, Fn, Hb, HNTC, ICC, Lns; KJV, RSV]: as it happened and as you know. In this case, the apostle appeals for confirmation to two things, the fact that it happened and the experience of the people [Ea, Fn, Hb]. Some make the preceding clause the content of what they know: it happened, just as you know [WBC; NASB, NEB, NIV, NJB], or changing the order: as you know, that is what happened [Hn; TEV, TNT].

3:5 Because of-this[a]

LEXICON—a. διὰ τοῦτο: 'because of this', 'on account of this' [Lns], 'for this reason' [Hn; NASB, NIV, RSV], 'for this cause' [KJV], 'that is why' [NAB, NJB, TEV, TNT], 'and thus it was that' [NEB], 'therefore' [WBC], 'wherefore' [ICC], 'so' [HNTC].

QUESTION—What relationship is indicated by this phrase?
1. 'This' refers back to verse 4 [Alf, Ea, El, Hb, Lns, My, NCBC, Wd]: because you had been afflicted, I sent Timothy.
2. 'This' refers back to all of 2:17–3:4 [Hn, TH].
3. 'This' refers forward to the following clause [Fn, WBC]: because of this, that I could no longer bear not knowing about your faith, I sent Timothy.

no-longer bearing[a] **(it)**

LEXICON—a. pres. act. participle of στέγω (LN **25.176**): 'to bear' [BAGD; NEB, NJB, RSV, TEV, TNT], 'to endure' [BAGD, HNTC, ICC, LN; NASB], 'to forbear' [KJV], 'to stand' [BAGD, Hn, Lns; NAB, NIV], 'to hold out' [WBC]. See this phrase at 3:1.

QUESTION—What relationship is indicated by the participial form στέγων 'bearing'?
1. This is temporal [Hn; KJV, NAB, NASB, NEB, NIV, NJB, RSV]: when I could no longer bear it, I sent, etc.
2. This is the reason for the following clause [HNTC, ICC, WBC; TEV]: because I could no longer bear it, I sent, etc.

QUESTION—What couldn't he bear?

He could not bear to be without information about them [Hb, My, NCBC, TH, WBC], to be absent from them [ICC, NCBC, NIC, TH], or to be anxious about them [Bul (p. 14), EGT].

I-also[a]...sent[b] in-order to-know[c] your faith,[d]

LEXICON—a. κἀγώ: 'I also' [BAGD; NASB], 'I too' [BAGD, Hn, ICC], 'I for my part' [WBC], 'also I myself' [Lns], 'I' [HNTC; all versions except NASB].

b. aorist act. indic. of πέμπω (LN 15.66): 'to send' [BAGD, Hn, HNTC, ICC, LN, Lns, WBC; all versions]. See this word at 3:2.

c. aorist act. infin. of γινώσκω (LN 27.2; 28.1): 'to know' [LN, Lns; KJV, RSV, TNT], 'to find out about' [BAGD, LN; NAB, NASB, NEB, NIV, TEV], 'to learn about' [BAGD, Hn, HNTC, LN, WBC], 'to have knowledge of' [LN], 'to get knowledge' [ICC], 'to assure oneself' [NJB], 'to ascertain' [BAGD]. The aorist tense is ingressive, 'to get to know' [Hb, Hn, Lns, Rb, Wd].

d. πίστις (LN 31.85; 31.88): 'faith' [BAGD, Hn, HNTC, ICC, LN, Lns, WBC; all versions]. See this word at 3:2.

QUESTION—What is the significance of κἀγώ (καὶ ἐγώ) 'and/even/also I'?

1. This focuses on Paul's personal feelings [EBC, EGT, El, Er, Fn, Hb, HNTC, Mn, Mou (p. 167), NCBC, NIC, TH, WBC]: I, for my part. It does not imply that the others were less concerned [Hb]. However, it could be taken to mean that Paul was the most impatient one of the missionaries, and most responsible for sending Timothy [WBC].

2. This includes others [Alf, Ea, Hn, ICC, Lns, My]: I, also, as well as others. The others might be more easily worried, but even Paul felt this way [Lns]. The reference to 'others' means Silvanus [ICC].

QUESTION—Is there an implied object to the verb ἔπεμψα 'I sent'?

The implication is: I sent Timothy [Ea, Fn, Hb, HNTC, ICC, Lns, NCBC, NIC, TH; TEV, TNT].

QUESTION—What did Paul want to know about their faith?

He wanted to know if they still continued to have faith [Ea, Fn, HNTC, NCBC, NIC, TH], in God [NCBC], or Jesus Christ [TH], and how it was being maintained [Ea, Fn, Hb, My, TH]. This does not mean that Paul wanted to know what they believed [TH].

lest[a] the (one) tempting[b] tempted[c] you and in vain[d] should-become our labor.[e]

LEXICON—a. μή πως (LN 89.62): 'lest' [LN, WBC], 'lest by some means' [KJV], 'lest by any means' [Hn], 'lest in some way' [Lns], 'whether' [TNT]. Many make this introduce the contents of an implied verb 'fearing' [Hb, HNTC, ICC, Mn, NCBC, Rb, Wd; NAB, NASB, NEB, NIV, NJB, RSV]: 'fearing that' [ICC; NAB, NEB], 'fearing that in some way' [HNTC], 'to be afraid that' [NJB], 'to be afraid that in some way'

[NIV], 'for fear that' [NASB], 'for fear that somehow' [RSV], 'surely it could not be that' [TEV].
- b. pres. act. participle of πειράζω (LN 88.308; 12.36): 'to tempt' [LN]. All translate this as a substantive: 'the tempter' [BAGD, Hn, HNTC, ICC, LN, Lns, WBC; all versions except NJB, TEV], 'the Tester' [NJB], 'the Devil' [TEV]. The present tense indicates that a continual tempting is going on [Hb], it indicates Satan's characteristic activity [Fn, Mn].
- c. aorist act. indic. of πειράζω (LN 88.308): 'to tempt' [BAGD, Hn, HNTC, ICC, LN, Lns, WBC; KJV, NASB, NEB, NIV, RSV, TEV], 'to put to the test' [BAGD; NAB, NJB]. The aorist indicative implies that he feared that the temptation had already taken place [Ea, EBC, El, Fn, Hb, ICC, Mn, My, NCBC, NIC, TH].
- d. εἰς κενός (LN 89.53): 'in vain' [ICC, WBC; KJV, NASB, RSV, TNT], 'fruitless' [HNTC], 'useless' [Hn; NIV], 'pointless' [NJB], 'lost' [NEB], 'for nothing' [Lns; NAB, TEV], 'without result' [LN].
- e. κόπος (LN 42.47): 'labor' [BAGD, HNTC, ICC, WBC; KJV, NAB, NASB, NEB, RSV, TNT], 'toil' [BAGD, Hn, LN, Lns], 'work' [BAGD; NJB, TEV], 'hard work' [LN], 'efforts' [NIV]. See this word at 1:3 and 2:9.

QUESTION—Who was the tempter?

This is a reference to the Devil, Satan [EBC, Er, Fn, Hb, Hn, HNTC, ICC, Lns, Mn, My, NIC, TH, WBC; TEV], who is referred to by his characteristic activity [Hb].

QUESTION—What was the temptation?

It was the temptation to abandon their faith [Hb, NCBC, WBC].

QUESTION—What is the relationship between being tempted and the labor being in vain?
1. 'He tempted' means an attempt to get them do wrong without indicating whether the attempt was successful [Ea, EBC, El, Hb, HNTC, ICC, Mn, NCBC, NIC]: lest he tempted you and (lest you succumbed so that) our labor became in vain. Some think that the aorist indicative ἐπείρασεν 'he tempted' indicates that Paul assumed that Satan had actually tempted them and the subjunctive γένται 'it should be (in vain)' indicates that the outcome was uncertain as to whether they succumbed or not [Alf, Ea, EBC, El, Hb, HNTC, ICC, Mn]. Others think that the subjunctive puts doubt on the idea that the labor was in vain and implies that they had resisted the temptation [NIC].
2. 'He tempted' implies a successful act [EGT, My, TH, WBC]: lest he tempted you and (as a result) our labor became in vain. It was not known whether he had so tempted them.

QUESTION—What would make their labor to be in vain?

Paul's labor had been to bring the Thessalonians to faith. His labor would be in vain if their faith did not endure [Hb] and they succumbed to the temptation and gave up their faith [Er, NCBC, WBC].

DISCOURSE UNIT: 3:6–13 [Fn, Hb, Hn; NIV, NJB]. The topic is Timothy's report [Fn, Hb; NIV], thanksgiving for a good report [NJB]. This is further divided: 6, 7–10, 11–13 [Hb]; 6, 7–8, 9–10, 11, 12–13 [Fn].

DISCOURSE UNIT: 3:6–10 [EBC, Er, Hn, HNTC, ICC, Mn, WBC, Wd]. The topic is Timothy's report [HNTC, ICC, Wd], joy over the report [EBC, Er, Hn, WBC].

DISCOURSE UNIT: 3:6–8 [Alf, NIC]. The topic is Timothy's report about his visit to the Thessalonians.

3:6 But[a] now

LEXICON—a. δέ (LN 89.124): 'but' [Hn, ICC, Lns, WBC; KJV, NAB, NASB, NEB, NIV, RSV, TNT], 'however' [HNTC; NJB], not explicit [TEV].
QUESTION—What relationship is indicated by δέ 'but'?
   This indicates a contrast [El, Hb, Hn, HNTC, ICC, Lns, My, NIC, TH, WBC; all versions except TEV]. This contrasts the past and the present [El, Hb, My, NIC]. It contrasts Paul's attitude before Timothy was sent and his attitude now that he has returned [Hb, TH].
QUESTION—What verb does the adverb ἄρτι 'now' modify?
   1. It modifies ἐλθόντος 'coming' in the following phrase [Alf, Ea, EBC, Fn, Hb, Hn, HNTC, ICC, Lns, Mn, NIC, WBC; NEB, NIV, TEV, TNT]: but Timothy having now come..., we were comforted. One commentator adds that it is also connected with 'bringing good news' [Fn].
   2. It modifies παρεκλήθημεν 'we were comforted' in 3:7 [My; probably NAB, NASB, RSV]: but now, Timothy having come..., we were comforted.

Timothy coming to us from you and bringing-good-news[a] to-us of-the faith and the love of-you,

LEXICON—a. aorist mid. participle of εὐαγγελίζω (LN 33.215): 'to bring good news' [BAGD, ICC, Lns, WBC; NASB, NEB, NIV, RSV, TNT], 'to bring good tidings' [KJV], 'to bring glad tidings' [Hn], 'to bring welcome news' [TEV], 'to report good news' [NAB], 'to give good news' [NJB], 'to tell good news' [HNTC, LN], 'to announce the gospel' [LN].
QUESTION—What relationship is indicated by the use of the two participial forms ἐλθόντος 'coming' and εὐαγγελισαμένου 'bringing good news'?
   1. This genitive absolute construction indicates time [Ea, HNTC; KJV]: when Timothy came and brought good news. This sentence seems to have been left incomplete [HNTC], since 3:7 indicates that verse 6 is the cause of 'we were comforted' rather than the temporal setting.
   2. The first indicates the time of the second [Hb]: when Timothy came, he brought good news.
   3. They introduce the reason for 3:7 [Ea, Hn, HNTC, ICC, NCBC, WBC; NASB, NEB, NIV, NJB, RSV, TEV, TNT]: because Timothy came...and brought good news..., (because of this) we have been comforted. Some introduce the participial clauses with that [Hn, ICC, WBC; NASB, RSV]:

(now) that Timothy came and brought good news—because of this we have been comforted. Others translate the participial clauses as indicatives [NEB, NIV, NJB, TEV, TNT]: but now Timothy has come and brought us good news. Because of this we have been comforted.

QUESTION—To whom does ἡμᾶς 'us' refer?

It refers to Paul and Silvanus [Fn, Hb, Hn, HNTC, ICC]. In this case, the coming of Timothy and Silvanus (Silas) to Corinth (Acts 18:5) can be understood to mean that Silvanus actually arrived before Timothy [Hb, ICC]. If the two arrived together, then perhaps (1) 'us' refers to both Paul and Silvanus since Timothy had first returned to Silvanus and then to Paul along with Silvanus [perhaps implied by Fn], or (2) 'us' refers to Paul and the Christians in Corinth [mentioned as a possibility by HNTC], or it is a literary plural, referring only to Paul [possibly NCBC].

QUESTION—Towards whom is their faith directed?

They have faith in God [EBC, Hb, HNTC, NIC, TH, WBC]. Therefore the news was that their faith had remained firm since Paul had left them [Ea].

QUESTION—Towards whom is their love directed?

They love others [Ea, EBC, El, Hb, HNTC, NCBC, NIC, TH, WBC]. Most commentators think that this love is directed toward all people, with their special attitude toward Paul being discussed in the following clause [Hb, NCBC, NIC]. One mentions that the love is directed not only towards other people, but also towards God [NCBC]. One adds that this love is especially for the three missionaries [WBC].

and that you-have good[a] remembrance[b] of-us always,[c]

LEXICON—a. ἀγαθός (LN 88.1): 'good' [BAGD, LN, Lns; KJV], 'pleasant' [NIV], 'affectionate' [Hn], not explicit [NAB]. This adjective is also translated as an adverb with the verbal form of the noun it modifies: 'kindly' [BAGD, ICC, WBC; NASB, NEB, RSV, TNT], 'affectionately' [HNTC], 'well' [TEV], 'with pleasure' [NJB].

b. μνεία (LN **29.7**): 'remembrance' [BAGD, ICC, Lns; KJV], 'memories' [BAGD; NIV], 'recollection' [Hn]. This noun is also translated as a verb: 'to remember' [HNTC, LN, WBC; NAB, NJB, RSV, TNT], 'to think' [NASB, NEB, TEV]. The present tense ἔχετε 'you have' indicates that this is a constant attitude [Ea, Hb, Hn, ICC, NCBC; NAB].

c. πάντοτε (LN 67.88): 'always' [BAGD, HNTC, ICC, LN, Lns, WBC; all versions except NAB], 'constantly' [NAB], 'at all times' [Hn, LN], 'on every occasion' [LN].

QUESTION—What is a good remembrance?

It does not mean that they had a good, clear recollection of Paul, but that their memory of Paul was of enjoyable experiences and produced kindly affection towards him [EBC, El, Hb, HNTC, ICC, Mn, TH, WBC]. The 'good' focuses on having affection for him [Hn, ICC, NCBC, TH, WBC; NASB, NEB, NIV, NJB, RSV, TNT], although one seems to have it focus on the respect they have for him: they think well of him [TEV].

longing[a] to-see[b] us,
LEXICON—a. pres. act. participle of ἐπιποθέω (LN 25.18): 'to long' [BAGD, Hn, ICC, LN, Lns, WBC; NASB, NIV, RSV, TNT], 'to desire' [BAGD], 'to deeply desire' [LN], 'to desire greatly' [KJV], 'to be desirous' [NAB], 'to be anxious' [NEB], 'to want' [NJB, TEV], 'to wish' [HNTC]. The present tense is continuous [Hb].
  b. aorist act. infin. of ὁράω (LN 24.1): 'to see' [BAGD, Hn, HNTC, ICC, LN, Lns, WBC; all versions].
QUESTION—What relationship is indicated by the participial form ἐπιποθοῦντες 'longing'?
  1. This is translated as a coordinate statement with the preceding one [ICC, WBC; NAB, NEB, NIV, NJB, RSV, TEV, TNT]: you have good remembrance of us and you long to see us. The preceding clause is about their attitude concerning Paul's first visit with them. This adds to it their attitude about a return visit [NIC].
  2. This indicates the grounds for the preceding statement [HNTC]: you have a good remembrance of us, (and this is proved) since you long to see us.
  3. This indicates the result of the previous clause [Ea]: you have a good remembrance of us and therefore you long to see us.

just-as[a] also[b] we you,
LEXICON—a. καθάπερ (LN 64.15): 'just as' [BAGD, Hn, HNTC, LN, Lns; NASB, NIV, TNT], 'as' [ICC, WBC; KJV, NAB, NEB, RSV], 'just as much as' [TEV], 'quite as much as' [NJB].
  b. καί (LN 89.93): 'also' [Hn, HNTC, Lns; KJV, NASB, NIV], 'too' [ICC], not explicit [WBC; NAB, NEB, NJB, RSV, TEV, TNT].
QUESTION—What verbs are implied in this comparison?
  The full comparison is: just as we long to see you [Alf, Ea, El, Hn, HNTC, My, WBC; NASB, NIV, NJB, RSV, TEV, TNT]. Some omit one of the words: as we to see you [KJV, NAB, NEB]. There is equal longing [Ea, Hb, Lns, NIC].

3:7 because-of this[a] we-were-encouraged/comforted,[b] brothers, about/because -of[c] you
LEXICON—a. διὰ τοῦτο: 'because of this' [Lns], 'for this reason' [Hn, ICC; NASB, RSV], 'for that reason' [HNTC], 'therefore' [KJV, NIV], 'so' [TEV, TNT], 'and so' [NEB, NJB], 'why then' [WBC], not explicit [NAB].
  b. aorist pass. indic. of παρακαλέω (LN 25.150): 'to be/become encouraged' [BAGD, HNTC, ICC, LN; NIV, TEV], 'to be reassured' [WBC]; or 'to be comforted' [BAGD, Hn, Lns; KJV, NASB, RSV], 'to be consoled' [LN], 'to be much consoled' [NAB]. This is also translated actively, with 'faith' being the subject: 'to reassure' [NEB], 'to greatly cheer' [TNT], 'to be a great encouragement' [NJB]. See this word at 3:2.

c. ἐπί (LN 90.23; 89.27): 'about' [Hn, WBC; NASB, NEB, NIV, RSV, TEV], 'over' [Lns, NIC; KJV], 'with regard to' [WBC], or 'because of' [HNTC], 'in' [ICC]; not explicit [NAB, NJB, TNT].

QUESTION—What relationship is indicated by διὰ τοῦτο 'because of this'?

This indicates the result of Timothy's good news (verse 6) [Alf, Ea, El, Hb, HNTC, ICC, Lns, Mn, NCBC, NIC, TH, WBC]: because of Timothy's good news about you, we were comforted. The three items of the good news are considered as a whole by the use of the singular τοῦτο 'this' [Alf, Ea, El, Hb, Mn, My, NIC]. There is no main verb in verse 6 and it seems to have started out to be a temporal circumstance for what would follow [El, NCBC]. However, verse 7 seems to begin a new sentence, using verse 6 as a cause. Some think that verse 6 was left unfinished [El, HNTC, NCBC]. This is shown in some translations by ending verse 6 with a dash [HNTC, ICC, WBC; RSV]. Other translations translate the participles in verse 6 as main verbs so that a break is not evident [NAB, NEB, NIV, NJB, TEV, TNT].

QUESTION—What relationship is indicated by ἐπί 'about/because of', and how does this affect the meaning of the verb?

1. ἐπί means 'about' or 'concerning' and indicates that the feeling of anxiety about the continued faithfulness of the Thessalonians was removed [Alf, BAGD, Ea, Hn, Lns, My, WBC; KJV, NASB, NEB, NIV, RSV, TEV]: we were comforted or encouraged about you.
2. ἐπί means 'because of' and indicates that the report about the Thessalonians strengthened the missionaries to face difficult circumstances [BAGD, Ea, EBC, Er, Fn, Hb, HNTC, ICC, NCBC, NIC, TH; perhaps NAB, NJB, TNT]: we were strengthened because of you. This would then restate the initial διὰ τοῦτο 'because of this'.

in/concerning[a] all the distress[b] and affliction[c] of-us

LEXICON—a. ἐπί (LN 67.136; 90.23): 'in' [Hn, HNTC, Lns, WBC; KJV, NASB, NEB, NIV, RSV, TEV], 'throughout' [NAB], 'in the middle of' [NJB], 'to face' [ICC], not explicit [TNT].

b. ἀνάγκη (LN 22.1): 'distress' [BAGD, Hn, LN, Lns, WBC; NAB, NASB, NIV, NJB, RSV], 'trouble' [LN; TEV], 'calamity' [BAGD], 'difficulties' [NEB], 'affliction' [HNTC; KJV], 'privations' [ICC]. This noun is also translated as a verb: 'to be distressed' [TNT].

c. θλῖψις (LN 22.2): 'affliction' [BAGD, Hn, Lns, WBC; NASB, RSV], 'suffering' [LN; TEV], 'trial' [NAB], 'hardship' [NEB, NJB], 'persecution' [ICC, LN; NIV], 'distress' [KJV], 'tribulation' [BAGD, HNTC]. This noun is also translated as a verb: 'to be afflicted' [TNT]. See this word at 1:6.

QUESTION—What relationship is indicated by ἐπί 'in/concerning'?

1. This means 'in' and introduces the circumstances in which they are comforted or encouraged [Alf, BAGD, El, My, TH, WBC]: while we were in distress and affliction, we were comforted or encouraged. This indicates that the difficult circumstances continued [Hn, HNTC, My].

2. This means 'concerning' [EBC, ICC, NIC]: we were comforted or encouraged concerning our own troubles by the news of the faithfulness of the Thessalonians. They were strengthened to endure their afflictions [NIC].

QUESTION—What is the distinction between ἀνάγκῃ 'distress' and θλίψει 'affliction'?

Some say that there is no significant difference [Ea, HNTC, Lns, NCBC, TH, WBC]. It may refer to internal anxiety about the Thessalonians. Also the missionaries might have been wondering if God had really guided them to Macedonia where they had met such trouble [WBC]. Or it may refer to external troubles [Alf, Ea, EBC, El, Fn, Hb, HNTC, My, NCBC], such as persecution [NIC, NTC], or hard physical labor as they worked and ministered [Hn]. Or it may refer to both internal and external pressures [Hn]. πάσῃ 'all' refers to the intensity of the troubles, rather than the kinds of troubles [HNTC]. If distinctions are to be made, the first refers to difficulties in general and the second to opposition from people [EBC, Fn, ICC, My, NIC], or the first indicates that the troubles are unavoidable, while the second focuses on the pressure they bring [Ea, Hb, Lns], or the first refers to the distress resulting from pressures while the second refers to physical harm [TH].

because-of/through[a] your faith,[b]

LEXICON—a. διά (LN 89.26; 89.76): 'because of' [NIV]; or 'through' [Hn, HNTC, ICC, WBC; NASB, RSV], 'by' [KJV, NAB], 'by means of' [Lns]. Some indicate this relationship by making 'faith' the subject of the first verb in this verse [NEB, NJB, TEV, TNT].

b. πίστις (LN 31.85): 'faith' [BAGD, Hn, HNTC, ICC, LN, Lns, WBC; all versions]. See this word at 3:2.

QUESTION—What is implied in this phrase?

It is implied that 'the news' about their faith is what comforted or encouraged Paul [Bul (p. 25), Ea, Hb, HNTC, WBC; TNT]. Specifically, it was news that the Thessalonians' faith was holding firm [Hb, WBC], they depended on God to help them [EBC], and had a continuing trust in the Lord [TH]. Although the news included other points (1:3, 3:6), their faith was the key point and basic to the other good reports [Hb, Hn, HNTC, Lns, NIC].

QUESTION—What relationship is indicated by διά 'because of/through'?

1. This introduces the reason why they were comforted or encouraged [TH; NIV]. Since 3:6 also indicated a reason, this picks out the basic reason, πίστιν 'faith', and emphasizes it: because of that report (3:6) we were comforted/encouraged, and it was particularly because of the report about your faith.

2. This introduces the means by which they were comforted or encouraged [Ea, EBC, El, Hb, Hn, HNTC, ICC, Lns, NIC, WBC; NASB, RSV]: because of that report (verse 6) we were comforted/encouraged and your faith is the means by which we were.

3:8 because[a] now[b] we-live[c]

LEXICON—a. ὅτι (LN 89.33): 'because' [HNTC; TEV], 'for' [Hn, ICC; KJV, NASB, NIV, RSV], 'seeing that' [Lns], 'so much so that' [NAB], not explicit [WBC; NEB, NJB, TNT].
  b. νῦν (LN 67.38): 'now' [BAGD, Hn, HNTC, ICC, LN, Lns; KJV, NASB, NIV, NJB, RSV, TEV], not explicit [WBC; NAB, NEB, TNT].
  c. pres. act. indic. of ζάω (LN 23.88): 'to live' [BAGD, HNTC, ICC, LN, Lns; KJV, RSV], 'to really live' [Hn; NASB, NIV, TEV], 'to flourish' [NAB], 'it is life (to us)' [WBC], 'to be able to breathe again' [NJB], 'to be the breath of life' [NEB]. This is also translated as a clause: 'life is worth living' [TNT]. The present tense indicates a continuing state [Hb, Lns] and implies a continuing need for them to stand firm [Lns; NAB].

QUESTION—What relationship is indicated by ὅτι 'because'?
  This indicates the reason why their faith is so important to Paul [Ea, El, Hb, ICC, Lns, NCBC, WBC]: we were encouraged by your faith, because we live if you stand fast.

QUESTION—Is νῦν 'now' temporal or logical?
  1. It is temporal [Fn, Mn, NCBC]: now, in contrast with the time before Timothy returned with the good news.
  2. It is logical [Alf, BAGD, Ea, El, Hb, ICC, My]: under the circumstances, we now live. The 'if' clause supports this interpretation [Ea].

QUESTION—In what respect can they now live?
  They have a new sense of joy [HNTC], life is worth living [Bul (p. 829), Hb, TH; TNT], their spiritual life was strengthened by the knowledge of the progress of the converts [NCBC], they have renewed enthusiasm [EBC, HNTC], purpose [Fn], and satisfaction [Hb].

if[a] you stand-firm[b] in[c] (the) Lord.

LEXICON—a. ἐάν (LN 89.67): 'if' [BAGD, Hn, HNTC, ICC, LN, Lns, WBC; KJV, NASB, RSV, TEV, TNT], 'only if' [NAB], 'as' [NJB], 'since' [NIV], 'that' [NEB].
  b. pres. act. indic. of στήκω (LN 13.30): 'to stand' [LN], 'to stand firm' [BAGD, HNTC; NAB, NASB, NEB, NIV, TEV, TNT], 'to stand fast' [Hn, ICC, Lns, WBC; KJV, RSV], 'to hold firm' [NJB], 'to be steadfast' [BAGD].
  c. ἐν (LN 89.119; 89.76): 'in' [Hn, HNTC, ICC, Lns, WBC; all versions except TEV], 'in your life in union with' [TEV].

QUESTION—What is implied by ἐάν 'if'?
  This does not indicate doubt about their standing firm at the present [Hb, HNTC, Mn, NCBC, TH; NIV], yet it reminds them that they are responsible to continue standing firm in the future [Alf, Hb, Lns, Mn, NCBC].

QUESTION—In what way did they hold firm?
  They held firm in regard to a steady faith [Hb, Lns, WBC]. Faith characterized their lives [NIC]. They were to be faithful to every aspect of life as it related to obedience to the Lord [NCBC].

QUESTION—What is meant by standing firm ἐν κυρίῳ 'in the Lord'?
1. 'In' is local and indicates in what respect they stand firm [Hb, NCBC]: they stand firm in relation to their lives being in union with the Lord [Ea, Hb, HNTC, TH; TEV]. It means to be related to him by faith, love, hope in him [Hn, Lns].
2. 'In' is instrumental and indicates the means of standing firm [ICC]: they stand firm in regard to their faith by means of receiving power from the indwelling Christ [ICC].

DISCOURSE UNIT: 3:9–13 [NAB, TH]. The topic is Paul's prayer that they become holy.

DISCOURSE UNIT: 3:9–10 [Hb, NIC, TH]: The topic is a statement of satisfaction [NIC], thanksgiving and prayer [Hb].

3:9 Because/Then
LEXICON—γάρ (LN 89.23; 91.1): 'because', 'for' [Hn, Lns; KJV, NASB, RSV]; or 'then' [HNTC], 'now' [TEV], 'indeed' [ICC], not explicit [WBC; NAB, NEB, NIV, NJB, TNT].
QUESTION—What relationship is indicated by γάρ 'because/then'?
1. This indicates the reason or grounds for saying that they live if the Thessalonians stand fast [Alf, Ea, El, Hb, My, WBC]: we live if you stand firm because that is what we rejoice about. It also specifies what 'to live' means [Alf, Ea].
2. This explains why they said that they were so encouraged through the faith of the Thessalonians [Fn, ICC]. [ICC]: we were encouraged by your faith because now we live if you stand fast and since we are so thankful for you. This is parallel in meaning to ὅτι 'because' [ICC] in 3:8.
3. This indicates the result of being encouraged by the good news [EBC, HNTC, NCBC]: we were encouraged about you, therefore we thank God. When γάρ is used in a question it means 'then' [HNTC, NCBC].

what thanks[a] are-we-able to-return[b] to-God concerning[c] you
LEXICON—a. εὐχαριστία (LN 33.349): 'thanks' [BAGD, ICC, Lns; KJV, NAB, NASB, NEB, TEV], 'thanksgiving' [BAGD, Hn, HNTC, LN, WBC; RSV], 'rendering of thanks' [BAGD]. This is also translated as a verb: 'to thank' [NIV, NJB, TNT].
b. aorist act. infin. of ἀνταποδίδωμι (LN 57.154): 'to return' [BAGD, HNTC, ICC; NEB], 'to render' [WBC; RSV], 'to render in return' [NASB], 'to render again' [KJV], 'to give' [NAB, TEV], 'to give back' [BAGD, LN], 'to offer in return' [Hn], 'to repay, to pay back' [LN], 'to give in due return' [Lns]. This verb is conflated with the noun 'thanks' by some: 'to thank' [NJB, TNT], 'to thank in return' [NIV].
c. περί (LN 89.6; 90.24; 89.36): 'concerning' [Hn, Lns], 'for' [HNTC, ICC, WBC; all versions except NAB, TNT], 'because of' [NAB], 'on your account' [TNT].

QUESTION—What is implied by this rhetorical question?

It is implied that God has done so much that they cannot adequately or sufficiently thank him [Alf, Ea, EBC, El, Er, Fn, Hb, Hn, HNTC, ICC, Lns, My, NCBC, TH, WBC, Wd; NIV, NJB, TNT]. This is indicated in some translations which supply adverbs with the verb; 'to thank God adequately' [Hn, ICC, WBC], 'to thank God enough' [NIV, NJB], 'to thank God sufficiently' [Alf, Ea, El, NCBC; TNT]. It is also implied that God is responsible for keeping the Thessalonians steadfastly faithful [Fn, Hb, HNTC, ICC, NCBC, NIC]. Christian growth is due both to the working of God and the activity of the believer, so that Paul can thank God for the results and also urge the Thessalonians to grow in their faith [NCBC]. The verb is also considered by some to have here the component of returning what is due and adequate [Alf, Ea, El, Fn, Hb, Hn, ICC, Lns, Mn, My, NCBC, NIC, TH, Wd; NASB, NIV, NJB], and perhaps this is also involved in supplying the adverbs. Thanksgiving is regarded as something owed for the blessings from God [El]. They can never thank God enough to recompense him for the good thing he did in regard to the Thessalonians [Hb, Wd]. They can never thank God enough to match their joy [Lns, My, TH]. Some commentators, however, do not seem to consider this component to be in focus here [WBC; NAB, NASB, RSV]

for[a] all the joy[b] (with) which we-rejoice[c] because-of[d] you

LEXICON—a. ἐπί (LN 89.27; 90.23): 'for' [Hn, ICC; all versions], 'at' [WBC], 'in' [HNTC, Lns].
- b. χαρά (LN 25.123): 'joy' [BAGD, Hn, HNTC, ICC, LN, Lns, WBC; all versions], 'gladness' [LN].
- c. pres. act. indic. of χαίρω (LN 25.125): 'to rejoice' [Hn, HNTC, LN, Lns, WBC; NASB, NEB], 'to joy' [KJV], 'to be glad' [LN]. This is also conflated with the noun 'joy': 'the joy we feel' [NAB, NJB, RSV], 'the joy we have' [NIV, TEV, TNT], 'the joy we express' [ICC]. The present tense indicates that the joy continues on [Hb].
- d. διά (LN 90.44): 'because of' [Lns; NAB, NIV, TEV], 'on account of' [Hn, HNTC, WBC; NASB, NJB, TNT], 'brought by' [NEB]; or 'for the sake of' [ICC; KJV, RSV].

QUESTION—What relationship is indicated by ἐπί 'for'?

This introduces the reason for giving thanks [BAGD, Ea, El, Hb, ICC, Mn, NCBC, TH]; it follows that this is also the topic of the statement of thanksgiving.

QUESTION—What is meant by πάσῃ 'all'?

This indicates the intensity of the joy [Alf, HNTC, ICC, NCBC, TH], not different kinds joy nor different sources. Or, some speak of it as meaning joy regarded in its fullest, its sum total [Ea, El, Fn, Hb, My], it lacks nothing to make it complete [El].

QUESTION—What relationship is indicated by διά 'because of'?
> This indicates that the Thessalonians are the reason for rejoicing [Ea, Fn, Hb, Hn, HNTC, Lns, Mn, TH, WBC; NAB, NASB, NEB, NIV, NJB, TEV, TNT]: we rejoice because of how you have shown yourselves to be.

before^a our God,
LEXICON—a. ἔμπροσθεν (LN 83.33): 'before' [BAGD, HNTC, LN, Lns; KJV, NASB, NEB, NJB, RSV], 'in front of' [LN], 'in the presence of' [BAGD, Hn, ICC, WBC; NAB, NIV, TEV, TNT]. See this word at 1:3 and 2:19.
QUESTION—What does this phrase mean?
> It is connected with 'we rejoice' [Ea, Hb, ICC, Mn, My, NCBC]. It means that the missionaries are conscious of being in God's presence as they pray to him [Hb, HNTC, Lns, WBC], or their joy is expressed to God in prayer [Hb, ICC, NCBC, TH]. 'Our' includes the readers [HNTC, ICC, TH].

3:10 night and day earnestly^a asking^b
LEXICON—a. ὑπερεκπερισσοῦ (LN **78.34**): 'earnestly' [NJB, RSV], 'most earnestly' [ICC; NASB, NEB, NIV, TNT], 'with intense earnestness' [Hn], 'with extreme earnestness' [LN], 'with deep earnestness' [HNTC], 'with the utmost earnestness' [WBC], 'as earnestly as possible' [BAGD], 'exceedingly' [Lns; KJV], 'fervently' [NAB], 'with all one's heart' [TEV].
  b. pres. pass. (deponent = active) participle of δέομαι (LN 33.170): 'to ask' [BAGD, Lns; NAB, TEV], 'to beg' [ICC, LN], 'to plead' [LN], 'to pray' [Hn, HNTC, WBC; KJV, NASB, NEB, NIV, NJB, RSV, TNT]. The present tense indicates repeated asking [Hb; NASB].
QUESTION—What relationship is indicated by the participial form δεόμενοι 'asking'?
> This indicates a circumstance which occurs with a preceding verb [Alf, Ea, EBC, El, Fn, Hb, HNTC, Lns, My; NAB, NASB, NEB]: as/while we ask. This accompanies their rejoicing [EBC, HNTC], or it accompanies their attempts to thank God [Alf, Ea, El, Fn, Hb, Lns, My].

QUESTION—What is meant by praying νυκτὸς καὶ ἡμέρας 'night and day'?
> This does not mean two different times for prayer, but it means continued, regular, and frequent prayer [EBC, HNTC, ICC, NIC, TH, Wd], we prayed again and again both during the night and during the day [Hb]. In English idiom, the order would be reversed to 'day and night' [Lns]. See this same order at 2:9.

that/in-order-that to-see your (plural) face
QUESTION—What relationship is indicated by εἰς τό 'that/in order that' with the infinitive ἰδεῖν 'to see'?
> This indicates the content of their prayers [Hb, Hn, HNTC, ICC, Lns, Mn, NCBC, WBC; TNT]: we pray that we will see your face, etc. It also indicates their purpose for praying [Alf, Ea, El, Fn, My, NCBC, WBC]: we

pray in order that we will see your face, etc. There is one article to unite both clauses; his desire to see them includes the purpose of completing what is lacking [Ea, Fn, Hb, Hn, HNTC, Lns, NCBC].

QUESTION—What does ἰδεῖν ὑμῶν τὸ πρόσωπον 'to see your face' mean?

'Face' is a metonymy for the whole person and this means to see them [NEB, NIV], to see them personally [TEV], to see them face to face [Hb, WBC; NAB, NJB, RSV, TNT]. It implies fellowship [Hb, Hn, TH].

and to-complete/correct^a the deficiencies^b of-your faith?

LEXICON—a. aorist act. infin. of καταρτίζω (LN 75.5): 'to complete' [BAGD, Lns; NASB], 'to make up' [ICC; NJB], 'to make good' [HNTC, WBC; TNT], 'to make adequate' [LN], 'to perfect' [KJV], 'to supply' [Hn; NIV, RSV, TEV], 'to furnish completely' [LN]; or 'to remedy' [NAB], 'to mend' [NEB].

b. ὑστέρημα (LN 57.38; 85.29): 'deficiencies' [Hn, HNTC, ICC, WBC], 'shortcomings' [BAGD; NAB, NJB], 'backward things' [Lns], 'what is lacking' [BAGD, LN; KJV, NASB, NIV, RSV, TNT], 'absence' [LN], 'what is needed' [LN; TEV], 'where it falls short' [NEB]. The noun is plural and implies more than one deficiency [Hb, NIC].

QUESTION—What is meant by καταρτίσαι 'to complete/correct'?

1. It means that their faith required further teaching to complete it [BAGD, Ea, El, Fn, Hb, Hn, Lns, Mn, NCBC, TH, WBC]: to supply what is lacking. Paul's short stay did not give enough time to teach them all that he wants them to know [Hb, Lns, NCBC]. Perhaps they were also slow in their spiritual growth [NCBC]. What he taught in 4:1–5:22 indicates some areas still lacking and this was given in the event that he would not see them soon [TH, WBC]. Their 'faith' refers to the Christian doctrine [Hn, Lns, WBC], and also to their active trust in Christ [Hn, Lns].
2. It means that their faith was defective and needed to be corrected or restored to what it had been [Er, NIC]: to correct what is wrong.
3. It means both of the above [EBC, HNTC, ICC, Wd]. There probably were some moral failures and also the previous instructions were inadequate because of the brevity of Paul's ministry among them [HNTC].

DISCOURSE UNIT: 3:11–13 [Alf, EBC, Er, Hb, Hn, HNTC, ICC, Mn, NCBC, NIC, TH, WBC, Wd]. The topic is prayer for the Thessalonians [Er, Hb, HNTC, ICC, Mn, NCBC, NIC, TH, WBC, Wd]. This is the ending of the first part of the letter [Alf, HNTC, Mn, NCBC, WBC, Wd].

3:11 Now/But^a

LEXICON—a. δέ (LN 89.94; 89.124): 'now' [Hn, HNTC, ICC, Lns, WBC; KJV, NASB, NIV, RSV], not explicit [NAB, NEB, NJB, TEV, TNT].

QUESTION—What relationship is indicated by this conjunction?

1. This is transitional and introduces a new section of the letter [Ea, EBC, El, Fn, Hb, HNTC, ICC, Lns, TH; KJV, NASB, NIV, RSV]: now. This paragraph expands what is said about their prayer for the Thessalonians in

the previous paragraph [EBC, Hb, Lns]. It indicates what is needed to supply the lack in their faith [Hb].
2. This is adversative [Alf, My]: but. It contrasts Paul's plans with God's plans.

he/himself[a] the God and Father of-us and the Lord of-us Jesus
LEXICON—αὐτός (LN 92.11; 92.37): 'he' [Hn, Lns]; or 'himself' [BAGD, HNTC, ICC, WBC; all versions].
QUESTION—Does αὐτός function as emphatic 'he' or reflexive 'himself'?
1. It is emphatic [Hb, Hn, Lns]: he. It goes with ὁ θεὸς καὶ πατήρ 'our God and Father' [Hb]: may he, our God and Father, and our Lord Jesus, or it goes with both persons (in agreement with the singular verb which goes with both persons) [Hn, Lns]: may he, our God and Father and our Lord Jesus, direct our path to you.
2. It is reflexive [Ea, EBC, El, Fn, HNTC, ICC, Mn, My, NCBC, Rb, WBC, Wd; all versions]: himself. It goes with 'God' [Ea, El, Mn, My; KJV, NAB]: God himself, who is our Father; or it goes with both titles [Fn, HNTC, Rb, WBC; NASB, NEB, NIV, NJB, RSV, TEV, TNT]: our God and Father himself; or it goes with both persons (in agreement with the singular verb which goes with both persons) [EBC, ICC, NCBC]: may our God and Father and our Lord Jesus himself direct our path to you.

QUESTION—What is the first ἡμῶν 'of us' connected with?
1. It is connected only with πατήρ 'Father' [Alf, Ea, El, My; KJV, NAB, NJB]: God our Father.
2. It is connected with both titles [EBC, Fn, Hb, Hn, HNTC, ICC, Lns, NIC, Rb, TH, WBC; NASB, NEB, NIV, RSV, TEV, TNT]: our God and Father.

QUESTION—What is the second ἡμῶν 'of us' connected with?
It is connected with ὁ κύριος 'the Lord'. Then the name 'Jesus' stands in apposition with 'our Lord', identifying the Lord to be Jesus [Hb, Lns; NASB]: our Lord, Jesus. Most do not indicate this apposition and merely translate 'our Lord Jesus' [EBC, Hn, HNTC, ICC, WBC; all versions except NASB].

may-he-direct/make-straight[a] our path[b] to you;
LEXICON—a. aorist act. optative of κατευθύνω (LN 36.1): 'to direct' [BAGD, Hn, HNTC, ICC, LN, Lns, WBC; KJV, NASB, RSV], 'to guide' [LN], 'to make straight' [BAGD; NAB], 'to clear' [NIV], 'to prepare' [TEV], 'to ease' [NJB]. This is also conflated with the noun ὁδόν 'way': 'to bring (us) direct' [NEB], 'to guide' [TNT]
b. ὁδός (LN 15.19): 'path' [HNTC; NAB, NJB], 'way' [BAGD, Hn, ICC, Lns, WBC; KJV, NASB, NIV, RSV, TEV], 'journey' [LN].

QUESTION—Why is the verb singular with the two subjects, God and the Lord Jesus?
It indicates that the writer is thinking of them both as the one God [Alf, Ea, EBC, EGT, El, Fn, Hb, Hn, ICC, Lns, Mn, NCBC, NIC, Rb, TH], or at least,

as regularly and intimately associated together in what they do [HNTC, My, WBC]. Two subjects often take a singular verb which agrees with the nearer of the two subjects [WBC].

QUESTION—What does the metaphor mean?
1. The illustration is: like someone puts a person on a desired path. Probably this is meant by those who translate: 'may God direct our way/path to you' [Hn, HNTC, ICC; KJV, NASB, RSV], and 'may God guide us to you' [TNT]. The point of comparison is getting to the right destination. The nonfigurative statement is: may God direct or cause us to come to you.
2. The illustration is: like someone makes a path straight to the destination. The point of comparison is the removal of detours [Lns, Mn, WBC; NAB, NEB]. The nonfigurative statement is: may God cause us to come to you soon [WBC].
3. The illustration is: like someone levels a path. The point of comparison is the removal of obstacles [EBC, Hb, HNTC, Mn, NCBC, NIC, TH; NIV, NJB, TEV]. The nonfigurative statement is: may God remove the hindrances that keep us from coming to you.

3:12 and/but[a]

LEXICON—a. δέ (LN 89.94; 89.124): 'and' [Hn, HNTC, ICC, Lns, WBC; KJV, NAB, NASB, NEB, RSV]; or 'but' [Hb, NIC]; not explicit [NIV, NJB, TEV, TNT].

QUESTION—What relationship is indicated by this conjunction?
1. This is coordinate [Hn, HNTC, Lns, Mn, TH, WBC; KJV, NAB, NASB, NEB, RSV, and probably the rest of the versions]: and. It continues the prayer with two more wishes [TH, WBC].
2. It is contrastive [Ea, El, Fn, Hb, ICC, Mn, NCBC, NIC]: may the Lord do that for us, but as for you, may the Lord do the following. The emphatic position of ὑμᾶς 'you' at the beginning of the clause supports this contrast [Hb, ICC, NCBC].

you may the Lord make-to-increase[a] **and make-to-abound**[b] **in-love**[c] **to one-another and to all (people),**

LEXICON—a. aorist act. optative of πλεονάζω (LN **78.32**): 'to cause/make (one) to increase' [BAGD, ICC, Lns; KJV, NAB, NASB, RSV], 'to cause/make (one) to abound' [Hn, HNTC], 'to enlarge (someone)' [WBC], 'to make (love) to mount' [NEB], 'to make (love) increase' [NIV], 'to increase (love)' [NJB]. The two verbs are also conflated: 'to make (love) grow more and more' [TEV], 'to help (someone to love) with an overflowing abundance' [TNT], 'to greatly increase (love)' [LN].

b. aorist act. optative of περισσεύω (LN **78.32**): 'to cause/make (one) to abound (in love)' [BAGD, ICC, Lns, WBC; KJV, NASB, RSV], 'to cause (one) to overflow (in love)' [Hn, HNTC; NAB], 'to make (love) overflow' [NEB, NIV], 'to enrich (love)' [NJB].

c. ἀγάπη (LN 25.43): 'love' [BAGD, Hn, HNTC, ICC, LN, Lns, WBC; all versions], 'loving concern' [LN]. This noun is also translated as a verb: 'to love' [TNT].

QUESTION—Who is the Lord?
1. 'Lord' refers to Jesus [Ea, EBC, El, Fn, Hb, Hn, HNTC, ICC, Mn, My, NCBC, NIC, Rb, TH, WBC]. Probably Paul was not consciously making a distinction between God the Father and the Lord Jesus [NIC, TH].
2. 'Lord' refers to God the Father [Alf].
3. This refers to both persons [Lns]. This goes along with the view that both persons were considered as one in the previous verse.

QUESTION—What does τῇ ἀγάπῃ 'in love' go with?
1. The phrase goes with both preceding verbs [Ea, EBC, El, Hb, Hn, HNTC, ICC, Lns, My, NCBC, NIC, TH; NEB, NIV, NJB, TEV, TNT]: may the Lord cause you to both increase and abound in love. The two verbs are almost the same in meaning [Ea, Hb, Hn, HNTC, Lns, NCBC, NIC] and they are used together to make an emphatic statement [Hb, HNTC, Lns, NCBC, NIC]. He assumes that they already have love and he asks that their love may be increased until it overflows [EBC, Hb, Hn, Lns].
2. The phrase goes only with the immediately preceding verb [Alf, WBC; NAB]: may the Lord make you to increase and also to abound in love. The wish that they may 'increase' refers to general spiritual enlargement [WBC], or to growth in the number of members in the congregation and also to an increase in faith, knowledge and spiritual gifts [Alf].

as[a] also[b] we to you,

LEXICON—a. καθάπερ (LN 64.15): 'as' [HNTC, WBC; KJV, NAB, NEB, RSV, TEV, TNT], 'just as' [BAGD, Hn, ICC, Lns; NASB, NIV].
b. καί (LN 89.93): 'also' [Hn, Lns; NASB], 'too' [ICC], 'even' [WBC; KJV, NAB], 'so that it matches' [NJB], not explicit [HNTC; NEB, NIV, RSV, TEV, TNT].

QUESTION—What relationship is indicated by καθάπερ 'as'?
This compares the love that Paul desires the Thessalonians to have with the love he already has for them. He gives himself and his companions as an example [Hb, ICC, Lns, Mn, NCBC, NIC], and as a standard of such love [EBC, Hb, HNTC].

QUESTION—What verb is implied in this clause?
Most supply a generic verb 'do' [Hb, Hn, HNTC; KJV, NAB, NASB, NEB, NIV, RSV]: as we do to you. More specific verbs are also supplied from the previous clause: as we abound in love towards you [WBC], as we increase and abound in love [Ea, Fn, Hn, HNTC, ICC, My], as we love you [Lns; TNT].

3:13 so-that[a]

LEXICON—a. εἰς (LN 89.48; 89.57): 'so that' [HNTC, Lns; NASB, RSV], 'in order that' [Hn, ICC], 'so as to' [WBC], 'to the end' [KJV], 'in this way' [TEV], not explicit [NAB, NEB, NIV, NJB, TNT].

QUESTION—What relationship is indicated by this conjunction?

This introduces the purpose of the prayer in the preceding verse [Alf, BAGD, Ea, EBC, El, Fn, Hb, Hn, HNTC, ICC, Mn, My, NCBC, NIC, Rb, TH, WBC, Wd; KJV, NASB, RSV], or the contemplated result of the Lord's action [Lns; TEV]: may the Lord cause you to increase and abound in love, so that he may establish your hearts. εἰς τό with the infinitive indicates purpose [Ea, Fn, Hb, HNTC, Mn, Rb]. Some begin a new sentence here without a relational word [NAB, NEB, NIV, NJB, TNT]: may the Lord cause you to increase and abound in love. May he establish your hearts.

to-establish[a] your hearts[b]

LEXICON—a. aorist act. infin. of στηρίζω (LN 74.19): 'to establish' [BAGD, Lns, WBC; KJV, NASB, RSV], 'to strengthen' [BAGD, Hn, HNTC, ICC, LN; NAB, NIV, TEV], 'to make strong' [TNT], 'to make firm' [NEB], 'to make more firm' [LN], 'to confirm' [BAGD; NJB]. See this word at 3:2.

b. καρδία (LN 26.3): 'hearts' [BAGD, Hn, HNTC, ICC, LN, Lns, WBC; all versions except TEV, TNT], 'inner selves' [LN], 'minds' [LN], 'you' [TEV, TNT]. See this word at 2:4.

QUESTION—Who is the implied agent of the infinitive form στηρίξαι 'to establish'?

It is the Lord (from the preceding clause) [Alf, Ea, EBC, El, Hb, Hn, HNTC, ICC, My, TH]: in order that the Lord may establish your hearts. The Lord uses their growing love to establish their holy character [Hb, Hn, NCBC]. Love makes them the kind of people whom the Lord can strengthen [HNTC].

QUESTION—In what respect are they 'established'?

They are to be established in their whole person [HNTC], their inner life [Hb, HNTC, NCBC, NIC, TH, Wd], their will and motives [Hb, Hn, ICC, WBC], or their characters [Hb, HNTC]. Although not directly commenting on this, some appear to take this to mean that he prays that the Lord will cause and make permanent a state of holiness so that they will be unblamable in respect to such holiness at God's judgment [Ea, Hb; KJV, NAB, NASB, NJB, RSV]. Some further explanations are that it means stability in ethical conduct and motives [Hb, WBC], steadiness of Christian character [NCBC], the ability to be unmoved by future circumstances [Hb, NIC], the lasting assurance of security [Fn], the possession of understanding and courage [TH].

blameless[a] in[b] holiness[c] before[d] the God and Father of-us

LEXICON—a. ἄμεμπτος (LN 88.317): 'blameless' [BAGD, Hn, HNTC, ICC, LN, Lns, WBC; NAB, NIV, NJB, TNT], 'without blame' [LN], 'unblamable' [KJV, NASB, RSV], 'faultless' [BAGD; NEB], 'perfect' [TEV].

b. ἐν (LN 89.5): 'in' [Hn, HNTC, ICC, Lns, WBC; KJV, NASB, NJB, RSV]. Some translate this preposition as a coordinate conjunction: 'and' [NAB, NEB, NIV, TEV, TNT].

c. ἁγιωσύνη (LN 88.25; **53.45**): 'holiness' [BAGD, Hn, HNTC, ICC, Lns, WBC; KJV, NASB, NJB, RSV], 'consecration' [LN]. This noun is also translated as an adjective: 'holy' [NAB, NEB, NIV, TEV, TNT].

d. ἔμπροσθεν (LN 83.33; 90.20): 'before' [BAGD, HNTC, LN, Lns; KJV, NAB, NASB, RSV], 'in front of' [LN], 'in the presence of' [BAGD, Hn, ICC, WBC; NIV, TEV, TNT], 'in the sight of' [LN; NJB], 'in the opinion of' [LN]. It is also translated as a verb phrase: 'to stand before' [NEB]. See this word at 1:3, 2:19, and 3:9.

QUESTION—How is ἀμέμπτους 'blameless' related to the verb στηρίξαι 'to establish'?

It will be the result of the Lord establishing them [Alf, Ea, EBC, El, Fn, Hn, HNTC, ICC, Mn, My, NCBC, WBC, Wd; NEB, NIV, TNT]: may the Lord strengthen your hearts so that you will be blameless.

QUESTION—What relationship is indicated by ἐν 'in' in the phrase in holiness?

This indicates in what respect they will be blameless [Alf, Ea, El, HNTC, ICC, My; probably KJV, NASB, RSV]: may the Lord strengthen your hearts so that you will be blameless in respect to holiness. Some describe this use of ἐν as the sphere in which their blamelessness is shown [Alf, El, My].

QUESTION—What is implied in the phrase ἔμπροσθεν τοῦ θεοῦ 'before God'?

It means that they will be blameless in his judgment [Ea, EBC, El, Fn, Hb, Hn, HNTC, Lns, Mn, My, NCBC, WBC, Wd]. This refers to the final judgment at the coming of Christ [EBC, Hn, HNTC, Lns, NCBC, WBC, Wd], or their presentation to God by Christ [Hb]. A state of blameless holiness is attained only at the time they stand before God at the coming of Christ [Hb, Hn, WBC]. However, some commentators say that this establishment can take place in the present and will be disclosed at the future judgment [Fn, NCBC].

QUESTION—What does ἡμῶν 'of us' go with?

1. It goes with both titles [Hn, HNTC, ICC, Lns, WBC; all versions except KJV]: our God and Father.
2. It goes only with πατρός 'Father' [KJV]: God, who is our Father.

at[a] the coming[b] of the Lord of-us Jesus

LEXICON—a. ἐν (LN 67.33; 89.5): 'at' [Hn, HNTC, WBC; KJV, NAB, NASB, RSV], 'when' [ICC; NEB, NIV, NJB, TEV, TNT]; or 'in connection with' [Lns]. See this word at 2:19.

b. παρουσία (LN 85.25; 15.86): 'the coming' [BAGD, Hn, LN; KJV, NAB, NASB, RSV], 'parousia' [HNTC, Lns], 'advent' [BAGD, WBC], 'presence' [LN]. This noun is also translated as a verb: 'to come' [ICC; NEB, NIV, NJB, TEV, TNT]. See this word at 2:19.

QUESTION—What relationship is indicated by ἐν 'at'?
This indicates the time at which they will be judged by God to be blameless [Ea, El, Fn, Hb, Hn, HNTC, Lns, Mn, NCBC, WBC, Wd]: blameless at the judgment that takes place when the Lord Jesus comes.

with[a] all his saints.
LEXICON—a. μετά (LN 89.108): 'with' [BAGD, Hn, HNTC, ICC, LN, WBC; all versions], 'together with' [LN, Lns], 'in the company of' [LN].
  b. ἅγιος (LN 11.27): 'saints' [Hn, Lns; KJV, NASB, RSV], 'holy ones' [BAGD, HNTC, WBC; NAB, NIV, NJB], 'those who are his own' [NEB], 'God's people' [LN], '(those) who belong to him' [TEV, TNT], 'angels' [ICC].
QUESTION—How is this phrase connected to what precedes?
  1. It is connected with the coming of the Lord Jesus; he will be accompanied by his saints [Ea, El, Fn, Hb, Hn, HNTC, ICC, Mn, NCBC, NIC, WBC]: at the coming of the Lord Jesus with all his saints. If this refers to believers, then they have previously died and gone to be with the Lord, and will accompany him as he returns [Fn, Hb].
  2. It is connected with their hearts being blameless in holiness [EBC, Lns]: so that you will be blameless in holiness along with all of his other saints when the Lord Jesus comes.
QUESTION—Who are his saints?
  1. They are believers [EBC, Fn, Hb, Hn, Lns, TH].
  2. They are the angels [BAGD, HNTC, ICC, NCBC].
  3. They are both believers and angels [Alf, Ea, El, Mn, NIC, WBC, Wd].

Amen.
TEXT—This word is omitted in some manuscripts. GNT includes it in brackets with a C rating, indicating a considerable degree of doubt in including it. It is omitted by most commentaries and versions.
QUESTION—What is the function of this word?
If original, it is the customary response to the mention of the return of Christ [WBC].

DISCOURSE UNIT: 4:1–5:24 [Alf, Hb, Mn, WBC, Wd]. The topic is exhortations [Hb, WBC], exhortations and teaching [Alf, Mn, Wd]. This is the second main part of the letter [Hb].

DISCOURSE UNIT: 4:1–5:22 [EBC, HNTC, ICC]. The topic is exhortations [EBC, HNTC, ICC]. Further divisions in this unit separate the types of exhortations: 4:1–2, 4:3–8, 4:9–10a, 4:10b–12, 4:13–18, 5:1–11, 5:12–13, 5:14a–c, 5:14d–15, 5:16–18, 5:19–22 [ICC].

DISCOURSE UNIT: 4:1–5:11 [EGT]. The topic is special teaching.

DISCOURSE UNIT: 4:1–12 [Alf, EBC, EGT, Fn, GNT, Hb, Hn, Mn, My, NCBC, NIC, Wd; NAB, NIV, NJB, TEV]. The topic is exhortations [Alf], exhortations about Christian living [EBC, Hb, Hn, NCBC, NIC], teaching about

Christian morals [EGT, Fn, Mn], holiness [Wd], a life that pleases God [GNT; NIV, TEV], chastity and love [NAB], holiness and love [NJB].

DISCOURSE UNIT: 4:1–8 [Alf, My, NCBC]. The topic is exhortation to holy living [Alf], sexual morals [NCBC].

DISCOURSE UNIT: 4:1–2 [EBC, Hb, HNTC, ICC, Mn, My, NIC, TH, WBC, Wd]. The topic is general exhortations [Mn, NIC], exhortation to please God [Hb], keeping the teachings [WBC], improvement [EBC], encouragement [Wd]. This section introduces the following sections of exhortations [HNTC, ICC, NCBC, TH, WBC, Wd].

4:1 **For-the-rest**[a] **then,**[b] **brethren,**

LEXICON—a. λοιπόν (LN 89.98; 61.14): 'for the rest' [Hn, WBC], 'as for the rest' [Lns], 'furthermore' [LN; KJV], 'finally' [BAGD, ICC, LN, Mou (p. 161); NASB], 'as the last matter' [HNTC], 'in summary' [LN]. This word and οὖν are conflated by some: 'now' [NAB, TNT], 'and now' [NEB], and perhaps by those who have only 'finally' [NIV, NJB, RSV, TEV].

b. οὖν (LN 89.50; 91.7): 'then' [HNTC, Lns, WBC; KJV, NASB], not explicit [Hn, ICC].

QUESTION—What relationship is indicated by λοιπόν 'for the rest'?

This does not indicate that the letter is about to end [Hb, HNTC, NIC]. It marks a transition to another aspect of the letter [Alf, Ea, El, Hb, Hn, HNTC, ICC, Mn, My, NCBC, NIC, TH]. It marks a change from expressions of thanksgiving and prayer to exhortations about living the Christian life [ICC, NIC]. It also indicates that this second major portion of the letter is the concluding portion [Alf, Ea, EBC, El, HNTC, My, NCBC].

QUESTION—What relationship is indicated by οὖν 'therefore'?

1. This indicates a conclusion [Alf, Ea, EBC, El, Er, Hb, HNTC, My, NCBC]: therefore.
1.1 It supplies the practical implication of the first part of the letter [HNTC, NCBC], or it introduces a conclusion based on chapters 2–3 [EBC].
1.2 It introduces a conclusion based on the prayer in 3:13 [Alf, Ea, El, Hb, My]: after praying that they would be holy, he now exhorts them to be so.
2. This merely reinforces the transition and does not refer to a preceding reason [TH, WBC].

we-request[a] **of-you and we-urge**[b]

LEXICON—a. pres. act. indic. of ἐρωτάω (LN 33.161): 'to request' [BAGD, Hn, LN, Lns, WBC; NASB], 'to ask' [BAGD, HNTC, ICC; NIV, TNT], 'to beseech' [KJV, RSV], 'to beg' [NAB, NEB, TEV], 'to urge' [NJB].

b. pres. act. indic. of παρακαλέω (LN 33.168): 'to urge' [BAGD, Hn, ICC; NIV, TEV], 'to beg' [TNT], 'to pray' [NEB], 'to appeal' [BAGD, LN, WBC; NJB], 'to request' [HNTC, LN], 'to exhort' [BAGD; KJV, NAB, NASB, RSV], 'to admonish' [Lns].

QUESTION—What is the difference between the two verbs ἐρωτῶμεν 'we request' and παρακαλοῦμεν 'we urge'?
1. There is no significant difference intended here [HNTC, ICC, Lns, NCBC, NIC, TH]. They are practically synonymous [HNTC, ICC, NCBC]. This combination of verbs gives emphasis to the request [Lns, NIC, TH].
2. There is a significant difference between the verbs [EBC, Fn, Hb, My, WBC]. The first is a friendly request, the second is an urgent exhortation [EBC, Hb, My], and includes an authoritative note [EBC, My]. The second is an exhortation, implying a possible indifference on the part of those asked [Fn]. The second is more emphatic and formal than the first [WBC].

in[a] (the) Lord Jesus,
LEXICON—a. ἐν (LN 89.119; 89.5): 'in' [Hn, HNTC, ICC, Lns, WBC; NAB, NASB, NIV, NJB, RSV], 'by' [KJV], 'by our fellowship with' [NEB], 'in the name of' [TEV], 'as fellow Christians' [TNT].
QUESTION—What relationship is indicated by ἐν 'in'?
1. This indicates an appeal to authority [Fn, Mn, NCBC, NIC, TH, Wd; KJV, TEV]: we beseech you with the authority given us by the Lord Jesus.
2. This indicates close fellowship with the Lord [Ea, Er, Hb, Hn, HNTC, ICC, My, WBC; NEB, TNT]: we beseech you, we (excl./incl.) being in union with the Lord Jesus. The fact that Thessalonians and missionaries are all united in their union with the Lord should make the appeal carry weight [Hb, HNTC]. Or, the missionaries make their appeal as a result of their own fellowship with the Lord [My; NEB]. Or, the fact that the Lord indwells and inspires the missionaries should give authority to what they request [Ea, Hn, ICC].
3. This defines the area of the requests [EBC, El, Lns]: we beseech you about matters in connection with the Lord. All are saved and belong to the Lord and all know that the missionaries are sent with authority from the Lord [Lns], the requests deal with matters of the Lord [EBC].

that, as[a] you-received[b] from us how it-is-necessary[c] (for) you to-walk[d]
LEXICON—a. καθώς (LN 64.14): 'as' [Hn, ICC, Lns, WBC; KJV, NASB, RSV], 'even as' [NAB], 'just as' [HNTC], 'in accordance with' [TNT]. Some translate this as a separate sentence and omit the relational word [NEB, NIV, NJB, TEV].
b. aorist act. indic. of παραλαμβάνω (LN **27.13**; 33.238): 'to receive' [BAGD, HNTC, Lns, WBC; KJV], 'to receive instructions' [Hn, ICC; NASB], 'to receive rules for behavior' [TNT], 'to learn' [BAGD, LN; NAB, RSV, TEV]. This verb is also translated with a reciprocal verb: 'we passed on to you the tradition' [NEB], 'we instructed you' [NIV, NJB]. See this word at 2:13.

c. pres. act. indic. of δεῖ (LN 71.21; 71.34): 'it is necessary' [BAGD, Lns], not explicit [WBC; NAB, NIV, NJB, TNT]. This impersonal verb is also translated with 'you' or 'we' as the subject: 'you ought' [BAGD, Hn, HNTC, ICC; KJV, NASB, RSV], 'you should' [TEV], 'we must' [NEB].

d. pres. act. infin. of περιπατέω (LN 41.11): 'to walk' [BAGD, ICC, Lns; KJV, NASB], 'to walk around' [BAGD], 'to conduct oneself' [BAGD, Hn, WBC; NAB], 'to live' [BAGD, LN; NEB, NIV, NJB, RSV, TEV], 'to behave' [LN; TNT], 'to progress' [HNTC]. See this word at 2:12.

QUESTION—Why is it necessary for them to do so?

It is a moral obligation brought about by Jesus being their Lord [Fn, Hb, NIC], or by gratitude for their redemption [Hn]. If the next phrase is taken as the purpose or contemplated result of this verb, such a goal logically compels them to walk in a certain way so as to please the Lord.

and[a] to-please[b] God,

LEXICON—a. καί (LN 89.92; 89.87): 'and' [Hn, ICC, Lns; KJV, NASB, RSV], 'in order to' [NIV, TEV], 'and so' [HNTC], 'so as to' [WBC], 'to' [NEB]. This is also explicitly connected to the preceding verb: '(to walk) in a way that pleases' [NAB, NJB], '(to receive instructions) as being acceptable' [TNT].

b. pres. act. infin. of ἀρέσκω (LN 25.90): 'to please' [BAGD, Hn, HNTC, ICC, LN, Lns, WBC; all versions except TNT], 'to be acceptable to' [TNT]. See this word at 2:4.

QUESTION—What relationship is indicated by καί 'and'?

1. This indicates the purpose or intended result of such a walk [Alf, Ea, El, Hb, HNTC, ICC, Mn, My, NIC, TH, WBC; NEB, NIV, TEV]: how to walk *in order to* please God, or how to walk *and so* please God.
2. This indicates the kind of walk intended [Bul (p. 671); NAB, NJB]: how to walk *in a way that* pleases God.
3. This separates two subjects of instruction [Fn]: how to walk, *and also* how to please God.

as[a] indeed[b] you-are-walking,

TEXT—This clause is omitted in some manuscripts. GNT includes it without a note. It is omitted only by KJV.

LEXICON—a. καθώς (LN 64.14): 'as' [Hn, ICC, Lns, WBC; NIV], 'just as' [HNTC; NASB, RSV]. This is also translated as a relative clause: 'which you are doing' [NAB], or as a separate statement 'you are already' [NEB], 'you are so living' [NJB], 'this is the way you have been living' [TEV]. It is also implied by translating the verb 'to go on behaving' in the preceding clause [TNT].

b. καί (LN 89.93; 91.12): 'indeed' [HNTC; NAB, NEB], 'actually' [NASB], 'in fact' [Hn, ICC; NIV], 'of course' [TEV], 'also' [Lns], 'even' [WBC], not explicit [NJB, RSV, TNT].

QUESTION—What is indicated by the use of the present tense form περιπατεῖτε 'you are walking'?

Paul recognizes that the Thessalonians are already obeying his instructions [Hb, WBC], and continue to do so [NIC, TH].

that[a] you-abound[b] more.[c]

LEXICON—a. ἵνα (LN 90.22): 'that' [Hn, HNTC, ICC, Lns; NASB, TNT], 'so' [KJV, NAB], not explicit [WBC; NEB, NIV, NJB, RSV, TEV].
  b. pres. act. subjunctive of περισσεύω (LN **78.31**): 'to abound' [Hn, ICC, Lns, WBC; KJV], 'to excel' [BAGD, HNTC; NASB], 'to make progress' [NAB, NJB], 'to do thoroughly' [NEB], 'to do something more' [NIV, RSV, TEV, TNT], 'to do so even more' [LN]. See this word at 3:12.
  c. μᾶλλον (LN 78.28): 'more' [BAGD, Hn, ICC, LN; NIV, RSV, TNT], 'more and more' [HNTC, Lns, WBC; KJV], 'still more' [NASB, NJB], 'yet more' [NEB], 'even more' [LN; TEV], 'still greater' [NAB].

QUESTION—What relationship is indicated by ἵνα 'that'?

Because of the intervening two καθώς 'as' clauses, this repeats the preceding ἵνα 'that' and introduces the object of his request [Alf, Ea, EGT, Fn, Hb, ICC, Lns, Mn, NCBC, WBC]: we ask and beseech you that, (as, etc.) (as, etc.), that you abound even more. However, the two intervening clauses complicate the grammar so that the intervening clauses cannot merely be omitted to get to the main clause [Alf, EGT, HNTC, Mn]. This clause depends on the first intervening clause to indicate in what they are to abound: that you abound in walking to please God [HNTC, ICC, WBC]. The fact that they are to 'abound even more' builds on the second intervening clause, which states that they are already so walking [EGT, Hb, ICC, NCBC].

4:2 Because[a]

LEXICON—a. γάρ (LN 89.23): 'because', 'for' [Hn, HNTC, ICC, Lns, WBC; KJV, NASB, NEB, NIV, RSV, TEV], not explicit [NAB, NJB, TNT].

QUESTION—What relationship is indicated by this conjunction?
  1. This indicates the grounds for the statement that they had learned from the missionaries how they ought to live to please the God [Alf, Ea, El, Hb, ICC]: it is true that you received instructions from us how to live to please God, *since* you know what instructions we gave you.
  2. This explains and amplifies the previous statement [Lns, NCBC, TH]: you received knowledge from us how to live to please God, *that is,* you know the instruction we gave you, etc. It emphasizes the former statement by repetition [NCBC, TH].

you-know what instructions[a] we-gave you through[b] the Lord Jesus.

LEXICON—a. παραγγελία (LN 33.328): 'instructions' [BAGD, Hn, HNTC, ICC; NAB, NIV, NJB, RSV, TEV, TNT], 'commandments' [KJV, NASB], 'commands' [BAGD], 'orders' [BAGD, LN, Lns; NEB], 'charges' [WBC].

b. διά (LN 90.4): 'through' [Hn, HNTC, Lns, WBC; RSV], 'by' [KJV], 'by the authority of' [NASB, NIV, TEV], 'on the authority of' [NJB], 'in the name of' [NEB], 'in' [NAB], 'from' [TNT], 'prompted by' [ICC].

QUESTION—What relationship is indicated by διά 'through'?

Some commentators find it hard to specify a meaning for διά here [HNTC, NCBC, NIC], but several point out that it does not mean what the grammar might suggest, that the missionaries issued orders which were then transmitted through the Lord Jesus to the Thessalonians [Hb, HNTC, Lns]. One suggestion is that it indicates that they gave instructions which came from the Lord Jesus [Alf, Hb, Lns, My; TNT], under his prompting [El, ICC], at his command [Hn]. Another is that the instructions they gave were given by authority derived from the Lord Jesus [EBC, Hb, Hn, WBC; NASB, NIV, NJB, TEV], or the instructions were enforced through the Lord Jesus [Fn]. Another is that they gave instructions through the action of the Lord Jesus who was with them and who enabled them to communicate what originated with the Lord [Ea, HNTC]. Another is that it means the same as ἐν 'in' the Lord (4:1) and means by the authority of the Lord [EGT, Mou (p. 57), TH]. Another is that the Lord Jesus is the one through whom the instructions could be carried out [Mn].

DISCOURSE UNIT: 4:3–8 [EBC, Hb, HNTC, ICC, Mn, My, NIC, TH, WBC, Wd]. The topic is sex [HNTC, Wd], sexual purity [EBC, NIC, TH, WBC], warning about impurity [Mn], exhortation to sanctification [Hb], real sanctification [ICC].

4:3 For[a]

LEXICON—a. γάρ (LN 89.23; 91.1): 'for' [Hn, HNTC, Lns, WBC; KJV, NASB, RSV], not explicit [ICC; NAB, NEB, NIV, NJB, TEV, TNT].

QUESTION—What relationship is indicated by this conjunctioin?

This is explanatory [Alf, Ea, El, Hb, ICC, Lns, My, NCBC]. It explains how they ought to live to please God [Hb, ICC, Lns]: you ought to live to please God, *that is*, God's will is that you be sanctified. It explains what their instructions (4:2) were [Alf, Ea, El, ICC, Lns, My, NCBC]: you know the instructions we gave you, that is, God's will is that you be sanctified.

this is (the) will[a] **of-God, your sanctification,**[b]

LEXICON—a. θέλημα (LN 25.2): 'will' [BAGD, Hn, HNTC, ICC, Lns, WBC; KJV, NAB, NASB, NEB, NIV, RSV], 'what (God) wants' [TNT], 'wish' [LN], 'desire' [LN]. This noun is also translated as a verb: 'to will' [NJB], 'to want' [TEV].

b. ἁγιασμός (LN 53.44): 'sanctification' [BAGD, Hn, Lns, WBC; KJV, NASB, RSV], 'holiness' [BAGD; TNT], 'consecration' [BAGD, LN], 'dedication' [LN]. This noun is also translated as a verb phrase: 'to grow in holiness' [NAB], 'to be holy' [NEB, NJB, TEV], 'to be consecrated' [ICC], 'to be sanctified' [NIV], 'to sanctify oneself' [HNTC].

QUESTION—What is the significance of the lack of an article before θέλημα 'will' in the Greek?

It indicates that this sanctification is one aspect of all that God wills [Hb, HNTC, My, NCBC, NIC, Wd]. There are other aspects of his will which are not specified here. For instance, it is also God's will that they give thanks (5:18) [Hb]. It may be due to the influence of Hebrew [ICC]. Even so, the total content of the will of God is not indicated here [ICC]. The absence of the article may be explained as marking the predicate part of the statement [Alf, Lns, WBC] or as the part following the verb [El].

QUESTION—What is meant by ἁγιασμός 'sanctification'?

The word used here means the process of becoming holy [Hb, HNTC, ICC, NCBC, NIC, TH, WBC]. It means to become more and more in line with what God wants us to be [Hb]. The noun can be taken passively, 'that you may be sanctified' [Lns; NIV], probably implying that they are sanctified by God's action [Lns, TH]. Or, it can be taken reflexively, 'that you sanctify yourselves' [HNTC, ICC, My], and this is supported by the fact that the passage is concerned about what the believers are to do [HNTC].

(for) you to-abstain[a] from fornication,[b]

LEXICON—a. pres. mid. infin. of ἀπέχω (LN 13.158): 'to abstain' [BAGD, Hn, HNTC, ICC, WBC; KJV, NAB, NASB, NEB, RSV, TNT], 'to avoid' [NIV], 'to avoid doing' [LN], 'to keep away from' [BAGD; NJB], 'to restrain from' [LN], 'to hold oneself away' [Lns], 'to be completely free from' [TEV]. The present tense is continuative [Hb, Lns]: to keep on avoiding fornication.

b. πορνεία (LN **88.271**): 'fornication' [BAGD, ICC, Lns, WBC; KJV, NEB], 'immorality' [Hn; NAB], 'sexual immorality' [LN; NASB, NIV, NJB, TEV], 'sexual vice' [TNT], 'sexual sin' [HNTC], 'unchastity' [BAGD; RSV].

QUESTION—What relationship is intended by the use of the infinitive forms here and in 4:4–6?

They are in apposition to ἁγιασμός 'sanctification' and explain it [Alf, Ea, El, Hb, Hn, HNTC, ICC, Lns, NCBC, Rb; NAB, NASB, NEB, NIV, RSV, TNT]: God wills that you be sanctified, *that is,* that you abstain from fornication, etc. Some take the infinitives to be examples of the preceding instruction [Ea, EBC]: God wills that you be sanctified, *for example,* that you abstain from fornication, etc. There is some disagreement about how the five infinitives are related in verses 3–6. One view is that three infinitives, here, 4:4, and 4:6, are in apposition to 'sanctification' [Hb, Hn]: God wills your sanctification, that is, that you abstain, etc., that each one knows how to take a vessel in holiness, etc., and that no man transgress, etc. Another view is that the three infinitives, here, 4:4a, 4:4b, are in apposition to 'sanctification' [ICC]: God wills your sanctification, that is, that you abstain, etc., that each one respects his wife, that each one takes a wife in holiness, etc. Another view is that the two infinitives, here and 4:6, are in apposition

1 THESSALONIANS 4:3

to 'sanctification' [Lns]: God wills your sanctification, that is, that you abstain, etc., and that no man transgress, etc. All agree that the first of the series begins here. These do not include all that is involved in sanctification, but are important aspects that needed to be stressed for the Thessalonians [Alf, Ea, ICC, NIC, WBC].

QUESTION—What is meant by πορνεία 'fornication'?

Here it means all kinds of illicit sexual relationships [BAGD, Hb, NIC, WBC, Wd], all kinds of sexual immorality [EBC, HNTC, ICC, Lns, NCBC, TH], all kinds of sexual intercourse other than what takes place within the marriage relationship [NCBC]. It therefore includes adultery as well as fornication.

4:4 to-know-how/respect[a] each-one of-you his-own vessel[b] to-possess[c]

LEXICON—a. perf. act. indic. of οἶδα (LN 28.7): 'to know how' [BAGD, Hn, HNTC, LN; KJV, NASB, NJB, RSV, TEV, TNT], 'to know' [Lns], 'to learn' [WBC; NEB, NIV], or 'to respect' [ICC]. This verb is also conflated with the following one: 'to guard' [NAB].

b. σκεῦος (LN **23.63; 8.6; 10.55**): 'vessel' [Lns, WBC; KJV, NASB], 'body' [BAGD, LN; NEB, NIV, NJB, TNT], 'sexual life' [LN], 'member' [NAB]; or 'wife' [BAGD, Hn, HNTC, ICC, LN; RSV, TEV].

c. pres. mid. infin. of κτάομαι (LN 57.58): 'to possess' [KJV, NASB], 'to control' [NIV, NJB, TNT], 'to gain control over' [WBC], 'to guard' [NAB], 'to gain mastery over' [NEB], 'to keep' [HNTC]; or 'to take' [BAGD, Hn; RSV], 'to acquire' [BAGD, LN, Lns], 'to get' [BAGD, ICC, LN], 'to live with' [TEV].

QUESTION—What relationship is indicated by the use of the infinitive form of the verb εἰδέναι 'to know how/to respect'?

1. This is parallel with the preceding infinitive and gives a second explanation of sanctification [Ea, El, Hb, Hn, ICC, Mn, My, Rb].
2. This explains the preceding infinitive clause [Lns, NCBC, NIC]: to abstain from fornication, *that is,* to know how to possess his vessel in sanctification and honor.

QUESTION—What area of meaning is intended by the first verb?

1. It means 'to know how' to do the following verb [Ea, EGT, El, Fn, Hb, Hn, HNTC, Lns, My, NCBC, Rb, WBC; all versions except NAB]: to know how to possess his vessel in sanctification and honor.
2. It means to know the value of, to respect [ICC]. Then this clause ends after 'vessel' (taken to mean wife). It refers to the man who has a wife. The next clause carries over 'each one' as the subject and 'vessel' as the object and refers to a man who is not yet married: that each man (who is married) respect his wife, that each man (who is unmarried) obtain his own wife in sanctification and honor.

QUESTION—What is the metaphor intended by the use of σκεῦος 'vessel' and how does this affect the meaning of the verb?
1. 'Vessel' means a person's own body [Hb, Mn, NCBC, NIC, WBC; NASB, NEB, NIV, NJB, TNT]. The verb, then, means to possess his body so as to use it in the right way [Mn], or to control himself from performing sinful acts with his body: to control his own body. Probably the point of comparison is being a container [Fn, HNTC, Mn]: like a vessel is a container for some substance, a body is a container for the soul of a person. This would especially refer to a man's body in reference to sexual activity [NCBC] and it would apply to any person, married or unmarried [HNTC]. This would not mean that the body is considered apart from the soul, but the whole being of a person is considered to be engaging in some physical activity [HNTC]. Besides regarding the body to be a container of the soul, it might also be considered to be the instrument of the soul [Hb, Mn]. Another approach is to consider 'vessel' to be an euphemism for a man's genital organ [NCBC].
2. 'Vessel' means a man's wife [Alf, BAGD, Ea, EBC, EGT, El, Er, Fn, Hn, HNTC, ICC, Lns, My, Rb, Wd; RSV, TEV]. Probably the point of comparison is the role of an instrument [Fn, ICC]: like a vessel is an instrument meant for a certain use, so a wife is meant for a pure and honorable relationship.
   2.1 The verb pertains to an unmarried man and means to become married [Ea, EGT, Fn, Hn, ICC, Lns, Rb]: to acquire a wife for himself.
   2.2 The verb pertains to a married man and means to possess his wife sexually [Er, HNTC, Wd; TEV]: to live with, or have sex with, his wife. Reference is made to a Hebrew idiom in support of this [HNTC], or to regarding 'possess' as an euphemism for sexual intercourse [NCBC, Wd].

in[a] sanctification[b] and honor,[c]

LEXICON—a. ἐν (LN 89.80; 89.84): 'in' [Hn, HNTC, Lns, WBC; KJV, NAB, NASB, RSV], 'in a way' [NIV, NJB, TEV], 'in the spirit of' [ICC], not explicit [NEB, TNT].
b. ἁγιασμός (LN 53.44): 'sanctification' [BAGD, Hn, HNTC, Lns, WBC; KJV, NASB], 'sanctity' [NAB], 'holiness' [BAGD; RSV], 'consecration' [BAGD, ICC, LN], 'dedication' [LN], 'a way that is holy' [NIV, NJB, TEV]. This noun is also translated as a verb: 'to hallow' [NEB], 'to keep pure' [TNT]. See this word at 4:3.
c. τιμή (LN 87.4): 'honor' [Hn, HNTC, ICC, LN, Lns, WBC; KJV, NAB, NASB, RSV], 'respect' [LN], 'respectability' [BAGD], 'a way that is honorable' [NIV, NJB]. This noun is also translated as an adjective: '(to be) honorable' [TEV]; and as a verb: 'to honor' [NEB], 'to show respect' [TNT].

QUESTION—What relationship is indicated by ἐν 'in'?
1. It indicates the circumstance that is to accompany the action [Ea, El, Hb, ICC]. It is spoken of as being the sphere or atmosphere in which the event is done [Ea, Hb, ICC].
2. It indicates the manner in which one follows the instruction [Lns, Mou (p. 78), NCBC; NIV, NJB, TEV].
3. It indicates the means for maintaining the marriage [EBC].

QUESTION—What is meant by ἁγιασμῷ 'sanctification'?
1. He is to do so in a way that seeks to obey and please God [ICC, Lns, NCBC].
2. He is to regard his body as belonging to the Lord and consecrated to him [Hb, NIC, WBC]. He is to keep his body pure [Hb, NIC, Rb; TNT].
3. He is to appreciate his wife as being also one of God's holy people and not just an object to satisfy his lusts [HNTC].

QUESTION—What is meant by τιμῇ 'honor'?
1. He is to do so in a way that is considered honorable by society [Lns; probably NIV, NJB, TEV which translate it 'honorable':].
2. He is to treat someone with honor [EBC, HNTC, ICC, NCBC]. In reference to controlling his own body, he is to treat all women with honor [NCBC]. In reference to acquiring a wife, he is to treat his wife with honor [EBC, HNTC, ICC, NCBC].
3. He is to honor his body [Hb, NIC; TNT]. Fornication would dishonor it.

4:5 not in passion[a] of-lust[b]

LEXICON—a. πάθος (LN **25.30**): 'passion' [BAGD, Hn, HNTC, ICC, Lns, WBC; NASB, RSV], 'lust' [KJV], 'desire' [LN; TEV], 'inclinations' [TNT]. This is also translated as an adjective: 'passionate' [NAB, NIV]. The following translate the two nouns as a unit: 'to give way to lust' [NEB], 'to give way to selfish lust' [NJB].
b. ἐπιθυμία (LN **25.20**): 'lust' [Hn, ICC, LN, Lns; NIV, RSV], 'desire' [BAGD, LN; NAB], 'evil desires' [LN], 'concupiscence' [KJV]. This noun is also translated as an adjective: 'lustful' [HNTC, WBC; NASB, TEV, TNT].

QUESTION—How are πάθος 'passion' and ἐπιθυμία 'lust' differentiated?
πάθος 'passion' is a strong or ungovernable desire [Fn, Hb, Lns, NCBC, NIC], while ἐπιθυμία 'desire/lust' is here a strong evil desire [Hb, NCBC, NIC].

QUESTION—How are the two nouns related in the genitive construction πάθει ἐπιθυμίας 'passion of lust'?
These are both attributes of the event of desiring. Some take the second to modify the first [HNTC, WBC; NASB, TEV, TNT]: lustful passion. Others take the first to modify the second [NAB, NIV]: passionate lust. Some describe the combination as having a passion with which their lust consents [Lns], having passion overcome by lust [Mn], or having desires overcome by passion [Ea].

as[a] **also**[b] **the heathen,**[c] **those not knowing**[d] **God,**

LEXICON—a. καθάπερ (LN 64.15): 'as' [HNTC; NAB, TNT], 'even as' [KJV], 'like' [Hn, Lns, WBC; NASB, NEB, NIV, RSV, TEV], 'just like' [NJB], 'as is the case with' [ICC].

  b. καί (LN 89.93): 'also' [Hn, Lns], 'even', [HNTC], not explicit [ICC, WBC; all versions].

  c. ἔθνος (LN 11.37): 'heathen' [BAGD, Hn, LN; NIV, RSV, TEV], 'pagans' [BAGD, HNTC, LN, Lns; NEB], 'nations' [BAGD; NJB], 'Gentiles' [BAGD, ICC, WBC; KJV, NAB, NASB, TNT], 'non-Christians' [Hb, NIC].

  d. perf. act. participle of οἶδα (LN 28.1; 87.12): 'to know' [BAGD, Hn, HNTC, ICC, LN, Lns; KJV, NAB, NASB, NIV, RSV, TEV, TNT], 'to acknowledge' [NJB], 'to have knowledge of' [LN, WBC], 'to honor, to respect' [LN]. This is also translated by conflating the negative with the verb: 'to be ignorant of' [NEB].

QUESTION—What relationship is indicated by the participial form εἰδότα 'knowing'?

It describes the pertinent characteristic of the 'heathen' [El, Hb, Hn, HNTC, ICC, Lns, Mn, NCBC, WBC, Wd; all versions]: the heathen who do not know God. Many of the Thessalonian Christians were Gentiles in the sense of not being Jews [NIC]. This refers to Gentiles who were not Christians [NIC]. This also implies that not knowing God is the reason why they act sinfully [Ea, EBC, Fn, Hb, Mn, NCBC, NIC, WBC]. It implies that their ignorance of God is deliberate, that they refuse to know God [EBC, Fn, ICC, Lns, NCBC, NIC, WBC, Wd]. It does not mean that they do not know 'about' God, but that they do not take account of God [TH].

4:6 **not to-wrong**[a] **and to-defraud**[b] **his brother in the matter,**[c]

LEXICON—a. pres. act. infin. of ὑπερβαίνω (LN 88.296): 'to wrong' [NIV], 'to do wrong to' [NEB, TEV], 'to go beyond' [KJV], 'to go beyond what is proper' [Hn], 'to overreach' [NAB], 'to go too far' [Lns], 'to outdo' [TNT], 'to injure' [HNTC], 'to disregard' [ICC], 'to transgress' [BAGD; NASB, RSV], 'to trespass' [BAGD, WBC], 'to sin' [BAGD; NJB], 'to sin against' [LN].

  b. pres. act. infin. of πλεονεκτέω (LN 88.144): 'to defraud' [BAGD, Hn; KJV, NASB], 'to cheat' [BAGD; NAB], 'to take advantage of' [BAGD, ICC, LN; NIV, NJB, TEV], 'to invade one's rights' [NEB], 'to wrong' [RSV], 'to take selfish advantage of' [TNT], 'to exploit' [HNTC], 'to behave covetously against' [WBC], 'to overreach' [Lns].

  c. πρᾶγμα (LN 42.9; 56.2): 'matter' [BAGD, Hn, HNTC, ICC, WBC; all versions], 'lawsuit' [BAGD, LN], 'case' [LN], 'matter of business' [Lns], 'undertaking' [LN].

QUESTION—What is indicated by the use of the infinitive form ὑπερβαίνειν 'to wrong'?
1. It indicates another explanation of what is meant by sanctification (4:3a) [Alf, Ea, EBC, El, Hb, Hn, Lns, Mn; NAB, NASB, NEB, NIV, NJB, RSV]: your sanctification, *that is*, to abstain from fornication, etc., and not to wrong your brother. This is the second or the third explanation, according to whether 'to know how to possess one's vessel' is considered to be parallel with the other two infinitive clauses (see 4:3–4).
2. It indicates another explanation of the statement about abstaining from fornication (4:3b) [Fn, HNTC]: to abstain from fornication, etc., *that is*, each one is to know how to possess his own vessel, and he is not to wrong his brother in this matter.
3. It explains the statement about acquiring a wife (4:4) [Er, NCBC]: each one is to know how to possess his own vessel, *that is*, he is not to wrong his brother in this matter.
4. It gives another explanation of 'God's will' [My, TH]: this is God's will: your sanctification, *and also* that no one wrong and defraud his brother.
5. It indicates purpose [ICC, Rb, WBC].
5.1 He should know how to acquire his own wife in sanctification and honor in order that he not wrong his brother [ICC].
5.2 He should be sanctified in order that he not wrong his brother [Rb].

QUESTION—What matter is being discussed?
1. This refers to the matter already under discussion, the matter of sexual relations [Alf, Ea, EBC, EGT, El, Fn, Hb, Hn, HNTC, ICC, Mn, NCBC, NIC, Rb, TH, WBC, Wd]. 'Matter' is an euphemistic reference to sexual sins [EGT, Hb, HNTC, NCBC]. This is a new stage, dealing with the social aspect of such sin [EGT, El].
2. This refers to a new topic, the matter of business dealings [Lns, My]. The word is a commercial term used in business [Lns, My].

QUESTION—What relationship is indicated by καί 'and'?
1. This indicates coordination [TH; KJV, NASB, RSV]: to wrong *and* defraud his brother. The same act of lust constitutes both wronging and defrauding his brother. The two verbs are virtually synonymous so that adding the second verb makes the statement emphatic [TH].
2. This indicates alternation [Alf, HNTC, ICC, WBC; NAB, NEB, NIV, TEV, TNT]: to wrong *or* to defraud his brother.
3. This indicates a restatement of the preceding action [Lns, Mn, My]: to do wrong, *that is*, to defraud his brother.
4. This indicates the means of doing the preceding action [NJB]: to wrong *by* defrauding.
5. This indicates the result of the preceding action [Wd]: to wrong *and thus* to defraud.

QUESTION—What is meant by the two verbs?
The verbs are sometimes used in business contexts. Some take the first verb to be intransitive [Fn, Hn, Lns, Mn, My], others take it to be transitive so that

τὸν ἀδελφὸν αὐτοῦ 'his brother' is the object of both verbs [Alf, Ea, EGT, El, HNTC, ICC, NIC].
1. The following suggestions follow the interpretation that the matter concerns sexual sins. The verbs are business terms used metaphorically [EGT], and together they indicate that the marriage rights of a brother are violated when someone has sexual relations with the wife of that brother [Ea, EBC, Fn, Hb, Hn, HNTC, NCBC, NIC, TH, WBC, Wd], or with an unmarried woman who will become the wife of that brother [EBC, Hb, NIC]. Some take it to concern the rights of a man to protect a female member of his family, such as a daughter [Hn, WBC].
2. The following suggestion follows the interpretation that this refers to business sins. It means to be so desirous of material gain that a brother is defrauded in business or at any other time [My].

QUESTION—Who is the 'brother'?
1. This means a man who is a fellow Christian man [Ea, EBC, El, HNTC, ICC, Lns, Mn, My, NCBC, TH, WBC]. This does not imply that it would be permissible if the person were not a Christian [HNTC, ICC, Lns, My, NCBC, WBC]. What was required among Christians would also apply to all relationships [Hb].
2. This means a fellowman and pertains to non-Christians as well as Christians [Fn, NIC].

because[a] (the) avenger[b] (is) (the) Lord concerning all these,
LEXICON—a. διότι (LN 89.26): 'because' [BAGD, Hn, HNTC, Lns, WBC; KJV, NASB, NEB, RSV], 'for' [ICC; NAB, TNT], not explicit [NIV, NJB, TEV].
b. ἔκδικος (LN **38.9**): 'avenger' [BAGD, Hn, HNTC, ICC, Lns, WBC; KJV, NAB, NASB, RSV], 'punisher' [LN]. This is also translated as a verb: 'to punish' [NEB, NIV, TEV], 'to pay back' [NJB], 'to exact retribution' [TNT].

QUESTION—What relationship is indicated by διότι 'because'?
This introduces the reason for obeying the preceding instructions [EBC, El, Hb, Hn, HNTC, ICC, Lns, My, NCBC, NIC, TH, WBC, Wd]. It provides a motive for obeying [Hb, ICC, Wd].
1. This is the reason for obeying the immediately preceding clause [NCBC; NASB, NEB, NJB, RSV]: no one is to wrong and defraud his brother *because* the Lord will avenge such acts.
2. This is the reason for obeying all the commands in 4:3b–6a [Hn, HNTC, ICC; probably NAB, NIV].

QUESTION—Who is the Lord?
1. The Lord is Jesus Christ [EBC, Fn, Hb, HNTC, ICC, Lns, Mn, NCBC, TH, WBC]. This refers to the final judgment [EBC, Fn, Hb, ICC, Mn, Rb]. He is God's agent to judge the world [Fn, Hb, Mn]. It is possible that this also refers to present judgments [HNTC, NCBC, Rb].

2. The Lord is God [NIC, Wd]. This refers to the final judgment [NIC, Wd], or judgment during one's present lifetime [Wd].

as^a indeed^b we-previously-told^c you

LEXICON—a. καθώς (LN 64.14): 'as' [Hn, HNTC, ICC, WBC; all versions except NASB, TEV], 'just as' [NASB], 'even as' [Lns], not explicit [TEV].
- b. καί (LN 89.93; 91.12): 'indeed' [HNTC, ICC, WBC], 'also' [Lns; KJV, NASB], not explicit [Hn; all versions except KJV, NASB].
- c. aorist act. indic. of προλέγω (LN 33.86; 33.423): 'to tell previously' [Hn], 'to tell before' [BAGD; NASB, NEB, NJB, TEV], 'to tell already' [NIV], 'to say already' [LN], 'to tell earlier' [HNTC], 'to tell in advance' [Lns], 'to predict' [ICC], 'to once indicate' [NAB], 'to forewarn' [KJV, RSV], 'to already warn' [TNT], 'to warn' [LN, WBC].

and solemnly-warned.^{a}

LEXICON—a. aorist mid. (deponent = active) indic. of διαμαρτύρομαι (LN 33.425; 33.223): 'to solemnly warn' [NASB], 'to strongly warn' [TEV], 'to warn' [LN; NIV], 'to solemnly testify' [BAGD, Hn], 'to strongly testify' [HNTC], 'to testify' [BAGD, LN, Lns; KJV], 'to assert' [LN], 'to solemnly affirm' [ICC]. This is also combined with the preceding verb in a phrase: 'to indicate by our testimony' [NAB], 'to tell before with all emphasis' [NEB], 'to tell before emphatically' [NJB], 'to solemnly forewarn' [RSV], 'to most solemnly warn' [TNT], 'to warn insistently' [WBC].

QUESTION—What relationship is indicated by καί 'and'?

This adds a similar, but stronger verb to the preceding one [El, TH] to indicate that the coming judgment will be a solemn matter [Hb, HNTC, Lns, Mn, TH] and that they had emphasized this [El, My, NCBC, TH].

4:7 Because^a

LEXICON—a. γάρ (LN 89.23): 'because', 'for' [Hn, HNTC, ICC, Lns, WBC; KJV, NASB, NEB, NIV, RSV, TNT], not explicit [NAB, NJB, TEV].

QUESTION—What relationship is indicated by this conjunction?
1. This indicates a second reason for obeying the preceding instructions (4:3b–6a) [EBC, Fn, HNTC, ICC, NCBC, NIC]: obey, because (διότι, 4:6b) the Lord will punish those who disobey by committing such sins and *because* (γάρ) he called us to be sanctified.
2. This gives the grounds for warning them that there is punishment for immoral people [Ea, Hb, Hn]: I had reason to warn you about being punished for immorality, *since* God called us in sanctification (and therefore holds us accountable to be sanctified).
3. This indicates the grounds for the necessity of giving these instructions [Lns]: I give you these instructions *since* God called you to be sanctified.

4. This gives the grounds for the preceding statement that the Lord is the avenger concerning all these things [El, My]: he will avenge failures to obey *since* he has called us to this.

God did not call[a] us to/on-the-basis-of[b] immorality[c]

LEXICON—a. aorist act. indic. of καλέω (LN 33.312): 'to call' [BAGD, Hn, HNTC, ICC, LN, Lns, WBC; all versions], 'to call to a task' [LN].
  b. ἐπί (LN 90.23; 89.13; 89.27; 89.60): 'to' [NAB, NEB], 'unto' [KJV], 'for' [Hn, ICC, WBC; RSV], 'for the purpose of' [NASB], 'to be' [NIV, NJB], 'to a life of' [TNT], 'to live in' [TEV]; or 'on the basis of' [Lns], 'because of' [HNTC].
  c. ἀκαθαρσία (LN 88.261): 'immorality' [BAGD, LN; NAB, TEV, TNT], 'impurity' [HNTC, ICC, LN, WBC; NASB, NEB], 'filthiness' [LN], 'uncleanness' [Hn, Lns; KJV, RSV]. This is also translated as an adjective: 'immoral' [NJB], 'impure' [NIV].

QUESTION—What relationship is indicated by ἐπί 'to/on the basis of'?
  1. This indicates purpose [Alf, BAGD, Ea, El, Fn, ICC, Mn, My, NIC, TH, WBC, Wd; all versions]: God did not call you *in order that* you be immoral. God had a purpose in calling them, but his purpose was not for them to be immoral [NIC].
  2. This indicates the basis on which he called them [Hb, HNTC, Lns, NCBC, Rb]. Explanations of what this means are varied. One explanation seems to make this equivalent to God's purpose in calling them [Hb, Rb]. Another, that God did not call them on the basis of accepting the continuation of their immorality [probably Lns, NCBC]. Or, God did not call them because they were immoral [HNTC].

but in[a] sanctification.[b]

LEXICON—a. ἐν (LN 90.23; 89.49; 89.80): 'in' [Hn, WBC; NASB, RSV], 'unto' [KJV], 'to' [NAB, NEB], 'to be' [ICC; NJB], 'so that we exist in' [HNTC], 'to a life of' [TNT], 'to live (in)' [NIV, TEV], 'in connection with' [Lns].
  b. ἁγιασμός (LN 53.30): 'sanctification' [BAGD, Hn, HNTC, Lns, WBC; NASB], 'holiness' [BAGD; KJV, NAB, NEB, RSV, TEV], 'purification' [LN], 'purity' [TNT], 'a holy life' [NIV]. This noun is also translated as an adjective: 'holy' [NJB], 'consecrated' [ICC]. See this word at 4:3.

QUESTION—What relationship is indicated by ἐν 'in'?
  1. This indicates purpose, God's goal in calling them. Some do not make any difference in the translation of the words ἐπί and ἐν, treating them both as the purpose for which God called them [NAB, NEB, NIV, NJB, TEV, TNT]. Probably those who speak of the state of holiness as a result of the call [HNTC, ICC, My] are to be included here: he called you so as to be sanctified. In effect it describes God's purpose for them, and implies the words 'so as to be' [HNTC, ICC].
  2. This describes the circumstance of their call. Some seem to describe this as an act of God which accompanies their call [Lns, NCBC, WBC]: God

called you and, as he called you, he sanctified you, setting you apart to be his people. One seems to describe this as specifying the aspect in which they are called [NCBC]: God called you in the matter of sanctification of your whole Christian life. Some talk about being called in the sphere, element, or atmosphere of sanctification [Alf, Ea, El, Hb, NIC, Rb, Wd]. It is further explained that sanctification is the sphere in which they were called to develop their lives [El, Hb, NIC].

4:8 Therefore[a]

LEXICON—a. τοιγαροῦν (LN 89.51): 'therefore' [BAGD, Hn, Lns, WBC; KJV, NEB, NIV, RSV], 'hence' [NAB], 'consequently' [HNTC, ICC; NASB], 'so then' [LN; TEV], 'in other words' [NJB], not explicit [TNT].

QUESTION—What relationship is indicated by this conjunction?
1. This is the conclusion of the preceding clause [El, Hb, Hn, My, NCBC, NIC]: he called you to be sanctified, *therefore* you reject God if you do not become sanctified.
2. This is the conclusion of the preceding passage, 4:3–7 [Ea, Fn, ICC, Lns]: since such commands for sanctification are God's will and God called you to be sanctified, *therefore* you reject God if you do not become sanctified.

the (one) rejecting,[a] **not man rejects,**[b] **but God**

LEXICON—a. pres. act. participle of ἀθετέω (LN 31.100): 'to reject' [BAGD, Hn, LN; NAB, NASB, NIV, NJB, TEV, TNT], 'to disregard' [WBC; RSV], 'to not rely on' [LN], 'to despise' [KJV], 'to spurn' [HNTC], 'to flout' [NEB], 'to set aside' [Lns]. This participle is also translated as a substantive: 'the rejector' [ICC]. The present tense is timeless, characterizing the person [Alf, Ea, El, Hb, Lns, My].
b. pres. act. indic. of ἀθετέω: 'to reject'. See this word above.

QUESTION—What is the implied object of the event in the participle ἀθετῶν 'rejecting'?
1. The implied objects are the instructions or rules about being sanctified [Ea, El, Hb, Hn, My, NCBC, WBC; NAB, NEB, NIV, TEV, TNT]: the one rejecting these instructions. Since the instructions were given by Paul, they indirectly rejected him [Hb, ICC, My, NCBC, WBC].
2. The implied object is 'his brother' whom he wrongs and defrauds [Alf]: the one rejecting his brother is not rejecting just a man, but also God.

the (one) even/also[a] **giving**[b] **his Holy Spirit to/into you.**

TEXT—Some manuscripts do not include καί 'indeed/also'. GNT includes it within a bracket but does not discuss the omission.

TEXT—Instead of διδόντα 'giving' (present tense), some manuscripts have δόντα 'having given' (aorist tense). GNT does not discuss the possibility of the alternative aorist tense. The aorist tense is accepted by Alf, Ea, El, My and KJV.

TEXT—Instead of ὑμᾶς 'you', some manuscripts have ἡμᾶς 'us'. GNT does not mention this alternative reading. Only KJV translates 'us'.

LEXICON—a. καί (LN 89.93; 91.12): 'even' [Hn], 'indeed' [WBC], '(the) very (one/God)' [HNTC; TNT], or 'also' [KJV], not explicit or following a text that does not include this word [ICC, Lns; all versions except KJV, TNT].
  b. pres. act. participle of δίδωμι (LN 57.71): 'to give' [BAGD, Hn, LN, Lns, WBC; KJV, NASB, NIV, NJB, RSV, TEV], 'to send' [BAGD; NAB], 'to bestow' [BAGD; NEB, TNT], 'to put' [ICC], 'to set' [HNTC].
  c. εἰς (LN 84.16; 90.59): 'to' [Hn, Lns; NASB, RSV], 'unto' [KJV]. Some translate without the preposition: 'who gives you' [WBC; NIV, NJB, TEV]. Some use another verb: 'who sends upon' [NAB], 'who bestows upon/on' [NEB, TNT], 'who sets within' [HNTC].

QUESTION—What is indicated by καί 'indeed/also'?
1. This means 'indeed, even' [Hn, WBC].
2. This means 'also' [Ea, El, Hb]. God called us and he also gives his Holy Spirit to you. God not only called us to be sanctified, but he also gave the Holy Spirit to accomplish it [Ea, El, Hb].

QUESTION—What is the significance of the present tense of the participle διδόντα 'giving'?
1. The present tense is timeless and characterizes God as the one who gives [EGT, Fn, Hb, HNTC, ICC, Lns, Mn, NCBC]: God, the giver of the Holy Spirit. God gave the Spirit to particular individuals at the different times he called them [ICC].
2. The present tense indicates that God continually gives the Holy Spirit throughout their lives [EBC, NIC]. This provides continued strength to resist immorality [EBC].

QUESTION—What is the significance of the phrase εἰς ὑμᾶς 'to/into you'?
1. This has the meaning 'to you' [Alf, Ea, Hn, Lns, My, WBC; NASB, NIV, NJB, RSV, TEV]: the one giving his Holy Spirit to you, or the one giving you his Holy Spirit. This is also described as indicating the direction of the giving [Alf, Ea] or of the location [My].
2. This has the meaning 'into you' and indicates that God gives the Holy Spirit to indwell the person [Ea, Hb, HNTC, ICC, Mn, NIC]: the one giving his Holy Spirit to be within you. A parallel is Gal. 4:6 where it says that God sent the Spirit 'into our hearts' (εἰς τὰς καρδίας ἡμῶν) [ICC].

DISCOURSE UNIT: 4:9–12 [Alf, Er, Hb, Hn, HNTC, My, TH, WBC, Wd]. The topic is brotherly love [Alf, HNTC, TH, WBC], brotherly love and being industrious [Er, Hb, Hn], love, peace, and work [Wd].

DISCOURSE UNIT: 4:9–10 [EBC, My, NIC]. The topic is brotherly love [EBC, NIC].

DISCOURSE UNIT: 4:9–10a [Alf, Hb, ICC, Mn]. The topic is brotherly love [Alf, Hb, ICC, Mn].

4:9 Now/But[a] concerning brotherly-love,[b]

LEXICON—a. δέ (LN 89.94; 89.124): 'now' [Hn, HNTC, ICC, Lns; NASB, NIV]; or 'but' [KJV, RSV]; not explicit [WBC; NAB, NEB, NJB, TEV, TNT].

b. φιλαδελφία (LN **25.34**): 'brotherly love' [BAGD, HNTC, Lns, WBC; KJV, NAB, NIV, NJB], 'love of the brethren' [NASB, RSV], 'love to the brothers' [BAGD, Hn, ICC], 'love for one's brotherhood' [NEB], 'love for fellow believers' [TEV], 'love for fellow Christians' [TNT], 'affection for fellow believers' [LN].

QUESTION—What relationship is indicated by δέ 'now/but'?

1. This is merely transitional [EBC, El, Hn, HNTC, ICC, Lns, Mn, My, TH; NASB, NIV]: now. It introduces a new subject [EBC, Hn, ICC, Mn, My].
2. This indicates contrast [Alf, Ea, Fn, Hb, NCBC; KJV, RSV]: you have need for us to write about sexual purity, but you do not have need for us to write about brotherly love.

you-have no need[a] (for me/us/anyone) to-write to-you;

TEXT—Instead of ἔχετε 'you have', some manuscripts have ἔχομεν 'we have'. GNT does not indicate the alternative reading. Some translate impersonally, 'there is no need' [NAB, NJB, TEV, TNT]. Only NIV follows the alternate reading.

LEXICON—a. χρεία (LN 71.23): 'need' [BAGD, Hn, HNTC, ICC, LN, Lns, WBC; NAB, NASB, NJB, RSV, TEV, TNT]. This noun is also translated as a verb: 'to need' [KJV, NEB, NIV]. See this word at 1:8.

QUESTION—Who are the implied writers?

1. Paul is implied [El, NIC; KJV, NAB, NEB]: you have no need for me to write to you.
2. The three mentioned at the beginning of the letter, Paul, Silvanus, and Timothy, are implied [Alf, HNTC, ICC, Lns, TH, WBC]: you have no need for us to write to you.
3. The need for anyone to write is rejected [Alf, Hn; NASB, RSV]: you have no need for anyone to write to you.

because[a] you yourselves are God-taught[b] to[c] to-love[d] one-another.

LEXICON—a. γάρ (LN 89.23): 'because', 'for' [Hn, HNTC, ICC, Lns, WBC; KJV, NASB, NEB, RSV, TNT], 'since' [NJB], not explicit [NAB, NIV, TEV].

b. θεοδίδακτος (LN **33.228**): 'God-taught' [Lns]. This is also translated as a verbal phrase: 'to be taught by God' [BAGD, Hn, HNTC, LN; NASB, NEB, NIV, RSV, TEV, TNT], 'to be taught of God' [ICC; KJV], 'to be divinely taught' [WBC], 'God has taught you' [NAB], 'you have learned from God' [NJB].

c. εἰς (LN 90.23; 89.48) 'to' [Hn, HNTC, ICC, WBC; all versions except TEV], 'how (to)' [TEV]; or 'so that' [Lns].

d. pres. act. infin. of ἀγαπάω (LN 25.43; 25.44): 'to love' [BAGD, Hn, HNTC, ICC, LN, Lns, WBC; all versions], 'to regard with affection'

[LN], 'to show/demonstrate one's love' [LN]. The present tense indicates that love is to be continuous [Hb].

QUESTION—What relationship is indicated by γάρ 'for'?

This indicates the reason why they do not need anyone to write them [Ea, Hb, ICC, WBC].

QUESTION—How did God teach them?

God, through the working of the Holy Spirit, directly impressed it upon their consciousness [EBC, Er, Hb, Hn, ICC, Mn, NCBC, NIC, TH, WBC], or applied the words spoken by the missionaries [Lns].

QUESTION—What relationship is indicated by εἰς 'to'?

1. This indicates the content of what was taught [Hn, ICC, Mn, WBC; KJV, NAB, NASB, NEB, NIV, NJB, RSV, TNT]: God taught you to love one another.
2. This indicates the purpose or intended result of the teaching [Alf, Ea, El, Fn, Hb, HNTC, Lns, My, TH]: God taught you so that you would love one another. At the same time, this also indicates the content of what was taught [Ea, El, My].

4:10a Because/And[a] indeed[b]

LEXICON—a. γάρ (LN 89.23; 91.1): 'because', 'for' [HNTC; NASB], 'indeed' [Lns], 'and' [all versions except NASB, TNT], 'in fact' [ICC], 'and in fact' [Hn], not explicit [WBC; TNT].

b. καί (LN 89.93; 91.12): 'indeed' [WBC; KJV, NASB, RSV, TNT], 'even' [HNTC], 'also' [Hn, ICC, Lns], 'in fact' [NEB, NIV, NJB, TEV], not explicit [NAB].

QUESTION—What relationship is indicated by γάρ 'for'?

1. This indicates the grounds for saying that they had been taught to love by God [Ea, EBC, El, Fn, Hb, ICC, My]: it is true you have been taught by God to love one another, *since* you, in fact, do love the brethren everywhere.
2. It indicates another reason that no one needed to write to them about loving one another [Er, ICC, NCBC]: no one needs to write you concerning brotherly love, *because* (γάρ) God has taught you about it and *because* (γάρ) you are already showing that you love all the brethren. The argument is from the greater to the less [ICC, NCBC, NIC], if they love all the brethren in all of Macedonia, they surely love the brethren in their own congregation.
3. This is an added statement to show that the teaching is effective [Hn, Lns, NIC]: God taught you to love one another, *and indeed* you *also* love all of your brothers everywhere.

you-do it toward[a] all the brothers, the (ones) in[b] all Macedonia.

LEXICON—a. εἰς (LN 90.41; 90.59): 'toward' [ICC, Lns; KJV, NASB, NEB, TEV, TNT], 'to' [Hn, HNTC, WBC], 'with respect to' [NAB], not explicit [NIV, NJB, RSV].

b. ἐν (LN 83.13): 'in' [Hn, HNTC, ICC, Lns, WBC; KJV, NASB, TEV]. This word is also conflated with the following word ὅλῃ 'all': 'throughout' [NAB, NEB, NIV, RSV, TNT], 'throughout the whole of' [NJB].

QUESTION—How could they show their love to all the brothers in Macedonia?
Thessalonica was the capital city of the province of Macedonia [Fn, Hb]. The Thessalonians could show their love to Christian brothers from other places in Macedonia when those brothers came to the capital. They could have shown their love by providing hospitality [Ea, Fn, Hb, HNTC, ICC, Lns, NCBC]. They could also provide help to churches in other towns [ICC, NCBC]. πάντας 'all' means all the brethren they came in contact with [Hn, NIC].

DISCOURSE UNIT: 4:10b–12 [Hb, ICC, Mn]. The topic is exhortations [Hb], idleness [ICC], call to work [Mn].

4:10b But[a] we-exhort[b] you, brothers, to-abound[c] more,[d]

LEXICON—a. δέ (LN 89.124): 'but' [Hn, HNTC, WBC; KJV, NASB, RSV], 'yet' [Lns; NAB, NEB, NIV], 'however' [ICC; NJB], 'so' [TEV], not explicit [TNT].

b. pres. act. indic. of παρακαλέω (LN 33.168): 'to exhort' [BAGD; NAB, RSV], 'to urge' [BAGD, Hn, ICC; NASB, NIV, NJB], 'to request' [BAGD, HNTC, LN], 'to beg' [TEV, TNT], 'to beseech' [KJV], 'to appeal to' [BAGD, LN, WBC; NEB], 'to admonish' [Lns]. See this word at 2:12 and 4:1.

c. pres. act. infin. of περισσεύω (LN 78.31; 59.52): 'to abound' [Hn, ICC, Lns, WBC], 'to increase' [KJV], 'to excel' [HNTC; NASB], 'to make progress' [NJB]. This is also translated as a phrase with the following word: 'to do better still' [NEB], 'to do so more and more' [NIV, RSV], 'to do even more' [TEV], 'to go even further' [TNT], 'to even greater progress' [NAB]. See this word at 3:12 and 4:1.

d. μᾶλλον: 'more'. See this word at 4:1.

QUESTION—What relationship is indicated by δέ 'but'?
This indicates a contrast of degree [Ea, Hb, Hn, HNTC, ICC, Lns; all versions except TEV, TNT]: you already show love to all the brethren, *but* we exhort you to show it more and more. The love they already had was commendable. But there is always a need for an increase of love [EBC, Er, Fn, Hb, Hn, Lns, NCBC]. There are always new needs for it to be exercised [HNTC, NIC].

DISCOURSE UNIT: 4:11–12 [EBC, Hb, My, NIC]. The topic is independence from the need to be helped.

4:11 and[a]

LEXICON—a. καί (LN 89.92): 'and' [Hn, HNTC, ICC, Lns; KJV, NASB, NJB], not explicit [WBC; NAB, NEB, NIV, RSV, TEV, TNT].

1 THESSALONIANS 4:11

QUESTION—How are this exhortation and the following two connected with the preceding exhortation and the section about love?
1. The following exhortations concern love. This continues the topic of love and indicates a way to show love for others [HNTC, Mn, NCBC, TH]. The further exhortations show how to abound in love [HNTC, NCBC]. They are the areas in which brotherly love was abused [Ea].
2. This begins a new and distinct topic. This is shown by separating the previous exhortation from this series of exhortations with a semicolon or period [WBC; KJV, NAB, NEB, TEV, TNT], or beginning a new paragraph at this point [NIV], or even by inserting a new outline title [EBC, Hb, NIC]. However, some commentators think that there is also a close connection with the duty of showing love to the brethren.

to-endeavor^a to-be-quiet^b

LEXICON—a. pres. mid. (deponent = active) infin. of φιλοτιμέομαι (LN 25.78): 'to endeavor', 'to strive' [ICC], 'to earnestly aspire' [LN], 'to make it one's aim' [WBC; TEV], 'to study' [KJV], 'to make it a point' [NJB], 'to make it a point of honor' [NAB], 'to aspire' [BAGD; RSV, TNT], 'to be ambitious' [Hn, HNTC, Lns], 'to make it one's ambition' [BAGD; NASB, NEB, NIV]. The present tense in this and the following infinitives indicate that these are to be their continual duties [Alf, Ea, Hb, Rb, TH].
b. pres. act. infin. of ἡσυχάζω (LN **88.103**): 'to be quiet' [BAGD, Lns; KJV], 'to be calm' [ICC], 'to keep calm' [NEB], 'to remain at peace' [NAB], 'to lead a quiet life' [WBC; NASB, NIV, TNT], 'to live a quiet life' [LN; TEV], 'to live quietly' [NJB, RSV], 'to live calmly' [Hn], 'to live unobtrusively' [HNTC].

QUESTION—In what respect are they to be quiet?
1. This refers to a peaceful life in relation to others [Alf, Fn, HNTC, Lns, My, NCBC, NIC, TH, WBC; NASB, NIV, TEV, TNT]: endeavor to lead a peaceful life. They should live a simple life [NIC]. They are not to be agitators [WBC]. They might have been so taken up with the approaching day of the Lord's coming that they lost all desire to keep up ordinary living [WBC], especially in the matter of earning their own livelihood [NIC]. The following two instructions explain what such a life involves [Lns, NCBC, NIC]: lead a quiet life, that is, mind your own business and work with your hands.
2. This refers to an inner calmness of mind [Ea, El, Er, Hb, Hn, ICC; NEB]: aspire to be calm. Some might have been fanatically excited about the imminent coming of the Lord [Ea, Hb, ICC]. This attitude would lead to the need for the two following exhortations [Hn, ICC].

and to-do^a (your) own-things^b

LEXICON—a. pres. act. infin. of πράσσω (LN 42.8): 'to do' [BAGD, LN; KJV]. This verb appears to be combined with the following noun as an idiom: 'to attend to one's own affairs' [WBC; NAB], 'to attend to one's

1 THESSALONIANS 4:11

own business' [Lns; NASB, NJB], 'to mind one's own affairs' [HNTC; RSV], 'to mind one's own business' [ICC; NIV, TEV, TNT], 'to be engaged in one's own affairs' [Hn], 'to look after one's own business' [NEB].
   b. ἴδιος (LN 57.4): 'own things', 'your own affairs' [BAGD, Hn, HNTC, WBC; NAB, RSV], 'your own business' [ICC, Lns; KJV, NASB, NEB, NIV, NJB, TEV, TNT].

QUESTION—What is this exhortation concerned with?
   1. This refers to a person's personal affairs, the opposite of being involved in other people's affairs [Ea, EBC, Er, Fn, Hn, ICC, My, NCBC, NIC, TH, WBC, Wd]. One suggestion is that some might try to interfere in the running of the church and tried to manage things themselves [Hn, ICC, NIC, Wd]. Or this refers to meddling in the personal affairs of other people [EBC, Hb, Hn, My, NCBC, NIC, TH]. There is a positive side to this, that they are to tend to their own personal affairs and responsibilities [Ea, EBC, El, Hb, My, TH].
   2. This concerns business affairs [Lns]. This would be a different group from the following group: businessmen are to attend to their business affairs, and laborers are to be satisfied to work with their hands [Lns].

and to-work[a] with-your hands,

LEXICON—a. pres. mid. (deponent = active) infin. of ἐργάζομαι (LN 42.41): 'to work' [BAGD, Hn, HNTC, ICC, LN, Lns, WBC; KJV, NAB, NASB, NEB, NIV, RSV, TNT], 'to labor' [LN]. This verb is also conflated with the following phrase: 'to earn your (own) living' [NJB, TEV].

QUESTION—What is the intent of this exhortation?
The point is not that they are to do only manual work, but that they were to earn their own living instead of asking the church to support them [Ea, EBC, Hn, ICC, TH, Wd]. The reference to the hands is due to the fact that most did manual labor [Ea, Hb, Hn, HNTC, My, TH]. Some commentators speculate that the cause for idleness was the disdain Greeks had for common manual labor [EBC, NIC], or that the anticipation of the coming of Christ took up time and thought [Ea, NCBC], or that they took advantage of the brotherly love of other Christians to provide for the needs of the poorer ones [Ea, EBC, NCBC, WBC].

as[a] we-instructed[b] you,

LEXICON—a. καθώς (LN 64.14): 'as' [ICC, WBC; KJV, NAB, NEB, RSV, TNT], 'just as' [Hn, HNTC, LN; NASB, NIV, NJB, TEV], 'even as' [Lns].
   b. aorist act. indic. of παραγγέλλω (LN 33.327): 'to instruct' [BAGD, HNTC; TNT], 'to tell' [NIV, NJB, TEV], 'to direct' [BAGD; NAB], 'to command' [BAGD, LN; KJV, NASB], 'to order' [LN; NEB], 'to give orders' [BAGD, Lns], 'to charge' [Hn, ICC, WBC; RSV].

QUESTION—With what is this phrase connected?
1. It is connected with all three of the preceding exhortations [EBC, El, Hn, HNTC, My, NCBC].
2. It is connected with only the immediately preceding exhortation [Fn, Hb, ICC, NIC; NAB]: work with your own hands as we instructed you.

4:12 in-order-that/that[a]

LEXICON—a. ἵνα (LN 89.59; 90.22): 'in order that' [Hn, ICC], 'so that' [HNTC, WBC; NAB, NASB, NEB, NIV, NJB, RSV], 'in this way' [TEV], 'so' [TNT]; or 'that' [Lns; KJV].
QUESTION—What relationship is indicated by this conjunction?
1. It indicates the purpose or contemplated result of the preceding exhortation(s): do so *in order that* you may walk becomingly.
   1.1 It is the purpose of all of the preceding exhortations [Alf, Ea, EBC, El, Hn, HNTC, Mn, My, NCBC, TH; NASB, TEV, TNT]: we exhort you to abound in love, to live quietly, to mind your own affairs, and to work, *in order that* you may walk becomingly and not have need of any thing/person. If the exhortations have been divided so that 4:10a is separated from the series in 4:11, then the purpose would apply to those in 4:11.
   1.2 It is the purpose of only the last exhortation [Hb, ICC, NIC; NAB]: work with your hands as we instructed you, *in order that* you may walk becomingly and not have need of any thing/person. These also take interpretation 2 in the preceding phrase. Idleness discredited Christianity in the community and it put them in need, making them dependent on charity [ICC].
2. It indicates the content of what they instructed the Thessalonians to do [Lns]: as we instructed you *that* you should walk becomingly and should have need of nothing.

you-may-walk[a] becomingly[b] toward[c] the (ones) outside[d]

LEXICON—a. pres. act. subj. of περιπατέω (LN 41.11): 'to walk' [HNTC, Lns; KJV], 'to behave' [LN; NASB], 'to behave oneself' [ICC], 'to live' [LN], 'to conduct oneself' [Hn, WBC]. This verb is also translated with the adverb as a unit: 'to give a good example' [NAB], 'to command respect' [NEB, RSV], 'to earn respect' [NJB], 'to win respect' [TEV, TNT], 'your daily life may win respect' [NIV]. See this word at 2:12 and 4:1.
b. εὐσχημόνως (LN 88.50; 66.4): 'becomingly' [BAGD, HNTC, ICC, WBC], 'in a becoming manner' [LN], 'properly' [Hn; NASB], 'with propriety' [LN], 'decently' [BAGD, LN], 'in seemly fashion' [Lns], 'honestly' [KJV], 'proper' [LN].
c. πρός (LN 89.7; 90.20): 'toward' [Lns, WBC; KJV, NASB], 'to' [NAB], 'with respect to' [Hn], 'in reference to' [ICC], 'in the judgment of' [HNTC].

d. ἔξω (LN 11.10): 'outside'. This is translated as a substantive: 'outsiders' [Hn, HNTC, LN; NAB, NASB, NIV, NJB, RSV], 'those (that are) without' [Lns; KJV], 'those outside your own number' [NEB], 'those who are outside your ranks' [WBC], 'those outside the church' [TNT], 'those who are not believers' [TEV], 'unbelievers' [ICC].

and you-may-have need[a] of-nothing/no-one.
LEXICON—a. χρεία (LN 57.40): 'need' [BAGD, ICC, LN, Lns, WBC; NASB], 'want' [NEB], 'lack' [LN; KJV]. The noun is also conflated with the verb 'to have': 'to want' [NAB], 'to be dependent on' [Hn; NIV, NJB, RSV, TEV], 'to be dependent on one for one's needs' [TNT], 'to require help' [HNTC].
QUESTION—Is the word μηδενός neuter ('nothing') or masculine ('no one')?
Whichever way the grammar is taken, the other point is implied [NIC].
1. It is neuter [Alf, Fn, Hb, Lns, Mn, My, WBC, Wd; KJV, NAB, NASB, NEB]: you may have need of *nothing*. If they work, then they will be able to pay for all their needs.
2. It is masculine [Ea, EBC, El, Hn, HNTC, ICC, NCBC; NIV, NJB, RSV, TEV, TNT]: you may have need of *no one*. If they work, then they will not need to have other people supply what they need.

DISCOURSE UNIT: 4:13–5:11 [Alf, EBC, GNT, Hn, Mn, My, NCBC, NIC, Wd; NIV]. The topic is teaching about the Lord's coming again [Alf, EBC, GNT, Hn, My, NCBC; NIV], problems about the Lord's coming [Mn, NIC, Wd].

DISCOURSE UNIT: 4:13–18 [Alf, EBC, Er, Fn, Hb, Hn, HNTC, ICC, Lns, Mn, My, NCBC, NIC, WBC, Wd; NAB, NJB, TEV]. The topic is what happens to believers who die before the Lord comes.

4:13 Now/But[a]
LEXICON—a. δέ (LN 89.94; 89.124): 'now' [Hn, ICC, Lns, WBC]; or 'but' [KJV, NASB, RSV]; not explicit [HNTC; NAB, NEB, NIV, NJB, TEV, TNT].
QUESTION—What relationship is indicated by this conjunction?
1. It indicates a transition to a new subject [Ea, EBC, El, Hb, Hn, HNTC, ICC, Lns, NCBC, TH, WBC]: now.
2. It indicates a contrast [KJV, NASB, RSV]: but. If these translations intend to indicate a contrast here, perhaps it is a change from exhortations to instruction, or from a change of subject from the readers to the deceased Christians.

we-do-not-want[a] you to-be-ignorant,[b] brothers, concerning the (ones) sleeping,[c]
TEXT—Instead of οὐ θέλομεν 'we do not want', some manuscripts have οὐ θέλω 'I do not want'. GNT does not mention this alternative. Only KJV uses the singular form.

TEXT—Instead of the present tense κοιμωμένων 'are sleeping', some manuscripts have the perfect tense κεκοιμημένων 'having fallen asleep'. GNT does not mention this alternative.

LEXICON—a. pres. act. indic. of θέλω (LN 25.1): 'to want' [BAGD, LN, Lns; NASB, NIV, NJB, TEV, TNT], 'to wish' [BAGD, Hn, HNTC, ICC, LN, WBC; NEB], '(we) would have' [KJV, NAB, RSV].

   b. pres. act. infin. of ἀγνοέω (LN **28.13**): 'to be ignorant' [BAGD, HNTC, Lns, WBC; KJV, NIV, RSV], 'to be in ignorance' [Hn, ICC], 'to remain in ignorance' [NEB, TNT], 'to be uninformed' [NASB], 'to be unaware' [LN]. This is also translated without the negative: 'to be quite certain' [NJB], 'to be clear' [NAB], 'to know the truth' [TEV].

   c. pres. pass. (deponent = active) participle of κοιμάω (LN 23.104): 'to sleep' [BAGD, HNTC, ICC], 'to be asleep' [WBC; KJV, NASB, RSV], 'to fall asleep' [BAGD, Hn, Lns; NIV, NJB]. This is also translated with the nonfigurative meaning made explicit: 'to sleep in death' [NAB, NEB], 'to die' [LN; TEV], 'to be dead' [LN]. It is also translated as a substantive: 'the dead' [TNT]. The present tense may mean a continuing state of sleeping [Alf, Hb, NIC]; or a repeated event as different people fall asleep at different times [EBC, Hb, Mn, Rb]; or it is a timeless present which refers to a class of people as 'the sleepers' [ICC].

QUESTION—What figure of speech is the phrase οὐ θέλομεν ὑμᾶς ἀγνοεῖν 'we do not want you to be ignorant'?

It is a litotes [Hb, NCBC, WBC; probably NAB, NJB, TEV]. The denial of the negative statement makes an emphatic statement of the positive: we very much want you to know.

QUESTION—What metaphor is intended by the use of the verb κοιμωμένων 'sleeping'?

This refers to death and some call this an euphemistic term, which would mean that it was selected to avoid using the verb 'to die' [Hb, ICC, My, NCBC, WBC, Wd]. It was already in use by non-Christians [EBC, El, Hb, HNTC, ICC, Lns, NCBC, WBC]. However, some commentators think that Christians used this metaphor because of the meaning it conveyed and not merely to avoid the use of a direct reference to dying [EBC, Er, Lns, Mn, My, WBC]. Suggestions about the point of comparison are: the stillness of the body at rest [Ea, Hb, NCBC], rest from labor [Ea, El, Fn, Hn], the temporary condition that will end with an awakening [Ea, EBC, El, Fn, Hb, Lns, My, NIC, WBC], the continued existence of the soul during sleep [Ea, El]. This refers to the state of the body, and does not imply that the soul is asleep [EBC, Hb, Lns]. Or it refers to the soul in relation to the world and does not imply that the soul is not awake somewhere else [Hn].

in-order-that you-not-grieve[a] as indeed[b] the rest,[c] those not having hope.[d]

LEXICON—a. pres. pass. subj. of λυπέω (LN 25.275): 'to grieve' [BAGD, Hn, ICC, Lns, WBC; NASB, NEB, NIV, NJB, RSV], 'to sorrow' [HNTC; KJV, TNT], 'to yield to grief' [NAB], 'to be sad' [BAGD, LN; TEV].

b. καί (LN 91.12): 'indeed'. The phrase καθὼς καί 'as indeed' is translated 'even as' [HNTC; KJV], 'as' [Hn, ICC; NASB, NJB, RSV, TEV, TNT], 'like' [WBC; NAB, NEB, NIV], 'as also' [Lns].
c. λοιπός (LN 63.21): 'rest'. This is translated as a substantive: 'the rest' [BAGD, Hn, ICC, LN, Lns; NASB], 'the rest of men' [HNTC; NEB, NIV], '(the) others' [BAGD, WBC; KJV, NJB, RSV], 'those' [NAB, TEV], 'non-Christians' [TNT].
d. ἐλπίς (LN 25.59): 'hope' [BAGD, Hn, HNTC, ICC, LN, Lns, WBC; all versions].

QUESTION—What relationship is indicated by ἵνα μή 'in order that not'?

This indicates the purpose the writer had for wanting them to know about believers who die [Alf, Ea, El, Hb, ICC, TH].

QUESTION—What relationship is indicated by καθώς 'as'?

This compares two classes of people in the matter of grieving [Ea, EBC, El, Hb, HNTC, ICC, My, NCBC, TH]: that you will not grieve about the condition of a believer who dies, unlike the outsiders who grieve about those who die. Because Christians have hope, they have no reason to grieve at all [Ea, ICC]. This does not measure degree ('that you will not grieve as much as the outsiders') [Ea, El, Hb, HNTC, ICC, Mn, My, TH]. However, some add that this concerns grieving about the fate of the deceased believers and it does not imply that they are forbidden to grieve about their own sense of personal loss in the death of a loved one [Alf, Ea, EBC, HNTC, NCBC].

QUESTION—Why would Christians grieve about the death of other Christians?

They thought that those who had died or will yet die before the Lord's return would miss participating in the blessedness of that great event [Ea, EBC, El, Er, Fn, Hb, My, NIC, WBC], or at least experience it later than those who were still alive [Hb]. Some commentators say that they might have thought that those who died before the return of the Lord would miss out altogether in being in the future kingdom [Alf, Fn, Lns, NCBC].

QUESTION—What is the content of the hope?

They had the hope that their bodies will be resurrected [Alf, El, Hb, Hn, HNTC, Lns, WBC], the hope that they will be with Christ after death [HNTC, ICC], the hope that the deceased will be able to participate in the future state of salvation connected with the Lord's return [Ea, EBC, Fn, NCBC], the hope of a future blessed life after death [My, TH], or a knowledge of God [NIC].

4:14 Because[a]

LEXICON—a. γάρ (LN 89.23): 'because', 'for' [Hn, HNTC, ICC, Lns, WBC; KJV, NAB, NASB, RSV], not explicit [NEB, NIV, NJB, TEV, TNT].

QUESTION—What relationship is indicated by this conjunction?

1. This indicates the reason why they should not grieve about those who have died [Alf, Ea, EBC, El, Er, Hb, HNTC, ICC, My, NCBC, TH]: do not grieve for them, *because* God will bring them with Jesus at his return.

2. This indicates the reason why such implied ignorance is inexcusable [Hn]: you should not be ignorant concerning those who are asleep in death, *because* since you believe that Jesus died and rose again, you should know that God will bring them with him.

if[a] we-believe[b] that Jesus died and rose-again,[c]

LEXICON—a. εἰ (LN 89.30; 89.65): 'if' [Hn, HNTC, ICC, Lns, WBC; KJV, NAB, NASB], 'since' [RSV], not explicit [NEB, NIV, NJB, TEV, TNT].
  b. pres. act. indic. of πιστεύω (LN 31.35): 'to believe' [BAGD, Hn, HNTC, ICC, LN, Lns, WBC; all versions], 'to think to be true' [LN].
  c. aorist act. indic. of ἀνίστημι (LN 23.94): 'to rise again' [Hn; all versions except NAB], 'to rise' [BAGD, HNTC, ICC, WBC; NAB], 'to arise' [Lns], 'to raise to life again' [LN].

QUESTION—What relationship is indicated by εἰ 'if'?
  This is a condition of reality [EGT, El, Fn, Hb, HNTC, ICC, Lns, NCBC, NIC, Rb, TH, Wd; NEB, NIV, NJB, RSV, TEV, TNT]: if we believe this, and we do. Some take it to be equivalent to 'since' [Hb; RSV], so that it introduces the grounds for the following conclusion: since you believe this, therefore the conclusion is, etc. However, others take this to be a conditional statement that introduces the premise of a syllogism [Alf, Ea, Hn, Mn, My]: if you believe this, then it follows that, etc.

QUESTION—To whom does 'we' refer?
  'We' refers to the writer and the recipients of the letter [Hb, HNTC, Lns] and all Christians [Hb, HNTC]: we Christians believe this.

QUESTION—Why is not the metaphor 'to sleep' used here of Jesus as it is used of believers before and after this clause?
  'To die' stresses the stark fact of Jesus' death. The restful and comforting aspects implied by using 'sleep' when speaking of the death of the believer were brought about by his death for our sins [EBC, Hb, Lns, Mn, NIC, WBC].

thus/so[a] also God, the (ones) having-fallen-asleep[b] through[c] Jesus will-bring[d] with[e] him.

LEXICON—a. οὕτως (LN 61.9): 'so'. The phrase οὕτως καί 'so also' is translated 'so also' [Hn, HNTC, ICC, WBC], 'thus also' [Lns], 'even so' [KJV, NASB, RSV], 'and so' [NIV, TEV], 'and so it will be' [NEB], 'so it will be' [TNT], 'and that in the same way' [NJB], not explicit [NAB].
  b. aorist pass. participle of κοιμάω (LN 23.104): 'to sleep'. See this word at 4:13. The aorist tense refers to the moment of dying [Hb, WBC], or it looks back from the standpoint of the coming of Christ and includes all who will have died before Christ's return [Fn, Hb].
  c. διά (LN 90.4): 'through' [Hn, HNTC, ICC, Lns, WBC; RSV], 'in' [KJV, NASB, NIV, NJB]. This is also translated as a phrase: 'believing in' [NAB, TEV, TNT], 'as Christians' [NEB].
  d. fut. act. indic. of ἄγω (LN 15.165): 'to bring' [Hn, HNTC, LN, Lns; KJV, NASB, NIV, NJB, RSV], 'to bring forth' [NAB], 'to bring to life' [NEB],

'to bring back' [WBC], 'to bring back again' [TNT], 'to lead' [LN], 'to lead on' [ICC], 'to take back' [TEV].
   e. σύν (LN 89.107): 'with' [Hn, HNTC, Lns, WBC; all versions], 'along with' [ICC].

QUESTION—What relationship is indicated by οὕτως καί 'thus/so also'?
   1. This indicates the conclusion of a grounds clause [Hb, Hn, HNTC, Lns, NCBC, NIC, TH; NIV, TEV]: since we believe that Jesus died and arose, *therefore* we (should) also conclude/believe that God will bring the believers who have died with him. The argument is not based on whether or not one's belief is firm, but states what we should believe [HNTC, Lns, NCBC, NIC, TH]. The fact that they believe this implies a church creed [HNTC] and could be omitted from the argument [TH], since the argument is merely: Jesus died and rose again, thus one can conclude that God will bring deceased believers with him [HNTC, Lns, TH]. Implied is the fact that the God who raised Jesus is the God who raises the dead [NCBC, NIC]. The logical step about God raising the dead is taken for granted and is passed over to the result, that the dead will share in the second coming by being with Christ [NCBC, TH].
   2. This indicates a comparison [Alf, Ea, El, Fn, ICC, Mn, My]. Some speak of the grammar as not following a strict logical structure [Alf, Ea, El, Fn, Mn, My]. The preceding clause appears to be a grounds or condition expecting this to be a conclusion or result instead of a comparison. There seem to be implicit steps in the argument. One explanation is that the implied comparison is: as we believe that Jesus died and that God raised him from death, so we must also believe that God will raise believers from death and bring them with Jesus [Alf, Bul (p. 91), Ea, ICC]. The function of this clause as a conclusion is only implicit [Ea], the relational word indicates a likeness between the fate of Jesus and the fate of believers, each dying and being resurrected [Ea, El, My].

QUESTION—With what is διά 'through' connected, and what relationship is indicated by it?
   1. This is connected with the preceding phrase [Alf, Ea, EBC, El, Fn, Hb, Hn, ICC, Mn, NCBC, NIC, Rb, TH, WBC, Wd; KJV, NAB, NASB, NEB, NIV, NJB, TEV, TNT]: the ones having fallen asleep through Jesus.
      1.1 διά 'through' indicates that Jesus is God's agent for bringing about their state of temporary sleep in place of a permanent state of death [Alf, Ea, EBC, El, Fn, Hb, Hn, Mn, NIC, WBC]: the ones having fallen asleep, who escape the curse of death so that they are merely asleep, waiting to be awakened by what Jesus has accomplished in his atonement for them.
      1.2 διά indicates an attendant circumstance [Mou (p. 57), TH; all versions except RSV]: the ones having fallen asleep in relationship with Jesus when they died. Some take this to mean that they died believing in him [NAB, TEV, TNT]. Some translate this as equivalent to the phrase 'in Christ' [KJV, NASB, NIV, NJB], or 'as Christians' [Mou (p. 57); NEB].

Probably this means that their deaths did not take place apart from Jesus [NCBC].
2. This is connected with the following phrase [Bul (p. 91), EGT, HNTC, Lns, My; RSV]: God will bring them through Jesus. διά 'through' indicates means [EGT, HNTC, Lns, My]: Jesus is the agent by which God brings about the resurrection and the gathering of the deceased believers.

QUESTION—What is meant by God bringing them with Jesus?
1. God will bring the deceased believers from heaven to where the living believers are when Jesus returns [Hb, Hn, HNTC, NCBC, NIC]. Jesus will come the second time in company with the souls of those believers who have been with him in heaven, then they will be reunited with their resurrected bodies, in which they go to meet him in the air [Hn]. That God 'brings' them does not mean that God comes with the dead, but that he will cause them to accompany Jesus [Hn, NCBC].
2. God will bring the deceased believers to the living believers by resurrecting them at Jesus' coming and together with Jesus they will come to them [Alf, Ea, WBC]. This does not refer to their souls coming from heaven [Alf, Ea].
3. God will bring or take the resurrected believers to himself in heaven with Jesus [EBC, ICC, TH]. The believers will accompany Jesus when he returns to heaven to hand over the kingdom to his Father [ICC].

4:15 Because[a]

LEXICON—a. γάρ (LN 89.23): 'because', 'for' [Hn, HNTC, ICC, Lns, WBC; KJV, NASB, NEB, RSV], not explicit [NAB, NIV, NJB, TEV, TNT].

QUESTION—What relationship is indicated by this conjunction?
1. This indicates the grounds for the preceding statement [Alf, EBC, El, Hb, ICC, My, NCBC]: it is true that you need not grieve about those that sleep in death, etc., *since* Jesus' word is that the living will not precede those who sleep. This also elaborates on the previous verse [El, ICC, NCBC].
2. This explains and expands on the previous statement [Ea, Er, Hn, HNTC, Lns, TH].

this we-say[a] to-you by[b] a-word[c] of-(the) Lord,

LEXICON—a. pres. act. indic. of λέγω (LN 33.69): 'to say' [Hn, HNTC, LN; KJV, NAB, NASB], 'to tell' [ICC, LN, Lns, WBC; NEB, NIV, NJB, TNT], 'to declare' [RSV], 'to teach' [TEV].
b. ἐν (LN 89.76): 'by' [Hn, WBC; KJV, NASB, RSV], 'in' [HNTC, ICC], 'according to' [NIV], 'in connection with' [Lns], 'as if (the Lord had said it)' [NAB], 'as' [NEB], 'from' [Mou (p. 79); NJB]. This is also translated as a phrase: '(what we teach) is' [TEV], 'something which (the Lord said)' [TNT], 'as a message from the Lord' [Mou (p. 79)].
c. λόγος (LN 33.98): 'word' [Hn, HNTC, ICC, LN, Lns, WBC; KJV, NASB, NEB, NIV, RSV], 'teaching' [NJB, TEV], 'message' [LN]. This noun is also translated as a verb: 'to say' [NAB, TNT].

1 THESSALONIANS 4:15

QUESTION—To what does τοῦτο 'this' refer?

It refers to what follows [Alf, Ea, Hb, ICC, Lns, My, NCBC, TH, WBC, Wd; TNT]: this we say: that we who are alive, etc. There are various views as to the extent of what the Lord's word was. It is either the whole passage 4:15b–17 [TH], or 4:15b is Paul's summary of the Lord's word, which he then reports in essence in 4:16–17 [HNTC, NCBC, Wd]. The original saying would have been in third person forms rather than in the first person plural that Paul gives [HNTC].

QUESTION—When and how was the word received by Paul?

This word may have been contained in written reports which were credited by tradition to the teachings of Jesus and were apart from the four Gospels [Hn, ICC, NCBC, NIC, WBC], or it is a summary of all of the Lord's teaching on the subject [Lns], or it was a prophetic message by someone who spoke for the Lord [EBC, HNTC, WBC], or it was a prophetic message given directly to Paul by the Lord [Alf, Bul (p. 457), Ea, EBC, EGT, El, Er, Fn, Hb, Hn, My].

that we, the (ones) living, the (ones) remaining[a] until[b] the coming[c] of-the Lord,

LEXICON—a. pres. pass. participle of περιλείπομαι (LN **85.66**): 'to remain' [BAGD, Lns; KJV, NASB], 'to survive' [HNTC, ICC, WBC; NAB], 'to be left' [BAGD, Hn; NIV, RSV], 'to be left behind' [BAGD, LN]. This is also combined with the preceding verb: 'to be still alive' [LN; NJB], 'to be left alive' [NEB, TNT], 'to be alive' [TEV].

b. εἰς (LN 67.119): 'until' [Hn, ICC; NAB, NASB, NEB, NIV, RSV], 'unto' [KJV], 'for' [Lns; NJB], 'to' [HNTC, WBC], 'when' [TNT], 'on (the day)' [TEV].

c. παρουσία (LN 15.86): 'the coming' [BAGD, Hn, ICC, LN; KJV, NAB, NASB, NIV, NJB, RSV], 'parousia' [HNTC, Lns], 'advent' [BAGD, WBC]. This noun is also translated as a verb: 'to come' [NEB, TEV, TNT]. See this word at 2:19.

QUESTION—To whom does ἡμεῖς 'we' refer?

Paul includes himself and the readers since they are all presently living [Alf, Ea, EBC, El, Fn, Hb, NCBC, Rb, TH]. People are divided into two classes, those who are alive and those who have died at the time of the Lord's coming [Ea, El, Hb, NIC]. Some commentators emphasize that this does not indicate that Paul knows that he will be alive when the Lord comes [Ea, EBC, El, Fn, Hb, HNTC, Lns, NCBC, NIC, Rb, TH], but the possibility is that he might be [Ea, EBC, Hb, HNTC, Lns, NCBC]. The present tense of the two participles can be considered to be timeless, indicating the time of the future verbs [Hb]: the ones who are living and remaining when the Lord comes. However, the meaning could be that those who were living at the time of the writing would be alive when the Lord comes [El]. In line with this, some hold that Paul wrote as though he thought that he would be alive when the Lord came [Alf, ICC, My, WBC].

not[a] **shall-precede/have-advantage-over**[b] **the (ones) having-slept.**

LEXICON—a. οὐ μή (LN 69.5): 'not not'. This emphatic double negative is translated 'in no way' [Lns; NAB], 'certainly not' [HNTC; NIV, TNT], 'not' [KJV, NASB, NEB, NJB, RSV, TEV], 'no' [Hn, WBC], 'by no means' [ICC, LN].

    b. aorist act. subj. of φθάνω (LN **15.141**): 'to precede' [BAGD; NASB, NIV, RSV], 'to go ahead' [TEV], 'to go before' [LN], 'to be ahead of' [Lns], 'to prevent' [KJV], 'to forestall' [NEB], 'to anticipate' [ICC]; or 'to have an advantage over' [Hn, HNTC; NAB, NJB], 'to take precedence over' [TNT], 'to have precedence over' [WBC].

QUESTION—What area of meaning is intended by φθάνω 'to precede/to have advantage over'?

    1. This refers to temporal order [Alf, El, ICC, Lns, Rb, TH; NASB, NIV, RSV, TEV]: we who are alive will not go to meet the Lord before those who have died.

    2. This refers to having an advantage over the others [Ea, Hb, Hn, HNTC, Mn, NCBC, NIC, WBC; NAB, NJB, TNT]: we who are alive will not have an advantage over those who have died. Specifically, the advantage is being present at the Lord's coming [WBC], having a resurrection body [Hn], going to meet the Lord [Ea, Hb], and participating in the glory of it [Ea, Hb, WBC].

4:16 because/that[a] **the Lord himself,**

LEXICON—a. ὅτι (LN 89.33; 90.21): 'because' [HNTC, ICC, WBC; NEB], 'for' [Hn; KJV, NASB, NIV, RSV, TNT]; or 'that' [Lns]; not explicit [NAB, NJB, TEV].

QUESTION—What relationship is indicated by ὅτι 'because/that'?

    1. This indicates the grounds for the preceding statement by explaining more fully [Alf, Ea, EBC, El, Fn, Hb, Hn, HNTC, ICC, Mn, My, NCBC, WBC; KJV, NASB, NEB, NIV, RSV, TNT]: it is true that the living shall not precede the dead, *since* what will happen is that the dead shall rise first, etc.

    2. This is a second thing that the Thessalonians are told [Lns]: we say to you by the word of the Lord *that* we who are alive shall not precede those who have fallen asleep, and *that* the Lord will descend from heaven, etc.

QUESTION—What is the significance of the intensifier αὐτός 'himself'?

This emphasizes that this is not done through angelic representatives [Ea, EBC, Hb, NIC, WBC], and that the Lord Jesus will personally come in his glorified body [Hb].

with[a] **a shouted-command,**[b] **with a-voice**[c] **of-an-archangel**[d] **and with a-trumpet**[e] **of-God,**

LEXICON—a. ἐν (LN 89.80): 'with' [Hn, WBC; KJV, NASB, NIV, RSV], 'at' [ICC, Mou (p. 78); NAB, NEB, NJB], 'accompanied by' [HNTC], 'in connection with' [Lns], 'there will be' [TEV, TNT].

b. κέλευσμα (LN **33.324**): 'shouted command' [Hn], 'shout of command' [WBC; TEV], 'word of command' [LN; NAB, NEB, TNT], 'a cry of command' [BAGD; RSV], 'a loud command' [NIV], 'a shout' [KJV, NASB], 'a command' [HNTC, ICC, Lns], 'a signal' [NJB], 'a signal shout' [Alf, Ea].
   c. φωνή (LN 33.103; 33.80): 'voice' [BAGD, Hn, ICC, LN, Lns, WBC; KJV, NASB, NIV, NJB, TEV, TNT], 'sound of the voice' [NAB, NEB], 'call' [BAGD; RSV], 'cry' [BAGD, HNTC].
   d. ἀρχάγγελος (LN **12.31**): 'archangel' [BAGD, Hn, HNTC, ICC, LN, Lns, WBC; all versions].
   e. σάλπιγξ (LN 6.93): 'trumpet' [Hn, HNTC, ICC, Lns, WBC; NASB], 'trump' [KJV], 'trumpet call' [BAGD; NEB, NIV, TNT], 'sound of a trumpet' LN; [NAB, RSV, TEV], 'trumpet blast' [LN], 'signal given by a trumpet' [NJB].

QUESTION—How are these three phrases related?

These phrases each begin with the preposition ἐν 'with', which indicates the circumstances accompanying the Lord's descent [Alf, Ea, Fn, Hb, HNTC, ICC, Mn, Mou (p. 78)]. The circumstances may be taken as the time at which the Lord descends [ICC] or as simultaneous events with his descent [NCBC].
1. There are three events in which sounds are made. The Lord shouts a command, the archangel shouts a command, and the trumpet is blown [EBC, NIC, TH]. This is further explained: the Lord will give a shout of command for the dead to awaken, the archangel will add his voice to that call, and then a trumpet will be sounded to stress the glory of that day [NIC].
2. There are two events in which sounds are made. The Lord shouts a command and the archangel makes a sound by means of blowing a trumpet [Hn, Lns]. This is further explained: the Lord shouts a command to the dead to arise and the archangel adds to the summons by blowing the trumpet [Hn].
3. There are two events in which sounds are made. A command is given and this command is explained as being given by the voice of the archangel, and also by the trumpet call [Alf, El, HNTC, ICC, Mn, My; NJB]: with a command, that is, the voice of the archangel and the sound of a trumpet. This is further explained: the Lord or God is the source of the command for the dead to arise, but the command is given through the call of the archangel, and also through the sounding of the trumpet [HNTC, Mn]. The one who blows the trumpet may be the archangel who both uses his voice and blows the instrument [My]. Another view is that the command is given by the archangel to the angels under him and a trumpet is blown [El].
4. There is one event and one sound. The command of the Lord is explained as being accomplished by his agent, the archangel, calling out, and the call is further explained as being a trumpet blast [Fn]: the Lord will command

the dead to arise by having an archangel call them forth by sounding a trumpet.

QUESTION—How are the two nouns related in the genitive construction σάλπιγγι θεοῦ 'a trumpet of God'?

This is described as a trumpet which belongs to God [Alf, Ea, Hb, Hn, TH], a trumpet used in the service of God [Alf, Ea, El, Hb], or a trumpet used to proclaim God's signal [Hn].

will-descend[a] from heaven, and the dead in[b] Christ will-rise[c] first,[d]

LEXICON—a. fut. mid. (deponent = active) indic. of καταβαίνω (LN 15.107): 'to descend' [Hn, HNTC, LN, Lns, WBC; KJV, NASB, NEB, RSV, TNT], 'to come down' [BAGD, ICC, LN; NAB, NIV, NJB, TEV].

b. ἐν (LN 89.119): 'in' [Hn, HNTC, ICC, Lns, WBC; KJV, NAB, NASB, NIV, NJB, RSV]. This is also translated as a phrase: 'to believe in' [TEV], and it is also conflated with the noun 'Christ': 'Christian' [NEB, TNT].

c. fut. mid. indic. of ἀνίστημι (LN 23.94): 'to rise' [BAGD, Hn, HNTC, WBC; all versions except TEV], 'to arise' [ICC, Lns], 'to rise to life' [LN; TEV].

d. πρῶτος (LN 60.46): 'first' [BAGD, Hn, HNTC, LN, Lns, WBC; all versions], 'first of all' [ICC].

QUESTION—What relationship is indicated by καί 'and'?

This indicates the result of the descent of the Lord and the accompanying commands [Ea, EBC, El, ICC, Lns, My]: and, as a result, the dead will rise. Or it indicates the two events that will follow the sound [Hb].

QUESTION—What relationship is indicated by ἐν 'in'?

1. This refers to the relationship the dead have with Christ after death [Ea, Fn, Hb, Hn, ICC, Mn, NCBC, TH, WBC]: the people who had died and were now in union with Christ. Those who were in this relationship with Christ before death, remain in the same relationship after death [Ea, Hb, Hn, ICC, WBC].

2. This refers to the relationship the dead had before and when they died [HNTC; probably NAB, NJB]: the people who had been in union with Christ at the time of their death.

QUESTION—In what respect do the dead rise?

This refers to their bodies which rise from the grave [Ea, Hb, Lns].

QUESTION—What does πρῶτον 'first' signify?

This is the first result of the Lord's coming [Ea, My, WBC]. It is first in relation to the following temporal event introduced by ἔπειτα 'then', which is concerned with those still living [Alf, Ea, El, Fn, Hb, Lns, My, NCBC, NIC, TH, WBC]. It does not have any reference to a second resurrection consisting of the unsaved [Alf, Ea, El, Fn, Hb, Lns, My, NIC, WBC].

4:17 Then[a] we, the (ones) living, the (ones) remaining, at-the-same-time/place[b] with them we-shall-be-caught-up[c] in/by-means-of[d] clouds

LEXICON—a. ἔπειτα (LN 67.44): 'then' [BAGD, Hn, HNTC, ICC, LN, Lns, WBC; all versions except NIV, NJB], 'after that' [NIV, NJB], 'afterwards' [LN].
  b. ἅμα (LN 67.34; 89.114): 'at the same time' [LN], 'at the same place'. This is translated with σύν 'with' as follows: 'at the same time with' [ICC], 'simultaneously with' [HNTC], 'together with' [BAGD, Hn, LN, Lns, WBC; KJV, NASB, NIV, NJB, RSV, TNT], 'at that time along with' [TEV], 'with' [NAB]. This is also translated as a verbal phrase: 'we shall join them' [NEB].
  c. fut. pass. indic. of ἁρπάζω (LN 18.4): 'to be caught up' [Hn; KJV, NAB, NASB, NEB, NIV, RSV, TNT], 'to be caught away' [WBC], 'to be caught and carried' [ICC], 'to be taken up' [NJB], 'to be taken away' [LN], 'to be gathered up' [TEV], 'to be snatched up' [HNTC], 'to be snatched' [BAGD, Lns], 'to be snatched away' [LN].
  d. ἐν (LN 83.13; 89.76): 'in' [Hn, HNTC, Lns, WBC; all versions], 'by means of' [ICC].

QUESTION—What is meant by ἅμα 'simultaneously/together'?

As an adverb, it indicates the time the survivors are caught up [Ea, El, HNTC, ICC, Rb, Wd]: we shall be caught up at the same time the resurrected believers are caught up. It may also be considered to be closely connected with the preposition σύν 'with' and be taken in a local sense rather than temporal [Fn, Mn, TH, WBC]: we will be caught up in company with, or together with, the resurrected believers. Since all are caught up together as one group, they are caught up at the same time, so either interpretation implies the other.

QUESTION—What is implied by the verb ἁρπαγησόμεθα 'we shall be caught up'?

The passive voice implies that the actor is God [Hb, HNTC, Mn, TH]: God will catch us up. The verb contains the ideas of suddenness [Ea, Fn, Hb, Hn, HNTC, Mn, NIC, Wd], swiftness [Hn, HNTC, My], and being accomplished by great power [Ea, Fn, Hb, Hn, HNTC, Mn, My, NIC, Wd]. This verb also occurs at 2 Cor. 12:2, 4; Acts 8:39; and Rev. 12:5.

QUESTION—What relationship is indicated by the preposition ἐν 'in'?

1. This means that they will be in the midst of clouds, [EBC, Hb, My, TH, Wd]: we will be caught up and taken to a meeting place amidst the clouds where we will meet the Lord. Perhaps this only indicates that the meeting place 'in the air' is where the clouds are located [TH].
2. They will be carried by means of the clouds to meet the Lord [HNTC, ICC, Lns, Mn, NCBC]: we will be caught up and brought on clouds to meet the Lord.
3. This includes both of the above meanings [Ea, El, Fn, WBC]: we will be caught up to be in the midst of clouds which will take us to meet the Lord.

for/to a-meeting^a of-the Lord in air.^b

LEXICON—a. ἀπάντησις (LN **15.78**): 'meeting' [HNTC, Lns]. This noun is also translated as a verb: 'to meet' [BAGD, Hn, ICC, LN, WBC; all versions].

b. ἀήρ (LN 1.6): 'air' [BAGD, Hn, HNTC, ICC, LN, Lns, WBC; all versions].

QUESTION—What is the significance of the noun ἀπάντησιν 'meeting'?

This is used in Greek literature as a technical term to describe how the citizens of a city go out to meet and welcome a visiting dignitary and escort him back to the city [EBC, EGT, Hb, Hn, HNTC, NCBC, NIC, TH, WBC]. This can also refer to any type of important meeting [EBC, HNTC, NIC, TH]. This account does not say where the Lord goes after this meeting. Some take this to mean that the Lord comes as far as the atmosphere, waits to be met by all those who believe, and then continues on with them to the earth to judge it [Alf, EGT, El, Lns, NCBC]. Some take it to mean that the Lord comes as far as the atmosphere, where he is met by all those who believe, and then returns to heaven with them [EBC, ICC, Mn]. Others caution that it is not explicit whether the Lord continues on to earth (post tribulational rapture) or goes back to heaven for a time (pretribulational and mid-tribulational raptures) [Ea, Fn, Hb, Hn, HNTC, My, Rb, WBC].

and so^a always we-shall-be with (the) Lord.

LEXICON—a. οὕτως (LN 61.9): 'so, thus' [LN], 'in this way' [LN]. The phrase καὶ οὕτως 'and so' is translated 'and so' [Hn, HNTC, ICC; KJV, NIV, RSV, TEV], 'and thus' [Lns; NASB], 'thus' [WBC; NEB], 'this is the way' [NJB], 'this is how' [TNT], 'thenceforth' [NAB].

QUESTION—What relationship is indicated by οὕτως 'so'?

This indicates the result of the preceding meeting [Ea, El, Hb, ICC, Rb, WBC, Wd]: by means of, or because of, the preceding catching up of believers to meet the Lord, *the result is that* we will be with the Lord forever.

4:18 Therefore^a

LEXICON—a. ὥστε (LN 89.52): 'therefore' [Hn; NASB, NIV, RSV], 'wherefore' [Lns; KJV], 'so then' [HNTC, ICC; TEV], 'so' [WBC], 'then' [NEB, NJB, TNT], not explicit [NAB].

QUESTION—What relationship is indicated by this conjunction?

This indicates an exhortation based on the preceding account about the fate of believers who have died [Ea, EBC, El, Fn, Hb, Lns, My, NCBC, NIC]: because of the preceding teaching, *therefore* you must comfort/encourage one another.

comfort/encourage^a one-another with^b these words.^c

LEXICON—a. pres. act. impera. of παρακαλέω (LN 25.150): 'to comfort' [BAGD, Lns, WBC; KJV, NASB, RSV, TNT], 'to console' [LN; NAB, NEB]; or 'to encourage' [BAGD, Hn, HNTC, ICC, LN; NIV, NJB, TEV].

The present tense of the imperative means that this is a continuing duty [Fn, Hb].
b. ἐν (LN 89.76): 'with' [Hn, HNTC, ICC, Lns, WBC; all versions].
c. λόγος (LN 33.98): 'words' [Hn, ICC, LN, Lns, WBC; all versions except NAB, NJB], 'message' [LN; NAB], 'thoughts' [NJB], 'arguments' [HNTC].

QUESTION—What relationship is indicated by ἐν 'with'?
This indicates the means by which one is to comfort another [Ea, El, Fn, Mn, WBC]: comfort each other *by means of* telling these words.

DISCOURSE UNIT 5:1–22 [NJB]. The topic is watching for the Lord's coming.

DISCOURSE UNIT: 5:1–11 [Alf, EBC, EGT, Fn, Hb, Hn, HNTC, ICC, Mn, TH, WBC; NAB, TEV]. The topic is the times and seasons [EGT, HNTC, ICC, WBC], the coming of the day of the Lord [EBC, Fn], an exhortation to be prepared for the Lord's coming [Alf, Hb, Mn; NAB, TEV].

DISCOURSE UNIT: 5:1–3 [Alf, My, NIC, Wd]. The topic is the time when the Lord comes [NIC], the unexpectedness of the day [Alf, My, Wd].

DISCOURSE UNIT: 5:1–2 [EBC, Hb]. The topic is the coming of the day [EBC], the uncertainty of the time it comes [Hb].

5:1 Now/But[a]

LEXICON—a. δέ (LN 89.94; 89.124): 'now' [Hn, HNTC, ICC, Lns; NASB, NIV]; or 'but' [WBC; KJV, RSV]; not explicit [NAB, NEB, NJB, TEV, TNT].

QUESTION—What relationship is indicated by this conjunction?
1. This indicates a transition to a new topic [Ea, EBC, Hb, Hn, HNTC, ICC, Lns, NCBC, TH; NASB, NIV]: now. The vocative ἀδελφοί 'brothers', also marks the transition [EBC, HNTC, Lns, NCBC, TH]. Several commentators think that this topic is in answer to a question asked by the Thessalonians and communicated to Paul by letter or by Timothy's report of his visit [EBC, Hn, HNTC, ICC]. Others consider this view to be unlikely [Ea, Lns], since Timothy had just been there [Lns].
2. This indicates a contrast [WBC; KJV, RSV]: but. The contrast may be: you needed to be instructed about what happens when the Lord comes, but you already know about the unexpected-ness of his coming [TH, WBC], or the Lord's coming is certain, but the time is uncertain [Hb].

concerning[a] the times[b] and the seasons,[c] brothers,

LEXICON—a. περί (LN 89.6): 'concerning' [Hn, Lns], 'as regards' [NAB], 'with regard to' [WBC], 'as to' [ICC; NASB, RSV, TNT], 'about' [NEB, NIV, NJB, TEV], 'on the subject of' [HNTC], 'of' [KJV].
b. χρόνος (LN 67.1; 67.78): 'times' [ICC, LN, Lns, WBC; KJV, NASB, NIV, NJB, RSV, TEV, TNT], 'specific times' [NAB], 'occasions' [LN],

'dates' [HNTC; NEB], 'duration periods' [Hn], 'periods of time' [LN], 'eras' [Hb].

c. καιρός (LN 67.1; 67.145): 'seasons' [ICC, Lns, WBC; KJV, RSV, TNT], 'appropriate seasons' [Hn], 'epochs' [NASB], 'specific moments' [NAB], 'times' [HNTC, LN; NEB], 'dates' [NIV, NJB], 'occasions' [LN; TEV], 'crises' [Hb], 'ages' [LN], 'eras' [LN].

QUESTION—What do τῶν χρόνων 'the times' and τῶν καιρῶν 'the seasons' relate to and how do the terms differ?

1. This is an idiom for referring to the time when the day of the Lord will come [HNTC, ICC, NCBC, TH]: you do not need anyone to inform you about the time when the Lord will come. This phrase is a traditional doublet or technical term [HNTC, ICC, NCBC, TH, WBC]. The plural forms may not be significant [HNTC, ICC].

2. This means the occurrence of the times and the events that would enable one to predict when the day of the Lord will come [Ea, EBC, EGT, El, Hb, Lns, NIC]. It is implied from the reason clause in 5:2 that the forecast of the time of the coming of the day of the Lord is in focus: you do not need anyone to inform you about the periods of times and the events that will take place in order for you to know when the day of the Lord will come. Some consider the phrase to be a technical term for the signs signaling the approach of the day of the Lord and the events accompanying that day [WBC]. Others make a distinction between the two terms [Alf, Ea, EBC, El, Fn, Hn, Lns, Mn, My, NIC, Rb, Wd]. 'Time' refers to the matter of duration, the temporal passage of time [Ea, EBC, El, Fn, Hb, Hn, Lns, Mn, My, NIC, Rb, Wd]. 'Season' refers to the character and quality of the time [Alf, Ea, EBC, Hb, Mn, NIC], to the kinds of events which distinguish various periods of time [Fn, Hb, Lns, NIC], or it refers to a definite period of time [Ea, Rb], or it means the proper, opportune time [EGT, El, Hb, Hn, My, Wd]. The plurals in this phrase refer to the different eras that must occur before that day and the events that will distinguish those eras [Ea, Hb, Lns, Mn].

you-have no need[a] to-be written[b] to-you

LEXICON—a. χρεία (LN 71.23): 'need' [Hn, HNTC, ICC, LN, Lns, WBC; KJV, NASB, NJB, RSV, TEV, TNT]. The phrase 'you have no need' is translated 'we do not need (to write)' [NAB, NEB, NIV]. See this word at 1:8 and 4:9.

b. pres. pass. infin. of γράφω (LN 33.61): 'to be written' [Hn, HNTC, ICC, LN, Lns, WBC; NASB, RSV]. This passive infinitive is also translated as an active verb: 'to write' [KJV, NAB, NEB, NIV, NJB, TEV, TNT].

QUESTION—Why does Paul write this paragraph if there was no need?

He wants to remind them about what they had been taught [Fn, Hn, NCBC, NIC] and they need to relate the teaching to their present circumstances [NIC]. They need encouragement rather than instruction in this matter [ICC].

5:2 because[a] you-yourselves well[b] know

LEXICON—a. γάρ (LN 89.23): 'because', 'for' [Hn, HNTC, ICC, Lns; all versions except NAB, TNT], not explicit [WBC; NAB, TNT].

b. ἀκριβῶς (LN 72.19): 'well' [NJB, RSV], 'very well' [Hn; NAB, NIV, TEV], 'full well' [NASB], 'perfectly well' [WBC; NEB, TNT], 'perfectly' [KJV], 'accurately' [HNTC, ICC, LN, Lns].

QUESTION—What relationship is indicated by γάρ 'because'?

This indicates the reason for the preceding clause [Alf, Ea, El, Fn, Hb, ICC, My, WBC]: you have no need to have anyone write to you about the times and seasons *because* you know that the day of the Lord will come unexpectedly. This could also be taken as the grounds for making his statement: I say that you have no need to have anyone write to you, *since* you already know about it. This view seems to take the reference to τῶν χρόνων καὶ τῶν καιρῶν 'the times and seasons' to mean the specific time when that day comes [HNTC, ICC, NCBC]: you have no need to have anyone write to you about the subject of when the day of the Lord will come because you already know all there is to know about the subject from previous teaching, specifically that the date cannot be known. Some who take 'times and seasons' to refer to the times and events which lead up to and include the day of the Lord explain this by saying that they did not need to have anything written to them about the times and seasons because they had already been taught all of this.

QUESTION—What is meant by ἀκριβῶς 'well'?

Some focus on the degree of knowledge [My, NIC]: you know very well. They do not need additional knowledge. Others focus on the quality of their knowledge [Ea, El, Fn, HNTC, ICC, Lns, Mn, NCBC, Rb]: you know very accurately. They do not need to have their knowledge corrected. Either degree or quality implies the other and some explain the word in terms of both [EBC, Hb, Hn, WBC]. Several mention a touch of irony here: you know full well that nothing can be known about when this day will come [NIC], or you know precisely that nothing precise can be known about when the day comes [Fn, HNTC]. This is also called a paradox [Hb].

that (the) day[a] of-(the)-Lord so[b] comes[c] as[d] a-thief[e] in[f] (the) night.

LEXICON—a. ἡμέρα (LN 67.178): 'day' [BAGD, Hn, HNTC, ICC, LN, Lns, WBC; all versions].

b. οὕτως (LN 61.9): 'so' [BAGD, ICC, LN, Lns; KJV], not explicit [Hn, HNTC, WBC; all versions except KJV]. The combination 'so...as' stresses the similarity between the two things being compared [El, Hb, Lns, My].

c. pres. mid. (deponent = active) indic. of ἔρχομαι (LN 15.81): 'to come' [BAGD, Hn, HNTC, ICC, LN, Lns, WBC; all versions]. The present tense is prophetic or futuristic [Rb], it is used to emphasize the prophetic certainty of the future event [Alf, Ea, El, Hb, My, NIC, Rb], or it is gnomic and general [Hn, ICC], or it is the tense used in doctrinal

140   1 THESSALONIANS 5:2

statements to indicate abiding truth [Hb, Lns]. It is also translated in the future tense: 'it will come' [NASB, NIV, RSV, TEV, TNT].

d. ὡς (LN **64.12**): 'as' [BAGD, HNTC, ICC, Lns; KJV, TEV, TNT], 'like' [BAGD, Hn, LN, WBC; NAB, NEB, NIV, NJB, RSV], 'just like' [NASB].
e. κλέπτης (LN 57.233): 'thief' [BAGD, Hn, HNTC, ICC, LN, Lns, WBC; all versions].
f. ἐν (LN 67.136): 'in' [Hn, HNTC; all versions except TEV], 'at' [ICC, Lns; TEV], 'by' [WBC].

QUESTION—To whom does 'Lord' refer?
   This refers to Jesus Christ [Ea, Hb, HNTC, ICC, NCBC, TH, WBC].
QUESTION: How are the two nouns related in the genitive construction ἡμέρα κυρίου 'the day of the Lord'?
   This means the time when the Lord comes to judge the world [EBC, El, Hb, NCBC, NIC, WBC], to save his people [EBC, NCBC, WBC], and to set up his kingdom [Hb].
QUESTION—Does ἡμέρα 'day' refer to an event or to a period of time?
   1. It refers to the event of Christ's coming [Alf, Ea, Er, Hn, ICC, Lns, TH, WBC, Wd].
   2. It refers to a period of time beginning with Christ's coming [Ea, EBC, Fn, Hb, HNTC, Mn, My, NCBC, NIC].
QUESTION—What is the point of comparison between the coming of the day of the Lord and the coming of a thief at night?
   The point of comparison is the suddenness of the event [Alf, Ea, El, Hb, Hn, HNTC, ICC, My, Rb, Wd] and its unexpectedness [Ea, EBC, Fn, Hb, Hn, HNTC, ICC, Lns, My, NCBC, NIC, Rb, TH, WBC]. Other points of comparison are mentioned as applying only to unbelievers: unpreparedness of the ones who suffer [Hn, ICC, Lns], the unwelcome and dreadful result of the event [Alf, Fn, NCBC].

DISCOURSE UNIT: 5:3 [EBC, Hb]. The topic is the result of being unprepared [Hb], the unbelievers and the day of the Lord [EBC].

5:3 When[a] **they-say peace**[b] **and security,**[c]

TEXT—Some manuscripts add γάρ 'because'. GNT does not mention this possibility. Only KJV includes it.
LEXICON—a. ὅταν (LN 67.30): 'when' [BAGD, Hn, ICC, LN, Lns, WBC; KJV, NJB, RSV, TEV], 'just when' [NAB, TNT], 'while' [NASB, NEB, NIV], 'at a time when' [HNTC].
   b. εἰρήνη (LN 22.42; 25.248): 'peace' [BAGD, Hn, HNTC, LN, Lns, WBC; KJV, NAB, NASB, NEB, NIV, RSV], 'tranquility' [LN], 'freedom from worry' [LN]. This is also translated as an adjective: '(to be) quiet' [NJB, TEV], '(to be) peaceful' [TNT], '(to be) well' [ICC].
   c. ἀσφάλεια (LN **21.9**): 'security' [BAGD, HNTC, LN, WBC; NAB, NEB, RSV], 'safety' [BAGD, Hn, Lns; KJV, NASB, NIV]. This is also

1 THESSALONIANS 5:3   141

translated as an adjective: '(to be) safe' [ICC; TEV], '(to be) peaceful' [NJB], '(to be) secure' [TNT].

QUESTION—How is this clause related to the preceding one?

This explains in more detail the reference to the day of the Lord coming like a thief in the night [Alf, Fn, ICC, My, NCBC]. It is an illustration of the unexpectedness of the day of the Lord [NIC].

QUESTION—Who says this?

This refers to people in general [Alf, HNTC, ICC, Lns, NCBC, TH; NAB, NIV, NJB, RSV, TEV, TNT]. With the contrast with ὑμεῖς ἀδελφοί 'you, brothers' in the next verse, most consider this to be a reference to unbelievers at the time of the coming of the day [Alf, Ea, EBC, El, Fn, Hb, Hn, ICC, Lns, Mn, My, NCBC, NIC, TH]: when unbelievers are saying peace and security.

QUESTION—What is the difference between εἰρήνη 'peace' and ἀσθάλεια 'security'?

1. There is no significant difference between the words [HNTC, ICC, TH].
2. There is a difference intended [Ea, EBC, El, Hb, NIC]. Peace refers to inward peace of mind, while safety refers to the absence of outward events or circumstances that would threaten to disturb their way of life [Ea, EBC, El]. Or, peace refers to outward circumstances which do not present a threat to the person [Hb, NIC] and safety refers to the feeling of being secure from enemies or danger [El, Hb].

QUESTION—To what circumstance do the terms refer?

1. This refers to their sense of security from adverse world conditions or conditions of their environment [probably many of those who do not state the second interpretation].
2. This refers to their sense of security from God's intervention in their lives [Hb, Lns], by bringing an end to the universe [NIC].

then[a] sudden[b] destruction[c] comes-on[d] them,

LEXICON—a. τότε (LN 67.47): 'then' [BAGD, Hn, HNTC, ICC, LN, Lns, WBC; KJV, NASB, RSV, TEV], not explicit [NAB, NEB, NIV, NJB, TNT].

b. αἰφνίδιος (LN 67.113): 'sudden' [BAGD, Hn, HNTC, ICC, LN, Lns, WBC; KJV, NJB, RSV]. This adjective is also translated as an adverb: '(come) suddenly' [NASB, NIV, TEV, TNT], 'all at once' [NEB]. This is also translated as a noun which makes explicit the point of comparison: '(with) the suddenness (of pains)' [NAB].

c. ὄλεθρος (LN 20.34): 'destruction' [BAGD, Hn, ICC, LN, Lns, WBC; KJV, NASB, NIV, NJB, RSV, TEV], 'ruin' [BAGD; NAB], 'disaster' [HNTC; TNT], 'calamity' [NEB].

d. pres. mid. indic. of ἐφίσταμαι (LN 13.119): 'to come on/upon' [BAGD, Hn, ICC, LN, Lns, WBC; KJV, NASB, NIV, RSV], 'to be upon' [NEB, TNT], 'to fall on' [NAB, NJB], 'to hit' [TEV], 'to overtake' [HNTC].

QUESTION—In what way will they be destroyed?
It does not refer to cessation of existence [EBC, Hb, ICC, Mn, NIC, TH], but to the loss of everything that makes existence worthwhile [EBC, Hb, Mn, NIC], to separation from God and Christ [Hb, ICC, NIC], to God's judgment and punishment [TH]. This is the opposite of salvation [EBC, Hb]. While most commentators take a theological meaning of the word, one takes this as a proverb and considers 'destruction' to be an indefinite word which describes many types of calamities [HNTC].

as[a] the labor-pain[b] to the pregnant[c] woman,
LEXICON—a. ὥσπερ (LN 64.13): 'as' [BAGD, ICC, LN; KJV, NEB, NIV, NJB, RSV, TEV], 'like' [Hn, WBC; NASB, TNT], 'just as' [BAGD, HNTC, LN, Lns], not explicit [NAB].
  b. ὠδίν (LN **23.54**): 'labor pains' [NIV, NJB], 'birth pains' [BAGD, LN], 'birth pangs' [Hn, WBC; NASB, TNT], 'pangs' [NEB], 'pains in labor' [NAB, TEV], 'pain of childbirth' [HNTC], 'travail' [ICC, Lns; KJV, RSV].
  c. γαστήρ (LN 23.50): 'pregnant' [BAGD, Hn, HNTC, LN; NIV, NJB, TNT], 'with child' [ICC, Lns, WBC; KJV, NASB, NEB, RSV], not explicit [NAB, TEV].
QUESTION—What is the metaphor here?
The point of comparison is that both events are sudden (which is supported by the preceding clause) [Ea, El, Fn, Hb, ICC, Lns, Mn, TH, WBC, Wd; NAB, NEB, NJB, TEV], and unexpected [Alf, Ea, EBC, El, Hb, NCBC, TH], or inescapable (which is supported by the following clause) [Fn, Hb, Hn, HNTC, Lns, NCBC, NIC, WBC]. A few refer to the intense pain which accompanies both [Fn, HNTC, NCBC].

and they-will not escape.[a]
LEXICON—a. aorist act. subj. of ἐκφεύγω (LN 21.14): 'to escape' [BAGD, Hn, HNTC, ICC, LN, Lns, WBC; KJV, NASB, NIV, TEV, TNT]. This is also translated as a noun: '(there will be no) escape' [NAB, NEB, NJB, RSV].
QUESTION—To whom does 'they' refer?
This refers to the people upon whom the sudden destruction comes, those who say, 'Peace and safety' [Hb]. They will be the people living on earth at the time the Lord comes and they will not escape the judgment that brings about their destruction [Hb, HNTC].

DISCOURSE UNIT: 5:4–11 [EBC, Hb, My, NIC, Wd]. The topic is believers and the day of the Lord [EBC, NIC], the conduct of believers [Hb], the need for alertness [My, Wd].

5:4 But[a] you, brothers,
LEXICON—a. δέ (LN 89.124): 'but' [Hn, HNTC, ICC, Lns, WBC; all versions except NAB], not explicit [NAB].

QUESTION—What relationship is indicated by δέ 'but'?

This conjunction indicates contrast [Ea, EBC, El, Hb, Hn, HNTC, ICC, Lns, Mn, My, NCBC, NIC, TH, WBC, Wd; all versions except NAB]: the day of Lord will suddenly come on the unprepared for their destruction, but you will not be surprised by it. The contrast is emphasized by the explicit reference to ὑμεῖς 'you' [Hb, Lns, Mn, NCBC, NIC, TH], and the vocative ἀδελφοί 'brothers' [Hb, Hn, Lns, Mn].

are not in[a] darkness,[b]

LEXICON—a. ἐν (LN 13.8): 'in' [Hn, HNTC, ICC, Lns, WBC; all versions].

b. σκότος (LN 14.53; 88.125): 'darkness' [BAGD, Hn, HNTC, ICC, LN, Lns, WBC; KJV, NASB, NIV, RSV, TEV, TNT], 'the dark' [NAB, NEB, NJB], 'realm of evil' [LN].

QUESTION—What is meant by being in darkness?

They are located in the dark. It may continue the picture of the homeowner being in the darkness of night, the time when the thief comes [NCBC]. But darkness is also to be taken as the moral darkness in which unbelievers live [Ea, El, Hb, My, NCBC, NIC; NJB]. Darkness is a symbol of sin [Hb, Hn, My, NCBC, TH], evil [Hb], wickedness [EBC, ICC], moral ignorance [Alf, EBC, El, Hb, Mn, NCBC, TH], unbelief [Hb, Hn, HNTC], and separation from God [Hb, Mn, My, Wd]. This is the condition of all unbelievers [Hb, ICC].

so-that[a]

LEXICON—a. ἵνα (LN 89.49): 'so that' [Hn, Lns; NIV], 'that' [HNTC, ICC; KJV, NAB, NASB, NEB, NJB], 'for' [WBC; RSV]. This is also translated as an independent clause: 'and the day should not, etc.' [TEV, TNT].

QUESTION—What relationship is indicated by this conjunction?

This indicates the result of living in darkness [BAGD, EBC, Fn, Hb, Hn, HNTC, ICC, Lns, Mn]: you are not in darkness, the result of which would be to have that day overtake you. Some commentators consider this word to indicate God's purpose [Alf, El, My]. However, that would seem to imply that God is responsible for putting people in darkness as the means of accomplishing his purpose of having that day overtake them and no one seems to take it in that way. Rather, they explain that all results are purposed by God [Alf], or that God's plan for those who are in darkness is that the day would take them by surprise [My], or that by means of taking them out of darkness, it was God's purpose to prevent them from being overtaken by surprise on that Day [El].

the day should-overtake/seize[a] you as[b] a-thief.[c]

TEXT—Instead of the nominative singular form κλέπτης 'thief', some manuscripts have the accusative plural form κλέπτας 'thieves'. GNT accepts the singular form with an A rating, indicating virtual certainty. Only ICC and Mn take the accusative plural form.

LEXICON—a. aorist act. subj. of καταλαμβάνομαι (LN **13.119**; 37.108; 39.48; 37.19): 'to overtake' [BAGD, WBC; KJV, NASB, NEB], 'to catch off guard' [NAB], 'to surprise' [HNTC, ICC; NIV, RSV], 'to take one unawares' [NJB], 'to take one by surprise' [TEV], 'to steal on one' [TNT], 'to come upon' [BAGD, LN]; or 'to seize' [Hn], 'to catch' [Lns].
  b. ὡς (LN 64.12): 'as' [Hn, ICC, Lns; KJV], 'like' [HNTC, WBC; all versions except KJV].
  c. κλέπτης (LN 57.233): 'thief' [BAGD, Hn, HNTC, LN, Lns, WBC; all versions], 'thieves' [ICC, Mn]. See this word at 5:2.

QUESTION—What day does this refer to?
  1. This refers to the Day of the Lord (5:2) [EBC, Fn, Hb, Hn, HNTC, ICC, Lns, Mn, My, NCBC, TH, WBC; NJB, TEV, TNT]. The contrast with darkness adds to the reference the 'time' when the Lord comes, the idea that the day also includes daylight [ICC, WBC].
  2. This refers to daytime in contrast with the darkness of nighttime [Alf, Ea, El]. This, however, is practically the same as saying the day of the Lord [El].

QUESTION—What is the metaphor here in relation to the textual variants in the singular and plural forms for 'thief'?
  1. The singular form refers to much the same metaphor as in 5:2 [Alf, Ea, EBC, Fn, Hb, Hn, HNTC, Lns, NCBC, NIC, WBC; all versions].
    1.1 The verb is taken to mean 'overtake', in the sense that the person will be surprised when the day unexpectedly comes [Alf, EBC, Fn, HNTC, NCBC, NIC, Wd]: the day will surprise the unprepared person, as a thief surprises a homeowner when he comes to steal his possessions.
    1.2 The verb is taken to mean 'seize' [Ea, Hb, Hn, Lns]: the day will seize the unprepared person as a thief will seize the homeowner in order to take his possessions. What is meant by saying that the day will seize the unbelievers is that it will catch them unprepared [Hn, Lns]. Or, the idea of surprise is meant, as in the preceding interpretation [Ea, Hb]. Or, perhaps it means that it will prevent them from escaping the consequences of its coming [TH].
  2. The plural form indicates that the dawn surprises the thieves as they are engaged in their act of theft which was begun in the dark [ICC, Mn]: that day will overtake and surprise the unprepared as daylight will overtake and surprise thieves occupied in their thievery.

5:5 Because[a]

TEXT—Some manuscripts do not have this word. GNT includes it without comment. It is omitted by KJV. Probably the others who do not translate it explicitly consider the sequence of statements sufficient to indicate the meaning implicitly.

LEXICON—a. γάρ (LN 89.23): 'because', 'for' [Hn, HNTC, ICC, Lns; NASB, RSV], not explicit [WBC; KJV, NAB, NEB, NIV, NJB, TEV, TNT].

QUESTION—What relationship is indicated by this conjunction?
1. This indicates the reason they will not be surprised by the coming of the day [Ea, Hb, ICC, My]: you are not in darkness that you would be surprised by that day *because* you are sons of light and day.
2. This gives the grounds for making the previous statement [Alf, El, HNTC]: it is true that you are not in darkness that you would be surprised by that day, *since* you are sons of light and day.
3. This explains and reinforces his statement about them not being in darkness by restating that negative statement with a positive one [EBC, Mn; probably NAB, NCBC which begin the clause with 'No']: you are not in darkness, *that is,* you are sons of light and day.

all you are sons[a] of-light[b]
LEXICON—a. υἱός (LN 11.14): 'sons' [BAGD, Hn, HNTC, ICC, Lns, WBC; NASB, NIV, RSV], 'children' [KJV, NAB, NEB, NJB], 'people' [LN], '(people who) belong to' [TEV, TNT].
   b. φῶς (LN 14.36): 'light' [BAGD, Hn, HNTC, ICC, LN, Lns, WBC; all versions].
QUESTION—What is the significance of the fronted position of πάντες 'all' and ὑμεῖς 'you'?
'All' is emphatic [Hb, HNTC, ICC, Lns, NCBC, TH, Wd]. None are excepted [Lns, NCBC, NIC]. This emphasis is meant to encourage the fainthearted [ICC, Wd]. 'You' is also emphatic [Hb].
QUESTION—How are the two nouns related in the genitive construction υἱοὶ φωτός 'sons of light'?
This is a Hebrew expression in which υἱοί 'sons' means people whose lives are characterized by the word in the genitive case [Fn, Hb, HNTC, ICC, NIC, TH], or people who belong to such a sphere [Alf, El, Hb, My, NCBC; TEV, TNT]. In this verse it means that they are people whose natures are characterized and controlled by light [Hb, Lns, WBC], who live in light instead of in darkness [Hb, NCBC], who are destined for the place of heavenly light because the light is already in their hearts [Hn]. 'Light' is a symbol of righteousness [NCBC], moral purity [Fn], knowledge [Fn], salvation [Fn, NCBC], or God [WBC].

and sons of-day.[a]
LEXICON—a. ἡμέρα (LN 14.40; 67.186): 'day' [BAGD, Hn, HNTC, ICC, LN, Lns, WBC; all versions], 'daylight' [LN].
QUESTION—How are the two nouns related in the genitive construction υἱοὶ ἡμέρας 'sons of day' and how is this clause connected with the preceding one?
1. 'Day' means daytime in contrast to 'night' and does not directly refer to the day of the Lord [Ea, EBC, Fn, Hb, HNTC, ICC, Lns, My, TH; NEB, NJB, TEV, TNT]: you are people who are conducting yourselves as people do in the exposure of daylight. It pertains to the following illustration about nighttime and daytime. There seems to be little difference between light and the daytime [LN, Lns, My, TH]. If a

difference is intended, light describes their character, day is the realm in which they live [Hb, ICC], or it especially refers to the future kingdom [ICC]: you belong to God's kingdom and glory.
2. 'Day' refers to the preceding reference to the day of the Lord [Mn, NCBC, NIC]: you are people who will participate in the glorious events of that day. This day is also associated with light [NCBC].

We-are not of-night^a nor of-darkness.^b

LEXICON—a. νύξ (LN 14.59): 'night' [BAGD, Hn, HNTC, ICC, LN, Lns, WBC; all versions].

b. σκότος (LN 14.53): 'darkness' [BAGD, Hn, HNTC, ICC, LN, Lns, WBC; all versions].

QUESTION—Why is there a change from the second person ὑμεῖς 'you' to the first person 'we'?

The statements just made are the beginning of the grounds for the exhortation about to be made. The missionaries want to unite themselves with the readers in the responsibilities entailed by their position as believers, so they include themselves in the last statement of the grounds for the following exhortation [Hb, ICC, Lns]. This shows that the following exhortations are applicable to all believers [EBC, Hb, ICC, Lns, Mn, NIC]. By tactfully including themselves, the exhortation is less harsh [EBC, Hn, HNTC, ICC, NIC]. This last point is also denied [Lns].

QUESTION—What is indicated by the use of the genitive case for νυκτός 'night' and σκότους 'darkness'?

1. This genitive phrase goes with the verb ἐσμέν 'we are' and describes the people [Alf, Ea, El, Fn, Hb, Hn, HNTC, ICC, Lns, Mn, My, WBC; all versions]: we are people who do not belong to night and darkness. This does not imply the Hebrew figure 'sons of night', but it can be considered to be equivalent to such a phrase [ICC]. To be νυκτός οὐδὲ σκότους 'of the night and darkness' is a stronger statement than to be ἐν σκότει 'in darkness' (5:4) [Hb]. It means that they are not controlled by night and darkness [Lns].
2. This depends on υἱοί 'sons' in the preceding clauses [EBC]: we are not sons of night, sons of darkness.

QUESTION—What is meant by the combination of the words νυκτός 'night' and σκότους 'darkness'?

This parallels, in chiastic order (a, b, b, a), the use of the words φωτός 'light' and ἡμέρας 'day' in the preceding sentence [Hb, HNTC, ICC, NIC, TH]. If 'day' is taken to refer to daylight, probably these terms for the time of darkness will mean the opposite of what is meant by their counterparts of light and day. If there is a difference intended between the nonfigurative meanings of night and darkness, day and night refer to periods of time, light and darkness refer to the characteristics of those periods [Ea, ICC], night is the state of ignorance and separation from God while darkness is the description of an evil way of life [Fn], night is the state of separation from

God and darkness means sin [Hb], night indicates that they will not participate in the glory of the day of the Lord and darkness describes their spiritual condition [NIC].

5:6 So therefore^a

LEXICON—a. ἄρα οὖν: 'so therefore', 'so then' [ICC, WBC; NASB, NIV, RSV, TEV], 'well then' [HNTC], 'accordingly, then' [Lns]. The two words are also translated as one word: 'therefore' [KJV, NAB], 'so' [NJB, TNT] 'accordingly' [Hn], 'and' [NEB].

QUESTION—What relationship is indicated by this phrase?

This introduces an exhortation which is a logical conclusion of the preceding statement [Ea, EBC, El, Er, Fn, Hb, Hn, HNTC, ICC, Lns, Mn, My, NCBC, NIC, Rb, TH, WBC, Wd; all versions]: since you (and we) are sons of light and day and we are not of the night and darkness, *therefore* let us not sleep (which naturally goes with the night, not with the day).

let-us-not-sleep^a as^b the rest,^c

LEXICON—a. pres. act. subj. of καθεύδω (LN 23.66): 'to sleep' [BAGD, Hn, HNTC, ICC, LN, Lns, WBC; all versions except NAB, NIV], 'to be asleep' [LN; NAB, NIV].

b. ὡς (LN 64.12): 'as' [BAGD, Hn, ICC, WBC; KJV, NASB, NJB, RSV, TNT], 'like' [BAGD, HNTC, Lns; NAB, NEB, NIV, TEV].

c. λοιπός (LN 63.21): 'the rest' [Hn, HNTC, LN, Lns; NAB, NEB], 'others' [BAGD, LN, WBC; KJV, NASB, NIV, RSV, TEV], 'everyone else' [NJB, TNT], 'unbelievers' [ICC]. See this word at 4:13.

QUESTION—What is indicated by the use of the present tense?

1. The present tense indicates that they must continually avoid such sleep [Hb, Lns]: let us never sleep.
2. It indicates that they should stop doing what they have been doing [Rb; NJB]: let us stop sleeping, let us not go on sleeping.

QUESTION—What is meant by 'sleeping'?

This is connected with the illustration about sleeping during the night [ICC, Lns] and also refers to being asleep when the thief comes in the night (5:2) [HNTC, WBC]. As a metaphor, the point of the comparison would be unawareness of what goes on. Spiritual or moral sleep means indifference and insensitivity to the spiritual things which pertain to God [Ea, EBC, El, Er, Fn, Hb, Mn, NCBC, NIC, Wd], being morally lax in general [Hn, ICC], being unconcerned about the coming day of the Lord and thus unprepared for it [EBC, Er, Hn, HNTC, My, WBC].

QUESTION—Who are the rest of the people who are asleep?

They are all the rest of mankind, [WBC], those who do not believe [Ea, El, Hb, My, NIC], those of the night [Lns, NCBC].

but let-us-keep-awake^a and let-us-be-sober.^b

LEXICON—a. pres. act. subj. of γρηγορέω (LN 23.72; 27.56): 'to keep awake' [WBC; NEB, RSV], 'to stay awake' [LN], 'to stay wide awake' [NJB],

'to be awake' [NAB, TEV]. This verb is also translated as to its nonmetaphorical meaning: 'to watch' [ICC, Lns; KJV], 'to be watchful' [BAGD, Hn, LN; TNT], 'to be alert' [HNTC, LN; NASB, NIV], 'to be vigilant' [LN]. The present tense used here and for the next verb mean that these are continuous conditions [Lns].
- b. pres. act. subj. of νήφω (LN **30.25**; **88.86**): 'to be sober' [BAGD, Hn, ICC, LN, Lns, WBC; all versions except NIV], 'to be sober-minded' [LN]. This verb is also translated in its extended meaning: 'to be self-controlled' [BAGD; NIV], 'to be clear-headed' [HNTC].

QUESTION—What relationship is indicated by ἀλλά 'but'?

This indicates contrast by giving the positive statement of the preceding negative one [Ea, Hb].

QUESTION—What is meant by being 'awake'?

This is the opposite of being asleep [Hb, ICC, NIC]. It is a metaphor for being spiritually alert [Hb, Hn, ICC, NCBC, Wd], being watchful and alert against being overcome by sin [Hb, ICC], being aware of what is happening [HNTC], being occupied with serving Christ and being occupied with the thought of his return [Fn, Hn]. It means being prepared for the coming day of the Lord [Hn, NCBC].

QUESTION—What is meant by being 'sober'?

This is the opposite of being drunk in the following clause [Hb, Lns].
1. This refers specifically to avoiding drunkenness [Fn, WBC].
2. This has an extended meaning [EBC, El, Hb, Hn, HNTC, ICC, Lns, Mn, NCBC, NIC, Rb, TH, Wd]. It refers to all aspects of being self-controlled [EBC, Hb, ICC], to be earnest about spiritual things, neither fanatical nor indifferent [Hn], to be calm and sane [Hn, ICC], to be prepared to meet whatever comes [Hb], to avoid any excess that would make one insensitive to the things of God [NCBC]. It is virtually synonymous with the preceding word 'awake' [Hn].

5:7 Because[a]

LEXICON—a. γάρ (LN 89.23): 'because', 'for' [Hn, HNTC, ICC, Lns, WBC; KJV, NASB, NIV, RSV], not explicit [NAB, NEB, NJB, TEV, TNT].

QUESTION—What relationship is indicated by this conjunction?
1. This adds another grounds for the preceding exhortation [Ea, El, Fn, Hb, ICC, My, NCBC]: since we are not of the night, therefore let us not sleep, rather let us watch and be sober, since the opposite actions of sleeping and being drunk are what people belonging to the night do. The negative part of the exhortation seems to be grounded especially on the preceding clause (5:5), while the positive part of the exhortation seems to be especially grounded on this following clause.
2. This explains more fully the reference to the remaining people who are sleeping [Alf, EBC]: let us not sleep as the rest do. Those people who are sleepers sleep at night and thus are people who belong to the night.

the (ones) sleeping sleep at-night and the (ones) being-drunk are drunk at-night.

QUESTION—How exact is this statement?

Nighttime is when these events usually and characteristically take place [EBC, El, Hb, HNTC, NCBC, NIC, Rb, TH, WBC]. It is unusual to do these things in the daytime [HNTC]. 'At night' is emphatic [ICC].

5:8 but[a] we,

LEXICON—a. δέ (LN 89.124): 'but' [Hn, HNTC, ICC, Lns, WBC; all versions except NAB], not explicit [NAB].

QUESTION—What relationship is indicated by δέ 'but'?

This indicates a contrast between the actions of the believers and the people who belong to the night [Alf, Ea, Hb, Hn, HNTC, ICC, Lns, NIC, TH, WBC, Wd; all versions]: the rest, who belong to the night, sleep and are drunk, but we, who belong to the day, must be sober. 'We' is emphasized [Ea, Fn, Hb, NIC, Wd].

being[a] of-(the) day,

LEXICON—a. pres. act. participle of εἰμί (LN 58.67): 'to be' [BAGD, LN; KJV, NASB]. This whole phrase is translated 'who live by day' [NAB] 'belonging to the day/daylight' [BAGD, Hn, HNTC, ICC, Lns, WBC; NEB, NIV, NJB, RSV, TEV, TNT]. See the parallel expression 'we are not of the night' in 5:5.

QUESTION—What relationship is indicated by the participial form ὄντες 'being'?

1. This indicates the grounds for the following exhortation [Ea, EBC, El, Er, Fn, Hb, Hn, HNTC, ICC, Lns, Mn, Mou (p. 103), NCBC, NIC, TH, Wd; NASB, NIV, RSV]: *since* we are of the day, let us be sober.
2. This describes 'us' [WBC; KJV, NAB, NEB, TNT]: let us, who are of the day, be sober. This description also implies that this fact is the grounds for the following exhortation.
3. This is also translated as an independent clause [NJB, TEV]: we are of the day and we should be sober.

let-us-be-sober,

LEXICON—pres. act. subj. of νήφω (LN **88.86**; 30.25): 'to be sober' [BAGD, Hn, ICC, LN, Lns, WBC; KJV, NASB, NEB, NJB, RSV, TEV, TNT], 'to not be drunk' [LN]. This verb is also translated with its extended meaning: 'to be alert' [NAB], 'to be self-controlled' [BAGD; NIV]. Because of the following reference to the armor of a soldier, some shift the meaning to the action of a soldier on sentry duty: 'to be vigilant' [HNTC, NCBC]. The present tense indicates that this must be a continuing state [Hb, Lns, WBC, Wd; NEB]. See this word at 5:6.

1 THESSALONIANS 5:8

having-put-on[a] **a-breastplate**[b] **of-faith**[c] **and of-love**[d]

LEXICON—a. aorist mid. participle of ἐνδύω (LN 49.1): 'to put on' [BAGD, Hn, HNTC, ICC, LN, Lns, WBC; KJV, NAB, NASB, NIV, NJB, RSV, TNT], 'to wear' [TEV], 'to be armed with' [NEB].

b. θώραξ (LN **6.39**): 'breastplate' [BAGD, Hn, HNTC, ICC, LN, Lns, WBC; all versions except NEB], 'coat of mail' [NEB].

c. πίστις (LN 31.85): 'faith' [BAGD, Hn, HNTC, ICC, LN, Lns, WBC; all versions].

d. ἀγάπη (LN 25.43): 'love' [BAGD, Hn, HNTC, ICC, LN, Lns, WBC; all versions].

QUESTION—What relationship is indicated by the aorist participial form ἐνδυσάμενοι 'having put on'?

1. Some commentators speak of this participle as being one of identical action [HNTC, ICC]. Perhaps it is meant that this is the specific intention of a generic statement: be sober, that is, put on the armor. Yet, some explanations are not that definite, and the comments seem to suggest that this can be considered to be coordinate action [EBC, El, HNTC, Mn, NCBC]: let us be sober and let us put on armor.
2. This indicates the means by which they can become and remain sober [Ea, Fn, Mn]: let us be sober *by* putting on the armor.
3. This indicates a temporal circumstance, preceding the main verb [El, Hb]: let us be sober, *after* having put on the armor.
4. This indicates the grounds for the exhortation [Wd]: let us be sober *since* we have put on the armor.

QUESTION—How are the nouns related in the genitive construction θώρακα πίστεως καὶ ἀγάπης 'a breastplate of faith and of love'?

The breastplate consists of the two qualities [Ea, El, Fn, Hb, Hn, HNTC, ICC, Lns, Mn, My, Wd]: the breastplate which represents faith and love.

QUESTION—Toward whom or what is faith directed?

Faith is directed towards Christ [Ea, Fn, Hb, HNTC, My], God [EGT, Fn, Hn, HNTC, NCBC, TH], God's promises [Hn], or the fact that one's sins are forgiven [Hn].

QUESTION—Toward whom is love directed?

Love is directed towards people [Fn, Hb, HNTC, Mn, My], other believers [EGT, Hb], God [Hn, TH], both God and people [Ea].

QUESTION—Why are the figures, breastplate and helmet, used?

They are metaphors. The point of comparison is protection. Like armor protects one from being harmed by enemy soldiers, so the qualities of faith, love, and hope protect a believer.

1. The protection is from the influence of outside spiritual enemies, specifically Satan [ICC, TH], evil influences [Ea, Hb, My], the world [Hb, Hn], or troubles and trials in their lives [EBC, El, Mn].
2. The protection is from their own fleshly nature [My], which hinders vigilant watching for the coming of the day of the Lord [HNTC], or which cause doubts [EBC] and indifference [EGT], or moral evil [Er, Hn].

3. The protection is from being surprised by being unprepared for the day of the Lord [Alf, Fn, HNTC, NIC, Wd].
4. The protection is from God's punishment which will be given in the time of judgment at the coming of the Lord [WBC].

and a-helmet[a] (which is the) hope[b] of-salvation.[c]
LEXICON—a. περικεφαλαία (LN 6.38): 'helmet' [BAGD, Hn, HNTC, ICC, LN, Lns, WBC; all versions].
  b. ἐλπίς (LN 25.59): 'hope' [BAGD, Hn, HNTC, ICC, LN, Lns, WBC; all versions].
  c. σωτηρία (LN 21.25; 21.26): 'salvation' [BAGD, Hn, HNTC, ICC, LN, Lns, WBC; all versions].
QUESTION—How are the two event nouns related in the genitive construction ἐλπίδα σωτηρίας 'hope of salvation'?
  Salvation is what they firmly hope for [Ea, El, Hb, HNTC, ICC, Lns, Mn, Rb, TH, Wd]: they hope that they will be saved. This is salvation in all the completeness that occurs at the day of the Lord [Ea, Hb, Hn, HNTC, ICC, Lns, NIC, WBC]. It is salvation from the coming wrath and judgment [Fn, Hb, ICC, Lns, WBC, Wd] and, in a positive sense, it is salvation to eternal life [Wd], and fellowship with the Lord [ICC].

5:9 Because[a]
LEXICON—a. ὅτι (LN 89.33): 'because' [HNTC, Lns, WBC], 'for' [Hn, ICC; KJV, NASB, NEB, NIV, RSV, TNT], not explicit [NAB, NJB, TEV].
QUESTION—What relationship is indicated by this conjunction?
  This indicates the grounds for saying that they should put on the helmet of hope for salvation [Alf, Ea, EBC, El, Fn, Hb, Hn, HNTC, ICC, Lns, My, NCBC, NIC, Wd]: it is reasonable to hope in our future salvation, *since* God destined us to obtain this salvation.

God did-not destine[a] us for[b] wrath,[c]
LEXICON—a. aorist mid. indic. of τίθημι (LN 37.96; **90.86**): 'to destine' [BAGD, HNTC; NAB, NASB, NEB, NJB, RSV, TNT], 'to appoint' [BAGD, Hn, ICC, LN, Lns, WBC; KJV, NIV], 'to choose' [TEV], 'to designate' [LN], 'to put (in the church)' [TH], 'to subject someone to' [LN].
  b. εἰς (LN 89.57): 'for' [Hn, HNTC, WBC; NAB, NASB, NJB, RSV], 'to' [ICC; KJV, NEB], 'unto' [Lns], 'with a view to' [Alf], 'to suffer' [NIV, TEV, TNT].
  c. ὀργή (LN 88.173; 38.10): 'wrath' [BAGD, Hn, ICC, Lns, WBC; KJV, NAB, NASB, NIV, RSV, TNT], 'anger' [BAGD, HNTC, LN; TEV], 'punishment' [LN], 'retribution' [NJB], 'the terrors of judgment' [NEB]. See this word at 1:10.
QUESTION—What is meant by God's wrath?
  God's wrath is directed towards evil and sin [Ea, Hb, NCBC, NIC]. God did not destine us to experience the outcome of his wrath [Ea, El, Lns, My,

NCBC, NIC]. This specifically refers to the judgment at the end time when he will punish sinners [Ea, EBC, Hb, HNTC, ICC, Lns, NCBC, WBC].

but for possession[a] of-salvation[b]

LEXICON—a. περιποίησις (LN **90.74; 57.62**): 'possession' [LN, Lns], 'full attainment' [NEB]. This noun is also translated as a verb: 'to possess' [TEV], 'to obtain' [BAGD, Hn, HNTC, WBC; KJV, NASB, RSV], 'to acquire' [NAB], 'to receive' [NIV], 'to win' [ICC; NJB], 'to gain' [BAGD; TNT], 'to experience' [LN].

b. σωτηρία (LN 21.25; 21.26): 'salvation' [Hn, HNTC, ICC, LN, Lns, WBC; all versions]. See this word at 5:8.

QUESTION—How are the two event words related in the genitive construction περιποίησιν σωτηρίας 'possession of salvation'?

1. People are the actors of the event 'to possess' and the genitive σωτηρίας 'of salvation' indicates the object of that event [Alf, Ea, El, Fn, Hb, Hn, HNTC, ICC, Mn, NCBC, NIC, Rb, TH, WBC; all versions]: God destined us to possess salvation. Some consider this to mean more than that God destined us to be saved. They take it to mean that we must receive the salvation that is made possible [Hb, Hn, HNTC, NCBC, NIC; NIV, NJB, TNT]: God destined us to receive salvation for ourselves. Some also take it to mean that a person may fail to obtain that final salvation by lack of vigilance [HNTC], while others point out that there is nothing of human merit in accepting what has been provided [Hb, NCBC, NIC]. Believers are saved from the wrath just mentioned [Ea, Lns, WBC] and are saved to fellowship with Christ [Hb, ICC].

2. God is the actor of the event 'to possess' and the genitive σωτηρίας 'of salvation' is in apposition [EBC, My]: God destined us to be possessed or adopted by him, that is, God determined to save us.

through[a] the Lord of-us Jesus Christ,

LEXICON—a. διά (LN 89.76): 'through' [Hn, HNTC, ICC, Lns, WBC; all versions except KJV], 'by' [KJV].

QUESTION—What relationship is indicated by διά 'through'?

This indicates the means by which we are saved [Ea, EBC, El, Er, Fn, Hb, Hn, ICC, Mn, NCBC, TH, WBC]. Salvation is made possible by means of what Christ did for us [Ea, Er, NCBC, NIC].

1. This is explained by the following verse [Ea, Er, Mn, NCBC, NIC, WBC]: it is specifically by means of Christ's death for us that we receive salvation.

2. This refers to Christ's indwelling presence in us [ICC]: it is by means of Christ indwelling us. He empowers us to be righteous [ICC].

3. This means both of the preceding views [Hn]: it is by means of his death for us and his power working in us.

4. This refers to the means by which salvation is ours [My]: through our faith in Christ.

1 THESSALONIANS 5:10

5:10 the (one) having-died[a] for[b] us,

TEXT—Instead of ὑπέρ 'for, on behalf of, for the benefit of', some manuscripts have περί 'for, concerning'. GNT does not mention this alternate wording. The reading περί is followed by Fn, Hb, Hn. Some argue that the words have no significant difference and are interchangeable [Fn, HNTC, ICC, Mn, NCBC, Rb].

LEXICON—a. aorist act. participle of ἀποθνῄσκω (LN 23.99): 'to die' [Hn, HNTC, ICC, LN, Lns, WBC; all versions].

  b. ὑπέρ (LN 90.36): 'for' [Hn, HNTC, ICC, LN; all versions], 'in behalf of' [LN, Lns], 'for the benefit of' [NCBC], 'for the sake of' [LN].

QUESTION—Why is this description of Christ given at this point?

1. This explains the means by which the Lord Jesus Christ made salvation available [Ea, EBC, El, Fn, HNTC, Lns, Mn, NCBC, NIC]: God destined us to obtain salvation through Christ, specifically through Christ's dying for us.
2. This is a comment about the Lord [ICC, My]: through Christ who died for us.

QUESTION—What relationship is indicated by 'for'?

1. The reading ὑπέρ is followed [Ea, EBC, El, Lns, My, TH, WBC]: he died on behalf of us, for our benefit. A few argue that this preposition includes the idea of his dying as a substitute for us [Hb, Lns, WBC]: he died in place of us.
2. The reading περί is followed [Fn, Hb, Hn]: he died in reference to us.

in-order-that[a] whether we-are-awake[b] or we-sleep[c]

LEXICON—a. ἵνα (LN 89.59): 'so that' [Lns, WBC; NEB, NIV, NJB, RSV, TNT], 'that' [ICC; KJV, NAB, NASB], 'in order that' [Hn, HNTC; TEV].

  b. pres. act. subj. of γρηγορέω (LN 23.72; **23.97**): 'to be awake' [Hn, HNTC, WBC; all versions except KJV, RSV, TEV], 'to wake' [Hn; KJV, RSV], 'to be alive' [LN; TEV], or 'to watch' [ICC, Lns]. See this word at 5:6.

  c. pres. act. subj. of καθεύδω (LN 23.66; **23.104**): 'to sleep' [ICC, Lns; KJV, RSV], 'to be asleep' [HNTC, WBC; NAB, NASB, NEB, NIV, NJB, TNT], 'to be dead' [LN; TEV]. See this word at 5:6 and 7.

QUESTION—What relationship is indicated by ἵνα 'so that'?

This indicates Christ's purpose in dying for us [Ea, El, Er, Fn, Hb, Hn, HNTC, ICC, Mn, NCBC, NIC, TH, WBC; TEV]: he died for us *in order that* we might live together with him. With practically the same meaning, some refer to this as the contemplated result [Lns]: he died for us so that we shall live together with him.

QUESTION—What is meant by being awake or asleep?

1. 'Asleep' is used in the same sense as κοιμάομαι 'to sleep' in 4:14, that is, both verbs for sleep refer to physical death.

  1.1 'Awake' refers to physical life [Alf, Ea, EGT, El, Fn, Hb, Hn, HNTC, ICC, Mn, My, NCBC, NIC, Rb, TH, WBC, Wd]: whether we are

physically alive or physically dead. The words for being awake and asleep are used in a different sense here than the way they were used in 5:6.
- 1.2 'Awake' refers to moral preparedness [Er, Lns]: whether we are watching for his coming or have died at the time of Christ's coming. The word for awake is used in the same way as in 5:6 and implies that they are alive to do so.
2. 'Asleep' is used in the sense of 5:6 where it refers to moral unpreparedness and 'awake' refers to moral preparedness [EBC]: whether we believers are watching for his coming or are unprepared. Our salvation is dependent on Christ's death for us, not our preparedness, and so we will be with him no matter how prepared we are [EBC].

we-may-live[a] together[b] with him.

LEXICON—a. aorist act. subj. of ζάω (LN 23.88): 'to live' [BAGD, Hn, HNTC, LN, Lns, WBC; all versions], 'to have life' [ICC], 'to be alive' [LN]. This may be taken as an ingressive aorist [HNTC, Wd]: that we might begin to live, that we might gain life. Or it may simply state the fact of living with him to indicate that the goal has been reached [Hb].

b. ἅμα (LN 89.114): 'together' [ICC, Lns, WBC; KJV, NAB, NASB, NIV, TEV], 'together with' [LN], 'simultaneously with' [HNTC]. The phrase ἅμα σύν 'together with' is also translated as a unit: 'in company with' [NEB], 'united to' [NJB], 'with' [RSV, TNT], 'in fellowship with' [Hn].

QUESTION—When do we live with Christ?
1. This refers to the resurrection life which begins when Christ comes again [EBC, Er, Hb, Hn, HNTC, ICC, My, NCBC, WBC; TEV].
2. This refers to the believer's present life and means his fellowship with Christ which began when he believed [Fn, Mn, NIC]. It means much the same as the phrase 'in Christ' [NIC]. Even those who have died are living with Christ at the present [Fn, Mn].

QUESTION—What is the connection with ἅμα 'together'?
1. This refers to the believers being together with Christ [EBC, Lns, Rb; NEB, NJB, RSV, TNT]: we will live together with Christ.
2. This refers to the believers being together with each other [Alf, Ea, El, Hb, Hn, HNTC, My; NAB]: we, both living and dead believers together, will live with Christ.

5:11 Therefore[a]

LEXICON—a. διό (LN 89.47): 'therefore' [Hn, HNTC, Lns, WBC; NAB, NASB, NEB, NIV, RSV], 'wherefore' [KJV], 'so then' [ICC], 'so' [NJB, TNT], 'and so' [TEV].

QUESTION—What relationship is indicated by this conjunction?
This indicates an exhortation grounded on the preceding statements [Alf, Ea, El, Er, Fn, Hb, ICC, Mn, My, NCBC, NIC, TH; all versions]: since all of this is so, *therefore* encourage/comfort one another.

1 THESSALONIANS 5:11

encourage/comfort[a] **one-another and build-up**[b] **one the other,**

LEXICON—a. pres. act. impera. of παρακαλέω (LN 25.150): 'to encourage' [BAGD, Hn, HNTC, ICC, LN, WBC; NASB, NIV, RSV, TEV, TNT], 'to give encouragement to' [NJB], 'to hearten' [NEB]; or 'to comfort' [BAGD, Lns; KJV, NAB], 'to console' [LN]. See this word at 2:12 and 4:18. The present tense of this and the following verb mean that they should habitually do these things [NIC, TH].

b. pres. act. impera. of οἰκοδομέω (LN 74.15): 'to build up' [Hn, HNTC, ICC, LN, Lns, WBC; NASB, NIV, RSV], 'to upbuild' [NAB], 'to edify' [BAGD; KJV], 'to fortify' [NEB], 'to strengthen' [BAGD, LN; NJB, TNT], 'to help' [TEV].

QUESTION—In what sense are people built up?

This means to help people grow spiritually [Hb, Lns, NCBC, NIC, WBC], to help them to know God better [Lns, NIC] and love him [NIC].

as[a] **indeed/also**[b] **you-do.**

LEXICON—a. καθώς (LN 64.14): 'as' [Hn, ICC, WBC; KJV, NAB, NEB, NJB, TNT], 'just as' [HNTC; NASB, NIV, RSV, TEV], 'even as' [Lns].

b. καί: 'indeed' [WBC; NAB, NEB, TNT], 'even' [KJV], 'in fact' [Hn, ICC; NIV], 'already' [NJB]; or 'also' [Lns; NASB].

QUESTION—Why did he tell them to do this if they already were doing it?

The majority were doing so, but some needed this exhortation [WBC]. They were doing so, but they needed to be exhorted to do so even more [Ea, EBC, EGT, Er, Hb, NIC].

DISCOURSE UNIT: 5:12–28 [GNT, Hn; NIV, TEV]. The topic is final instructions [NIV], instructions and greetings [GNT; TEV], exhortations about proper behavior [Hn].

DISCOURSE UNIT: 5:12–24 [Alf, My, NCBC]. The topic is various instructions [Alf, My], instructions about church life [NCBC].

DISCOURSE UNIT: 5:12–22 [EBC, EGT, Er, HNTC, Mn, NIC, TH; NAB]. The topic is general exhortations [EGT, Er, NIC], church life [EBC, HNTC], teaching about church life and holy living [Mn], Christian behavior [NAB].

DISCOURSE UNIT: 5:12–15 [Fn, Hb, Wd]. The topic is instructions about the Christian community [Fn, Hb, Wd].

DISCOURSE UNIT: 5:12–13 [Alf, EBC, Hb, Hn, ICC, WBC, Wd]. The topic is instructions about their responsibilities to their leaders [Alf, EBC, Hb, Hn, ICC, Wd], respect for leaders [WBC].

5:12 Now/But[a]

LEXICON—a. δέ (LN 89.94; 89.124): 'now' [Hn, HNTC, Lns, WBC; NIV], 'and' [KJV], 'furthermore' [ICC]; or 'but' [NASB, RSV]; not explicit [NAB, NEB, NJB, TEV, TNT].

QUESTION—What relationship is indicated by this conjunction?
1. This indicates a transition to a new topic [Ea, El, Hb, Hn, HNTC, ICC, Lns, Mn, My, NCBC, TH, WBC; KJV, NIV]: now. Paul is continuing on with more exhortations to follow those given in 4:1–12 [Hb, ICC].
2. This indicates contrast [NASB, RSV]: but. It is not clear what is being contrasted. Perhaps the contrast is: you yourselves should seek to build up one another, but you must also appreciate and esteem your leaders who have the work of leading and admonishing you [My].

we-ask[a] you, brothers, to-know/appreciate[b] the (ones) working-hard[c] among[d] you

LEXICON—a. pres. act. indic. of ἐρωτάω (LN 33.161): 'to ask' [BAGD, HNTC, ICC, LN, WBC; NIV, TNT], 'to request' [BAGD, Hn, LN, Lns; NASB], 'to beseech' [KJV, RSV], 'to beg' [NAB, NEB, TEV], 'to appeal to' [NJB]. See this word at 4:1.
  b. perf. (= pres.) act. infin. of οἶδα (LN **87.12**): 'to know' [Lns, WBC; KJV], 'to appreciate' [Hn, ICC; NASB], 'to respect' [BAGD, HNTC, LN; NAB, NIV, RSV], 'to acknowledge' [NEB], 'to be considerate to' [NJB], 'to pay proper respect' [TEV], 'to pay due regard' [TNT].
  c. pres. act. participle of κοπιάω (LN 42.47): 'to work hard' [BAGD, HNTC, LN, WBC; NEB, NIV, NJB, TNT], 'to work' [TEV], 'to labor' [Hn, ICC, LN; KJV, RSV], 'to labor diligently' [NASB], 'to toil' [BAGD, LN, Lns]. This verb is also translated as a noun phrase: 'whose task it is' [NAB]. This verb is cognate with the noun κόπος 'labor' in 1:3.
  d. ἐν (LN 83.9): 'among' [Hn, HNTC, ICC, Lns, WBC; all versions]. This indicates the sphere of their work [ICC].

QUESTION—What area of meaning is intended by οἶδα 'to know/appreciate'?
  They are to know their true characters and work [Ea, El, Er, Fn, Hb, Lns, My, NIC]. This implies that they will recognize their true value [Ea, Er, Hb, Hn, Mn, My, NCBC, NIC, TH] and the verb in this context means to appreciate and respect them [Bul (p. 554), EBC, Er, Hb, Hn, HNTC, ICC, Mn, My, NCBC, NIC, TH; NAB, NASB, NIV, RSV, TEV, TNT].

and directing/caring-for[a] you in[b] the Lord and instructing/admonishing[c] you,

LEXICON—a. pres. mid. participle of προΐστημι (LN **36.1**; 35.12): 'to direct', 'to guide' [LN; TEV], 'to be over someone' [Hn; KJV, NIV, RSV], 'to have charge over' [NASB], 'to exercise authority' [NAB], 'to be one's leader' [NEB, NJB, TNT], 'to act as leaders' [ICC], 'to superintend' [Lns]; or 'to care for' [BAGD, HNTC, WBC].
  b. ἐν (LN 89.5; 89.119; 89.76): 'in' [Hn, HNTC, ICC, Lns, WBC; KJV, NAB, NASB, NIV, NJB, RSV]. This phrase is translated 'in the Christian life' [TEV], 'within the Christian fellowship' [TNT], 'in the Lord's fellowship' [NEB].
  c. pres. act. participle of νουθετέω (LN **33.231**; 33.418; 33.424): 'to instruct' [BAGD, LN, WBC; TEV], 'to give instruction' [NASB], 'to be

1 THESSALONIANS 5:12

one's adviser' [TNT], 'to be one's counselor' [NEB], or more specifically, 'to admonish' [BAGD, Hn, HNTC; KJV, NAB, NIV, NJB, RSV], 'to warn' [BAGD, ICC], 'to remonstrate' [Lns].

QUESTION—How are the three participles related?

The single article governs all three participles and indicates that one group of people is being described by all three of the participles [Alf, Ea, EBC, El, Er, Fn, Hb, Hn, HNTC, ICC, Lns, Mn, My, NCBC, NIC, Rb, WBC, Wd]: the ones who are working, leading, and admonishing.

1. The first participle is a generic term for the following two specific activities [Ea, EBC, EGT, El, Hb, HNTC, ICC, My, NIC, TH, Wd; NAB, TEV]: the ones who work among you, that is, the ones who lead and admonish you. It can mean that these two activities are the only ones intended by the use of the generic term [Hb, My], but some commentators understand the generic term to include more that these two which are especially emphasized [EBC, HNTC, ICC, NIC].
2. Each of the three participles describes different activities that are coordinate with each other [Er, Hn, Lns, Mn, NCBC, Rb, WBC]: the ones who work, and who direct, and who admonish.

QUESTION—What is meant by προϊσταμένους 'directing/caring for'?

1. The idea of leadership is primary [Alf, Ea, El, Fn, Hb, Hn, ICC, Lns, Mn, My, NIC, TH; all versions]: who direct you. Probably this refers to the group of elders [Ea, El, Fn, Hb, Hn, Lns, Mn, My, NIC], but some say that it is not a technical designation for officers of a church [Fn, Lns, Mn, NIC, WBC].
2. The idea of taking care of the congregation is primary [HNTC, WBC]: who take care of you.
3. Both leadership and the care this involves are intended [EBC, NCBC]: who care for and direct the church.

QUESTION—What relationship to the participle νουθετοῦντας 'directing/caring for' is indicated by ἐν 'in (the Lord)'?

1. Their leading was in relation to spiritual matters, not secular [Alf, Ea, EGT, El, Er, Hb, Mn, My, NCBC, NIC]: who lead you in matters pertaining to the Lord.
2. Their leading or taking care of Christians was one of the activities involved in serving the Lord [HNTC]: who care for you as a part of their Christian responsibilities.
3. Their position of leadership was appointed or prompted by the Lord [Fn, Hn, ICC]: who lead you because the Lord has appointed them to this work. He also equipped them for leadership [Hn].
4. Their leading was done in a Christian manner [Lns]: who lead you in a way a Christian leader should.

QUESTION—What is meant by νουθετοῦντας 'instructing/admonishing'?

1. This means to instruct in general [Ea, My, WBC; NASB, NEB, TEV, TNT]: who are instructing you. This would include admonition when needed [Ea, My, WBC].

2. This means rebuking and warning the people concerning things which need to be corrected or avoided [EBC, El, Fn, Hb, Hn, HNTC, ICC, Lns, Mn, NCBC, NIC, TH; KJV, NAB, NIV, NJB, RSV]: who are admonishing or warning you.

5:13 and to-esteem[a] them exceedingly[b] in[c] love[d]

LEXICON—a. pres. mid. (deponent = active) infin. of ἡγέομαι (LN 31.1): 'to esteem' [BAGD, Hn, HNTC, WBC; KJV, NAB, NASB, RSV], 'to hold in esteem' [NEB], 'to hold in regard' [NIV], 'to have respect' [NJB], 'to treat with respect' [TEV], 'to show respect' [TNT], 'to consider (them very much)' [LN, Lns], 'to regard' [LN], 'to rate (them highly)' [ICC]. The present tense indicates that they are to continue in this attitude [Hb].

b. ὑπερεκπερισσοῦ (LN 78.34): 'exceedingly', 'very highly' [Hn, HNTC, ICC, WBC; KJV, NASB, RSV], 'extremely' [LN], 'the highest possible' [NEB], 'highest' [NIV, TNT], 'greatest' [NAB, NJB, TEV], 'very much' [Lns].

c. ἐν (LN 89.80; 89.26; 89.84): 'in' [Hn, ICC, Lns, WBC; KJV, NASB, NEB, NIV, RSV], 'with' [HNTC; NAB, TEV].

d. ἀγάπη (LN 25.43): 'love' [BAGD, Hn, HNTC, ICC, LN, Lns, WBC; KJV, NAB, NASB, NIV, RSV, TEV], 'affection' [NEB, NJB, TNT].

QUESTION—What relationship is indicated by καί 'and'?

1. This coordinates this clause with the preceding one as the second part of the request [EBC, Hb, ICC, NIC]: we ask you to know/appreciate them... *and* to esteem them.
2. This is a restatement of verse 12 [TH]: we ask you to appreciate those who work among you, *that is*, to esteem them because of their work.

QUESTION—What relationship is indicated by ἐν 'in'?

1. This indicates the circumstance in which they are to regard them with esteem [Hb, Hn, HNTC, Mn]: to esteem them highly while loving them. It may be taken to imply that love is the instrument by which they show their esteem [HNTC]: show your esteem for them by loving them. It implies that love is being urged as well as esteem [Hb, HNTC, ICC, NIC]: esteem them highly and love them. Some translate this as a parallel command and seem to apply the adverb to both events [NEB, NJB, TEV, TNT]: have the highest esteem and love for them. Some connect the adverb with the event of loving [Alf; NAB]: to esteem them with the greatest love.
2. This indicates that love is to be the motive or reason for accepting and appreciating their leadership [ICC, Lns, NCBC, NIC]: esteem them, not from fear or thought of reward, but from love. Since another reason is explicitly stated in the next clause, this may be considered the inward motive, while the following is the outward motive [Lns].
3. 'Love' is the manner in which they are to regard them [El, Fn, My]: regard them with love in the highest degree. This does not take the verb to

mean 'esteem', rather, the phrase becomes equivalent to 'love them very much' [Fn, My].

because-of^a their work.^b

LEXICON— διά (LN 89.26): 'because of' [Hn, HNTC, WBC; NAB, NASB, NIV, NJB, RSV, TEV, TNT], 'on account of' [Lns], 'for' [NEB], 'for the sake of' [ICC; KJV].
- b. ἔργον (LN 42.42): 'work' [BAGD, Hn, ICC, LN, Lns, WBC; all versions], 'what they do' [HNTC].

QUESTION—What relationship is indicated by διά 'because of'?

This indicates the reason for esteeming them [EBC, El, Er, Hb, HNTC, Lns, Mn, NCBC, NIC, TH, WBC]: esteem them *because of* their work. This may imply that their work is done well [Hb, HNTC, TH]: esteem them because they work well. Or, it may imply that the nature of their work, being the Lord's work, merits such esteem [NCBC, NIC, WBC, Wd]: esteem them for the sake of the type of work they do. Or, it may mean both that their work is done well and also that the nature of the work demands it [Ea, EGT, El, Er, Mn, My].

Be-at-peace^a among^b yourselves.

LEXICON—a. pres. act. impera. of εἰρηνεύω (LN 88.102): 'to be at peace' [BAGD, Hn, ICC, Lns, WBC; KJV, NAB, NJB, RSV, TEV, TNT], 'to behave peacefully' [LN], 'to live in peace' [LN; NASB, NIV], 'to live at peace' [HNTC; NEB]. The present tense indicates that they are to continue on with this attitude [Fn, Hb, Lns, TH; NAB].
- b. ἐν (LN 83.9): 'among' [Hn, HNTC, ICC, Lns, WBC; KJV, NEB, NJB, RSV, TEV, TNT], 'with (one another)' [NAB, NASB, NIV].

DISCOURSE UNIT: 5:14–22 [Alf, WBC]. The topic is their various duties [Alf, WBC].

DISCOURSE UNIT: 5:14–15 [EBC, Hb, Wd]. The topic is instructions about Christians with faults [Hb], responsibilities towards all people [EBC], responsibilities towards Christians [Wd].

5:14 And/But^a we-exhort^b you, brothers,

LEXICON—a. δέ (LN 89.94; 89.124): 'and' [Hn, HNTC; NASB, NEB, NIV, RSV], 'now' [Lns, WBC; KJV] 'further' [ICC], not explicit [NAB, NJB, TEV, TNT].
- b. pres. act. indic. of παρακαλέω (LN 33.168): 'to exhort' [BAGD; KJV, NAB, RSV], 'to urge' [BAGD, Hn, ICC; NASB, NEB, NIV, NJB, TEV], 'to beg' [TNT], 'to request' [BAGD, HNTC, LN], 'to appeal' [BAGD, WBC], 'to admonish' [Lns]. See this word at 4:1 and 10.

QUESTION—What relationship is indicated by δέ 'and/but'?
1. This is transitional and indicates a new set of exhortations [Ea, EBC, Hb, Hn, HNTC, ICC, Lns, Mn, WBC; NASB, NEB, NIV, RSV]: and now.

2. This indicates a contrast in the attitudes they were to have [NCBC]: appreciate and honor those who labor among you, but do the following for special types of people among you.

QUESTION—Who are the brothers now being addressed?
1. They are the same brothers as the ones in 5:12, that is, the whole church [Alf, Ea, EBC, EGT, El, Er, Hb, Hn, HNTC, ICC, Lns, Mn, My, NCBC, NIC, TH, WBC, Wd]. These forms of service are a special responsibility of the leaders, but they are also ways in which all Christians can encourage and build up one another [Ea, Hb, ICC, Lns, WBC].
2. They are the leaders whose work included admonishing the believers [Fn].

admonish[a] the idle/disorderly,[b]

LEXICON—a. pres. act. impera. of νουθετέω (LN **33.418; 33.424**): 'to admonish' [BAGD, Hn, HNTC, LN, WBC; NAB, NASB, NEB, NJB, RSV], 'to warn' [BAGD, ICC, LN; KJV, NIV, TEV, TNT], 'to remonstrate' [Lns]. Some commentators take the present tense of the commands in this verse to indicate that this is a continuing duty [Hb, Lns]. Others do not think that it has to be taken as continuous [Hn]. See this word at 5:12.

b. ἄτακτος (LN **88.247**): 'idle'. This adjective is translated as a substantive: 'the idle' [BAGD; TEV], 'the idlers' [ICC; RSV, TNT], 'those who are idle' [NIV], 'those who are lazy' [LN], 'loafers' [HNTC]; or 'the unruly' [NAB, NASB], 'those who are unruly' [KJV], 'the disorderly' [BAGD, Hn, Lns, WBC], 'those who are undisciplined' [NJB], 'the careless' [NEB].

QUESTION—What is meant by τοὺς ἀτάκτους 'the idle/disorderly'?
1. The focus is on their failure to perform their orderly duties [Alf, El, Er, Fn, Hb, Hn, Lns, My]: the disorderly people. It includes their idleness [Hb, Hn, My].
2. The focus is on the specific form of disorderliness, that of refusing to work and to conform to the normal, orderly way of gaining a living [EGT, HNTC, ICC, NCBC, NIC, TH, WBC, Wd; NIV, RSV, TEV, TNT]: the idle people.

encourage/comfort[a] the fainthearted,[b]

LEXICON—a. pres. mid. (deponent = active) impera. of παραμυθέομαι (LN **25.153**): 'to encourage' [BAGD, Hn, HNTC, ICC, LN, Lns; NASB, NEB, NIV, NJB, RSV, TEV, TNT]; or 'to comfort' [WBC; KJV], 'to cheer' [NAB]. See this word at 2:12.

b. ὀλιγόψυχος (LN **25.290**): 'fainthearted'. This adjective is translated as a substantive: 'the fainthearted' [BAGD, Hn, ICC, Lns, WBC; NAB, NASB, NEB, RSV, TNT], 'the timid' [NIV, TEV], 'the apprehensive' [NJB], 'the worried' [HNTC], 'those who are losing heart' [LN], 'the feebleminded' [KJV].

QUESTION—In what sense are they fainthearted?

They are fearful [Er, HNTC, TH], they feel themselves inadequate [WBC], and are discouraged and despondent [Er, Hb, HNTC, Mn, My, NCBC, NIC, Wd]. Some reasons suggested for this attitude are persecution or trials in life [EGT, Hb, Lns, Mn, My, NCBC, NIC], worry about Christians who had died (4:13–17) [Ea, EBC, El, Er, Hb, Hn, ICC, Mn, My, NCBC], a sense of their sinfulness [Hb, My], a doubt that they can live a Christian life [Hb, My], or even a doubt about their own salvation (5:9–11) [Er, Hb, Hn, ICC, My].

help[a] the weak,[b]

LEXICON—a. pres. mid. impera. of ἀντέχω (LN **35.1**): 'to help' [BAGD, Hn, HNTC, WBC; NASB, NIV, RSV, TEV, TNT], 'to be of help' [LN], 'to support' [Lns; KJV, NAB, NEB, NJB], 'to cling to' [ICC].
- b. ἀσθενής (LN 88.117): 'weak'. This adjective is translated as a substantive: 'the weak' [BAGD, Hn, HNTC, ICC, Lns, WBC; all versions], 'morally weak' [LN], 'without moral strength' [LN].

QUESTION—In what sense are they weak?
1. They are morally weak [Er, ICC, LN, NCBC, Rb]. They were tempted to impurity (4:3–8) [EBC, Er, Hb, Hn, ICC, NCBC, Rb], or were afraid of persecution [EBC, Er].
2. They were spiritually weak [Alf, Ea, El, Fn, HNTC, Mn, My, NIC, WBC]. They are weak in their faith [Ea, EBC, El, Fn, NIC, WBC].
3. This means both of the above [EBC, Hb, Hn, Lns].

be-patient[a] with all.

LEXICON—a. pres. act. impera. of μακροθυμέω (LN 25.168): 'to be patient' [BAGD, HNTC, ICC, LN, WBC; all versions], 'to exercise patience' [Hn], 'to be longsuffering' [Lns].

QUESTION—Who are πάντας 'all'?
1. This refers to all people, both Christians and non-Christians [Alf, Ea, El, Er, Hb, Hn, ICC, Lns, My, NIC, TH]: be patient with all people.
2. This refers to all Christians [EBC, Fn]: be patient with all Christians. It is the next verse that specifically deals with non-Christians [EBC].
3. This is restricted to the three foregoing types of people [EGT, NCBC; NEB, RSV]: be patient with them all.

5:15 See[a] (that) not anyone returns[b] evil[c] for[d] evil[c] to-anyone,

LEXICON—a. pres. act. impera. of ὁράω (LN 13.134): 'to see (that)' [HNTC, Lns; KJV, NAB, NASB, RSV, TEV, TNT], 'to see to it' [BAGD, Hn, ICC, LN, WBC; NEB], 'to make sure' [NIV, NJB]. The present tense indicates a continuing duty [Hb, Mn, Wd].
- b. aorist act. subj. of ἀποδίδωμι (LN 38.16): 'to return' [NAB], 'to repay' [NASB, NJB, RSV, TNT], 'to pay back' [HNTC, ICC; NEB, NIV, TEV], 'to render' [BAGD, Hn, Lns, WBC; KJV], 'to recompense' [LN]. The aorist tense indicates that not even one instance of returning evil is to occur [Hb].

c. κακός (LN 88.106): 'evil' [BAGD, Hn, HNTC, ICC, LN, WBC; KJV, NAB, NASB, NJB, RSV, TNT], 'wrong' [BAGD; NEB, NIV, TEV], 'meanness' [Lns].

d. ἀντί (LN 57.145): 'for' [BAGD, Hn, ICC, LN, Lns, WBC; all versions except NAB], 'in place of' [LN], 'with' [HNTC]. This is left implicit in the verb: 'to return evil' [NAB].

QUESTION—How is this verse connected with the preceding verse?

This explains the last clause of the preceding verse, when πάντας 'all' refers to all people everywhere, by giving a negative and positive restatement [Hb, HNTC]: be patient with all, that is, do not return evil, but seek the good of all. When all refers only to the preceding groups, then this enlarges on the previous statement [NCBC]: be patient with them all, and even more, do not return evil at all, but seek the good of all people.

QUESTION—What is meant by κακόν 'evil'?

It is a harmful act caused by evil intent [Hb].

but[a] always seek[b] the good[c] for one-another and for all.

LEXICON—a. ἀλλά (LN 89.125): 'but' [Hn, HNTC, ICC, Lns, WBC; all versions except NAB, NJB], not explicit [NAB, NJB].

b. pres. act. impera. of διώκω (LN 68.66): 'to seek' [NAB] 'to seek eagerly' [HNTC], 'to seek (to do)' [RSV], 'to seek after' [BAGD; NASB], 'to aim at' [NJB], 'to aim (at doing)' [NEB], 'to make it one's aim (to do)' [TEV], 'to follow' [ICC; KJV], 'to try (to be/do)' [NIV, TNT], 'to do with effort' [LN], 'to strive toward' [LN], 'to pursue' [BAGD, Hn, Lns, WBC]. The present tense indicates that this is to be a continuous attitude [Hb, Lns, NIC].

c. ἀγαθός (LN 88.1): 'good' [BAGD, LN; NAB, RSV, TEV, TNT], 'kind' [NIV]. This adjective is also translated as a substantive: 'the good' [HNTC, ICC], 'what is good' [Hn, Lns, WBC; KJV, NASB], 'the best you can' [NEB], 'what is best' [NJB].

DISCOURSE UNIT: 5:16–24 [Fn, Hb]. The topic is instructions for the Christian life [Fn, Hb].

DISCOURSE UNIT: 5:16–22 [Hb, Mn, Wd]. The topic is exhortations [Wd], principles for a holy life [Hb], religious responsibilities [Wd].

DISCOURSE UNIT: 5:16–18 [EBC, Fn, Hb, Hn, HNTC, ICC, TH]. The topic is commands about the inner life [Hb, Hn, HNTC], personal responsibilities [EBC].

5:16 Always[a] rejoice,[b]

LEXICON—a. πάντοτε (LN 67.88): 'always' [BAGD, Hn, HNTC, ICC, LN, Lns; all versions except KJV], 'evermore' [KJV], 'at all times' [BAGD, LN, WBC].

b. pres. act. impera. of χαίρω (LN 25.125): 'to rejoice' [BAGD, ICC, LN, Lns, WBC; KJV, NAB, NASB, RSV, TNT], 'to be joyful' [Hn, HNTC;

NEB, NIV, NJB, TEV], 'to be glad' [LN]. The present tense here and in the two following commands indicate that these are to be continuous actions [Ea, Hb].

QUESTION—Why is πάντοτε 'always' emphasized by being placed first in this sentence?

This stresses the fact that rejoicing is not dependent on circumstances [Hb]. Rejoicing is based on the fact that they are in Christ (5:18) [EBC, Hb, NIC, WBC], that Christ is in them [ICC], that they are saved [Lns, NCBC], that they are forgiven, accepted by God, and receive present and future blessings from God [Hb, NCBC, NIC, TH].

5:17 **unceasingly[a] pray,[b]**

LEXICON—a. ἀδιαλείπτως (LN 68.55): 'unceasingly' [BAGD, HNTC], 'without ceasing' [KJV, NASB], 'ceaselessly' [Hn, Lns], 'unceasingly' [LN], 'continually' [ICC; NEB, NIV], 'continuously' [LN], 'constantly' [BAGD, WBC; NJB, RSV, TNT], 'at all times' [TEV]. This adverb is also translated as a verb phrase: 'never cease' [NAB]. See this word at 1:2 and 2:13.

b. pres. mid. (deponent = active) impera. of προσεύχομαι (LN 33.178): 'to pray' [BAGD, Hn, HNTC, ICC, LN, Lns, WBC; all versions].

QUESTION—How literally is ἀδιαλείπτως 'unceasingly' to be taken?

One commentator classifies this word as a hyperbole [TH]. Many point out that it does not mean that they were to speak to God without stopping [Ea, EBC, Er, Hb, NIC]. It means frequent, recurring prayer [EBC, Hb, Hn, NIC]. Many refer this to an attitude that shows itself in frequent prayer [Alf, Ea, EBC, EGT, El, Er, Hb, HNTC, Lns, NCBC, NIC]. This attitude is spoken of as one of devotion [Ea, El, Er], consciousness of God's presence [Ea, Er, Hb, NIC], and dependence on him [Ea, EBC]. Many mention that this word for prayer is a general, comprehensive term [Hb, Hn, HNTC, ICC, NIC]. Since thanksgiving is specified in the following clause, some think that this general term for prayer probably refers specifically to petition for themselves and intercession for others [HNTC, NCBC].

5:18 **in[a] everything give-thanks;[b]**

LEXICON—a. ἐν (LN 89.5): 'in' [Hn, ICC, Lns, WBC; KJV, NASB, NIV, RSV, TEV], 'for' [NJB], 'in connection with' [Lns]. The prepositional phrase is also translated as an adverbial phrase: 'constant' [NAB], 'whatever happens' [HNTC; NEB], 'whatever the circumstances' [TNT].

b. pres. act. impera. of εὐχαριστέω (LN 33.349; 25.100): 'to give thanks' [BAGD, Hn, HNTC, ICC, Lns, WBC; KJV, NASB, NEB, NIV, NJB, RSV, TNT], 'to thank' [LN], 'to render thanks' [BAGD; NAB], 'to be thankful' [LN; TEV], 'to be grateful' [LN]. See this word at 1:2.

QUESTION—What does παντί 'everything' refer to?

They are to give thanks in every circumstance [Alf, EBC, El, Er, Fn, Hb, Hn, HNTC, ICC, Mn, My, NCBC, NIC, TH, WBC, Wd; NIV, RSV, TEV, TNT], in every situation [WBC], in everything [Ea, El, Hb, Lns, NIC; KJV, NASB,

NEB]. A few commentators think that it could possibly refer to giving thanks at all times [HNTC, NCBC, TH]. However, either interpretation implies the other [NCBC]. Some seem to think that this means that one should thank God for the difficult circumstances [Er, NIC, Wd]. One can thank God that he is working all things out for good to those who love him [EBC, Hb, Lns, NCBC, NIC] and that one has the opportunity to strive for God [Wd]. Others think that it does not mean to thank God for the difficulties themselves, but to thank him in the midst of all circumstances for the blessings they are receiving from God [HNTC, NCBC]. Suggestions of the kind of blessings are salvation [Ea, HNTC, NCBC], and having Christ indwell them [ICC].

since[a] this (is) the will[b] of God in[c] Christ Jesus concerning[d] you.
LEXICON—a. γάρ (LN 89.23): 'since', 'for' [Hn, HNTC, ICC, Lns, WBC; KJV, NASB, NEB, NIV, RSV, TNT], not explicit [NAB, NJB, TEV].
  b. θέλημα (LN 25.2; 30.59): 'will' [BAGD, Hn, HNTC, ICC, LN, Lns, WBC; KJV, NAB, NASB, NIV, NJB, RSV], 'wish, desire' [LN], 'what God wills' [NEB], 'what God wants' [TEV, TNT].
  c. ἐν (LN 89.23): 'in' [Hn, HNTC, Lns, WBC; all versions except TEV, TNT], 'in your life in union with' [TEV], 'as (a Christian)' [TNT], 'operating in' [ICC].
  d. εἰς (LN 89.23; 90.59): 'concerning' [KJV], 'in regard to' [Lns], 'for' [Hn, HNTC, ICC, WBC; NAB, NASB, NEB, NIV, NJB, RSV], 'from' [TEV]. This preposition is also translated as the object of a verb: '(wants) you to do' [TNT].
QUESTION—What relationship is indicated by γάρ 'since'?
  1. This indicates the grounds for the preceding three commands [EBC, EGT, Er, Fn, Hb, Hn, HNTC, ICC, Lns, Mn, NCBC, NIC, TH, WBC, Wd]: rejoice, pray, and give thanks, *since* God wills that you do so. The singular form τοῦτο 'this' refers to all three commands as a unit [Fn, Hb, Mn, NIC].
  2. This indicates the grounds for only the immediately preceding command [Ea, El, My]: give thanks *since* God wills that you do so.
QUESTION—What relationship is indicated by ἐν 'in'?
  1. This is to be connected with ὑμᾶς 'you' [WBC; TEV, TNT]: this is God's will for you who are in union with Christ Jesus.
  2. This is to be linked with God's will [Alf, Ea, EGT, El, Er, Fn, Hb, Hn, HNTC, ICC, Lns, Mn, My, NCBC, NIC, Wd; KJV, NEB]: this is God's will in Christ Jesus for you. The explanations are varied and hard to classify. Some take it to mean that God's will was shown in Christ's life [Ea, El, Er, Hn, Mn, NIC], God's will operated in Christ's life [ICC], God's nature was made known by Christ's life [Wd], Christ is the model for such a life [EGT, Hb], God's will was communicated by means of Christ [Alf, Ea, El, My], Christ empowers them to obey such commands

[EGT, Er, Hb, ICC, NCBC, NIC, Wd], Christ is the means through whom God's will is made effective [Mn].

DISCOURSE UNIT: 5:19–22 [EBC, Hb, Hn, ICC]. The topic is rules for living together in the church [EBC, Hb], spiritual gifts [Hn, ICC].

5:19 The Spirit do-not quench,[a]

LEXICON—a. pres. act. impera. of σβέννυμι (LN **68.52**): 'to quench' [BAGD, Hn, ICC, WBC; KJV, NASB, RSV], 'to extinguish' [HNTC, Lns], 'to put out the fire' [NIV], 'to stifle' [BAGD; NAB, NEB, NJB, TNT], 'to restrain' [TEV], 'to stop' [LN]. Some commentators understand the present tense with the negative μή, here and in the following negative imperative, to indicate that the Thessalonians are being told to stop what they have been doing [EBC, Hb, HNTC, Mn, NIC, Rb]: stop quenching the Holy Spirit. Others think that this does not imply that they are guilty of doing this, but that these two negative present imperatives should be taken the same as the present imperatives without a negative particle and mean that this is to be a habitual action [Lns, Rb, WBC]: continually refrain from quenching the Holy Spirit.

QUESTION—What is meant by this metaphor?

Many have noted that the Holy Spirit, or his presence, or his activity, has been spoken of as fire in various verses (Matt. 3:11; Luke 3:16; 12:49; Acts 2:3; Rom. 12:11; 2 Tim. 1:6) [Ea, EBC, El, Fn, Hb, HNTC, ICC, Mn, NCBC, NIC, TH, WBC, Wd]. Because of that, it is appropriate to use quench as a metaphor. Probably the point of comparison is the preventing of a person or thing from performing his or its function [Fn]. Like a fire is not to be quenched, so the Spirit is not to be prevented from doing his work. Some take the reference to 'the Spirit' to be a metonymy in which Spirit represents his activity [Hb, Hn, HNTC, Lns] since the Spirit cannot be quenched in regard to his being, but his activity or gifts can be resisted.

1. This command refers to any activity of the Holy Spirit in the believer's life [Hb, Lns, NIC]: do not quench what the Spirit is doing in you, or do not quench the Spirit's work in you. Quenching is accomplished by ignoring the Spirit's promptings, or by committing or tolerating immorality among the members of the church [Hb, NIC], or by being idle [NIC]. Probably the suppression of prophetic utterances is the primary activity in this context [Hb, WBC]. A prophet might refuse to speak the message the Spirit gives him [WBC], others might try to prevent someone from speaking such a message [Hb, WBC], or the fervor of the prophet is suppressed by criticism and disapproval [Hb].

2. This command specifically refers to suppressing spiritual gifts [Alf, Bul (p. 540), Ea, EBC, El, Er, Hn, HNTC, ICC, Mn, My, NCBC, Rb, Wd]: do not quench what the Spirit is doing through spiritual gifts, or do not quench spiritual gifts which are inspired by the Spirit. Quenching is accomplished by depreciating what the Holy Spirit is doing [El, Hn], by not allowing people to use the gifts [Bul (p. 540), EBC, El, Er, HNTC,

ICC, Mn], by suppressing their own gifts [Er], or ignoring what such people say or do [HNTC].

5:20 prophecies[a] do-not despise;[b]

LEXICON—a. προφητεία (LN 33.460): 'prophecies' [BAGD, LN; NAB, NIV], 'prophesyings' [Lns, WBC; KJV, RSV], 'prophetic utterances' [Hn; NASB, NEB, TNT], 'prophetic revelations' [HNTC], 'inspired messages' [BAGD; TEV], 'inspired utterances' [LN], 'the gift of prophecy' [NJB], 'cases of prophesying' [ICC].

b. pres. act. impera. of ἐξουθενέω (LN 88.195): 'to despise' [Hn, HNTC, LN, WBC; KJV, NAB, NASB, NEB, RSV, TEV], 'to despise with contempt' [NJB], 'to treat with contempt' [NIV], 'to make little of' [TNT], 'to make light of' [ICC], 'to set at naught' [Lns].

QUESTION—How is this verse related to the preceding one?

This specifies one way in which the Spirit is quenched [Ea, El, Hb, Hn, HNTC, ICC, My, NCBC, TH, WBC, Wd]: do not quench the Spirit, especially do not quench him by despising prophecies.

QUESTION—What is meant by προφητείας 'prophecies'?

This refers to the utterances of members of the church who spoke messages directly inspired and revealed by the Holy Spirit [Ea, EBC, El, Er, Fn, Hb, Hn, HNTC, ICC, Mn, My, WBC, Wd] or, instead of direct revelation, this refers to teaching revelations that had already been given by God to others in the Old Testament and to the apostles [Lns]. The messages gave instruction and guidance about the present and prophetic revelations about the future [Hb, Hn, HNTC].

QUESTION—What is indicated by the plural form of the word προφητείας 'prophecies'?

The plural form denotes the various instances in which individuals uttered prophecies [EBC, Hb, ICC], or because there were various forms of expressing prophecy [ICC].

QUESTIONS—Why would Christians despise prophecies?

They might depreciate them because they valued the spectacular gifts more [Alf, Hb, WBC], or the more staid members reacted against the more spectacular gifts, such as speaking with tongues, by resisting all manifestations of spiritual gifts [Hb, HNTC, NCBC], or they did not receive the message seriously [Lns, WBC], or impostors had made wrong speculations, perhaps about the coming of Christ, and this discredited all prophecies [Ea, EBC, Hb, Hn, My, NIC], or idlers had wrongly used prophesying [EBC, ICC].

5:21 but[a] all (things) test,[b]

TEXT—Some manuscripts do not have δέ 'but'. GNT includes it with a C rating, indicating a considerable degree of doubt in doing so.

LEXICON—a. δέ (LN 89.124): 'but' [Hn, HNTC, WBC; NASB, NEB, RSV], 'however' [Lns], 'on the other hand' [ICC], not explicit or following the text that omits this word [KJV, NAB, NIV, NJB, TEV, TNT].

1 THESSALONIANS 5:21

b. pres. act. impera. of δοκιμάζω (LN 27.45): 'to test' [Hn, HNTC, ICC, LN, Lns, WBC; NAB, NIV, NJB, RSV, TNT], 'prove' [KJV], 'to examine' [LN], 'to examine carefully' [NASB], 'to put to the test' [BAGD; TEV], 'to bring to the test' [NEB], 'to try to determine the genuineness of' [LN]. The present tense here and in the two following imperatives indicates that these were to be continuing practices [Fn, Hb].

QUESTION—What relationship is indicated by δέ 'but'?

This is contrastive [Ea, EBC, El, Hb, HNTC, ICC, Lns, Mn, My, NIC, Rb, TH]. It contrasts the two preceding prohibitions with the following three positive commands [Hb, NIC]: do not do those two things, but do these three things. Or, do not despise prophecies, but rather test them and everything else [El, Lns]. Or, we should accept these gifts, but not without testing to see if they are truly inspired [HNTC, ICC, Mn].

QUESTION—What does πάντα 'all things' refer to and how can they be tested?

1. This refers specifically to prophetic utterances [Ea, Hn, My, NCBC, TH, WBC; NEB]: do not despise prophecies, but test all utterances which claim to be prophecy in order to determine whether or not they are truly inspired by the Holy Spirit. Some tests are determining if they are consistent with previous revelation [Hb, Hn, NCBC, WBC], noting if they recognize Christ as Lord (1 Cor. 12:3) [WBC].
2. This refers to all spiritual gifts [Alf, EBC, El, HNTC, ICC]: do not quench the Spirit, especially prophecies, but test all things involved in spiritual gifts to see if they are truly inspired by the Holy Spirit. This includes testing the aforementioned prophecies [ICC]. They are to judge if it promotes what is good for the church [EBC, ICC].
3. This is a general principle that applies to all things that affect their spiritual lives [Fn, Hb, Lns, NIC]: test all things. Some things that appear good on the surface may be found to be evil upon examination [NIC]. This includes the testing of prophetic utterances [Fn, Hb]. They are tested in regard to how they conform to scripture [Lns].

the good[a] hold-fast;[b]

LEXICON—a. καλός (LN 65.22; 88.4): 'good' [LN]. This adjective is translated as a substantive: 'the good' [BAGD, Hn, ICC; NIV], 'what is good' [HNTC, WBC; KJV, NAB, NASB, NEB, NJB, RSV, TEV, TNT], 'the excellent thing' [Lns].

b. pres. act. impera. of κατέχω (LN 31.48): 'to hold fast' [BAGD, HNTC, ICC, Lns, WBC; KJV, NASB, RSV, TNT], 'to hold on to' [Hn; NIV, NJB], 'to retain' [BAGD; NAB], 'to keep' [NEB, TEV], 'to continue to believe and practice' [LN].

QUESTION—How is this clause connected to the preceding one?

1. When the testing of all things in the preceding clause specifically refers to prophetic utterances, this indicates the result of such testing in regard to what is found to be good [Ea, EGT, Hn, My, NCBC, Rb, TH, WBC, Wd;

NEB]: test all prophetic utterances, and hold fast to those utterances that are good. 'Good' means that they are truly inspired [WBC]. A person can hold to them by being attentive to them and acting in accordance with them [NCBC, TH, WBC, Wd].
2. When the testing of all things in the preceding clause refers to spiritual gifts in general:
2.1 This indicates the result of such testing in regard to what is found to be good [EBC, El, HNTC, ICC]: test all that is done by those who claim to have a spiritual gift, and hold fast to what is good in such gifts. They are good if they edify the church and bring about mutual love [EBC, ICC], or are simply morally good [El].
2.2 This begins a new sentence with a general statement [Alf]: test all that is done by those who claim to have a spiritual gift. In this and in all things, hold fast to what is good.
3. When the testing of all things in the preceding clause refers to a general principle, this indicates the result of such testing in regard to what is found to be good [Hb, Lns, NIC]: test all things, hold fast to whatever is good.

5:22 from every form/appearance^a of-evil^b abstain.^c

LEXICON—a. εἶδος (LN 58.14): 'form' [Hn, LN, Lns; NASB, NJB, RSV], 'kind' [BAGD, HNTC, ICC, WBC; NEB, NIV, TEV, TNT]; or 'appearance' [LN; KJV], 'semblance' [NAB].
b. πονηρός (LN 88.110): 'evil' [BAGD, ICC, LN], 'wicked' [LN]. This adjective is translated as a substantive: 'evil' [BAGD, Hn, WBC; all versions except NEB], 'whatever is evil' [HNTC], 'the bad' [NEB], 'what is wicked' [Lns].
c. pres. mid. impera. of ἀπέχω (LN 85.16): 'to abstain' [BAGD, WBC; KJV, NASB, RSV, TNT], 'to hold aloof' [ICC], 'to hold off' [Lns], 'to be away from' [LN]. This verb is also conflated with the preposition ἀπό 'from': 'to avoid' [NAB, NEB, NIV, TEV], 'to shun' [NJB], 'to hold off' [Hn], 'to keep clear of' [HNTC].

QUESTION—How is this clause related to the preceding one?
1. This is the negative counterpart to the preceding positive command.
1.1 When the preceding clause is taken to refer specifically to prophecies. Instead of treating 'evil' as a substantive, it could be considered an adjective [NCBC, WBC]: test all prophetic utterances; hold fast to the good utterances, but abstain from every evil kind of utterance. In this case, an evil prophecy would be one that was contrary to the gospel teachings and practices [WBC].
1.2 When the preceding clause is taken to refer to spiritual gifts in general [EBC, HNTC, ICC]: test all claims of spiritual gifts; hold fast to those that promote what is good, but avoid every evil kind. Whether 'evil' is taken to be a noun, 'every kind of evil' [EBC], or an adjective, 'every

evil kind' [HNTC, ICC], the meaning is the same [ICC]. Evil is that which hinders the growth of the church.
1.3 When the preceding clause is taken to be a general principle [Fn, Hb, Lns, NIC, WBC, Wd]: test all things; hold fast to what is good, but abstain from every kind of evil. One form of evil, immorality, has been mentioned in 4:3 [Hb, WBC]. It includes perversions of the true teachings [Hb, Lns].
2. This is a general principle, broader than the reference to what is good.
2.1 When the preceding clause is taken to refer specifically to prophecies [Ea, Hn, My, TH]: hold fast to the good utterances. Avoid (evil kinds of prophetic advice and) every other form of evil.
2.2 When the preceding clause is taken to refer to spiritual gifts in general [El]: hold fast to the good gifts. Avoid (evil claims of gifts and) every form of evil.

QUESTION—What area of meaning is intended by εἴδους 'form/appearance'?
1. This refers to the form that evil takes or the kind of evil [Alf, Ea, EBC, El, Fn, Hb, Hn, HNTC, ICC, Lns, Mn, My, NCBC, NIC, Rb, TH, WBC, Wd; NASB, NEB, NIV, NJB, RSV, TEV, TNT]: every kind of evil.
2. This refers to even the appearance of evil [KJV, NAB]: every appearance of evil. This can be taken to mean to avoid anything that looks evil to others although, in itself, it may not be evil. However, some who mention 'appearance' as an alternate interpretation, take it to mean that they were to avoid any evil that appears [Hb, Mn, NIC].

DISCOURSE UNIT: 5:23–28 [EBC, Er, HNTC, Lns, NIC; NAB, NJB]. The topic is the conclusion [EBC, Er, Lns, NIC], prayer, exhortation, and benediction [HNTC], prayer and farewell greeting [NAB, NJB].

DISCOURSE UNIT: 5:23–24 [Alf, EBC, Hb, Hn, ICC, Mn, WBC, Wd]. The topic is prayer for the Thessalonians [EBC, ICC, Mn, WBC, Wd], prayer for their sanctification [Hb, Hn].

5:23 **Now/But**[a]
LEXICON—a. δέ (LN 89.94; 89.124): 'now' [HNTC, ICC, Lns, WBC; NASB], 'and' [Hn; KJV], not explicit [NAB, NEB, NIV, NJB, RSV, TEV, TNT].
QUESTION—What relationship is indicated by this conjunction?
1. This indicates transition to a new topic [Ea, Hb, Hn, HNTC, Lns, WBC; KJV, NASB]: now.
2. This indicates a contrast [Alf, El, Fn, ICC, My, NIC]: I have been urging you to do the preceding things, but it is God who will actually enable you to do so. It also introduces a new section [ICC].

(may) the God of-peace[a] **himself**[b] **sanctify**[c] **you completely,**[d]
LEXICON—a. εἰρήνη (LN 22.42; 25.248): 'peace' [BAGD, Hn, HNTC, ICC, LN, Lns, WBC; all versions], 'tranquility' [LN], 'freedom from worry' [LN]. See this word at 1:1 and the verb form at 5:13.

b. αὐτός (LN 92.37; 92.11): 'himself' [HNTC, ICC, WBC; NASB, NEB, NIV, RSV, TNT], 'the very' [KJV], 'he' [Hn, Lns], not explicit [NAB, NJB, TEV]. This word is emphatic [Ea, El, Hb, Lns, NCBC]. See this word at 3:11.

c. aorist act. opt. of ἁγιάζω (LN **88.26**): 'to sanctify' [BAGD, Hn, HNTC, Lns, WBC; KJV, NASB, NIV, RSV], 'to make holy' [LN; NAB, NEB, NJB, TEV, TNT], 'to consecrate' [BAGD, ICC]. The aorist tense indicates that the completion of sanctification is in view [Hb, WBC].

d. ὁλοτελής (LN **78.47**): 'completely' [HNTC, LN, WBC], 'entirely' [NASB, TNT], 'wholly' [BAGD, Lns; KJV, RSV], 'in every way' [TEV], 'in every part' [NEB], 'through and through' [BAGD, Hn, ICC; NIV]; or '(to make) perfect' [NAB, NJB]. This word is emphasized [Lns].

QUESTION—In what sense is εἰρήνης 'peace' meant here?
1. It refers to the peaceful relationship between God and people [EBC, Hb].
2. It refers to a feeling of tranquility [Ea, El].
3. It is a state in which material and spiritual matters are going well [Hn, ICC, NIC, TH].
4. It refers to all the blessings of salvation which accompany the gospel [HNTC, NCBC, WBC].

QUESTION—How are the two nouns related in the genitive construction ὁ θεὸς τῆς εἰρήνης 'the God of peace'?

God brings about peace [Ea, EBC, Er, Hb, HNTC, ICC, Lns, Mn, My, NCBC, Rb, TH, WBC; TEV, TNT]: the God who gives/establishes peace. When the peace is between God and believers, it means that he has made such a relationship possible by Christ's death [EBC]. When the peace refers to tranquility of heart, it means that he produces this state [Ea, El].

QUESTION—In what way does God sanctify believers?

This is the same in meaning as strengthening their hearts unblamable in holiness before God (3:13) [WBC]. This means that God separates them from a life of sin [Hn], sets them apart for himself [EBC, Er, Hb, Hn, Lns, NIC] to be devoted to him [ICC] and to serve him [Er]. It also refers to a process in which their characters come to match this separation [Er, Hb, ICC, NIC, WBC, Wd]. The process started when they believed, but must be continued and completed [Mn, NCBC, TH]. He sanctifies them completely, so that nothing is lacking [Ea].

QUESTION—How is ὁλοτελής 'completely' related to the verb?
1. This indicates the degree in which God sanctifies [Ea, EBC, TH, WBC]: may God completely sanctify you. Sanctification is a process and here he has the completing of it in view [EBC, TH, WBC].
2. This indicates the extent [Hb, ICC, Lns, My, Rb]: may God sanctify every part of you, the whole of each of you. No part is to be neglected [Hb].

and[a]

LEXICON—a. καί (LN 89.92; 89.87): 'and' [Hn, HNTC, ICC, Lns, WBC; KJV, NASB, NEB, NJB, RSV, TEV], not explicit [NAB, NIV, TNT].

1 THESSALONIANS 5:23

QUESTION—What relationship is indicated by this conjunction?

This indicates a restatement of the previous clause [Alf, Ea, El, Er, Hb, HNTC, ICC, Lns, My, NCBC, NIC, WBC, Wd]: may God sanctify you wholly, *that is*, may he keep every aspect of your being whole and blameless at the coming of Christ. It elaborates on the previous statement [Hb, HNTC, ICC, Lns, Wd]. It adds the time that this is to be completed [NCBC]. It details the effects of sanctification [Alf]. It is a more specific petition of the preceding general prayer [Ea, El].

(may) sound/whole^a your spirit^b and soul^c and body^d blamelessly^e be kept^f

LEXICON—a. ὁλόκληρος (LN **59.30**): 'sound' [BAGD; NEB, RSV], 'undamaged' [BAGD; TNT], 'without flaw' [Hn], 'entire' [LN], 'intact' [BAGD, ICC, Wd], 'whole' [BAGD, HNTC; KJV, NIV, TEV], 'whole and entire' [NAB], 'entire' [Lns], 'in entirety' [WBC], 'complete' [BAGD; NASB], not explicit [NJB]. This word is in an emphatic position [Alf, Lns].

b. πνεῦμα (LN 26.9): 'spirit' [BAGD, Hn, HNTC, ICC, LN, Lns, WBC; all versions].

c. ψυχή (LN **26.4**; 23.88): 'soul' [BAGD, Hn, HNTC, ICC, Lns, WBC; all versions except NJB], 'life' [BAGD, LN; NJB].

d. σῶμα (LN 8.1; 9.8): 'body' [BAGD, Hn, HNTC, ICC, LN, Lns, WBC; all versions].

e. ἀμέμπτως (LN 88.317): 'blamelessly' [BAGD, Lns], 'blameless' [ICC, LN; KJV, NIV, NJB, RSV, TNT], 'without blame' [Hn, LN; NASB], 'without fault' [HNTC; NEB], 'free from every fault' [TEV], 'free from blame' [WBC], 'irreproachable' [NAB]. See this word at 2:10.

f. aorist pass. opt. of τηρέω (LN 13.32; 37.122): 'to be kept' [BAGD, Hn, ICC, LN; NIV, NJB, RSV], 'to be preserved' [BAGD, HNTC, Lns, WBC; KJV, NASB], 'to be guarded' [LN]. The passive voice is also translated actively: 'may he preserve' [NAB], 'may he keep' [NEB, TEV, TNT].

QUESTION—With what does ὁλόκληρον 'sound/whole' relate and which area of meaning is intended?

It is an adjective which is singular in number and neuter in gender, in agreement with the first noun following it, πνεῦμα 'spirit'. Most say that it refers to all three nouns, spirit, soul, and body, and takes the person and gender from the one that is nearest to it [Alf, Ea, EBC, ICC, Lns, Mn, My, NIC, WBC].

1. The adjective refers to extent [HNTC, ICC, Lns, TH; NIV, TEV]: may every part of your spirit, and of your soul, and of your body be kept blameless.

2. The adjective refers to ethical soundness [EBC, Hb, NCBC; TNT]: may your spirit, soul, and body be kept sound.

QUESTION—With what does ἀμέμπτως 'blamelessly' relate and how does this connect with the adjective?

It is an adverb. However, some point out that it does not describe the manner in which the implied actor, God, keeps the believers [ICC, Lns]. As an adverb it could modify an adjective: 'blamelessly sound'. However, commentaries speak of it as modifying the verb: it describes the manner in which spirit, soul, and body are to be preserved in this life [Lns], or it indicates the result of being kept [ICC].

1. May your whole spirit, soul, and body be kept blameless at Christ's coming [HNTC, TH; NIV, TEV].
2. May your spirit, soul, and body be kept whole and blameless at Christ's coming [Alf, EBC, Er; RSV].
3. May your spirit, soul, and body be kept whole, so as to be blameless at Christ's coming [Hb, ICC; TNT].
4. May your spirit, soul, and body be kept free from any fault [NCBC].
5. This implies the verb 'may it be' and it pertains only to 'spirit' [Hn]: may your spirit be sound (without flaw) and may your soul and body be kept blameless.

QUESTION—How distinct are the differences between the terms, spirit, soul, and body, intended to be?

Together, these three terms emphasize the completeness of sanctification in one's whole being [Er, Fn, Mn, NCBC, NIC, WBC, Wd]. The three are equivalent to 'your hearts' in 3:13 [WBC]. The body is the material part of a person and the soul and spirit are the immaterial parts [EBC, El, Hb, Hn, WBC]. There are different views about the distinction between spirit and soul. Dichotomists hold that the differences are functional, trichotomists hold that the differences are substantive [Hb].

1. 'Spirit' and 'soul' refer to the same immaterial part of a person with no clear distinctions intended [WBC, Wd], or with different functions of the same part in view [Er, Fn, Hn, HNTC, Lns, NIC, WBC]. 'Spirit' refers to the immaterial part of a person from the aspect of its relation to God [Er, Fn, Hn, Lns], it is the mind of the believer who is in fellowship with God [Wd]. 'Soul' refers to the immaterial part from the aspect of its sensations, affections, and desires [Hn]; it animates the body and receives impressions from the body [Lns]; it is one's personality [Fn].
2. 'Spirit' and 'soul' refer to separate immaterial parts of a person [Alf, EBC, El, My, NCBC]. Some distinctions that are made are: the 'spirit' is the life principle [Hb], the part of one's nature that has a relationship with God [Alf, EBC, NCBC]. The 'soul' is the self-conscious life, the personality of a person [EBC, El, Hb, NCBC], the center of one's will and emotion [EBC, El, NCBC].

1 THESSALONIANS 5:23

in[a] the coming[b] of the Lord of-us, Jesus Christ.

LEXICON—a. ἐν (LN 67.33): 'in', 'in connection with' [Lns], 'unto' [KJV], 'at' [Hn, HNTC, ICC, WBC; NAB, NASB, NIV, RSV, TEV], 'when' [NEB, TNT], 'for' [NJB].

b. παρουσία (LN 15.86): 'the coming' [BAGD, Hn, ICC, LN; KJV, NAB, NASB, NIV, NJB, RSV, TEV], 'advent' [BAGD, WBC], 'parousia' [HNTC, Lns]. This noun is also translated as a verb: 'to come' [NEB, TNT]. See this word at 2:19.

QUESTION—What relationship is indicated by ἐν 'in'?

They are to be kept through all that period before the moment he comes and so it implies that they are to be kept blameless *until* he comes [Hb, HNTC, ICC, NIC, TH, WBC]. However, the point that is in focus is when they will be pronounced blameless *at* the time he comes [Alf, Ea, Hb, HNTC, ICC, NIC, Rb, TH, WBC]. Preservation occurs during one's life before the coming of Christ and so this is all done *in connection* with his coming [Lns].

5:24 Faithful[a] (is) the (one) calling[b] you,

LEXICON—a. πιστός (LN 31.87): 'faithful' [BAGD, HNTC, ICC, LN, Lns, WBC; KJV, NASB, NIV, RSV, TEV], 'trustworthy' [BAGD, LN; NAB, NJB, TNT], 'to be trusted' [NEB], 'dependable' [BAGD, LN], 'reliable' [Hn, LN].

b. pres. act. participle of καλέω (LN 33.312): 'to call' [BAGD, Hn, HNTC, ICC, LN, Lns, WBC; all versions]. The present tense is timeless and characterizes God as the one who calls people [Ea, El, Fn, Hb, Hn, ICC, Lns, My, NIC, Rb, WBC], or it means a continuing call to them [HNTC, NIC, TH, Wd].

QUESTION—Who is the one who calls them?

It is God [Alf, Ea, EBC, Er, Fn, Hb, ICC, Mn, My, NIC, WBC], the Father [TH]. This is made specific at 2:12 and 4:7 [TH]. He called them through the preaching of the gospel [Hb, ICC].

QUESTION—What does God call them to be?

God calls them to be consecrated to himself [Fn], to be sanctified [ICC, WBC], to be his people [NCBC, TH], to enter his kingdom [My, NCBC].

QUESTION—In what respect is God faithful?

He can be trusted to do all that he has said and planned [Ea, Hb, Hn, Lns], he keeps his promises [Ea, El, My, NCBC, TH], and he is faithful to his own nature [El]. He is faithful to help believers respond to and obey his call to be sanctified [Ea, EGT, ICC, WBC], and to answer Paul's prayer [EBC].

who indeed[a] will-do (it).

LEXICON—a. καί (LN 89.93; 91.12): 'indeed' [TNT], 'also' [Hn, ICC, Lns; KJV, NASB], 'and' [HNTC; NIV, NJB, RSV], 'therefore' [NAB], not explicit [WBC; NEB, TEV].

QUESTION—What relationship does this phrase have to the preceding one?

This indicates the conclusion of the preceding grounds: since he is faithful, *therefore* he will do it [ICC, NCBC, TH; NAB, TEV].

174   1 THESSALONIANS 5:24

QUESTION—What will he do?
He will enable them to respond to, and carry out, his call [Ea, Fn, Hb, WBC], he will sanctify and keep them (5:23) [Alf, Ea, EBC, EGT, El, Hb, Hn, ICC, Lns, My, WBC].

DISCOURSE UNIT: 5:25–28 [Alf, Fn, Hb, Mn, NCBC, WBC, Wd]. The topic is the conclusion of the letter [Alf, Fn, Hb, WBC], concluding requests and benediction [Mn, NCBC, Wd].

DISCOURSE UNIT: 5:25–27 [EBC, EGT, ICC, My]. The topic is final requests [ICC], concluding counsel and prayer [EGT], the way the Thessalonians should respond [EBC].

5:25 Brothers, pray[a] also[b] concerning[c] us.
TEXT—Some manuscripts omit καί 'also'. It is included in brackets by GNT with a C rating, indicating a considerable degree of doubt in doing so. It is omitted or not translated by El, KJV, NASB, NIV, NJB, and RSV.
LEXICON—a. pres. mid. (deponent = active) impera. of προσεύχομαι (LN 33.178): 'to pray' [BAGD, Hn, HNTC, ICC, LN, Lns, WBC; all versions except TNT]. The clause is also restructured: 'we need your prayers' [TNT]. The present tense indicates that the Thessalonians are to keep on praying for them [Hb, Lns, NIC, Wd].
 b. καί (LN 89.93): 'also' [HNTC, WBC; NEB, TEV], 'too' [NAB, TNT], 'as well' [ICC].
 c. περί (LN 89.6; 90.36; 90.24): 'concerning', 'about' [Mou (p. 63)], 'for' [Hn, HNTC, ICC, Lns, WBC; all versions except TNT].
QUESTION—What is inferred by the use of καί 'also'?
 1. This is connected with the prayers of the missionaries (5:23) [Fn, HNTC, Mn, My, NCBC, WBC]: we have prayed for you, you also should pray for us.
 2. This is connected with the others the Thessalonians pray for (5:17) [EBC, ICC]: as well as praying for yourselves and others, pray for us also.

5:26 Greet[a] all the brothers with a-holy[b] kiss.[c]
LEXICON—a. aorist mid. (deponent = active) impera. of ἀσπάζομαι (LN 33.20): 'to greet' [BAGD, Hn, HNTC, ICC, LN, WBC; all versions], 'to salute' [Lns].
 b. ἅγιος (LN 88.24): 'holy' [BAGD, Hn, HNTC, ICC, LN, Lns, WBC; all versions except NEB, TEV], 'pure' [LN], 'brotherly' [TEV]. This is also translated with the name it later acquired: '(kiss) of peace' [NEB].
 c. φίλημα (LN 34.62): 'kiss' [BAGD, Hn, HNTC, ICC, LN, Lns, WBC; all versions except NAB]. This is also translated with a cultural substitute: 'embrace' [NAB].
QUESTION—Who are involved in the greeting?
 1. The missionaries want to greet the members of the church by having people present in Thessalonica greet others on their behalf [Ea, EGT, Er, Fn, Hb, HNTC, ICC, Lns, Mn, NCBC, NIC]: greet all the brothers for us

to show our love for them. Some commentators specify that the elders are to greet the other members on behalf of the missionaries [Alf, Ea, EBC, El, Fn, Hb]. Others think that all the members are to greet one another on behalf of the missionaries [HNTC, ICC, Lns, Mn, NCBC]. Each member would greet several others so that no one was left out [NCBC].
2. The members of the church are to greet one another to express their own love for each other and also their unity [WBC]: greet all the brothers to show your love for them.

QUESTION—How was this kissing done?

Some commentators understand that the men and women were segregated in the meetings [Ea, Hb], so men kissed men and women kissed women [EBC, Hb, NIC, WBC]. Others do not rule out the possibility that one might kiss either sex [Ea, Er]. The kiss was not on the lips [HNTC], but on the cheek [Hb]. Greeting with a kiss was already a custom practiced in that society [Ea, El, Er, Fn, Hb, HNTC, NCBC, NIC].

QUESTION—Why is it called a holy kiss?

The kiss is a mark of a Christian relationship [Ea, EBC, Hn, NCBC] and shows Christian love rather than romantic love [EGT, Hb, ICC, NCBC] or worldly, secular esteem [Ea, EBC, EGT, NCBC]. It indicated brotherly love for all those within the spiritual family [Hb]. It was given between those who are holy (saints) [HNTC].

5:27 I adjure[a] you (by)[b] the Lord
LEXICON—a. pres. act. indic. of ἐνορκίζω (LN **33.467**): 'to adjure' [BAGD, ICC, Lns, WBC; NAB, NASB, NEB, RSV], 'to charge' [HNTC; KJV, NIV], 'to solemnly charge' [Hn; TNT], 'to urge' [TEV], 'my orders are' [NJB], 'to ask one to swear' [LN].
b. accusative case: 'by' [HNTC, ICC, Lns, WBC; KJV, NAB, NASB, NEB, RSV], 'before' [Hn; NIV], 'by the authority of' [TEV], 'in (the Lord's) name' [NJB, TNT]. The accusative case is commonly used to name the person involved in an oath [WBC].

QUESTION—To whom does ὑμᾶς 'you (plural)' refer?

This is addressed to whomever the letter was first handed [Lns]. Some take it to refer to the leaders of the church [Alf, Fn, Hb, HNTC, My, WBC], since they presumably would have been the original recipients of the letter [Hb, HNTC]. Another view is that it refers to the congregation as a unit [ICC].

QUESTION—To whom does 'the Lord' refer?

It refers to Jesus Christ [Hb, ICC, TH].

for the letter[a] to-be-read[b] to-all the brothers.
TEXT—Some manuscripts modify 'brothers' with ἁγίοις 'holy'. GNT omits this adjective with a B rating, indicating some degree of doubt in omitting it. It is included only by KJV.
LEXICON—a. ἐπιστολή (LN 6.63; 33.48): 'letter' [HNTC, ICC, LN, Lns, WBC; all versions except KJV], 'epistle' [Hn; KJV].

176   1 THESSALONIANS 5:27

b. aorist pass. infin. of ἀναγινώσκω (LN 33.68): 'to be read' [ICC, LN, Lns, WBC; KJV, NAB, NJB, RSV]. This passive is also translated 'to have it read' [Hn; NASB, NEB, NIV, TNT], 'to have it read aloud' [HNTC], 'to read' [TEV]. It should be read aloud publicly [El, Er, Hb, HNTC, Mn, NCBC, NIC, Rb]. The aorist tense indicates a definite occasion for reading to the congregation [Hb].

DISCOURSE UNIT: 5:28 [EBC, Hb, ICC]. The topic is the benediction [EBC, Hb, ICC].

5:28 **The grace^a of-the Lord of-us Jesus Christ (be) with^b you.**

TEXT—Some manuscripts add at the end, ἀμήν 'amen'. GNT omits it with a B rating, indicating some degree of doubt in omitting it. It is included only by KJV.

LEXICON—a. χάρις (LN 88.66): 'grace' [BAGD, Hn, HNTC, ICC, LN, Lns, WBC; all versions]. See this word at 1:1.

b. μετά (LN 90.60): 'with' [Lns]. This implies the verb εἴη or ἐστω 'be with' [Hn, HNTC, ICC, WBC; all versions].

EXEGETICAL SUMMARY OF 2 THESSALONIANS

DISCOURSE UNIT: 1:1–2 [Alf, EBC, EGT, Er, GNT, Hb, HNTC, ICC, Lns, Mn, My, NCBC, NIC, SSA, TH, WBC, Wd; NAB, NIV, NJB, TEV]. The topic is the greeting [EBC, Er, GNT, Hb, Lns, NCBC, NIC, TH, Wd; NAB], the address [EGT; NJB], the address and greeting [Alf, HNTC, Mn, My], the superscription [ICC, WBC].

1:1 **Paul and Silvanus and Timothy to-the church of-Thessalonians in God (the) Father of-us and (the) Lord Jesus Christ:**

This verse is identical with 1 Thess. 1:1a except that here ἡμῶν 'of us' is added after πατρί 'Father'. The pronoun ἡμῶν 'of us' is inclusive [EBC, Er, Hb, Hn, HNTC, ICC, Mn, NCBC, NIC, SSA].

1:2 **Grace to you and peace**

This clause is identical with 1 Thess. 1:1b.

from[a] God the Father of-us and (the) Lord Jesus Christ.

TEXT—Some manuscripts omit ἡμῶν 'of us' after πατρός 'Father'. GNT includes it in brackets with a C rating, indicating a considerable degree of doubt about including it. It is also included by Ea, WBC, KJV, and TEV.

LEXICON—a. ἀπό (LN 90.15): 'from' [BAGD, Hn, HNTC, ICC, LN, Lns, WBC; all versions except TEV]. This is also translated with an active verb: 'may (God and Christ) give (grace and peace to you)' [TEV].

DISCOURSE UNIT: 1:3–12 [Alf, EBC, GNT, Hb, HNTC, ICC, Lns, Mn, My, NCBC, NIC, SSA, TH, WBC, Wd; NIV, NJB, TEV]. The topic is thanksgiving [NCBC], prayer [NIC], encouragement [Hb], thanksgiving and prayer [ICC, Lns, Mn; NIV], thanksgiving, encouragement, and prayer [HNTC, WBC], thanksgiving, encouragement, and judgment [NJB], judgment [EBC, GNT, TH; TEV], vindication [Wd], introduction to the letter [Alf, My].

DISCOURSE UNIT: 1:3–10 [EBC, EGT, Er, ICC, Lns; NAB]. The topic is thanksgiving [EBC, EGT, Er, ICC, Lns], praise for the Thessalonians [NAB].

DISCOURSE UNIT: 1:3–5 [NIC]. The topic is thanksgiving.

DISCOURSE UNIT: 1:3–4 [Alf, Hb, SSA, WBC, Wd]. The topic is thanksgiving.

1:3 **We-ought[a] to-thank[b] God always[c] concerning[d] you, brothers,**

LEXICON—a. pres. act. indic. of ὀφείλω (LN 71.25): '(we) ought' [BAGD, HNTC, ICC, LN, SSA; NASB, NIV], '(we) must' [BAGD; NJB, TEV, TNT], 'to be bound (to thank God)' [WBC; KJV, RSV], 'to be obliged to' [Hn, Lns]. This is also translated by changing the subject of the verb: 'our thanks are due' [NEB]. This is also conflated with the following clause: 'it is no more than right' [NAB].

b. pres. act. infin. of εὐχαριστέω (LN 33.349): 'to thank' [HNTC, ICC, LN; KJV, NAB, NIV, NJB, TEV], 'to give thanks' [BAGD, Hn, Lns, WBC; NASB, RSV, TNT]. The present tense indicates that this should be continual or repeated [Hb, Rb]. See this word at 1 Thess. 1:2.

c. πάντοτε (LN 67.88): 'always' [BAGD, Hn, HNTC, ICC, LN, Lns, WBC; KJV, NASB, NEB, NIV, NJB, RSV], 'unceasingly' [NAB], 'at all times' [BAGD, LN; TEV]. This adverb is also translated negatively: 'we must not cease' [TNT]. In this last case, it avoids implying that they were not yet thanking God. This is considered a hyperbole meaning 'very frequently' [SSA]. See this word at 1 Thess. 1:2.

d. περί (LN 89.6): 'concerning' [BAGD, Lns], 'for' [Hn, HNTC, ICC, WBC; all versions]. See this word at 1 Thess. 1:2.

QUESTION—To whom does 'we' refer?

It refers to the three men mentioned in 1:1, Paul, Silvanus, and Timothy [El, Fn, Hb, Hn, Lns, Mn, My, SSA, TH, WBC]. Some commentators discuss the possibility that 'we' could be an editorial plural, referring only to Paul [Ea, EBC, Hb, HNTC, ICC, NCBC, NIC, Rb], but none have clearly supported this view. This is the same conclusion that was reached in 1 Thess. 1:2.

QUESTION—Which verb does the adverb πάντοτε 'always' modify?

1. It modifies the infinitive εὐχαριστεῖν 'to thank' [ICC, Mn, My, NCBC, SSA, WBC; probably KJV, NAB, NASB, NIV, NJB, RSV, TEV, TNT]: we ought to always be thanking God.
2. It modifies the indicative ὀφείλομεν 'we ought' [Hb, HNTC; NEB]: we always ought to thank God.

QUESTION—In what respect was it their obligation to thank God?

It was their personal obligation to God [EBC, Er, Hb, HNTC, Mn, NIC, Rb]. They felt the moral necessity of thanking God [Hb, Hn, Lns, TH, Wd]. God was responsible for the good actions of the Thessalonians and should be thanked [EBC, Rb]. Their joy over the news about the Thessalonians compelled them to thank God [NCBC]. It would be wrong not to thank God [NIC] and they could not help but thank God [Lns].

as^a it-is fitting,^b

LEXICON—a. καθώς (LN 64.14): 'as' [BAGD, Hn, HNTC, ICC, WBC; KJV, NASB, RSV], 'even as' [Lns], not explicit [NEB, TEV, TNT]. This is also conflated with the noun: 'it is no more than right' [NAB], 'and rightly so' [NIV], 'quite rightly' [NJB].

b. ἄξιος (LN 66.6): 'fitting' [BAGD, Hn, LN, WBC; NASB, RSV, TNT], 'right' [HNTC; NAB, NEB, TEV], 'proper' [BAGD, ICC, LN], 'meet' [KJV], 'worthy' [BAGD, Lns], 'worthy of' [LN]. This adjective is also translated as an adverb: 'rightly', [NIV, NJB].

QUESTION—What relationship is indicated by καθώς 'as'?

This relationship is variously described, even by the same commentators. Some say that it indicates the reason for the preceding statement [EBC, Hb, HNTC, ICC, Mn, My, NCBC, NIC, SSA]: I ought to thank God, because it is fitting that I do so. Others speak of a correspondence or harmony with the preceding statement [Hb, Hn], probably meaning that this adds a supporting comment [TH]: I ought to thank God, and indeed it is fitting that I do so. Many indicate that 'we ought' indicates the missionaries' subjective sense of responsibility to thank God, while 'it is fitting' indicates the objective merit of the Thessalonians' conduct [Alf, Ea, El, Er, Fn, Mn, My, Rb, SSA, Wd]. Or it resumes and explains the preceding [ICC]: I must thank God, and indeed it is fitting that I thank God. It is also described as indicating comparison, and this is explained as indicating a balance between the feeling of obligation to thank God and the worthiness of having such a feeling [Lns].

because/that[a] is-growing-abundantly[b] your faith

LEXICON—a. ὅτι (LN 89.33; 90.21): 'because' [Hn, HNTC, ICC, WBC; all versions except KJV, TNT], 'because that' [KJV], 'for' [TNT]; or 'that' [Lns].

b. pres. act. indic. of ὑπεραυξάνω (LN **78.6**): 'to grow abundantly' [WBC; RSV], 'to grow exceedingly' [ICC, Lns; KJV, TNT], 'to grow greatly' [HNTC], 'to grow apace' [NAB], 'to grow more and more' [NIV], 'to grow so much' [TEV], 'to grow so wonderfully' [BAGD; NJB], 'to grow beyond measure' [Hn], 'to be greatly enlarged' [NASB], 'to increase abundantly' [BAGD], 'to increase mightily' [NEB], 'to increase exceedingly' [LN]. This verb is in an emphatic position [Hb].

QUESTION—What relationship is indicated by ὅτι 'because/that'?

1. This indicates the two reasons that they feel that they ought to thank God [Ea, EGT, Fn, Hb, Hn, HNTC, ICC, Mn, NCBC, Rb, SSA, WBC]: we ought to thank God because your faith is growing and because your love is increasing. This also implies that the clause is, at the same time, the content of their thanksgiving [EGT, Fn].
2. This indicates the two grounds for saying that it is the right thing to do [Alf, EBC, El, Wd; NEB, TEV, TNT]: we ought to thank God, as it is the right thing to do since your faith is growing and since your love is increasing.
3. This indicates the content of what they thank God for [Lns, NIC, SSA]: we ought to thank God (as it is fitting to do) that your faith is growing and your love is increasing. This also implies that what they thank God for is the reason why they thank him.

QUESTION—What is involved in their faith?

Faith refers to their confidence and trust in God [Hb], in Christ [SSA, TH], and their acceptance of the gospel [Hb].

and the love[a] of-each one of-you all for one-another is-increasing,[b]

LEXICON—a. ἀγάπη (LN 25.43): 'love' [BAGD, Hn, HNTC, ICC, LN, Lns, WBC; all versions except KJV], 'charity' [KJV].

b. pres. act. indic. of πλεονάζω (LN 59.67; 59.48): 'to increase' [BAGD, Hn, ICC, Lns; NAB, NIV, NJB, RSV], 'to increase considerably' [LN], 'to multiply' [LN, WBC], 'to grow' [BAGD], 'to grow ever greater'

[NASB, NEB], 'to become greater' [TEV], 'to be on the increase' [TNT], 'to abound' [HNTC; KJV].

1:4 therefore[a]

LEXICON—a. ὥστε (LN 89.52): 'therefore' [NASB, NIV, RSV], 'so that' [BAGD, Hn, HNTC, ICC, Lns, WBC; KJV], 'so much so that' [NAB], 'that is why' [TEV], 'this makes us' [TNT], 'indeed' [NEB], not explicit [NJB].

QUESTION—What relationship is indicated by this conjunction?

This indicates the result of the preceding two clauses by stating the effect their growing faith and love had on the missionaries [BAGD, Ea, Hb, Hn, HNTC, ICC, Lns, My, NCBC, NIC, Rb, SSA, TH, WBC; KJV, NAB, NASB, NIV, RSV, TEV, TNT]: your faith is growing and your love is increasing, therefore we boast about you.

we ourselves in[a] you boast[b] in[c] the churches[d] of-God

LEXICON—a. ἐν (LN 89.5): 'in' [KJV, NJB], 'of' [Hn, ICC, WBC; NASB, RSV], 'about' [HNTC, Lns; NEB, TEV], not explicit [NAB, NIV, TNT].

b. pres. mid. (deponent = active) infin. of ἐγκαυχάομαι (LN 33.368): 'to boast' [BAGD, Hn, HNTC, ICC, LN, Lns, WBC; NEB, NIV, RSV, TEV], 'to speak proudly' [NASB], 'to speak with pride' [TNT], 'to glory' [KJV], 'to be able to boast' [NAB], 'to take special pride' [NJB]. The present tense indicates that this is their practice [Hb, Lns, SSA].

c. ἐν (LN 83.9): 'in' [Hn, HNTC, ICC, Lns, WBC; KJV, NAB, RSV, TEV], 'among' [NASB, NEB, NIV, NJB], 'to' [TNT].

d. ἐκκλησία (LN 11.32): 'churches' [BAGD, Hn, LN, Lns, WBC; all versions except NAB, NEB], 'congregations' [BAGD, LN; NEB], 'communities' [HNTC; NAB], 'assemblies' [ICC].

QUESTION—What is the significance of the emphatic αὐτοὺς ἡμᾶς 'we ourselves'?

1. This indicates the unexpectedness of their boasting [Fn, Hb, NCBC, NIC, Rb, SSA]: we ourselves, who usually do not boast, do so now. In spite of their usual modesty about work they had been involved in, the unusual growth of the converts brought about this unusual boasting [Hb].

2. This contrasts 'we ourselves' with the Thessalonians [EBC, Hn, ICC, Rb]: we ourselves boast, in contrast with you who don't think yourselves worthy of it. Perhaps the Thessalonians had said they were not worthy of the praise they had received in the first letter [Hn, ICC] and did not expect such praise from the missionaries [Rb].

3. This includes them with others [Alf, Ea, El, Lns, My]: we ourselves, as well as others who have heard about you, boast. Another view is that 'others' refers to the Thessalonians themselves [Mn]: we ourselves, as well as you, have reason to boast.

QUESTION—How are the two nouns related in the genitive construction ταῖς ἐκκλησίαις τοῦ θεοῦ 'the churches of God'?

1. This means the churches (congregations) which worship God [SSA].

2. This means the churches which belong to God [Hb, TH]. Also see this construction at 1 Thess. 2:14 where the two commentaries that discuss this construction take it to mean the churches which belong to God. Probably included in this interpretation is the translation 'the congregations of God's people' [NEB].

QUESTION—What relationship is indicated by ἐν 'in' in the phrase ἐν ταῖς ἐκκλησίαις 'in the churches'?

This indicates the places where they boasted [EBC, Hn, ICC, Lns]: we boast among the churches. This may indicate that the missionaries spoke to the congregations as they traveled about [Hb, NCBC]. However, it could also mean more than physical presence and oral communication. The missionaries could boast by means of written messages to some congregations, or by means of messages passed on by visitors from the churches or travelers going to the churches [EBC, Fn, Hb, Lns].

concerning/because-of[a] the steadfastness[b] of-you and faith[c]

LEXICON—a. ὑπέρ (LN 90.24; 89.28): 'concerning' [BAGD], 'of' [Hn, ICC; NAB], 'about' [BAGD, HNTC; NIV, TEV, TNT] 'for' [WBC; KJV, NASB, NJB, RSV], 'over' [Lns]; or 'because' [NEB]

b. ὑπομονή (LN 25.174): 'steadfastness' [BAGD; RSV, TNT], 'perseverance' [BAGD, Lns; NASB, NIV, NJB], 'endurance' [BAGD, Hn, HNTC, ICC, LN], 'constancy' [NAB], 'patience' [BAGD, WBC; KJV], 'the way you continue to endure' [TEV]. This noun is also translated as a verbal clause in connection with the following πίστεως 'faith': 'your faith remains so steadfast' [NEB].

c. πίστις (LN 31.85; 31.88): 'faith' [Hn, HNTC, ICC, LN, Lns, WBC; all versions except TEV], 'the way you continue to believe' [TEV], 'faithfulness' [BAGD, LN], 'trustworthiness' [LN].

QUESTION—What relationship is indicated by ὑπέρ 'concerning/be-cause of'?

1. This indicates the content of their boasting [BAGD, El, Hb, Hn, HNTC, ICC, Lns, My, NCBC, NIC, SSA]: we boast about you, specifically we boast about your steadfastness and faith.
2. This indicates the reason for their boasting [Hn, SSA; NEB]: we boast about you because of your steadfastness and faith.

QUESTION—How are ὑπομονῆς 'steadfastness' and πίστεως 'faith' related?

1. These are two separate qualities [El, Hb, Hn, ICC, My, NCBC, SSA, TH, WBC]: your steadfastness and your faith.
2. Steadfastness is an attribute of their faith [EGT, Wd; NEB]: your steadfast faith.

QUESTION—What did he boast about in relation to their steadfastness?

He boasted that they remained steadfast in their faith under persecution for their faith [El, Fn, Hb, HNTC, NCBC], they continued to be faithful to God [TH], and continued in their spiritual growth [EBC]. They bore persecution quietly and steadfastly with the expectation that God would give them a final deliverance [Ea].

QUESTION—What did he boast about in relation to their faith?

Some commentators take this to mean their faithfulness to God [BAGD, EBC, HNTC, My] so as to be similar in nature with 'steadfastness'; it is the proving of one's faith in Christ [My]. Most reject this meaning, and take it to be their active faith as in the preceding verse [Alf, Fn, ICC, Mn, TH], specifically, their faith in God [Hn, NCBC, NIC], in Christ [El, Hb, Lns, SSA], in both God and Christ [Ea], in God's faithfulness to them [NIC], and in God's promises [Hn]. They are keeping their trust in the Lord in the midst of persecution [Fn, Hb, Mn]. Their faith in God enabled them to be steadfast [Ea, Hb, NCBC, NIC].

in[a] all your persecutions[b] and the afflictions[c] which you-endure,[d]

LEXICON—a. ἐν (LN 89.80; 67.136): 'in' [Hn, HNTC, ICC, Lns, WBC; KJV, NAB, NIV, RSV], 'in the midst of' [NASB], 'under' [NEB, NJB], 'through' [TEV], 'during' [TNT].

b. διωγμός (LN 39.45): 'persecutions' [BAGD, Hn, HNTC, ICC, LN, Lns, WBC; all versions].

c. θλῖψις (LN 22.2): 'afflictions' [BAGD, Hn, ICC, Lns, WBC; NASB, RSV, TNT], 'tribulations' [BAGD, HNTC; KJV], 'persecutions' [LN], 'troubles' [NEB], 'trials' [NAB, NIV], 'hardships' [NJB], 'sufferings' [LN; TEV].

d. pres. mid. indic. of ἀνέχομαι (LN 25.171): 'to endure' [BAGD, Lns, WBC; KJV, NAB, NASB, NEB, NIV, RSV], 'to hold up under' [Hn], 'to bear' [HNTC, ICC; NJB], 'to have patience' [LN], 'to suffer' [TNT], 'to experience' [TEV]. The position of the verb makes it emphatic [ICC]. The present tense indicates that these difficulties were going on when the letter was being written, having continued from the first, or having been renewed [Alf, Ea, El, Fn, Hb, HNTC, ICC, Lns, Mn, My, NCBC, NIC, WBC]. It implies that they were successful in enduring trials [NCBC].

QUESTION—What relationship is indicated by ἐν 'in'?

This indicates the circumstances in which the Thessalonians displayed their steadfastness and faith [Hb, HNTC, ICC, SSA]: you showed your steadfastness and faith while you were being persecuted and while you were enduring afflictions.

QUESTION—How do the two nouns διωγμοῖς 'persecutions' and θλίψεσιν 'afflictions' differ from each other?

The first refers to acts of hostility towards the believers because they are believers [EBC, Hb, Mn, NIC, SSA], and of injury done to them, or to their property, by those who oppose the gospel [Ea]. The second is a more generic term [Ea, EBC, EGT, El, Fn, Hb, Hn, Lns, Mn, My, NIC, Rb, SSA, Wd], which includes sickness, hunger, poverty [Ea, SSA], and also loss of friends, and the breaking up of families [Ea]. But here some commentators say that it specifically means the difficult experiences they went through because of their faith [Fn, Hb, NIC]. Some take the two terms to be virtually synonymous [HNTC, ICC, NCBC, NIC], used for rhetorical effect [NCBC], or the second is the result of the first [Hn, Lns].

QUESTION—To what does αἷς 'which' refer?
1. It refers only to the preceding feminine noun θλίψεσιν 'afflictions' [Hn, My, WBC; NEB, RSV]: in all your persecutions, and in the afflictions you endure.
2. It refers to both of the two preceding nouns [HNTC, ICC, TH; NAB, NIV, NJB, TEV, TNT]: in all your persecutions and afflictions that you endure. It agrees in gender with the immediately preceding ταῖς θλίψεσιν 'the afflictions (feminine gender)' but includes τοῖς διωγμοῖς 'the persecutions (masculine gender)' [ICC]. One translation takes the last phrase to be the beginning of a sentence which is continued in the following verse [NAB]: You endure these as evidence of God's righteous judgment.

DISCOURSE UNIT: 1:5–12 [Fn]. The topic is the coming judgment.

DISCOURSE UNIT: 1:5–10 [Alf, Hb, SSA, WBC, Wd]. The topic is the encouragement of Christ's return [Alf, Hb, WBC], God's just judgment [SSA].

1:5 an-evidence[a] of-the just[b] judgment[c] of-God,

LEXICON—a. ἔνδειγμα (LN 28.52): 'evidence' [BAGD, LN; NIV, RSV], 'evidence' [LN], 'clear evidence' [TH], 'indication' [LN, Lns], 'plain indication' [BAGD; NASB], 'evident indication' [Hn], 'sure sign' [HNTC], 'sure token' [WBC], 'manifest token' [KJV], 'proof positive' [ICC], 'clear example' [TNT], 'expression' [NAB]. This noun is also translated as a verb: 'to bring out' [NEB], 'to show' [NJB], 'to show clearly' [SSA], 'to prove' [TEV].
b. δίκαιος (LN 88.12): 'just' [LN; NAB, NJB, TEV], 'righteous' [BAGD, Hn, HNTC, ICC, LN, Lns, WBC; KJV, NASB, RSV], 'right' [NIV]. This adjective is also translated as a noun: 'justice' [NEB, TNT]; and as an adverb: 'justly' [SSA].
c. κρίσις (LN **56.24**): 'judgment' [BAGD, Hn, HNTC, ICC, Lns, WBC; all versions], 'verdict' [LN]. This noun is also translated as a verb: '(God) will judge' [SSA].

QUESTION—How is this verse related to what precedes?
1. ἔνδειγμα 'evidence' is in the nominative case, functioning as a predicate nominative with ὅ ἐστιν 'which is' to be supplied [Alf, Ea, El, Fn, HNTC, Lns, My, SSA, WBC; KJV, NASB, NIV, RSV]: which is evidence of God's just judgment. Many begin a new sentence with this verse and translate 'this is evidence of God's just judgment' [HNTC; NASB, NIV, RSV].
2. ἔνδειγμα 'evidence' is in the accusative case and is in apposition to the preceding sentence [EBC, Hb, ICC, Mn]. It is in apposition to the whole idea of the preceding sentence [EGT, Mn]. This is essentially the same in meaning as the first interpretation [EGT, Hb].

QUESTION—When does the judgment take place and what is the evidence?
1. The judgment is future, at the coming of Christ (1:7) [EBC, EGT, El, Er, Fn, Hb, Hn, HNTC, ICC, Mn, My, Rb, SSA, TH, Wd].
    1.1 The evidence is their steadfastness and faith in the midst of their persecutions [EBC, El, Er, Fn, Hb, Hn, HNTC, ICC, Mn, My, SSA, TH, Wd]: the fact that you are steadfast in the midst of persecution and affliction is evidence of the justness of God's future judgment. Explanations of how this can be evidence are varied. Their conduct in response to persecution shows that God's future declaration that they are worthy of his kingdom is just [Hb, SSA]. It was evidence that the judgment is still future [Hb], and God's present grace in strengthening them indicated that he was on their side and would not let their suffering go without final vindication [Er, Fn, Hb]. When people who are steadfast and who continue believing must endure such persecution, it is a sign that God must judge in order to reward believers and punish the persecutors [TH]. Or, by God supplying them with steadfastness and faith in the midst of persecution, it is shown that God is just and this quality of being just will result in a final judgment [Hn].
    1.2 The evidence is the fact that they are being persecuted [WBC]: the fact that you undergo persecution and affliction is evidence of the justness of God's judgment. God's justice will be vindicated in their case and in the case of their persecutors when God judges all at Christ's coming [WBC].
    1.3 The evidence is the fact that Paul boasts of their faith and steadfastness in their persecution [HNTC]. The Thessalonians were not sure about their position. The fact that Paul actually boasts about them is a sign to them that God will count them worthy [HNTC].
2. The judgment is a present process of God's judging. [Lns, NCBC, NIC]. God is judging whether the Thessalonians are worthy of his kingdom. The trials and their good response to them are an evidence that God is carrying out a just process of judgment in order to determine that they are worthy of his kingdom [NCBC]. Or, their steadfastness and faith is evidence or an indication that God judges them to be worthy of his kingdom and that God is not unrighteous in allowing them to suffer persecution [Lns].
3. The judgment begins now, and will culminate at the future coming of Christ [Alf, Ea]. Their being subjected to persecutions and being strengthened to be steadfast and faithful is a proof that God is judging them justly [Alf]. God judges them with approval by giving them the gifts of steadfastness and faith and the presence of these are an evidence that in the final judgment, they will be brought into the kingdom and the persecutors will be punished [Ea]. The fact that they suffer now implies that under God's just government, there will be a future reward and penalty [Ea].

QUESTION—To whom is the evidence given?

It is given to the Thessalonians and also to the writer [SSA]: it is evidence to us (inclusive). It is especially given to the Thessalonians who needed assurance [Hb, HNTC, Lns]. It is evidence to whoever will consider it, including the persecutors [Fn].

so-that[a] **you be-counted/made-worthy**[b] **of-the kingdom**[c] **of-God,**

LEXICON—a. εἰς (LN **89.48; 89.57**): 'so that' [Lns, WBC; NASB, NJB], 'that' [HNTC, ICC; KJV, RSV], 'in order to' [NAB], 'in order that' [Hn], 'for the purpose of' [LN], 'as a result' [LN; NIV, TEV], 'and in the end' [TNT], not explicit [NEB].

b. aorist pass. infin. of καταξιόω (LN 65.18): 'to be counted worthy' [WBC; KJV, NIV, TNT], 'to be considered worthy' [BAGD; NASB], 'to be regarded as worthy of' [LN], 'to be deemed worthy' [Hn, ICC, Lns], 'to be thought worthy' [HNTC], 'to be found worthy' [NAB, NJB], '(it) will prove (you) worthy' [NEB], 'to be considered as meriting' [LN]; or 'to be made worthy' [RSV], 'to become worthy' [TEV]. The aorist tense refers to one particular act of declaring worthy, namely the one on the day of judgment [Hb].

c. βασιλεία (LN 37.64): 'kingdom' [BAGD, Hn, HNTC, ICC, Lns, WBC; all versions], 'rule, reign' [LN].

QUESTION—What relationship is indicated by εἰς 'so that'?

1. It indicates the result of God's judgment [Er, Lns, My]: God's just judgment will result in you being declared worthy of the kingdom. A verdict does not have a purpose other than being just, but it always has a result [Lns].
2. This is a specific restatement of the preceding clause since the judgment is the declaration [EBC, Mn, SSA]: he will justly judge, that is, he will declare you to be worthy of the kingdom.
3. It indicates the result of their steadfastness and faith in persecution [Mn, My, TH]: you are steadfast and have faith in the midst of persecution and, as a result, you will be counted worthy of the kingdom.
4. It indicates the purpose or contemplated result of the last clause in 1:4 [Hb]: you are persecuted and you endure afflictions in order that (or, so that) you will be counted worthy of the kingdom. This is God's purpose in permitting the present persecutions and afflictions [Hb].
5. It indicates the purpose of God's just judgment [Alf, Hn, ICC, NCBC, NIC, Rb, Wd]: God will judge justly in order to declare that you are worthy of the kingdom. The day of judgment will come in order to declare that the believers are deemed worthy of the kingdom [Hn]. When it is taken to refer to a present judgment, it is explained that the persecutions which God's people are enduring are evidence of a righteous process of judgment God is carrying out in order for him to see that they are worthy of his kingdom, and God uses the persecutions as the means of shaping

the believers into the condition where they might be declared worthy [NIC].

QUESTION—What is meant by καταξιωθῆναι 'to be counted/made worthy'?
1. This means to be 'counted' worthy [Alf, Ea, El, Fn, Hb, Hn, HNTC, ICC, Lns, Mn, My, NCBC, NIC, WBC, Wd; KJV, NAB, NASB, NEB, NIV, NJB, TNT]: so that you may be reckoned/declared to be worthy of the kingdom of God. This pertains to the outcome of God's judgment [Fn, SSA]. It means to be considered fit to enter God's kingdom [Lns].
2. This means to be 'made' worthy [RSV, TEV]: so that you may be made worthy of the kingdom of God.

on-behalf-of[a] which also/indeed[b] you-suffer,[c]

LEXICON—a. ὑπέρ (LN 90.36; 89.28): 'on behalf of' [Lns], 'for (which)' [Hn, HNTC, ICC, WBC; KJV, NASB, NEB, NIV, RSV, TEV, TNT], 'for the sake of' [NJB], 'in the interest of' [NIC], 'because of' [TH], 'since' [SSA], not explicit [NAB].
b. καί (LN 89.93; 91.12): 'also' [HNTC, Lns, SSA; KJV], 'too' [Hn, ICC]; or 'indeed' [WBC; NASB, NEB, TNT]; not explicit [NAB, NIV, NJB, RSV, TEV].
c. pres. act. indic. of πάσχω (LN 24.78): 'to suffer' [BAGD, Hn, HNTC, ICC, LN, Lns, SSA, WBC; all versions]. The present tense indicates that they continue to suffer at the time of writing [Hb, HNTC, ICC, NCBC, Rb, SSA, TH].

QUESTION—How is this clause related to the preceding one?
1. Most translate it as a relative clause which adds a comment about the kingdom [Hn, HNTC, ICC, Lns; all versions]: that you be counted worthy of the kingdom, the kingdom for which you are suffering.
2. It indicates the grounds for the preceding statement [SSA]: It is true that God will declare that you worthy of the kingdom since you are suffering on behalf of it now.
3. It indicates the reason for the preceding statement [Fn, My]: God will count you worthy of the kingdom because you are suffering for it now.

QUESTION—What relationship is indicated by ὑπέρ 'on behalf of'?
They are suffering because of their loyalty to the kingdom and its king, Christ [TH, WBC], and because they belong to it [SSA]. It indicates their motive for enduring suffering [Fn, Hb]. Their suffering is connected with and is in the interest of the kingdom [NCBC, NIC].

QUESTION—What is meant by καί 'indeed/also'?
1. This means 'also' [EBC, Hb, Hn, HNTC, ICC, Lns, NIC, Rb, TH; KJV]: you are also suffering.
2. This means 'indeed' [Fn, WBC; NASB, NEB, TNT]: you are indeed suffering.

DISCOURSE UNIT: 1:6–10 [Mn, NIC]. The topic is God's judgment [NIC], the Lord's coming [Mn].

2 THESSALONIANS 1:6   187

1:6 because[a]

LEXICON—a. εἴπερ (LN 89.66): 'because', 'since' [SSA, WBC], 'since indeed' [RSV], 'seeing' [KJV], 'for' [NJB], 'for after all' [NASB]; 'even if' [NAB], 'provided' [My], 'if indeed' [Hn, ICC, LN, Lns], 'it is surely' [NEB], 'if, as it surely is' [HNTC], not explicit [NIV, TEV, TNT].

QUESTION—What relationship is indicated by this conjunction?

Many commentators say that this indicates a conditional clause [Ea, El, Fn, Hb, Hn, HNTC, ICC, Lns, Mn, My, NCBC, NIC, Rb, SSA, TH, Wd]: if it is a just thing in God's estimation. However, all go on to say that the hypothetical condition is assumed to be true and no doubt is implied. The very certainty of it makes the hypothesis an effective rhetorical argument [Ea, El, Fn, Hb, Hn, HNTC, ICC, My, NIC].

1. It functions as the grounds for a previous statement [Alf, Ea, El, Hb, Hn, Lns, NCBC, SSA, WBC, Wd], since it is a just thing in God's estimation. There are various interpretations as to what is supported by this statement.

1.1 This indicates the grounds for saying that God will judge justly (1:5) [Alf, Ea, El, Hb, Lns, SSA]: it is true that God will judge justly, since it is a just thing in his estimation to punish the persecutors and to reward you.

1.2 It indicates the grounds for saying that God will count them worthy to enter his kingdom [Hn, NCBC]: it is true that God will count you worthy to enter his kingdom since it is a just thing in his estimation to punish the persecutors and to reward you.

1.3 This indicates the grounds for saying that their steadfastness and faith was evidence [WBC, Wd]: It is true that your steadfastness and faith are evidence of God's just judgment, since it is a just thing in God's estimation to punish your persecutors and reward you.

2. This is a restatement and expansion of the previous verse [HNTC, ICC, NIC, TH]: it is evidence of the just judgment of God, that is, it is just in God's estimation to punish the persecutors and reward you.

(it is) a-just-thing[a] with[b] God

LEXICON—a. δίκαιος (LN 88.12; 66.5): 'just' [HNTC, LN, SSA; NASB, NEB, NIV, RSV], 'righteous' [Hn, ICC, LN, Lns], 'right' [BAGD]. This neuter adjective is also translated as a substantive: 'a just thing', 'a righteous thing' [WBC; KJV], 'what is right' [TEV], 'justice' [NJB, TNT], 'strict justice' [NAB]. See this word at 1:5.

b. παρά (LN 90.3; 90.20): 'with' [Lns; KJV], 'for' [NASB], 'in (God's) estimation' [Hn], 'in the sight of' [BAGD, HNTC, ICC, WBC], '(God) deems' [RSV], not explicit [NAB, NEB, NIV, TEV, TNT].

to-repay[a] affliction[b] to-the-ones afflicting[c] you

LEXICON—a. aorist act. infin. of ἀνταποδίδωμι (LN 38.19): 'to repay' [BAGD, Hn, HNTC, LN, WBC; NASB, RSV], 'to pay back' [LN; NIV], 'to recompense' [ICC; KJV], 'to duly give in return' [Lns], 'to visit on' [NAB], 'to balance the account by sending' [NEB], 'to bring' [TEV], 'to

reward' [TNT], 'to inflict' [NJB]. The phrase 'to repay with affliction' is also conflated: 'to punish' [SSA]. The aorist tense views the repaying as a single event [Lns].
b. θλῖψις (LN 22.2): 'affliction' [BAGD, Hn, ICC, Lns, WBC; NASB, RSV], 'tribulation' [BAGD, HNTC; KJV], 'hardship' [NAB, NJB], 'trouble' [LN; NEB, NIV, TNT], 'suffering' [LN; TEV]. See this word at 1:4.
c. pres. act. participle of θλίβω (LN **22.21**): 'to afflict' [BAGD, Hn, ICC, Lns, WBC; NASB, RSV], 'to trouble' [SSA; KJV, NEB, NIV, TNT], 'to bring suffering on' [LN], 'to visit hardships on' [NAB], 'to inflict hardship on' [NJB], 'to cause someone tribulation' [HNTC], 'to make someone suffer' [TEV]. The present tense characterizes the people as repeatedly persecuting them [Hb].

QUESTION—Is the repetition of the words with the same root significant?
It is significant [NCBC]: to repay affliction to the ones who afflict you. They are paid back in kind [Alf, Ea, EBC, EGT, El, Fn, Hb, Mn, My, NCBC, SSA, Wd].

1:7 and^a to-you the (ones) being-afflicted^b rest^c with^d us,

LEXICON—a. καί (LN 89.92): 'and' [Hn, HNTC, ICC, SSA, WBC; all versions except NAB], 'and thus' [Lns], not explicit [NAB].
b. pres. pass. participle of θλίβω (LN 22.21): 'to be afflicted' [BAGD, Hn, ICC, Lns, WBC; NASB, RSV], 'to be troubled' [LN, SSA; KJV, NEB, NIV], 'to be in trouble' [TNT], 'to suffer' [TEV], 'to suffer hardship' [NJB], 'to suffer tribulation' [HNTC], 'to be sorely tried' [NAB], 'to be persecuted' [LN]. See this word at 1:6.
c. ἄνεσις (LN **22.36**): 'rest' [BAGD, Hn; KJV, RSV], 'relief' [BAGD, ICC, LN, SSA, WBC; all versions except KJV, RSV], 'peace' [HNTC], 'surcease' [Lns].
d. μετά (LN 89.108): 'with' [Hn, ICC, WBC; KJV, NJB, RSV], 'together with' [HNTC, SSA], 'in company with' [Lns], 'as well as' [NAB], 'and (to us) as well' [NASB, NEB, NIV, TEV], 'both (to you and to us)' [TNT].

QUESTION—What verb is implied in this clause?
This implies the verb of the preceding verse ἀνταποδοῦναι 'to repay' [EBC, HNTC, Wd; NEB]: he will repay affliction to those who afflict you, and he will repay rest to you who are afflicted. Or, it implies the first phrase of 1:6 also [SSA, WBC]: it is a just thing with God to repay affliction to those who afflict you and it is a just thing to repay rest to you who are afflicted. The verb 'repay' does not in itself indicate whether it is concerned with punishment or reward [WBC]. Some translations use different verbs according to whether it refers to punishment or blessing: 'to punish…to reward' [SSA], 'to repay…to give/grant' [Hn, NCBC; NASB, RSV], 'to pay back…to give' [NIV], 'to bring…to give' [TEV], 'to visit (hardships) on…to provide relief' [NAB], 'to reward (with trouble)…to grant' [TNT].

QUESTION—What is meant by ἄνεσιν 'rest'?
It means relief from persecution [Ea, Lns, WBC], and suffering [EBC, Er, Hb, ICC], absence of troubles and suffering [Hb, HNTC, My, NCBC, SSA, TH], and also the positive blessings of being in and enjoying God's kingdom [EBC, El, Hn, HNTC, Lns, WBC].

QUESTION—To whom does ἡμῶν 'us' refer?
This plural pronoun refers to the Paul and his two companions, Silvanus and Timothy [Alf, Ea, EBC, El, Er, Fn, Hb, HNTC, ICC, Lns, Mn, My, NCBC, WBC, Wd]. One commentator also includes all other Christians [Hn].

at[a] the revelation[b] of-the Lord Jesus from heaven

LEXICON—a. ἐν (LN 67.33): 'at' [Hn, HNTC, ICC, WBC], 'in connection with' [Lns], 'when' [BAGD; all versions].
  b. ἀποκάλυψις (LN 28.38): 'revelation' [BAGD, Hn, HNTC, ICC, LN, Lns, WBC]. This noun is also translated as a passive verb: 'to be revealed' [all versions except NJB, TEV]; or as an intransitive verb: 'to appear' [NJB, TEV]; or as an active transitive verb: '(God) reveals' [SSA].

QUESTION—What relationship is indicated by ἐν 'at'?
  1. This indicates the time when God will repay people [Alf, Ea, EBC, EGT, El, Er, ICC, My, NCBC, NIC, TH; all versions]: God will repay when the Lord Jesus is revealed.
  2. Some take it to indicate more than time. It also indicates the means by which the repayment (1:6) is accomplished, implying that such judgment is part of what is involved in the revelation of the Lord [Fn, Hb, HNTC, Mn, Wd]: God will repay by means of the appearing of the Lord Jesus, who will judge them.
  3. It indicates the means by which God will judge all justly (1:5) [SSA]: God will judge all people justly by means of him revealing the Lord Jesus.

QUESTION—How are the event word and person related in the genitive construction τῇ ἀποκαλύψει τοῦ κυρίου 'the revelation of the Lord'?
The Lord Jesus will be revealed [EBC, Fn, Hb, Hn, ICC, My, NCBC, NIC, TH, Wd; all versions except NJB, TEV], or the Lord Jesus will appear [Alf, Ea, Hb, HNTC; NJB, TEV], or God will reveal the Lord Jesus [SSA, Wd]. This refers to Christ's second coming [Ea, El, Hn, HNTC, My, NCBC, WBC, Wd].

QUESTION—In what way will the Lord be revealed ἀπό 'from' heaven?
Christ is now in heaven hidden from sight, but then he will come from heaven, appear, and be visible [Ea, El, Hb, Hn, HNTC, ICC, Lns, My, NCBC, NIC, SSA, Wd]. Christ's glory will be revealed to those who suffer [WBC] and to all others [Hb, Hn, NIC]. This implies that he will come with God's authority [NIC].

with[a] angels[b] of-power[c] of-him

LEXICON—a. μετά (LN 89.108): 'with' [Hn, HNTC, ICC, WBC; all versions], 'together with' [SSA], 'in company with' [Lns].

b. ἄγγελος (LN 12.28): 'angels' [BAGD, Hn, HNTC, ICC, LN, Lns, SSA, WBC; all versions].

c. δύναμις (LN 76.1): 'power' [BAGD, Hn, HNTC, ICC, LN, Lns; NJB]. This noun is also translated as an adjective: 'mighty' [BAGD, WBC; KJV, NAB, NASB, NEB, RSV, TEV, TNT], 'powerful' [SSA; NIV].

QUESTION—How are the persons related to the attribute and to each other in the double genitive construction ἀγγέλων δυνάμεως αὐτοῦ 'angels of power of him'?

1. 'Of him' is related to the phrase 'angels of power', and 'power' is an attribute of the angels [BAGD, Bul (p. 501), ICC, SSA, WBC; all versions except NJB]: with his powerful/mighty angels. This is a Hebraism [WBC].

2. 'Of him' is related to 'power' and therefore power is an attribute of the Lord [Alf, Ea, EBC, EGT, El, Fn, Hb, Hn, HNTC, Lns, Mn, My, NCBC, NIC, Rb, Wd; NJB]: with the angels of his power. This is further explained as angels through whom the Lord will exercise his power [El, Mn, My]; angels who manifest the Lord's power [Ea, EGT, El, Fn, Hn, Lns, My]; angels to whom the Lord gives his power [EBC, Wd], or the angels who belong to his power [HNTC, NCBC].

1:8 in[a] fire[b] of-flame,[c]

LEXICON—a. ἐν (LN 89.80): 'in' [Hn, HNTC, ICC, Lns, WBC; KJV, NASB, NEB, NIV, RSV], 'amid' [NJB], 'with' [SSA; NAB, TEV], 'there will be' [TNT].

b. πῦρ (LN 2.3): 'fire' [BAGD, Hn, HNTC, ICC, LN, Lns, SSA, WBC; all versions except NAB], 'power' [NAB].

c. φλόξ (LN 2.4): 'flame' [BAGD, ICC, LN; TNT]. This noun is also translated as an adjective which modifies 'fire': 'flaming' [BAGD, Hn, HNTC, Lns, WBC; KJV, NAB, NASB, NJB, RSV, TEV], 'blazing' [SSA; NEB, NIV].

QUESTION—With what is this phrase grammatically connected?

1. It is connected with the preceding clause [Alf, Ea, EBC, El, Fn, Hb, Hn, HNTC, ICC, Lns, Mn, My, NCBC, NIC, Rb, SSA, TH, WBC, Wd; NASB, NEB, NIV, RSV, TEV]: the Lord Jesus will be revealed in fire. Fire is connected with the brilliant appearance of God and Christ [Ea, Hb, Hn, HNTC, ICC, My, SSA, TH], similar to the brilliance accompanying the appearances of God in the Old Testament [Ea, EBC, El, Fn, Hb, HNTC, ICC, Mn, My, NCBC, SSA]. It is sign of God's presence [Ea, SSA, Wd], of his holiness [Hn], of his glory [Ea, El, Fn, Hb, HNTC, My, NIC], and also of his judgment [Fn, Hn, Mn, My, NCBC, Wd].

2. It is connected with the preceding noun, δυνάμεως 'power' [Lns]: he will be revealed with his power that is manifested in the angels by surrounding them with flames.

3. It is connected with the following clause [KJV, NAB, NJB]: in fire he will take vengeance.

giving[a] vengeance[b] to-the (ones) not knowing[c] God

LEXICON—a. pres. act. participle of δίδωμι (LN **90.90**; 90.51): 'to give' [BAGD, Lns], 'to take' [KJV], 'to inflict' [BAGD, Hn, HNTC; NAB, RSV, TNT], 'to deal out' [NASB], 'to mete out' [WBC], 'to render' [ICC], 'to impose' [NJB], 'to do' [NEB]. The phrase 'to give vengeance' is also translated 'to punish' [LN, SSA; NIV, TEV].

b. ἐκδίκησις (LN 38.8; 39.33): 'vengeance' [BAGD, Hn, HNTC, ICC, WBC; KJV, RSV], 'retribution' [LN; NASB], 'punishment' [BAGD, LN; NAB, TNT], 'penalty' [NJB], 'justice' [Lns; NEB].

c. perf. act. participle of οἶδα (LN 28.1; 87.12): 'to know' [BAGD, Hn, HNTC, ICC, LN, Lns, SSA, WBC; KJV, NASB, NIV, RSV, TNT], 'to be acquainted with' [LN], 'to acknowledge' [NAB, NEB, NJB], 'to honor, to respect' [LN]. This verb is also conflated with the negative: 'to reject' [TEV]. The present tense indicates the condition of the group [Lns] and marks the group by this characteristic [El, Hb].

QUESTION—What is meant by εἰδόσιν θεόν 'knowing God'?

It means to respect God [ICC], to worship God [ICC], to have faith in God [HNTC], to have a personal relationship with God [TH], to know him as their own God [Hn].

and to-the (ones) not obeying[a] the gospel[b] or-the Lord of-us Jesus,

TEXT—Some manuscripts add Χριστοῦ 'Christ' after 'Jesus'. This addition is not mentioned by GNT. Only KJV includes this word.

LEXICON—a. pres. act. participle of ὑπακούω (LN 36.15): 'to obey' [BAGD, Hn, HNTC, ICC, LN, SSA; KJV, NASB, NEB, NIV, RSV, TEV], 'to be obedient to' [TNT], 'to heed' [NAB], 'to accept' [NJB]. This verb is also conflated with the negative: 'to disobey' [WBC], 'to be disobedient' [Lns]. The present tense indicates their characteristic attitude [Hb].

b. εὐαγγέλιον (LN 33.217): 'gospel' [BAGD, Hn, HNTC, ICC, LN, Lns, WBC; KJV, NASB, NEB, NIV, NJB, RSV], 'good news' [BAGD, LN, SSA; NAB, TEV, TNT].

QUESTION—What relationship is indicated by καί 'and'?

1. It means 'even', and functions as a further description of the one group of people upon whom the Lord will take vengeance [Er, Fn, Hn, HNTC, Mn, NIC, WBC, Wd; probably KJV, NAB, NIV, NJB, TEV]: he will take vengeance on those who do not know God, even on those who do not obey the gospel or, he will take vengeance on those who do not know God and do not obey the gospel. This follows the parallelistic style of Old Testament prophecy and poetry to refer to the same subject [Fn, Mn, WBC]. The repetition of the article stresses the enormity of their sin in the rejection of the gospel [HNTC, NIC].

2. It is coordinate and indicates another group upon whom the Lord will take vengeance [Alf, Ea, EBC, EGT, El, Hb, ICC, Lns, My, NCBC, Rb; NASB, NEB, RSV, TNT]: he will take vengeance on those who do not know God and also on those who do not obey the gospel. The repetition of

the article is cited as support for this interpretation [Alf, Ea, EGT, Hb, Lns, My, Rb]. The people who do not know God are the Gentiles [Alf, Ea, EBC, EGT, El, Hb, ICC, Lns, My, NCBC, Rb] and the people who do not obey God are the unbelieving Jews [Alf, Ea, EBC, El, ICC, My, NCBC, Rb], or they are both Jews and pagans who have heard the gospel [EGT, Hb, Lns].

QUESTION—How are the two nouns related in the genitive construction τῷ εὐαγγελίῳ τοῦ κυρίου ἡμῶν Ἰησοῦ 'the gospel of our Lord Jesus'?
1. This means the gospel which tells about our Lord Jesus [Hb, SSA, TH; TEV].
2. This means the gospel which was brought by our Lord Jesus [Ea].

1:9 who will-pay[a] (the) penalty[b] eternal[c] destruction[d]

LEXICON—a. pres. act. indic. of τίνω (LN **90.77**): 'to pay' [BAGD, Hn, HNTC, WBC; NASB], 'to suffer' [Lns; NAB, NEB, RSV, TEV]. This verb is also conflated with the noun 'penalty': 'to be punished' [BAGD, ICC; KJV, NIV], 'their punishment is/will be' [NJB, TNT], 'to receive punishment' [LN, SSA].
  b. δίκη (LN **38.8**): 'penalty' [BAGD, Hn, HNTC, WBC; NAB, NASB], 'just penalty' [SSA], 'punishment' [BAGD, LN; NEB, NJB, RSV, TEV, TNT], 'as justice' [Lns].
  c. αἰώνιος (LN 67.96): 'eternal' [BAGD, HNTC, ICC, LN, Lns, WBC; NAB, NASB, NEB, RSV, TEV, TNT], 'everlasting' [Hn; KJV, NIV]. This adjective is also translated as an adverb: '(to be lost) eternally' [NJB], 'forever' [SSA].
  d. ὄλεθρος (LN 20.33): 'destruction' [BAGD, Hn, HNTC, ICC, LN, Lns, WBC; KJV, NASB, NIV, RSV, TEV, TNT], 'ruin' [BAGD, LN; NAB, NEB]. This noun is also translated as a verb: 'to be lost' [NJB], 'to be destroyed' [SSA], 'to be punished' [SSA].

QUESTION—What is the function of this relative clause?
This is the reciprocal of 1:8 [SSA]: the Lord Jesus will give vengeance to those who do not know God and do not obey the gospel; those people will pay the penalty. It focuses on the nature of the vengeance mentioned in the preceding verse [Hb, HNTC, ICC, NCBC].

QUESTION—Why was οἵτινες 'such as/who' used instead of οἵ 'who'?
1. This pronoun, instead of defining the preceding people themselves as οἵ would do, is a qualitative relative pronoun and refers to them as a class of people. Some say that this characterization also gives the reason why they must pay the penalty [Alf, Fn, Lns, My], while others speak against this implication [Ea, El].
   1.1 This pronoun characterizes the people just mentioned as a class of people of the kind just specified [Alf, Ea, El, Fn, Hb, HNTC, ICC, Mn, My, NCBC, NIC, Rb, SSA, TH, Wd]: such people as those who do not know God, or who do not obey the gospel, will pay the penalty of eternal destruction.

1.2 This pronoun characterizes the class of people as the kind that will pay the penalty [Hn, Lns; probably NIC]: the above-mentioned people are the kind of people who will pay the penalty of eternal destruction.
2. There is no significant difference between this preposition and the simple relative pronoun οἱ 'who' [WBC]: who will pay the penalty of eternal destruction.

QUESTION—How is the phrase ὄλεθρον αἰώνιον 'eternal destruction' related to what precedes it?

It is in apposition to 'penalty' [El, Fn, Hb, ICC, Rb, SSA, WBC]: who will pay the penalty, even eternal destruction. This specifies what the penalty is [Ea, NCBC, NIC, SSA].

QUESTION—What is meant by 'eternal destruction'?

Many commentators mention that it does not mean to cease to exist [EBC, Er, Fn, Hb, Hn, HNTC, ICC, Mn, NCBC, NIC, Rb, SSA, TH]. It is the opposite of 'eternal life' [Hb, Hn, HNTC, NCBC, NIC, TH, WBC], or of the life of the age to come [HNTC, NIC, WBC], which age is unending [NIC]. It means that the consequences of this destruction are eternal [El, Er, Hb, Hn, ICC, Mn, NCBC, Rb, Wd] and permanent [EBC], or characteristic of the age to come [HNTC, NIC, Rb, TH]. 'Destruction' refers to ruin [Ea, Fn, NIC, TH], the loss of all that is worthwhile in life [EBC, HNTC, NIC, TH]. Some think that this is explained by what follows, that is, they will be separated from the Lord [Er, Hb, Hn, HNTC, ICC, My, NCBC, NIC, Rb, SSA, TH, WBC, Wd], while others think that destruction is left unexplained, and the separation is the result of the destruction [EBC], or it means that the destruction will take place away from the presence of the Lord [Lns], or it means that the destruction both comes from the Lord and consists in separation from him [Wd].

from[a] (the) face[b] of-the Lord

LEXICON—a. ἀπό (LN 89.122): 'from' [ICC, SSA, WBC; KJV], 'apart from' [NAB], 'away from' [BAGD, Hn, Lns; NASB], 'out from' [HNTC], 'cut off from' [NEB], 'shut out from' [NIV], 'excluded from' [NJB], 'exclusion from' [RSV], 'separated from' [TEV], 'banishment from' [TNT], 'driven out from' [Bul (p. 47)].

b. πρόσωπον (LN 85.26): 'face' [BAGD, Hn, ICC, LN, Lns], 'presence' [BAGD, Bul (p. 874), HNTC, SSA, WBC; all versions].

QUESTION—What is indicated by ἀπό 'from'?

1. It indicates a spatial separation from the Lord 'away from' [Alf, BAGD, Ea, EBC, El, Er, Hb, Hn, HNTC, ICC, Lns, Mn, My, NCBC, NIC, Rb, SSA, TH, WBC]: eternal destruction away from the presence of the Lord. Here 'face of the Lord' refers to the presence of the Lord [Hb, HNTC, SSA, TH, WBC; all versions].
2. It indicates the source of eternal destruction, 'proceeding from' [Fn, Wd]: eternal destruction which comes from the Lord, that is, which is executed by the Lord. Here 'face of the Lord' seems to be an idiom for 'the Lord'

[Hb], although there is a comment about the hostile face the Lord has in regard to the guilty [Fn]. It is implied that the destruction consists in separation from the Lord's presence [Wd].

QUESTION—To whom does 'the Lord' refer?
1. It refers to the Lord Jesus Christ [Fn, Hb, Hn, HNTC, ICC, Lns, NCBC, SSA, TH, WBC].
2. It refers to God [Er].

and from the glory[a] of-the strength[b] of-him,

LEXICON—a. δόξα (LN 79.18; 14.49): 'glory' [Hn, HNTC, ICC, LN, Lns, SSA, WBC; KJV, NAB, NASB, NJB, RSV], 'brightness' [BAGD, LN], 'radiance' [BAGD, LN], 'shining' [LN], 'splendor' [BAGD, LN; NEB, TNT], 'majesty' [NIV]. This noun is also translated as an adjective modifying 'strength': 'glorious (might)' [TEV].

b. ἰσχύς (LN 79.62): 'strength' [BAGD, ICC, LN; NJB], 'power' [BAGD, WBC; KJV, NASB, NIV], 'might' [BAGD, Hn, HNTC, Lns; NAB, NEB, RSV, TEV]. This noun is also translated as an adjective modifying 'glory': 'mighty (splendor)' [TNT]; or modifying 'his': '(he is) powerful' [SSA].

QUESTION—How are the two nouns and the pronoun related in the double genitive construction τῆς δόξης τῆς ἰσχύος αὐτοῦ 'the glory of the strength of him'?

Most commentators take this to mean the glory which is manifested by his power [Alf, Ea, EBC, El, Er, HNTC, ICC, Mn, My], but some explain it as the glory that belongs to his power [Hb], or the glory he has because he is so powerful [SSA]. 'Glory' refers to the visible manifestation of the use of his power [EBC, Er, Lns], his power radiates glory [Mn], his reign is glorious [Lns], his power brings glory to his presence [ICC], or his power shows its glory in the blessed state of the believers [Alf, Ea, Hn, My], or in the act of judging people, he shows his power and his power bring glory to him [SSA].

1:10 when[a] he comes[b]

LEXICON—a. ὅταν (LN 67.30): 'when' [Hn, HNTC, ICC, LN, Lns, WBC; all versions except NIV], 'whenever' [SSA], not explicit [NIV].

b. aorist act. subj. of ἔρχομαι (LN 15.81): 'to come' [BAGD, Hn, HNTC, ICC, LN, Lns, SSA, WBC; all versions].

QUESTION—How is this phrase related to the preceding verse?

This indicates the time the people will pay the penalty (1:9) [Alf, Ea, El, Fn, Hn, HNTC, ICC, Lns, My, NCBC, SSA, WBC; NAB, NASB, NEB, NIV, NJB, RSV, TEV]: they will be paid the penalty of eternal destruction when the Lord comes. This resumes the topic of the Lord's return (1:5–7a) [EBC, Hn, ICC, NCBC, NIC, SSA]. It makes a contrast with the fate of the wicked [EBC, Er, Hb, HNTC, Lns, NCBC].

2 THESSALONIANS 1:10

to-be-honored[a] in[b] his saints[c]

LEXICON—a. aorist pass. infin. of ἐνδοξάζομαι (LN 87.9): 'to be honored' [BAGD, LN; TNT], 'to be praised' [SSA], 'to be glorified' [BAGD, Hn, HNTC, ICC, Lns, WBC; KJV, NAB, NASB, NEB, NIV, NJB, RSV], 'to receive honor' [LN], 'to receive glory' [TEV].

b. ἐν (LN 83.9; 90.6; 89.26): 'in' [Hn, HNTC, ICC, WBC; KJV, NAB, NASB, NIV, RSV], 'among' [Lns; NEB, NJB], 'from' [TEV], 'by' [TNT]; or 'because of' [SSA].

c. ἅγιος (LN 11.27): 'saints' [BAGD, Hn, HNTC, ICC, Lns; KJV, NASB, RSV], 'holy ones' [BAGD, WBC; NAB, NJB], 'holy people' [NIV], 'God's people' [LN], '(his) own' [NEB], '(his) people' [TEV], '(his) own people' [SSA], 'those who belong to him' [TNT].

QUESTION—What relationship is indicated by the infinitive form ἐνδοξασθῆναι 'to be honored'?

This indicates the purpose for the Lord's coming [Ea, El, Fn, Hb, Hn, Lns, My, NCBC, NIC, Rb, SSA, TH, Wd]: he will come in order to be honored. This is in addition to the purpose of punishing the wicked [SSA]. Some commentators think that it could just as well be considered to be the result of his coming [Hb, TH].

QUESTION—What relationship is indicated by ἐν 'in'?

1. This indicates the reason why he will be honored [Alf, Ea, EGT, El, Er, Hb, Hn, ICC, My, NIC, SSA, WBC]: he will be honored because of the saints. He will be honored because of what he has done for the saints in saving them and giving them glorified bodies [Ea, Hb, SSA, WBC, Wd], and what he has done in them by transforming their characters [Ea, Er, Hb, Hn, ICC]. Most explain this 'in' to mean that the Lord's glory will be seen in the persons of the saints who will reflect his glory [Alf, Ea, El, Hb, Hn, My, NIC, SSA, WBC]. It is suggested that the agents of the two passive verbs are the saints for which he has done so much [Ea, EGT, Hn, ICC, SSA, TH], and the angels [Hb, Hn, ICC].
2. This indicates the agents of the passive verb [TEV, TNT]: he will be honored by his saints, that is, his saints will praise him.
3. This indicates the location of the Lord [EBC, HNTC, Lns, NCBC; probably NEB, NJB]: he will be in the midst of the saints and, in that place, he will be honored by them. This pertains to the time Christ meets the saints in the air (1 Thess 4:17, 2 Thess. 1:7a) [EBC, HNTC]. Perhaps those who honor him include the angels [NCBC].

and to-be-admired[a] in[b] all the (ones) having-believed,[c]

TEXT—Instead of the aorist tense πιστεύσασιν 'they believed', some manuscripts have the present tense πιστεύουσιν 'they believe'. GNT chooses the aorist tense without mentioning the present tense alternative. Only KJV, NJB, and TEV translate in the present tense form.

LEXICON—a. aorist pass. infin. of θαυμάζω (LN 25.213): 'to be admired' [ICC; KJV], 'to be adored' [NAB, NEB], 'to be marveled at' [BAGD, Hn,

HNTC, LN, Lns, SSA, WBC; NASB, NIV, NJB, RSV], 'to receive honor' [TEV], 'to be revered' [TNT].
   b. ἐν (LN 90.6; 89.26): 'in' [Hn, HNTC, ICC, WBC; KJV, RSV], 'among' [Lns; NASB, NEB, NIV, TNT], 'by' [NAB, NJB], 'from' [TEV]; or 'because of' [SSA].
   c. aorist act. participle of πιστεύω (LN 31.85): 'to believe' [BAGD, Hn, HNTC, LN, Lns, SSA, WBC; all versions except NEB]. This verb and the article are also translated as a substantive: 'believers' [BAGD, ICC, Mn; NEB]. The aorist tense is used to refer to that decisive act of faith when they first believed the gospel rather than to their continuing belief [EBC, Hb, HNTC, ICC, NIC, TH, Wd], or the aorist tense looks back on their whole life of faith as a single unit [Ea, El, Fn].
QUESTION—How is this clause related to the preceding one?
   It is a second purpose, parallel with the preceding one [Hb, Lns, Mn, NCBC, SSA, TH, Wd]. It is virtually synonymous with the preceding one [Fn, Hb, Lns, SSA, TH, Wd], or it is a specific statement of the preceding general statement [ICC]. The way ἐν 'in' is interpreted in the preceding clause is also to be followed here [HNTC, Lns, My, SSA, TH, Wd].

because^a our testimony^b to^c you was-believed,
LEXICON—a. ὅτι (LN 89.33): 'because' [SSA, WBC; KJV, NIV, RSV, TEV], 'for' [Hn, HNTC, ICC, Lns; NAB, NASB, NEB, TNT], 'and' [NJB].
   b. ματύριον (LN 33.264): 'testimony' [BAGD, Hn, HNTC, ICC, LN, Lns, WBC; KJV, NASB, NEB, NIV, RSV, TNT], 'witness' [LN; NAB, NJB], 'the message that we told' [TEV]. This noun is also translated as a verb: 'to testify' [SSA].
   c. ἐπί (LN 90.57; 90.5): 'to' [Hn, HNTC, ICC, Lns, SSA, WBC; NAB, NASB, NIV, RSV], 'among' [KJV], not explicit [NJB, TEV]. The phrase 'our testimony to you' is also translated 'the testimony we brought (to) you' [HNTC; NEB, TNT]. It may have a double relation: 'our testimony to you was believed by you' [LN].
QUESTION—What relationship is indicated by ὅτι 'because'?
   The 'because' clause has an implied result clause [Hn, WBC, Wd]. This implies that they are included in the number of the believers, and gives a reason why they are included [Alf, Ea, EBC, EGT, El, Er, Hb, Hn, HNTC, ICC, Lns, My, NCBC, NIC, TH, WBC, Wd; NIV, TEV, TNT]: the Lord will be admired by/in the midst of/because of the believers. You are included among those believers because you have believed. Those who connect the following phrase 'in that day' with the first part of the verse consider this clause to be parenthetical [Alf, Ea, EGT, El, Fn, Hb, Hn, HNTC, ICC, Mn, My, NCBC, NIC, Rb, SSA, TH, WBC, Wd; KJV].

in^a that day.^{b}
LEXICON—a. ἐν (LN 67.33): 'in' [Hn, ICC; KJV, TNT], 'on' [HNTC, WBC; NAB, NASB, NEB, NIV, NJB, RSV, TEV], 'at' [SSA], 'in connection with' [Lns].

b. ἡμέρα (LN 67.178): 'day' [BAGD, Hn, HNTC, ICC, LN, Lns, WBC; KJV, NASB, NIV, NJB, RSV], 'Day' [NAB, NEB, TEV, TNT], 'time' [SSA].

QUESTION—What relationship is indicated by ἐν 'in'?
1. It indicates the time of his coming to be honored and admired [Alf, Ea, EBC, El, Fn, Hb, Hn, HNTC, Mn, My, NCBC, NIC, Rb, SSA, TH, WBC]. In many translations, this phrase is moved to the beginning of the verse and is closely connected with the verb ἔλθῃ 'he comes' [Hn, NIC, SSA; NAB, NEB, NIV, NJB, RSV, TEV, TNT]: when he comes on that day to be honored and admired. Some connect it more closely to the infinitives [Alf, Ea, El, Fn, Hb, HNTC, Mn, My, WBC]: when he comes to be honored and to be admired on that day. Some commentators think that its position at the end of the sentence in Greek indicates emphasis [EBC, Hb, Hn, Mn, NIC, TH], although one does not consider it to be emphatic [HNTC].
2. It indicates the content of the testimony [Lns]: you believed our testimony about the Day.

DISCOURSE UNIT: 1:11–12 [Alf, EBC, Er, Hb, ICC, Lns, NIC, SSA, WBC, Wd]. The topic is Paul's prayer for the Thessalonians.

1:11 For which[a] also[b] we-pray[c] always[d] for[e] you,

LEXICON—a. εἰς ὅ (LN 89.57; 90.23; 92.27): 'for which', 'to this/which end' [BAGD, ICC; NASB, RSV], 'with this in mind' [HNTC; NEB, NIV], 'with this in view' [BAGD, Hn], 'with this end in view' [WBC], 'in view of this' [NJB], 'in regard to which' [Lns], 'that/this is why' [TEV, TNT], 'wherefore' [KJV], not explicit [NAB].
b. καί (LN 89.93): 'also' [Hn, HNTC, Lns, SSA; KJV, NASB, NJB], 'too' [ICC], not explicit [WBC; NAB, NEB, NIV, RSV, TEV, TNT].
c. pres. mid. (deponent = active) indic. of προσεύχομαι (LN 33.178): 'to pray' [BAGD, Hn, HNTC, ICC, LN, Lns, SSA, WBC; all versions]. The present tense indicates that they pray regularly and this is reinforced by the word πάντοτε 'always' [Hb].
d. πάντοτε (LN 67.88): 'always' [BAGD, Hn, HNTC, ICC, LN, Lns; all versions except NIV, NJB], 'constantly' [WBC; NIV], 'continually' [NJB], 'very frequently' [SSA]. See this word at 1 Thess. 1:2.
e. περί (LN 90.24; 89.6): 'for' [Hn, HNTC, ICC, Lns, SSA, WBC; all versions except NJB], not explicit [NJB].

QUESTION—What relationship is indicated by the phrase εἰς ὅ 'for which'?
1. This indicates the purpose of the following prayer and refers to the Lord being honored in the saints (1:10) [Alf, Ea, Fn, ICC, SSA, TH, WBC]: in order that the Lord be honored in you and admired, we pray the following. Or it refers to all that is mentioned in 1:5–10 [Hb, Hn, Mn, NCBC, NIC, Rb, Wd]: in order that you may be counted worthy of entering the kingdom, that you may receive rest, and that the Lord may be honored in you, we pray the following. Or it refers specifically to the reference in 1:5

about being considered worthy of the kingdom, since the intervening material is a comment on that topic [EBC].
2. This is a less specific relationship meaning 'in reference to' what precedes (1:5–10) [El, HNTC, Lns, My]: in reference to the Lord's coming, the judgment, and his glorification in the saints, I pray for you.

QUESTION—What relationship is indicated by καί 'also'?
1. This adds to what Paul, Silvanus, and Timothy are already doing [Hb, NIC, TH; KJV, NASB, NJB]. There are various views about this. It is in addition to giving thanks (1:3) [EBC, EGT, Hn, HNTC, Lns, NCBC, NIC, SSA]: in addition to thanking God for you, we also pray for you. Or it is in addition to giving thanks for them (1:3) and boasting about them (1:4) [Hb, NIC, Wd]: in addition to thanking God for you and boasting about you in the churches, we also pray for you. Or it refers to the immediately preceding clause about their testimony (1:10) [Fn]: in addition to giving our testimony to you, we also pray for you. Or it implies that this was a wish before it was voiced in prayer [Alf, Ea, El]: not only do we wish that the following would happen for you, we also pray for you that it would.
2. There is no significance to this word and it is not translated [WBC; NAB, NEB, NIV, RSV, TEV, TNT].

QUESTION—How is πάντοτε 'always' to be understood?
This is referred to as hyperbole [SSA]. It means very frequently [SSA], regularly [Hb], every day [Hn].

that^a you our God may-consider-worthy/make-worthy^b of-the calling^c

LEXICON—a. ἵνα (LN 90.22): 'that' [Hn, HNTC, ICC, Lns, SSA, WBC; all versions except TEV], 'we ask God' [TEV].
b. aorist act. subj. of ἀξιόω (LN 65.18): 'to consider worthy' [SSA], 'to count worthy' [Hn, Lns, WBC; KJV, NASB, NEB, NIV, TNT], 'to deem worthy' [ICC], 'to judge worthy' [My], 'to regard as worthy' [LN]; or 'to make worthy' [BAGD, HNTC; NAB, NJB, RSV, TEV]. See the similar word, καταξιωθῆναι 'to be considered/made worthy', at 1:5.
c. κλῆσις (LN 33.313): 'calling' [BAGD, ICC, LN, Lns, WBC; KJV, NASB, NEB, NIV], 'call' [BAGD, Hn, HNTC; NAB, NJB, RSV, TNT], 'the life he has called you to live' [TEV], 'that for which he called you' [Bul (p. 602)], 'that to which he summoned you' [SSA].

QUESTION—What area of meaning is intended by the verb ἀξιώσῃ 'may consider/make worthy' and to what does the call refer?
1. The verb means 'to consider to be worthy' [Alf, Ea, EBC, EGT, El, Er, Fn, Hb, Hn, ICC, Lns, Mn, My, NCBC, NIC, Rb, SSA, WBC; KJV, NASB, NEB, NIV, TNT]: may God consider you to be worthy to receive the blessings he has summoned you to receive. Many commentators take the call to be the one that called them to salvation [Ea, El, Er, Fn, Hb, Hn, ICC, Lns, Mn, NCBC, NIC, Rb, SSA, TH], and this includes the conduct expected of God's people [El, Fn, Hn, Lns, SSA, TH]. Some also take it to refer to the consummation of salvation at the Lord's coming [Alf, EBC,

El, Er, Fn, Hb, Mn, My, NCBC, Rb, SSA]. Some think that the time God makes his evaluation will be at the judgment that will take place when the Lord Jesus is revealed from heaven (1:7) [EBC, Fn, Hn, NIC, WBC]. Others think that it is God's present estimation of his people [Lns]: may God consider you to be living as becomes the people who have received his call. Even though this means to 'consider' worthy, it is implied that the prayer is that Paul wants God to 'make' them worthy [NCBC]. This prayer implies that Paul wants the Thessalonians to so live that God will be able to pronounce them worthy [Hn, NIC, WBC].

2. The verb means 'to make worthy' [BAGD, HNTC, TH; NAB, NJB, RSV, TEV]: may God cause you to become worthy of the Christian life he has summoned you to live. The call is the past call to salvation [HNTC, TH] which included a call to the kind of life God intended them to live [TH].

and may-fulfill[a] every resolve[b] of-goodness[c]

LEXICON—a. aorist act. subj. of πληρόω (LN 13.106; 68.26): 'to fulfill' [ICC, LN, Lns, WBC; KJV, NAB, NASB, NIV, RSV], 'to bring to fulfillment' [Hn; NEB], 'to accomplish' [HNTC], 'to cause to happen' [LN], 'to bring to completion' [BAGD], 'to complete, to finish' [LN]. This verb has two objects and it has also been translated differently to collocate with those objects: 'fulfill...complete' [NJB, TEV], 'fulfill... perfect' [TNT].

b. εὐδοκία (LN 25.8): 'resolve' [Hn, HNTC, ICC; RSV], 'purpose' [NEB, NIV], 'intention' [NAB], 'desire' [BAGD, LN, WBC; NASB, NJB, TEV, TNT], 'good pleasure' [Lns; KJV], 'delight' [Rb].

c. ἀγαθωσύνη (LN 88.1): 'goodness' [BAGD, Hn, HNTC, ICC, LN, Lns, WBC; KJV, NASB, NJB, TEV, TNT], 'uprightness' [BAGD]. This noun is also translated as an adjective modifying 'resolve': 'good' [SSA; NEB, NIV, RSV], 'honest' [NAB].

QUESTION—What relationship is indicated by καί 'and'?

This is another petition in their prayers [EBC, Fn, Hb, NIC]. This also indicates the means by which God will enable them to be considered worthy [Ea, Er, Hb, Hn, ICC, My, SSA]. Or it indicates the two areas that God will make them worthy [HNTC]. Or it indicates the result of God's deeming them worthy [Lns].

QUESTION—Whose resolve is this and how are the event word and attribute related in the genitive construction εὐδοκίαν ἀγαθωσύνης 'resolve of goodness'?

1. This is the Thessalonians' resolve and the content of that resolve is goodness, that is, to be or to do good [Ea, EBC, El, HNTC, ICC, SSA, TH, Wd; NASB, NJB, TEV, TNT]: may God bring to completion the good you resolve to do. God will do this by enabling them to fully accomplish that good [SSA]. Or, this means 'may God cause you to delight in goodness' [Mn, My, Rb].

2. This is the Thessalonians' resolve and that resolve is the result of their goodness [Er, Fn, Hb, Hn, Lns, NIC]: may God bring to completion the

resolve you have which is prompted by your goodness. Their goodness refers to their regenerated nature which has been made good by God [Hb, Hn] and it has already been recognized earlier in the letter (1:3) [Fn].
3. This is the Thessalonians' resolve, and goodness is an attribute of that resolve [NAB, NEB, NIV, RSV]: may God fulfill every good resolve you have. This seems to mean the same as the first interpretation, a resolve for goodness.
4. This is God's resolve [KJV]: may God fulfill all the good pleasure of his goodness.

QUESTION—What is πᾶσαν 'every' connected with?

Πᾶσαν 'every' is feminine and is therefore grammatically connected with the feminine noun εὐδοκίαν 'resolve'. It is also connected in thought with the following neuter noun ἔργον 'work' [EGT, Fn, Hb, Hn, HNTC, ICC, Lns, NIC, SSA; NEB, NIV, NJB, TNT].

and work[a] of-faith[b]

LEXICON—a. ἔργον (LN 42.11): 'work' [BAGD, Hn, ICC, Lns, WBC; KJV, NAB, NASB, RSV, TEV, TNT], 'act' [LN; NEB, NIV], 'deed' [LN, SSA], 'manifestation' [BAGD], 'effort' [HNTC], 'all you have been doing' [NJB].

b. πίστις (LN 31.85): 'faith' [BAGD, Hn, HNTC, ICC, LN, Lns, WBC; all versions]. This noun is also translated as a verb: 'to believe' [SSA].

QUESTION—How are the two event words related in the genitive construction ἔργον πίστεως 'work of faith'? See this phrase at 1 Thess. 1:3.
1. This means work caused by faith [EBC, Er, Fn, Hb, Hn, HNTC, ICC, Lns, Mn, NCBC, NIC, Rb, SSA, TH, Wd; NEB, NIV, NJB, TNT]: may God enable you to do the good things that result from your believing in Christ.
2. This means the work characteristic of their faith [Ea, El].

in[a] power,[b]

LEXICON—a. ἐν (LN 89.84; 89.76): 'in' [ICC, WBC], 'with' [BAGD, Lns; KJV, NASB], 'by' [Hn; NAB, NIV, NJB, RSV, TEV, TNT]. This whole phrase is also translated as an adverb: 'mightily' [NEB], 'powerfully' [BAGD, HNTC, SSA].

b. δύναμις (LN 76.1): 'power' [BAGD, Hn, ICC, LN, Lns, WBC; all versions except NEB].

QUESTION—What relationship is indicated by ἐν 'in'?
1. This indicates the manner in which God will fulfill their resolve and work [Alf, BAGD, Ea, El, Fn, Hb, HNTC, Mn, My, SSA; NEB]: may God powerfully fulfill every resolve and work. 'Powerfully' implies that God will completely fulfill these [NCBC]. Its position at the end of the sentence makes it emphatic [Hb].
2. This indicates the means by which they will fulfill their resolve and work [EBC, Hn, ICC, Lns, NCBC, WBC, Wd; all versions except NEB]: may God fulfill every resolve and work by means of his power.

1:12 so-that[a]

LEXICON—a. ὅπως (LN 89.59): 'so that' [HNTC, WBC; NEB, NIV, NJB, RSV], 'in order that' [BAGD, Hn, ICC, Lns, SSA; NASB], 'that' [KJV, TNT], 'in this way' [NAB, TEV].

QUESTION—What relationship is indicated by this conjunction?

1. This indicates the purpose of the preceding prayer [BAGD, Ea, EBC, El, Er, Fn, Hb, Hn, HNTC, ICC, Lns, NCBC, NIC, SSA, WBC, Wd; NASB, NEB, NIV, NJB, RSV]: we pray for you in order that our Lord will be glorified, etc. Since εἰς ὅ 'for which', in 1:11a, indicated that the purpose of the prayer is in 1:10, some call this verse the reiteration of the purpose stated in 1:10 [El, Fn], or the ultimate or higher purpose [Er, Hb, Hn, ICC, NCBC, Wd]. It is similar, but more specific than the purpose given in 1:10 [El, ICC].
2. This indicates the result of God's actions in the preceding prayer [TH; NAB, TEV]: we pray for you. When our prayer is answered, the result will be that our Lord will be glorified, etc. Since this is an anticipated result of the preceding means, it implies that this is also the purpose for the prayer.
3. This is also translated as another topic of prayer [TNT]: we pray that God may consider you worthy. We pray that he will fulfill your desires and perfect your works. We pray that the name of our Lord Jesus will be glorified.

the name[a] of-the Lord of-us Jesus may-be-glorified[b] in[c] you,

TEXT—Some manuscripts add Χριστοῦ 'Christ' after 'Jesus'. This addition is not mentioned by GNT. Only KJV and NJB include this word.

LEXICON—a. ὄνομα (LN 9.19): 'name' [BAGD, Hn, HNTC, ICC, LN, Lns, WBC; all versions], not explicit [SSA].

b. aorist pass. subj. of ἐνδοξάζομαι (LN **87.9**): 'to be glorified' [BAGD, Hn, HNTC, ICC, Lns, WBC; all versions except TEV, TNT], 'to receive glory' [TEV], 'to receive honor' [LN], 'to be honored' [BAGD; TNT], 'to be praised' [SSA]. See this word at 1:10.

c. ἐν (LN 89.26; 89.119, 90.6): 'in' [Hn, HNTC, ICC, Lns, WBC; all versions except TEV, TNT], 'among' [TNT], '(to receive glory) from' [TEV], 'because of (what he has done for)' [SSA].

QUESTION—What is meant by τὸ ὄνομα 'the name'?

1. The use of 'name' is not significant and so 'the name of the Lord Jesus' means essentially the same as 'the Lord Jesus' [HNTC, NCBC, TH].
2. 'Name' has a special meaning. Some suggestions are that it means Jesus in his revealed character and attributes [Ea, EBC, El, Er, Fn, Hb, Hn, Lns, Mn, NIC, Rb, SSA, WBC, Wd], here specifically glorifying Jesus as Lord [Er, Fn, Hb, Hn, HNTC, ICC, My, NIC, Rb], as the man Jesus [NIC], and as the Savior [Er, Hn, SSA], or 'name' refers to the reputation of the Lord Jesus [WBC]. The difference between 'name of our Lord Jesus' and

simply 'our Lord Jesus' is so subtle that the translation of SSA leaves out 'name'.

QUESTION—What relationship is indicated by ἐν 'in'?

Some mention the similarity of the phrase 'may be glorified in you' with the phrase 'to be glorified on that day in his saints' in 1:10 [Fn, Hn, HNTC, Lns, SSA, WBC, Wd]. The meaning selected in 1:10 would be the same as selected here [Fn, Hn, SSA, WBC, Wd].

1. This indicates the reason for the Lord Jesus being glorified [Fn, Hn, HNTC, ICC, Lns, NCBC, NIC, SSA, WBC]: the name of the Lord Jesus will be glorified because of you. Some suggestions of the specific reasons are that he is praised by others because of the Thessalonians' good conduct, which brings credit to the one they serve [HNTC, NCBC, NIC, WBC]; he is praised, either by others or by the Thessalonians themselves, because of what he has done for the Thessalonians in saving them [SSA] and what he has done in them [Fn, Hn], because he has perfected the attributes of love and goodness in the Thessalonians [ICC], and has caused them to shine in glory [Fn, Hb, Lns].
2. This indicates the circumstance of the glorification and refers to spiritual union [EBC]: the Lord Jesus will be glorified as he is in union with you.
3. This indicates the agents of the event word 'glorification' [probably TNT]: the Lord Jesus will be glorified among you, that is, you will praise the Lord Jesus.

and you in him/it,

QUESTION—Is αὐτῷ to be taken as being in the masculine case, meaning 'him', or is it to be taken as being in the neuter case, meaning 'it'?

1. It refers to the immediately preceding masculine word 'Jesus' and means 'him' [Alf, Ea, EBC, El, Er, Fn, Hb, Hn, HNTC, NCBC, NIC, SSA, WBC, Wd; all versions]: and you in him.
2. It refers to the preceding neuter word 'name' and means 'it' [ICC, Lns, My]: and you in it. However, the meaning is the same as the first interpretation [Hn, ICC].

QUESTION—What verb is implied in this clause and what relationship is indicated by ἐν 'in'?

This is the grammatical reciprocal of the preceding clause [Hb, HNTC, ICC, NIC, SSA, Wd]: and in order that you may be glorified in him.

1. ἐν has a different meaning than in the preceding clause [Ea, Fn, Hn, SSA, TH, WBC, Wd; TNT]. While the Lord Jesus will be praised because of what he has done for them, they will be glorified by him [SSA]. Or his work in them brings glory to him, their nearness to him brings glory to them by their sharing his glory [Hn, Wd]. Some take it to refer to their relationship with Christ and the relationship to glorification is implicit: he will be honored among you, while you will be honored because you belong to him [TNT], he will be honored because of or by you and you

will be glorified because you are in union with him who is glorified [Ea, Fn, Hn].
2. This is the semantic reciprocal with ἐν 'in' to be taken in the same way as the preceding clause [EBC, HNTC, ICC, NCBC].

according-to^a the grace^b of-the God of-us and Lord Jesus Christ.

LEXICON—a. κατά (LN 89.8): 'according to' [Hn, ICC, Lns, WBC; KJV, NASB, NEB, NIV, RSV], 'in accord with' [NAB], 'in virtue of' [HNTC], 'by' [NJB, TEV], 'because' [SSA]. This relational word is also translated so as to begin a new sentence: 'May they make this come true' [TNT].
b. χάρις (LN 88.66): 'grace' [BAGD, Hn, HNTC, ICC, LN, Lns, WBC; all versions except NAB, TNT], 'the gracious gift' [NAB]. This noun is also translated as an adverb: 'graciously' [TNT]; or as a verb: 'to act graciously' [SSA].

QUESTION—What relationship is indicated by κατά 'according to'?
1. This indicates the reason that they are glorified in the preceding statement [Ea, EBC, Er, HNTC, NCBC, NIC, SSA, TH]: the glorification of the Lord Jesus and of you will take place because God and the Lord Jesus acted graciously toward you. This may be limited to the immediately preceding elliptical clause 'and you in him' [SSA, TH]: you will be glorified in him because God and the Lord Jesus acted graciously toward you.
2. This indicates the norm of the glorification and means 'in accordance with' [El, Fn, Hb, Hn, HNTC, ICC, Lns, Mn, My, WBC, Wd; KJV, NAB, NASB, NEB, NIV, RSV]: this mutual glorification will be in accordance with grace. This is further explained that the glory will be as great as the grace [Wd]. However, some who classify this as the norm of glorification also explain it to be the reason for glorification [El, Hb, Mn, Wd].

QUESTION—What is the significance of there being only one article with the two names?
1. This refers to two persons of the Godhead [Ea, EBC, El, Er, Fn, Hn, HNTC, Mn, My, NCBC, NIC, SSA, WBC]: the grace of our God and of the Lord Jesus Christ. 'Lord' can occur without the article when it is a name or title [SSA].
2. Both 'God' and 'Lord' describe the one person, Jesus [Hb, Lns, Wd]: the grace of him who is both our God and Lord, namely, Jesus Christ. The use of the one article with the two nouns refers both 'God' and 'Lord' to Jesus Christ.

DISCOURSE UNIT 2:1–17 [EBC, SSA, Wd]. The topic is the second advent. This is further divided 2:1–2, 3–5, 6–7, 8–10, 11–12, 13–14, 15–17 [Wd]; 2:1–2, 3–4, 5–7, 8–10, 11–12, 13–14, 15, 16–17 [EBC].

DISCOURSE UNIT: 2:1–12 [Alf, Er, Fn, GNT, Hb, Hn, HNTC, ICC, Lns, Mn, My, NCBC, NIC, SSA, TH, WBC; NAB, NIV, NJB, TEV]. The topic is the End [HNTC], the Day of the Lord [Alf, Hb, NCBC], the coming of the Lord

[Mn, My, NIC; NJB], the man of lawlessness [Fn, GNT, WBC; NIV, TEV], the coming of the Lord and the man of lawlessness [Er, TH], the restraining of the adversary [NAB], exhortation [ICC], exhortation not to be alarmed about messages that the day of the Lord has already come [SSA]. This unit indicates the theme of the letter [Hb, Lns, WBC]. This is further divided 2:1–2, 3–4, 5–7, 8–12 [WBC]; 2:1–2, 3– 8a, 8b–c, 9–12 [ICC]; 2:1–5 (1–2, 3–4, 5), 6–7, 8–12 [Hb]; 2:1–4, 5–7, 8–10, 11–12 [Mn]; 2:1–3, 3–10a, 10b–12 [TH]; 2:1–3a, 3b–5, 6–8, 9–12 [SSA].

2:1 **Now^a we-request^b you, brothers,**
LEXICON: a. δέ (LN 89.94; 89.124): 'now' [Hn, HNTC, ICC, Lns, WBC; KJV, NASB, RSV], 'and now' [NEB], not explicit [SSA; NAB, NIV, NJB, TEV, TNT].
   b. pres. act. indic. of ἐρωτάω (LN 33.161): 'to request' [BAGD, LN, Lns, SSA; NASB], 'to ask' [BAGD, ICC, LN; NIV], 'to beseech' [KJV], 'to beg' [HNTC, WBC; NAB, NEB, RSV, TEV, TNT], 'please' [NJB].
QUESTION—What relationship is indicated by δέ 'now'?
   1. This indicates transition to a new topic [El, Hn, HNTC, ICC, Lns, My, NCBC, NIC, SSA, TH, WBC; KJV, NASB, NEB, RSV]: now. The transition is from the thanksgiving and prayer in chapter 1 to an exhortation [ICC].
   2. This indicates contrast [Alf, Ea, Fn, Hb]: but. The contrast is between Paul's prayer for them and his correction of their errors [Hb]. It contrasts what he requests for them with what he requests of them [Alf, Ea]. Or, it contrasts the certainty of the Lord's coming with the disturbed state of the Thessalonian church about it [Fn].

concerning/by^a the coming^b of-the Lord of-us Jesus Christ and our assembling^c to^d him,
LEXICON—a. ὑπέρ (LN 90.24): 'concerning' [BAGD, Hn, SSA; NIV, RSV, TEV], 'about' [NEB, NJB, TNT], 'with/in regard to' [Lns, WBC; NASB], 'in connection with' [HNTC], 'in reference to' [ICC], 'on the question of' [NAB]; or 'by' [KJV].
   b. παρουσία (LN 15.86): 'the coming' [BAGD, Hn, ICC, LN; all versions], 'the parousia' [BAGD, HNTC, Lns], 'the advent' [WBC]. This noun is also translated as a verb: 'to return' [SSA].
   c. ἐπισυναγωγή (LN **15.126**): 'assembling' [BAGD, WBC; RSV], 'gathering' [NEB], 'gathering together' [Hn, ICC, Lns; KJV, NASB]. This noun is also translated as a verb: 'to be assembled together' [SSA], 'to be gathered' [NAB, NIV, NJB], 'to be gathered together' [HNTC, LN; TEV, TNT].
   d. ἐπί (LN 84.17): 'to' [HNTC, SSA, WBC; NAB, NASB, NEB, NIV, NJB], 'unto' [Lns; KJV], 'to meet' [Hn, ICC; RSV, TNT], 'to be with' [TEV].

QUESTION—What relationship is indicated by ὑπέρ 'concerning/by'?
1. This means 'concerning' [BAGD, Ea, Hn HNTC, ICC, Lns, Mn, NCBC, Rb, SSA, TH, WBC, Wd; all versions except KJV]: concerning the coming of our Lord and our assembling to him, we request that you not be shaken about the news that the day has already come. This is used in the sense of περί 'concerning' [HNTC, TH, WBC].
2. This means 'on behalf of' [Alf, EBC, El, Fn, Hb, My, NIC]: in interest of the truth about the coming of our Lord and our assembling to him, we request that you not be shaken by the news that the day has already come.
4. This means 'by', an adjuration appealing to these events for solemnity or certainty [KJV]: we request, by the coming of the Lord and our assembling to him, that you not be shaken by the news that the day has already come.

QUESTION—In what way will they assemble together to him?
This refers to the church being gathered together (passive sense of the noun) rather than its gathering together (active sense) [Wd]. This describes 1 Thess. 4:17 where believers will be gathered together at the resurrection and then brought to meet Christ in the air [Alf, EBC, El, Hb, Hn, HNTC, ICC, Lns, My, NCBC, NIC, Rb, SSA, TH, WBC, Wd].

2:2 that[a]
LEXICON—a. εἰς τό (LN 89.57; 90.23): 'that' [Lns, SSA; KJV, NASB], not explicit [Hn, HNTC, ICC, WBC; NAB, NEB, NIV, NJB, RSV, TEV, TNT].
QUESTION—What relationship is indicated by εἰς τό 'that'?
These words indicate the content of the preceding request (2:1) [EBC, Hb, HNTC, ICC, Lns, NCBC, SSA, WBC, Wd; NAB, NEB, NIV, NJB, RSV, TEV, TNT]: we request *that* you not be shaken or disturbed. At the same time, these words indicate the purpose for the request [Alf, Ea, El, Er, Hb, Mn, Rb].

you not to-be quickly/easily[a] shaken[b] from[c] the mind[d] nor to-be-disturbed,[e]
LEXICON—a. ταχέως (LN 67.56; 67.110): 'quickly' [BAGD, LN, SSA, WBC; NASB, RSV], 'soon' [LN; KJV], 'suddenly' [NEB, TNT]; or 'easily' [BAGD, Hn, Lns; NIV], 'so/too easily' [BAGD; NAB, NJB, TEV], 'readily' [HNTC, ICC].
b. aorist pass. infin. of σαλεύομαι (LN **25.242**): 'to be shaken' [BAGD, Hn, HNTC, Lns, WBC; KJV, RSV, TNT], 'to be unsettled' [ICC], 'to be confused' [TEV], 'to be troubled' [SSA], 'to be upset' [LN]. The phrase 'to be shaken from the mind' is also translated 'to be agitated' [NAB], 'to become unsettled' [NIV], 'to be thrown into confusion' [NJB], 'to be shaken from one's composure' [NASB], 'to lose one's head' [NEB]. The aorist tense refers to the initial shock of excitement [Fn, Hb, Hn, HNTC, Lns, Mn, NCBC, Rb, Wd], or it regards the action without reference to its progress [ICC].

c. ἀπό (LN 89.122): 'in' [ICC, SSA; KJV, RSV, TEV], 'from' [Hn, Lns], 'out of' [HNTC, WBC; TNT].
d. νοῦς (LN 30.5): 'mind' [BAGD, Hn, ICC, Lns, SSA; KJV, RSV], 'senses' [TNT], 'wits' [WBC], 'thinking' [TEV], 'way of thinking' [LN], 'sanity' [HNTC].
e. pres. pass. infin. of θροέομαι (LN **25.262**): 'to be disturbed' [BAGD, Hn, WBC; NASB], 'to be upset' [TEV], 'to be anxious' [HNTC], 'to be troubled' [Lns; KJV], 'to be nervously wrought up' [ICC], 'to be terrified' [NAB], 'to be alarmed' [LN, SSA; NIV, NJB, TNT], 'to alarm oneself' [NEB], 'to be excited' [RSV]. The present tense describes this as a continuous state [Hn, HNTC, ICC, Lns, Mn, NCBC, NIC, Rb, Wd]. It is a state of alarm that resulted from being shaken [Fn, Hb, Hn, HNTC, Lns, Mn, NCBC, Rb], although one commentator reverses that order and thinks that being shaken in mind is the result of being emotionally disturbed [TH].

QUESTION—What meant by ταχέως 'quickly/easily'?
1. This has the temporal meaning 'quickly' [Alf, Ea, Fn, My, NCBC, SSA, WBC]: I request that you not be shaken so quickly. This refers to the short time since they heard the false teaching [My, SSA].
2. This indicates manner, 'easily' [Ea, EBC, El, Hn, HNTC, ICC, Lns, Mn, TH] or 'rashly' [Alf, Ea, Hb, Mn, NIC]: I request that you not be shaken so easily/rashly. This means that they need to consider the teaching carefully [Hb, HNTC].

neither by[a] a-spirit[b] nor by[a] speech[c] nor by[a] a-letter[d] as[e] from/through[f] us,
LEXICON—a. διά (LN 90.4; 89.26): 'by' [Hn, ICC, Lns, SSA, WBC; KJV, NAB, NASB, NIV, NJB, RSV], 'in' [TNT], 'because of' [HNTC], 'while' [TEV], 'at' [NEB].
b. πνεῦμα (LN 12.33): 'spirit' [BAGD, Hn, HNTC, LN, Lns; KJV, NASB, RSV], 'prophecy' [NIV], 'prophetic utterance' [TNT], 'oracular utterance' [NAB, NEB], 'a spirit-inspired utterance' [WBC], 'the statement made by Spirit' [ICC], 'a message which someone claims to have been have been revealed by the Holy Spirit to us' [SSA], 'manifestation of the Spirit' [NJB]. This noun is also translated as a verb: '(while) prophesying' [TEV].
c. λόγος (LN 33.98; 33.99): 'speech', 'message' [BAGD, LN, SSA; NASB], 'word' [BAGD, Hn, LN, Lns; KJV, RSV], 'report' [BAGD; NIV], 'pronouncement' [NEB], 'statement' [BAGD, LN; NJB, TNT], 'speaking' [LN], 'a spoken word' [WBC], 'the statement made orally' [ICC], 'oral statement' [HNTC], 'rumor' [NAB]. This noun is also translated as a verb: '(while) preaching' [TEV].
d. ἐπιστολή (LN 6.63; 33.48): 'letter' [BAGD, Hn, HNTC, ICC, LN, Lns, SSA, WBC; all versions].
e. ὡς (LN 64.12): 'as' [Hn; KJV], 'as if' [ICC; NASB], 'as (claiming to come)' [Lns], 'alleged (to be)' [BAGD; NAB], 'purporting (to come/be)'

[HNTC, WBC; NEB, RSV, TNT], 'claiming (to come)' [NJB], 'which someone claims' [SSA], 'supposed (to have come)' [NIV], 'perhaps it is thought that we said this' [TEV].
- f. διά (LN 90.4): 'from' [Hn, HNTC; KJV, NASB, NEB, NIV, NJB, RSV, TNT], 'to be (ours)' [NAB], '(to be written) by' [WBC], '(we) had made it' [ICC]; or 'through' [Lns].

QUESTION—To what is the phrase ὡς δι' ἡμῶν 'as from us' to be connected?
1. It is connected to all three preceding means [EBC, Hb, HNTC, ICC, Lns, Mn, NCBC, NIC, SSA; TEV]: do not be shaken and troubled by means of a prophecy allegedly made by us, or by a message allegedly given by us, or by a letter allegedly from us.
2. It is connected to the last two means [Alf, Ea, El, Fn, Hn, My, Rb]: do not be shaken and troubled by means of a prophecy someone gives in the congregation, or by a message claimed to be given by us, whether they say we taught it or wrote it. It is to be noted that these two means are also connected in 2:15 [Alf].
4. It is connected to only the last means [EGT, Fn, WBC; probably KJV, NAB, RSV, TNT]: do not be shaken and troubled by means of a prophecy someone gives in the congregation, or by a message someone gives, or by a letter someone claims to have come from us.

QUESTION—What relationship is indicated by ὡς 'as'?
This can be taken to mean that someone claims that the message is from Paul and his companions although it really was not [Ea, El, Hb, Hn, Lns, Mn, My, NIC, SSA, WBC]. However, some commentators state that it does not definitely deny that it really was from them. Perhaps an authentic communication, such as the first letter to the Thessalonians (5:1–11), had been misunderstood [ICC, NCBC, WBC].

QUESTION—What relationship is indicated by διά 'from/through (us)'?
1. This indicates the originator or author of the communication [Hn, HNTC, ICC, Mn, My, Rb, SSA, WBC; all versions]: as from us.
2. This indicates the agency by which the communication came [Alf, El, Fn, Lns]: as through us.

as[a] that the day of-the Lord is-come.[b]
TEXT—Instead of κυρίου 'Lord', some manuscripts have Χριστοῦ 'Christ'. This alternative is not mentioned by GNT. Only KJV uses 'Christ'.
LEXICON—a. ὡς (LN 64.12; 90.21): 'as' [KJV], 'to the effect' [Hn, WBC; NASB, RSV], 'saying' [HNTC; NIV], 'which claims' [SSA], 'alleging' [NEB], 'suggesting' [NJB], 'by the claim' [TEV], 'any assertion' [TNT], not explicit [ICC, Lns; NAB].
- b. perfect act. indic. of ἐνίσταμαι (LN 67.41; 67.63; 13.109): 'to come' [BAGD, SSA; NASB, NIV, RSV, TEV], 'to be present' [BAGD, HNTC, ICC, LN, Lns, WBC], 'to arrive' [Hn; NJB], 'to be here' [NAB, NEB, TNT], 'to happen' [LN], 'imminent, impending' [LN], 'to be at hand' [KJV].

QUESTION—What is indicated by the use of the perfect tense ἐνέστηκεν 'is come'?
1. The perfect tense indicates that the Day is already present [Alf, Ea, EBC, EGT, El, Er, Fn, Hb, HNTC, ICC, Lns, Mn, NCBC, NIC, TH, WBC, Wd; all versions except KJV]: the day has come and is here.
2. It means that the Day is imminent [Rb; KJV]: the day is at hand. When it is intransitive in this tense, it means that it is near [Rb].

QUESTION—What is meant by 'the Day of the Lord'?
1. It means a period of time [Ea, EBC, El, Hb, Hn, ICC, NCBC, NIC]. The period has begun and the Lord may be expected at any moment [Hn, ICC]. Perhaps they were taught that they were in the period of tribulation that preceded the establishment of the kingdom [Ea, Hb].
2. It refers to the time of an event [HNTC, SSA]. It means the day when the Lord will come [HNTC] and judge people [BAGD, SSA].

2:3 Not anyone may-deceive^a you in not-any way;^b

LEXICON—a. aorist act. subj. of ἐξαπατάω (LN 31.12): 'to deceive' [BAGD, Hn, HNTC, ICC, LN, Lns, SSA, WBC; all versions except NAB], 'to deceive' [LN], 'to seduce' [NAB].
b. τρόπος (LN **89.83; 41.10**): 'way'. The phrase κατὰ μηδένα τρόπον 'in (not) any way' is translated 'in any way' [BAGD, Hn, HNTC, ICC, LN, Lns, SSA; NASB, NIV, NJB, RSV, TEV, TNT], 'in any way whatever' [NEB], 'by any means' [WBC; KJV], 'no matter how' [NAB].

because^a unless comes^b the apostasy^c first^d

LEXICON—a. ὅτι (LN 89.33): 'because' [Lns], 'for' [Hn, HNTC, ICC; KJV, NASB, NIV, RSV, TEV], 'since' [NAB], not explicit [SSA, WBC; NEB, NJB, TNT].
b. aorist act. subj. of ἔρχομαι (LN 13.117): 'to come' [BAGD, Hn, ICC, Lns, WBC; KJV, NASB, RSV], 'to occur' [NAB, NIV], 'to take place' [HNTC; NJB, TEV, TNT], 'to happen' [LN], not explicit [SSA; NEB]. This verb is in an emphatic position [Hb, Lns].
c. ἀποστασία (LN **39.34**): 'apostasy'. The phrase with the article is translated 'the apostasy' [BAGD, Hn, HNTC, ICC, Lns; NASB], 'the mass apostasy' [NAB], 'a falling away' [KJV], 'the rebellion' [BAGD, WBC; NIV, RSV], 'the final rebellion' [LN; TEV], 'the final rebellion against God' [NEB], 'the great Rebellion' [TNT], 'the Great Revolt' [NJB]. This noun is also translated as a phrase: 'many people will have rebelled against God' [SSA].
d. πρῶτος (LN 60.46; 67.18): 'first' [BAGD, HNTC, LN, Lns, WBC; KJV, NASB, RSV], 'first of all' [Hn, ICC], 'only after' [SSA], 'before' [LN], 'not until' [NIV, NJB, TEV, TNT], 'not before' [NEB], not explicit [NAB].

QUESTION—What relationship is indicated by ὅτι 'because'?
This indicates the grounds for the warning in the preceding verses [Hb, Hn, ICC, Lns, My, SSA, TH; all versions except NAB]: do not let anyone

deceive you into thinking that the day of the Lord has come, *since* the day will not come until certain things have taken place. This proves that the day has not yet arrived [EBC, NIC].

QUESTION—What is the implied apodosis on which the condition clause rests?

The implied apodosis is derived from the statement about the coming of day of the Lord (2:2) [Alf, Bul (p. 52), Ea, EBC, Fn, Hb, Hn, HNTC, ICC, Lns, Mn, My, NCBC, NIC, SSA, TH, WBC, Wd; all versions except NAB]: that day will not come unless the apostasy first comes and the man of lawlessness is revealed.

QUESTION—What is the significance of the article in the phrase ἡ ἀποστασία 'the apostasy' and what does the noun mean?

The article indicates that the particular apostasy to which he refers was already well know to the readers [Alf, Ea, Fn, Hb, Hn, HNTC, ICC, Lns, Mn, My, NCBC, NIC, Rb, SSA, WBC, Wd]. It also indicates that it is the apostasy that surpasses all others [SSA; NJB, TEV, TNT]: the great apostasy. 'Apostasy' means that people, in general, will rebel against God and his laws [ICC, My, NCBC, NIC, SSA, Wd], or it means that professed believers will defect [Ea, EBC, Er, Fn, Hb, Hn, Lns, Mn]. Some commentators say that besides being a religious revolt it also involves political revolt [WBC].

and is-revealed[a] the man of-lawlessness,[b]

TEXT—Instead of ἀνομίας 'of lawlessness', some manuscripts have ἁμαρτίας 'of sin'. GNT selects 'of lawlessness' with a C rating, indicating a considerable degree of doubt. Only KJV selects 'of sin'.

LEXICON—a. aorist pass. subj. of ἀποκαλύπτω (LN 28.38): 'to be revealed' [BAGD, Hn, HNTC, ICC, LN, Lns, SSA, WBC; KJV, NAB, NASB, NEB, NIV, RSV, TNT], 'to be made fully known' [LN]. The passive form is also translated actively: 'to appear' [NJB, TEV]. This verb is in an emphatic position [Fn, Hb, Lns, Mn].

b. ἀνομία (LN 88.139): 'lawlessness' [BAGD, Hn, ICC, LN, Lns, WBC; NAB, NASB, NIV, RSV, TNT], 'wickedness' [NEB], 'rebellion' [HNTC], 'the wicked one' [NJB, TEV]. This adjective is also translated as a verb phrase: '(the man who) will sin very greatly' [SSA].

QUESTION—What relationship is indicated by καί 'and'?

1. It indicates addition [EBC, Fn, Hb, ICC, Lns, NIC, SSA, WBC, Wd; all versions except NEB]: the apostasy comes first *and* then the man of lawlessness is revealed.
2. It indicates result [Alf, Ea, El, Mn, My]: the apostasy comes first, *with the result that* the man of lawlessness is revealed.
3. It indicates equivalence [EGT]: the apostasy comes first, *that is*, the man of lawlessness is revealed.
4. It indicates a temporal relationship [NEB]: the apostasy comes first, *when* the man of lawlessness is revealed.

QUESTION—How is the person related to the attribute in the genitive construction ὁ ἄνθρωπος τῆς ἀνομίας 'the man of lawlessness'?

The man is characterized by the quality of lawlessness [Bul (p. 501), Ea, EGT, Fn, Hb, HNTC, ICC, Lns, Mn, My, Rb, SSA, WBC], he is sin personified [Alf, El, Fn, Hb, Hn, HNTC, My], he does what is against the law EBC, [Mn].

the son of-perdition,[a]

LEXICON—a. ἀπώλεια (LN 20.31): 'perdition' [Hn, ICC, Lns, WBC; KJV, NAB, NEB, RSV], 'destruction' [BAGD, LN; NASB, NIV, TNT], 'hell' [TEV], 'doom' [HNTC], 'the lost (one)' [NJB]. This noun is also translated as a verb: 'to be destroyed' [SSA].

QUESTION—How is the person related to the event word in this genitive construction?

The man is the object of the event [Ea, EBC, ICC, SSA, TH, WBC]: the man who will be destroyed by God. Many take this to imply that he is destined for this destruction [Ea, EBC, EGT, Er, Fn, Hb, Hn, HNTC, ICC, Mn, My, NCBC, NIC, Rb, SSA, TH, WBC, Wd; NEB, NIV, TEV, TNT]: the man destined to be destroyed by God. 'Son of' is a Hebraism for a person who eminently embodies the characteristic of a class [EBC, Hb, HNTC, ICC, TH].

2:4 the (one) opposing[a] **and exalting-oneself**[b] **against**[c] **everything being-called**[d] **god or object-of-worship,**[e]

LEXICON—a. pres. mid. (deponent = active) participle of ἀντίκειμαι (LN 39.1): 'to oppose' [BAGD, Hn, HNTC, ICC, LN, Lns, WBC; KJV, NASB, NIV, RSV, TEV, TNT], 'to be hostile toward' [LN]. This participle with the article is also translated as a substantive: 'the adversary' [NAB], 'the enemy' [NEB, NJB], 'the supreme enemy of God' [SSA], 'the opposer' [My].

b. pres. mid. participle of ὑπεραίρομαι (LN 39.39): 'to exalt oneself' [BAGD, Hn, HNTC, ICC, Lns, SSA, WBC; KJV, NAB, NASB, NIV, RSV, TNT], 'to raise oneself' [NJB], 'to put oneself above' [TEV], 'to rise in pride' [NEB], 'to rise up in pride against' [LN].

c. ἐπί (LN 90.34; 37.9): 'against' [BAGD, Hn, HNTC, ICC, Lns; NEB, RSV, TNT], 'above' [SSA; KJV, NAB, NASB, NJB, TEV], 'over' [WBC; NIV], 'above' [BAGD].

d. pres. pass. participle of λέγω (LN 33.129; 33.131): 'to be called' [BAGD, Hn, HNTC, ICC, LN, Lns; KJV, NIV], 'so-called' [BAGD, WBC; NAB, NASB, NEB, NJB, RSV, TEV, TNT], 'to consider' [SSA].

e. σέβασμα (LN 53.55): 'object of worship' [BAGD, ICC, LN, Lns, WBC; NASB, NEB, NJB, RSV, TEV, TNT], 'sacred object' [HNTC], 'what/that is worshipped' [Hn, SSA; KJV, NIV], '(god) proposed for worship' [NAB].

2 THESSALONIANS 2:4

QUESTION—What does this man oppose?
1. 'Opposing' is separate from the following verb 'exalting himself' and it means that he opposes God [Alf, EBC, EGT, Hn, HNTC, Lns, NCBC, NIC, SSA] or, more specifically, he opposes Christ [Alf, Ea, El, Fn, Hb, My, Rb]: he opposes God and exalts himself above every so-called god.
2. 'Opposing' is coordinate with the following verb and its object is the last phrase [HNTC, Lns, NCBC, TH; TEV]: he opposes every so-called god and exalts himself above/against every so-called god.

so-that[a] into the temple[b] of-God he sits,[c]
LEXICON—a. ὥστε (LN 89.52): 'so that' [Hn, ICC, Lns, SSA, WBC; KJV, NASB, NIV, RSV], 'and even' [NEB], 'so as to' [HNTC], 'to' [NJB], not explicit [NAB, TEV, TNT].
  b. ναός (LN 7.15): 'temple' [BAGD, ICC, LN, SSA; KJV, NAB, NASB, NEB, NIV, RSV, TEV], 'sanctuary' [Hn, LN, Lns, WBC; NJB, TNT], 'shrine' [HNTC].
  c. aorist act. infin. of καθίζω (LN 17.12): 'to sit' [HNTC, ICC, LN; KJV], 'to sit down' [BAGD, LN; TEV], 'to take one's seat' [SSA, WBC; NASB, NEB, RSV, TNT], 'to seat one's self' [Hn, Lns; NAB]. This action is also translated to indicate its function as an official act: 'to set up one's self' [NIV], 'to enthrone one's self' [NJB]. This does not indicate whether the attempt is successful or not [HNTC, ICC].
QUESTION—What relationship is indicated by ὥστε 'so that'?
  This indicates the result of exalting himself [Ea, Fn, Hb, HNTC, Lns, Mn, NCBC, NIC, Rb, SSA]: he will exalt himself above every so-called god and object of worship, *with the result that* he will establish himself in the temple. Or, this indicates the natural consequence that the exaltation tends to produce and does not indicate that this is the actual result [Wd].
QUESTION—What is meant by εἰς 'into'?
  This implies the event of entering into the temple [Alf, Ea, Fn, Lns, SSA; TEV]: he will enter the temple and take his seat.
QUESTION—Where is the temple?
  This is the inner sanctuary of the temple [Ea, Fn, Hb, Hn, HNTC, Lns, NIC, WBC, Wd], where God was considered to dwell [HNTC, WBC]. It refers to the temple in Jerusalem [EBC, Hb, Mn, My, WBC, Wd], or in heaven [ICC]. Some take this to refer to a rebuilt temple in Jerusalem or somewhere else [EBC, El, Hb, NIC]. However, this may be taken as a metaphor, meaning that he will try to usurp the authority of God and receive the worship due God [Alf, Hn, NCBC, SSA, WBC, Wd].

proclaiming[a] himself that he-is God.
LEXICON—a. pres. act. participle of ἀποδείκνυμι (LN 28.65): 'to proclaim' [BAGD, Hn, HNTC, ICC, WBC; NIV, RSV, TNT], 'to publicly proclaim' [SSA], 'to declare' [NAB], 'to claim' [NEB, TEV], 'to show' [KJV], 'to show publicly' [LN], 'to show one's self off' [Lns], 'to display' [NASB], 'to demonstrate publicly' [LN], 'to flaunt the claim' [NJB].

QUESTION—What relationship is indicated by the participial form ἀποδεικνύντα 'proclaiming'?
This indicates what is implied by the act of seating himself in the temple [Hb, HNTC].

2:5 **Do-you not remember^a that yet^b being with you I-told^c you these-things?**

LEXICON—a. pres. act. indic. of μνημονεύω (LN 29.7): 'to remember' [BAGD, Hn, HNTC, ICC, LN, Lns, SSA, WBC; all versions], 'to recall' [LN].
  b. ἔτι (LN 67.128): 'yet' [BAGD, ICC, LN; KJV], 'still' [BAGD, Hn, LN, Lns, SSA, WBC; NAB, NASB, NEB, RSV, TNT], not explicit [HNTC; NIV, NJB, TEV].
  c. imperf. act. indic. of λέγω (LN 33.69): 'to tell' [BAGD, Hn, HNTC, ICC, LN, Lns, SSA, WBC; all versions]. The imperfect tense indicates that he repeatedly told them [Ea, Hb, Hn, HNTC, ICC, Lns, NIC, Rb, SSA; NAB, NASB, NIV, TNT].

QUESTION—What is the function of this rhetorical question?
It implies that Paul expects them to remember [Hb, ICC, SSA, Wd]. Some translate it to show that Paul assumes that they do remember [HNTC, ICC, SSA; NEB, NJB]: surely you remember. The mention of the topic would remind them of the details [Fn, Lns, NIC, Rb, WBC, Wd]. It is a mild rebuke [Alf, Ea, El, Er, Fn, Hb, Hn, HNTC, Lns, Mn, My, NCBC]: you should have remembered.

QUESTION—To what does ταῦτα 'these things' refer?
This refers to the preceding context 2:2–4 [Ea] or 2:3–4 [ICC, My, SSA].

2:6 **And now^a the (thing) restraining^b you-know,**

LEXICON—a. νῦν (LN 67.38): 'now' [BAGD, Hn, HNTC, LN, Lns, SSA, WBC; KJV, NASB, NEB, NIV, RSV, TEV], 'at present' [TNT], 'the present time' [ICC], not explicit [NAB, NJB].
  b. pres. act. participle of κατέχω (LN 13.150): 'to restrain' [BAGD, LN], 'to hinder' [LN]. The substantive is translated 'what restrains' [NAB, NASB, RSV, TNT], 'what is holding back' [Hn, WBC; NIV, NJB], 'the thing holding up' [Lns], 'what withholdeth' [KJV], 'the restraining hand' [NEB], 'something that keeps this from happening' [TEV], 'something which is preventing' [SSA], 'the spirit or power that detains' [ICC]. The present tense indicates that the restraint was then at work [Hb]. Its position makes this word emphatic [Alf, Hb].

QUESTION—With what does νῦν 'now' go?
  1. It goes with the participle κατέχον 'restraining' [EBC, Hn, Lns, SSA; NASB, RSV, TEV, TNT]: and you know what is now restraining him. This is in contrast with the future revealing at the proper time [EBC, Hn, SSA].
  2. It goes with the verb οἴδατε 'you know' with a contrast to what they knew previously [NCBC; NEB]: and you now know what is restraining

him. They have now come to the knowledge about the restrainer by experience [NCBC, Wd], or it could be taken in contrast with what precedes [NCBC]: you remember what I told you then, and now you know for yourselves by experience.
3. It focuses on the present circumstances [Fn, HNTC, ICC, Mn]: and as for the present time, you know what is restraining him. This present time is in contrast with ἐν τῷ αὐτοῦ καιρῷ 'in his own time' in the following phrase [Fn, HNTC, Mn] and with καὶ τότε 'and then' in 2:8 when the man of lawlessness will be revealed [ICC].
4. This goes with καί 'and' and has a resumptive or transitional, rather than a temporal, force [Alf, Ea, EGT, El, Hb, My, NIC, WBC]: and now to pass to a further point, you know what restrains him. It means 'now' in the argument [Alf, Ea, EGT]. Paul passes from a discussion about the future to present affairs [NIC].

QUESTION—What is meant by οἴδατε 'you know'?
Some commentators take it to mean that they know from previous instruction [Ea, ICC, Lns, My, SSA, WBC]: you know what has been taught you about the thing that restrains. Others take it to mean that they know from personal observation [Fn, HNTC, NCBC, TH, Wd]: you know from personal experience the power that is restraining the lawless one.

QUESTION—What is being restrained?
Many commentators supply 'him', or explain that it is the man of lawlessness [Alf, Ea, EBC, Hn, HNTC, ICC, Lns, Mn, NCBC, NIC, WBC]: you know what is restraining him. Others speak of restraining the act of revealing him (2:3) until the proper time comes [Hb, Lns, My, NIC, SSA]: you know what is keeping the man of lawlessness from being revealed.

QUESTION—What (neuter gender) is doing the restraining?
It is an unidentified power [Ea, El, Er, Fn, Hb, Hn, HNTC, ICC, Lns, Mn, My, NCBC, NIC, SSA, WBC], or principle [Fn, SSA, Wd], or spirit [EBC, ICC]. The power might be Rome [ICC], or more specifically, the government and its law and order [El, Fn, Hn, Mn, Wd]. Or it could be a spirit who is either the Holy Spirit [EBC, Hb], an angelic being [NCBC], or an unidentified supernatural being [ICC]. One commentator understands it to be the force of evil which occupies this world [HNTC]. Another commentator mentions the possibility that the phrase could mean that Satan is now holding sway [ICC], but none have accepted this interpretation.

so-that[a] he be-revealed[b] in[c] his time.[d]

LEXICON—a. εἰς (LN 89.57; 89.48; 67.119): 'so that' [Lns, WBC; NASB, NIV, RSV], 'in order that' [Hn, ICC, SSA], 'that' [KJV], 'which ensures that' [NEB], 'so as' [HNTC], 'from' [NJB], 'until' [NAB, TNT], not explicit [TEV].
  b. aorist pass. infinitive of ἀποκαλύπτω (LN 28.38): 'to be revealed' [BAGD, Hn, HNTC, ICC, LN, Lns, SSA, WBC; KJV, NAB, NASB, NEB, NIV, RSV, TNT], 'to be made fully known' [LN]. The passive

voice is also translated actively: 'to appear' [NJB, TEV]. See this word at 2:3.
  c. ἐν (LN 67.33): 'in' [Hn, HNTC, ICC, Lns; KJV, NAB, NASB, RSV], 'at' [SSA, WBC; NEB, NIV, TEV].
  d. καιρός (LN 67.1): 'time' [BAGD, HNTC, LN; KJV, NAB, NASB, RSV], 'season' [Lns]. The phrase 'his time' is translated 'the proper time' [NEB, NIV, TEV], 'his proper time' [WBC], 'the appointed time' [SSA; TNT], 'his appointed time' [ICC; NJB], 'his appropriate season' [Hn].

QUESTION—What relationship is indicated by εἰς 'so that'?
  1. This indicates the purpose for restraining the man of lawlessness [Alf, Ea, El, Fn, Hb, Hn, ICC, My, NCBC, Rb, SSA, WBC]: he is restrained *in order that* he may be revealed at the proper time. Some commentators speak of this as being God's purpose [Alf, Hb, Hn, ICC, My, SSA, WBC].
  2. This indicates the result of restraining the man of lawlessness [Lns, Wd]: the thing is restraining him *with the result that* he will be revealed at the proper time.
  3. It means 'until' [NAB, NJB, TNT]: you know what restrains him *until* the time comes for him to be revealed.

QUESTION—Who is the one who reveals the man of lawlessness?
  1. God reveals him [SSA]: so that he is revealed by God at the time determined by God.
  2. The man of lawlessness reveals himself [TH]: so that he will appear at the time determined by God. This assumes that the man's own activities will reveal who he is [TH].

QUESTION—What is meant by τῷ ἑαυτοῦ καιρῷ 'his time'?
  This means the time for him to be revealed [Alf, Ea, EBC, El, Fn, Hb, ICC, NCBC, NIC, SSA, Wd]. It is implied that God has determined this time [Alf, Ea, EBC, El, Fn, Hb, Hn, HNTC, ICC, Lns, Mn, My, NCBC, NIC, Rb, SSA, TH, WBC, Wd].

2:7 Because[a]

LEXICON—a. γάρ (LN 89.23): 'because', 'for' [Hn, HNTC, ICC, Lns, WBC; KJV, NASB, NEB, NIV, RSV, TNT], 'that is' [SSA], not explicit [NAB, NJB, TEV].

QUESTION—What relationship is indicated by this conjunction?
  1. This indicates an explanatory restatement of the preceding verse [Alf, Ea, EBC, EGT, El, Fn, HNTC, ICC, Lns, Mn, NCBC, SSA, Wd]: there is that which is restraining the lawless one in order that he may be revealed at the proper time, *that is,* the mystery of lawlessness is already at work, yet the one who is restraining him will continue to do so until he is removed and then the lawless one will be revealed.
  2. This indicates the grounds for the preceding statement [Hb, My]: there is one restraining him *since,* although the mystery of lawless is at work, there is one who restrains him until he is removed.

the mystery[a] of-lawlessness[b] already[c] is-at-work;[d]
LEXICON—a. μυστήριον (LN 28.77): 'mystery' [BAGD, Hn, HNTC, LN, Lns, WBC; KJV, NASB, NJB, RSV], 'secret' [BAGD, ICC, LN], 'secret force/power' [NAB, NEB, NIV]. This noun is also translated as an adjective: 'the Mysterious Wickedness' [TEV]; and as an adverb: '(to be) secretly (at work)' [TNT], 'secretly (causing people to reject God's law)' [SSA].
  b. ἀνομία (LN 88.139): 'lawlessness' [BAGD, Hn, ICC, LN, Lns, WBC; NAB, NASB, NIV, RSV, TNT], 'wickedness' [NEB, NJB, TEV], 'iniquity' [KJV], 'rebellion' [HNTC]. This noun is also translated as a verbal phrase: 'to reject God's law' [SSA]. See this word at 2:3.
  c. ἤδη (LN 67.20): 'already' [BAGD, Hn, HNTC, ICC, LN, Lns, SSA, WBC; all versions except TNT], 'even now' [TNT].
  d. pres. mid. indic. of ἐνεργέω (LN 42.3): 'to be at work' [BAGD, Hn, LN; all versions except KJV], 'to work' [BAGD, LN; KJV], 'to be set to work' [HNTC], 'to be active' [WBC], 'to be operating' [BAGD, Lns], 'to be set in operation' [ICC], 'to cause' [SSA].
QUESTION—How are the nouns related in the genitive construction τὸ μυστήριον τῆς ἀνομίας 'the mystery of lawlessness'?
  1. 'Mystery' refers to a secret, hidden activity or operation which is lawless [EGT, HNTC, NCBC, NIC, Rb, SSA, WBC, Wd]: the secret lawless activity. It is a secret rebellion, but it is known to Christians [HNTC].
  2. Lawlessness is the content of the mystery [Alf, Ea, El, Hb, ICC, My, TH]: the mystery concerning the lawlessness. 'Mystery' means facts that cannot be known unless they are revealed [Hb, TH]. The force of lawlessness is already at work in a hidden way, but it will become known when the man of lawlessness is revealed.

only[a] the (one) restraining now until[b] it-comes[c] out-of (the) midst.
LEXICON—a. μόνος (LN 58.50): 'only' [BAGD, Hn, ICC, Lns, WBC; KJV, NASB, NEB, RSV], 'but' [HNTC; NAB, NIV, NJB, TEV, TNT], 'nevertheless' [SSA].
  b. ἕως (LN 67.119): 'until' [BAGD, Hn, HNTC, ICC, LN, Lns, SSA, WBC; all versions except NJB, TNT], not explicit [NJB, TNT].
  c. aorist mid. (deponent = active) subj. of γίνομαι (LN 15.1): 'to come' [BAGD, LN]. The phrase ἐκ μέσου γένηται 'out from the midst it comes' is translated 'to be taken out of the way' [Hn; KJV, NASB, NIV, TEV], 'to be put out of the way' [ICC], 'to be out of the way' [HNTC; RSV], 'to get out of the way' [Lns], 'to be taken from the scene' [NAB], 'to disappear from the scene' [NEB], 'to no longer be there' [TNT], 'to be removed' [WBC; NJB], 'to be removed by God' [SSA].
QUESTION—What relationship is indicated by μόνον 'only' and what verb is implied in the clause?
  1. This indicates a contrast [Fn, HNTC, ICC, Lns, WBC; all versions except NEB]: the mystery of lawlessness is already at work, but *the apostasy will*

not come and the lawless one will not be revealed until the one who restrains it is removed [ICC], or the mystery of lawlessness is already at work, but *there is* one who restrains it until he is removed [Fn, HNTC, WBC].
2. This indicates a contraexpectation to the first part of the verse [My, NIC, SSA]: although the mystery of lawlessness is already at work, nevertheless the one who now is restraining *will continue to restrain* until that one is removed.
3. This indicates a temporal limitation [Ea, EBC, El, Hb, Hn, Mn, NCBC, Wd; NEB]: the mystery of lawlessness is already at work, *but it is a mystery* only until he who now restrains him is removed [Hn], or it is only at work until he who now restrains is removed [NCBC].

QUESTION—What is the significance of the change from neuter gender to masculine in the phrases τὸ κατέχον 'the (thing) restraining' (2:6) and ὁ κατέχων 'the (one) restraining' (here)?

There is not merely an impersonal force restraining the man of lawlessness, but there is a person behind that force [Fn, Hb, Hn, HNTC, Lns, Mn, My, NCBC, SSA].
1. The force of the Roman Empire which restrains the lawless one is concentrated in the Emperor [Fn, Hn, Mn].
2. The principle of law and order which restrains the lawless one is personified in the second mention of it [El].
3. The Holy Spirit is restraining the lawless one [Hb]. πνεῦμα 'Spirit' is a neuter noun, but the Spirit is a person who is also referred to by pronouns in the masculine gender.
4. The proclamation of the Gospel, a neuter concept, restrains the lawless one now and this is in charge of God's angel (masculine), who will be withdrawn [NCBC].

QUESTION—What is meant by the last phrase ἐκ μέσου γένηται 'it comes out of the midst'?
1. The passive sense is intended [Alf, Ea, Fn, Hn, ICC, Mn, My, NCBC, NIC, Rb, SSA, TH, WBC]: until he is removed. It is implied that God will remove him [SSA, TH].
2. The active sense is intended [Hb, HNTC, Lns]: until he comes out of the state of restraining, that is, until he ceases to restrain.

2:8 And then[a] the lawless[b] (one) will-be-revealed,[c]

LEXICON—a. τότε (LN 67.47): 'then' [BAGD, Hn, HNTC, ICC, LN, Lns, SSA, WBC; KJV, NASB, NEB, NIV, RSV, TEV], 'thereupon' [BAGD; NAB], 'at once' [TNT], not explicit [NJB].
b. ἄνομος (LN 88.140): 'lawless' [LN]. The substantive is translated 'lawless one' [BAGD, Hn, Lns, WBC; NAB, NASB, NIV, RSV, TNT], 'Wicked One' [NJB, TEV], 'that Wicked [KJV], 'wicked man' [NEB], 'Rebel' [HNTC], 'the Anomos' [ICC], 'man who rejects God's law' [SSA].

c. fut. pass. indic. of ἀποκαλύπτω (LN **28.38**): 'to be revealed' [Hn, HNTC, ICC, LN, Lns, SSA, WBC; all versions except NJB]. The passive voice is also translated actively: 'to appear openly' [NJB].

QUESTION—What time is referred to by τότε 'then'?

This refers to the time when the restrainer is removed (2:7) [Alf, Ea, El, Er, Hb, HNTC, Mn, My, NCBC, NIC, Rb, SSA, TH, WBC, Wd]: and then the time comes for him to be revealed. This word is emphatic [Alf, Ea, El, Hb, My, Rb, SSA]: at that very time the restrainer is removed. It contrasts with the words καὶ νῦν 'and now' in 2:6 [Hn, ICC]: now the lawless one is being restrained, then he will be revealed. Or it contrasts with ἄρτι 'now' in 2:7 [NCBC]: there is one who now restrains until he will be out of the way, then the lawless one will be revealed.

QUESTION—Who is the agent of the revealing?
1. God is the agent [SSA]: then the man of lawlessness will be revealed by God.
2. The Lord Jesus is the agent [Lns]: then the man of lawlessness will be revealed by the Lord. The Lord will reveal him by removing the restraining power so that he will have free course to show himself.
3. Satan is the agent [Hb]: then the man of lawlessness will be revealed by Satan.
4. He will reveal himself [Hn]: then the man of lawlessness will be revealed by his words and deeds.

whom the Lord Jesus will-destroy[a] by-the breath[b] of-his mouth

TEXT—Some manuscripts do not have the word Ἰησοῦς 'Jesus'. GNT includes it in brackets with a C rating, indicating more than a considerable degree of doubt about retaining it. It is omitted by KJV, NASB, NJB.

TEXT—Instead of ἀνελεῖ 'he will destroy', some manuscripts have ἀναλώσει 'he will consume'. GNT selects 'he will destroy' with a C rating, indicating a considerable degree of doubt. Only KJV selects 'he will consume'.

LEXICON—a. fut. act. indic. of ἀναιρέω (LN 20.71): 'to destroy' [BAGD, SSA, WBC; NAB, NEB, NJB, TNT], 'to slay' [BAGD, Hn, HNTC, ICC; NASB, RSV], 'to kill' [LN; TEV], 'to overthrow' [NIV], 'to make away with' [Lns].

b. πνεῦμα (LN **23.186**): 'breath' [BAGD, Hn, HNTC, ICC, LN, Lns, WBC; all versions except KJV, TNT], 'spirit' [KJV]. This noun phrase is also translated as a verbal phrase: 'to breathe upon' [TNT], 'what he will command' [SSA].

QUESTION—How will the Lord destroy him by means of τῷ πνεύματι τοῦ στόματος 'the breath of his mouth'?
1. This is to be taken figuratively.
   1.1 This refers to the words issuing from his mouth [Fn, Lns, SSA, Wd]: he will destroy him by a command that he be destroyed.

1.2 This expresses the ease with which the Lord will destroy him [Ea, Hn, Mn, My, NIC, Rb]: he will destroy him with just a mere puff. It emphasizes the Lord's power [El, Mn, My, TH].
2. This means that Jesus' breath will actually destroy him [EBC, Er, Hb, ICC]: he will destroy him by blowing on him. His breath will destroy like a blast of fire [Hb].

and will-bring-to-an-end^a by-the appearance/radiance^b of-his coming,^c

LEXICON—a. fut. act. indic. of καταργέω (LN 13.100): 'to bring to an end' [WBC; NASB], 'to cause to come to an end' [LN], 'to destroy' [HNTC, ICC; KJV, NIV, RSV, TEV], 'to annihilate' [NAB, NEB, NJB], 'to abolish' [BAGD, Lns], 'to take away all one's power' [TNT], 'to cause to become utterly powerless' [SSA], 'to utterly defeat' [Hn].

b. ἐπιφάνεια (LN 24.21): 'appearance' [BAGD, LN; NASB], 'appearing' [BAGD; RSV], 'manifestation' [Hn, HNTC, ICC], 'epiphany' [Lns], 'the dawning' [WBC]; or 'brightness' [KJV], 'radiance' [NEB], 'splendor' [NIV, TNT]; or 'glorious appearance' [NJB], 'dazzling presence' [TEV]. This noun is also translated as a verb: 'to manifest' [NAB]. The expression 'the appearance of his coming' is translated 'to be present' [SSA].

c. παρουσία (LN 15.86; 85.25): 'coming' [BAGD, Hn, ICC, LN; KJV, NASB, NEB, NIV, NJB, RSV], 'presence' [LN; NAB], 'parousia' [HNTC, Lns], 'advent' [BAGD, WBC]. This noun is also translated as a verb: 'to come' [TEV, TNT]. See this word at 2:1.

QUESTION—What is meant by ἐπιφάνεια 'appearance/radiance'?
1. This means 'appearance' [Alf, Ea, EBC, EGT, El, Fn, Hn, HNTC, ICC, Lns, Mn, My, NCBC, NIC, Rb, SSA, Wd; NAB, NASB, NJB, RSV]: the appearing of his coming. 'Appearance' may be considered a synonym for 'coming' [HNTC, ICC, NCBC]. Or a distinction may be made so that 'appearance' focuses on his presence and 'coming' on his arrival [ICC]. The appearance of his coming may occur just before he actually arrives [ICC], the first sign of his coming will be sufficient [Ea, Hn]. Some commentators take it to mean no more than his coming will be visible [EBC, El].
2. This means 'radiance' [Hb; KJV, NEB, NIV, TNT]. This shining refers to the visible presence of the Lord [Hb].

2:9 of-whom the coming^a is according-to/because-of^b (the) activity^c of-Satan

LEXICON—a. παρουσία (LN 15.86; 85.25): 'coming' [BAGD, Hn, ICC, LN; KJV, NASB, NEB, NIV, NJB, RSV, TNT], 'advent' [BAGD, WBC], 'parousia' [HNTC, Lns], 'presence' [Lns]. This noun is also translated as a verb: 'to appear' [NAB], 'to come' [TEV], 'to be present' [SSA]. See this word at 2:8.

b. κατά (LN 89.8): 'according to' [Hn, ICC, Lns, WBC], 'in accord/accordance with' [NASB, NIV], 'with' [TEV], 'as part of' [NAB], 'marked by'

[NJB], 'by' [RSV], 'after' [KJV], 'through' [HNTC; TNT], not explicit [NEB].
   c. ἐνέργεια (LN 42.3): 'activity' [BAGD, HNTC, WBC; NASB, RSV], 'working' [BAGD, LN, Lns; KJV, NAB], 'work' [NEB, NIV, NJB], 'energy' [Hn, ICC], 'power' [TEV, TNT].

QUESTION—To whom does οὗ 'of whom' refer?

Although the nearest antecedent is 'the Lord Jesus' (2:8b), this pronoun refers to the 'lawless one' (2:8a) [Alf, Ea, Er, Hb, Hn, HNTC, ICC, Lns, Mn, My, NCBC, NIC, Rb, TH, WBC, Wd; NAB, NEB, NIV, NJB, RSV, TEV, TNT].

QUESTION—Why is ἐστιν 'is' in the present tense?

The present tense is prophetic [Hn, ICC, Wd] and indicates the certainty of it being accomplished [Ea, El, Hb, Hn, My, NIC]: it will certainly be. Some translate it with the future tense form [NCBC; NAB, NEB, NIV, NJB, RSV, TEV, TNT]: it will be. Or, it indicates that at the future time of the coming of the man of lawlessness, Satan's work will be a present activity [HNTC]. Or, it is not concerned with the time when this will take place but only with the facts about it [Alf, Lns].

QUESTION—What is the verb ἐστιν 'is' connected with?

1. It is connected with the immediately following κατά 'according to' clause [Er, Hb, Hn, HNTC, Lns, NCBC, TH, Wd]: whose coming is according to Satan's activity.
2. It is connected with the following ἐν 'with' clause [Ea, Fn, My, WBC]: whose coming, according to Satan's activity, is with full power, etc. Then the κατά clause is parenthetical and especially modifies the following clause [Ea].
3. It is connected with the dative τοῖς ἀπολλυμένοις 'the ones perishing' (2:10) [ICC]: whose coming, which is according to Satan's activity, with all power...and with all deceit..., is for the disadvantage of those who will perish.

QUESTION—What relationship is indicated by κατά 'according to'?

Most commentators say that it indicates that the coming with power is in harmony with the way Satan works [Alf, Ea, El, Fn, Hb, Hn, ICC, Lns, My, Wd]: his coming will occur in the way Satan works. It indicates a standard of comparison [Hn, Lns, Wd]. The norm of Satan's work is lying, deception, and error [Lns]. Some take this to imply that the coming with power is the result of Satan's activity [Alf, BAGD, Ea, Hb, Hn, HNTC, ICC, My, NCBC, TH, Wd]: his coming with power will be caused by Satan's activity.

with[a] all power[b] and signs[c] and wonders[d] of-a-lie[e]

LEXICON—a. ἐν (LN 89.23; 89.48; 89.80; 89.84): 'with' [KJV, NASB, RSV, TEV], 'accompanied by' [NAB], 'attended by' [Hn, ICC, WBC; NEB, TNT], 'displayed in' [NIV], 'in' [HNTC; NJB], 'in connection with' [Lns].

b. δύναμις (LN 76.1; 76.7): 'power' [Hn, HNTC, ICC, LN, Lns, SSA, WBC; KJV, NAB, NASB, RSV], 'miracles' [BAGD, LN; NIV, NJB], 'mighty deed' [LN], 'mighty work' [TNT]. This noun is also translated as an adjective modifying the following two nouns: 'powerful' [NEB]; and as a verb: 'to perform' [TEV].

c. σημεῖον (LN 33.477): 'signs' [BAGD, Hn, HNTC, ICC, LN, Lns, WBC; all versions except TEV], 'supernatural signs' [SSA], 'miracles' [BAGD; TEV].

d. τέρας (LN 33.480): 'wonders' [BAGD, Hn, HNTC, ICC, Lns, WBC; KJV, NAB, NASB, NIV, NJB, RSV, TEV, TNT], 'signs' [LN], 'miracles' [NEB], 'amazing deeds' [SSA].

e. ψεῦδος (LN 33.254): 'falsehood' [BAGD, Hn, ICC, LN; NAB], 'lie' [BAGD, LN, Lns; NEB]. This noun is also translated as an adjective: 'false' [NASB, TEV, TNT], 'deceptive' [BAGD], 'lying' [KJV], 'counterfeit' [NIV, NJB], 'fraudulent' [WBC], 'pretended' [RSV]; and as a verbal phrase: 'intended to deceive' [HNTC].

QUESTION—What relationship is indicated by ἐν 'with'?

This indicates what accompanies the coming of the man of lawlessness [Er, Fn, Hn, HNTC, ICC, SSA; NAB, NEB, TNT]: he will come, accompanied by power, signs and wonders. It makes his coming known [Alf, Er, HNTC, Mn, My; NIV]. It tells in what sphere he will work [Ea, El, Hb, Mn]. It implies that he will perform these miracles himself [SSA].

QUESTION—What is meant by δυνάμει 'power' and what meaning of πάσῃ 'all' is involved?

1. This refers to the attribute 'power' [Fn, Hb, HNTC, ICC, Lns, NCBC, NIC, TH; KJV, NAB, NASB, RSV]: with all power. Some restrict 'all' to this word [TH], others take 'all' to modify all three nouns [Hb, ICC; NAB, NASB]. Some keep the same meaning for 'all' [Hb]: with *all kinds of* power, of signs, and of wonders. Others take the meaning of 'all' to change [ICC]: with *full* power and *all kinds of* signs and wonders.

2. This is another term for miracle and 'all' goes with each of the three nouns [Alf, Ea, EBC, El, Fn, Hn, Mn, My; NIV, NJB]: with all kinds of powerful demonstrations, signs, and wonders.

QUESTION—How are the nouns δυνάμει 'power' (singular) and the two following plurals, σημείοις 'signs' and τέρασιν 'wonders', related and which of them are modified by the genitive ψεύδους 'of a lie'?

1. 'Of a lie' indicates the attribute of the preceding two plural nouns [Fn, HNTC, Lns, SSA, TH, WBC, Wd; RSV, TEV, TNT]: with all power and false signs and wonders. 'Power' produces and shows itself in the following two plural nouns [Fn, HNTC, SSA, TH]: with all power, specifically with lying signs and wonders. The phrase 'signs and wonders' is an idiom used for miracles [HNTC].

2. 'Of a lie' modifies all three of the nouns [Alf, Ea, El, Hb, Hn, ICC, Mn, My, NCBC, NIC; NAB, NEB, NIV, NJB]: with all power and signs and wonders, all of which are related to falsehood. All three terms refer to

miracles by describing the miracles from three aspects: 'power' indicates the cause of the miracles, 'signs' indicates the meaning of the miracles, and 'wonders' indicates the effect they have on those who see them [Ea, Hb, Hn, ICC, NIC]. 'Signs' point to the supernatural power of the one who performs the miracles [Hn, ICC].

3. 'Of a lie' is an attribute of the third noun [KJV, NASB]: with all power and signs and lying wonders.

QUESTION: In what sense are the miracles false?

Only a few commentators think that this simply means that the miracles are faked [Ea, Lns, Mn]. Most think that these are real miracles [EBC, Er, Hb, Hn, HNTC, NCBC, NIC, SSA, TH, Wd]. 'Falsehood' then means that the miracles come from a false source [Alf, Ea, Fn, Hb, Hn, Lns, My, NCBC, SSA], seemingly done by God's power [SSA], and that they are intended to deceive people [Alf, Ea, EBC, Er, Hn, HNTC, Lns, Mn, My, NCBC, NIC, TH].

2:10 and with[a] all[b] deceit[c] of-unrighteousness[d] for-the[e] (ones) perishing,[f]

LEXICON—a. ἐν (LN 89.80; 89.84): 'with' [BAGD; KJV, NASB, RSV], 'by' [Hn, ICC, WBC; NAB], 'in' [HNTC; NIV], 'in connection with' [Lns], not explicit [NEB, NJB, TEV, TNT]. See this word at 2:9.

b. πᾶς (LN 59.23; 58.28): 'all' [Hn, ICC, Lns, WBC; KJV, NASB, NEB, RSV], 'every' [HNTC; NAB, NJB], 'every sort/kind of' [NIV, TEV], not explicit [TNT]. This adjective is also translated as an adverb: 'completely (deceive)' [SSA].

c. ἀπάτη (LN 31.12): 'deceit' [Hn, HNTC, ICC, Lns, WBC; TEV], 'deception' [BAGD, LN; NASB, NEB, NJB, RSV], 'deceivableness' [KJV], 'seduction' [NAB]. This noun is also translated as a verb: 'to deceive' [SSA; NIV], 'to be deceived' [TNT].

d. ἀδικία (LN 88.21): 'unrighteousness' [BAGD, Hn, ICC, LN, Lns, WBC; KJV], 'wickedness' [BAGD, HNTC; NASB], 'sinfulness' [NEB], 'evil' [NIV], 'the wicked' [NAB], 'wicked deeds' [SSA]. This noun is also translated as an adjective: 'wicked' [NJB, RSV, TEV]; and as an adverb '(to be) wickedly (deceived)' [TNT].

e. τοῖς, the article in the dative case: 'for those' [Hn, ICC, Lns, WBC; NAB, NASB, RSV], 'in them' [KJV], '(use deceit) on those' [TEV], 'towards the (ones)' [HNTC], 'aimed at those' [NJB], 'impose on them' [NEB]. Some translate the noun 'deceive' as a verb and make this the direct object: '(to deceive) them' [SSA; NIV, TNT]. This is the dative of disadvantage [Alf, Ea, El, My, NCBC], or the dative of the persons concerned [Fn, Rb].

f. pres. pass. participle of ἀπόλλυμι (LN 20.31): 'to perish' [BAGD], 'to be destroyed, to be ruined' [LN]. The substantive is translated 'those who perish' [KJV, NASB], 'those who are perishing' [Hn, Lns; NIV], 'the perishing' [HNTC], 'those destined to ruin' [NAB], 'those doomed/destined to destruction' [ICC; NEB, TNT], 'those on the way to destruction' [NJB], 'those on the way to perdition' [WBC], 'those who are to perish' [RSV], 'those who will perish' [SSA; TEV], 'those who are lost' [BAGD]. The article with the present tense indicates a class of people [Hb, HNTC, ICC]: the perishing ones. It describes them according to the process going on at the time in view [Alf, Ea, El, Fn, Hb, HNTC, Lns, NCBC, TH, WBC]: they are in the process of perishing, they are on their way to destruction. The present tense indicates the certainty of the future event [My].

QUESTION—How are the event noun and the attribute noun related in the genitive construction ἀπάτη ἀδικίας 'deceit of unrighteousness'?

    1. This means deceit resulting from unrighteousness [EBC, Fn, Hb, Hn, HNTC, ICC, Lns, SSA; NAB, NEB, NIV]. This could mean that unrighteousness is the attribute of the man of lawlessness or of his acts or motives and the reason for the deceit, or unrighteousness is an attribute of his acts and the means by which the deceit is accomplished. Most do not clarify the specific cause of the result.

    1.1 Unrighteousness is the means by which the man of lawlessness deceives [Hb, SSA]: he will deceive them by means of his unrighteous actions [SSA], or by means of his unrighteous plans [Hb].

    1.2 Unrighteousness is the cause for deceiving people [Hb, Hn, ICC; NAB]: he will deceive them because he has unrighteous motives [Hb, ICC].

    2. Unrighteousness is an attribute of deceit [WBC; NJB, RSV, TEV, TNT]: he will unrighteously deceive them.

    3. This means both of the above, 'unrighteousness' referring to both the origin and the character of the deceit [NCBC]: he will unrighteously deceive them because of/by means of unrighteousness.

    4. This means unrighteousness resulting from deceit: [My]: he will deceive people so that they become unrighteous or act unrighteously. Two commentators seem to hold both this interpretation and interpretation 2 [Alf, Ea].

because[a] (they) did not receive[b] the love[c] of-the truth[d]

LEXICON—a. ἀνθ' ὧν: 'because' [Hn, HNTC, ICC, Lns, Mou (p. 71), SSA, WBC; all versions].

    b. aorist mid. (deponent = active) indic. of δέχομαι (LN 31.51): 'to receive' [HNTC, Lns; KJV, NASB], 'to receive readily' [LN], 'to welcome' [ICC; TEV], 'to accept' [BAGD, Hn, LN, WBC; NJB, TNT], 'to open (one's heart)' [NAB], 'to open one's mind' [NEB], 'to believe' [LN]. This is also translated with the negative included in the verb: 'to refuse' [SSA; NIV, RSV]. The aorist tense refers to what they did before the final judgment [Hn, HNTC, Lns].

    c. ἀγάπη (LN 25.43): 'love' [BAGD, Hn, HNTC, ICC, LN, Lns, WBC; KJV, NASB, NEB, NJB], 'heart' [NAB]. This noun is also translated as a verb: 'to love' [SSA; NIV, RSV, TEV]; and as an adverb: 'gladly (accept)' [TNT].

d. ἀλήθεια (LN 72.2): 'truth' [BAGD, Hn, HNTC, ICC, LN, Lns, WBC; all versions], 'true message' [SSA].

QUESTION—What relationship is indicated by ἀνθ' ὧν 'because'?

1. This refers to the preceding participial phrase 'the ones perishing' and indicates the reason why they will perish [Alf, Ea, El, Hb, Hn, HNTC, ICC, Lns, NIC, Wd; NEB, NIV, TEV]: they will perish *because* they did not receive the love of truth.
2. This indicates the reason for their being deceived [EBC, Er, SSA; TNT]: those who will perish are completely deceived *because* they did not receive the love of truth.

QUESTION—How are the two nouns related in the genitive construction τὴν ἀγάπην τῆς ἀληθείας 'the love of the truth'?

'Truth' is the object of 'love' [Ea, EBC, EGT, El, Fn, Hb, Hn, HNTC, ICC, Lns, Mn, My, NCBC, NIC, SSA, WBC, Wd; NIV, RSV, TEV]: they did not love the truth. Some commentators consider 'the truth' to refer specifically to 'the true message', that is, the gospel [EBC, EGT, Fn, Hb, Hn, ICC, Lns, Mn, NCBC, NIC, SSA], or to any form of moral and religious truth [My]. 'Love' is included here because it is possible to receive the truth without loving the truth [Ea, EBC]. To fail to receive the 'love' of truth means to fail to want the truth and to be indifferent to its claims [Ea, El, Mn].

so-that[a] they be-saved.[b]

LEXICON—a. εἰς (LN 89.48; 89.57): 'so that' [BAGD], 'that' [Hn, Lns; KJV, TNT], 'in order to' [NAB], 'so as to' [HNTC, WBC; NASB, NEB, TEV], 'and so' [NIV, NJB, RSV], 'as a result' [SSA], 'unto' [ICC].

b. aorist pass. infin. of σῴζω (LN 21.27): 'to be saved' [BAGD, Hn, HNTC, LN, Lns, SSA; KJV, NAB, NASB, NIV, NJB, RSV, TEV], 'to find salvation' [WBC; NEB]. The passive form is also translated actively: 'to save' [TNT]. This verb is also translated as a noun: 'salvation' [ICC].

QUESTION—What relationship is indicated by εἰς 'so that'?

1. This indicates the result of receiving the love of the truth [BAGD, Fn, HNTC, Lns, NCBC, SSA, TH; NIV, NJB, RSV]: they did not love the truth, (and loving the truth) results in being saved. Since there is a negative in the first clause, the result did not happen [SSA]: they did not love the truth and as a result they were not saved.
2. This indicates the purpose of the love of the truth [Alf, Ea, El, Hb, Hn, ICC, My, NIC, Rb; NAB]: they did not love the truth, that truth that was intended to save them. This is God's purpose for giving them the truth [Hb]. Or, this would be their purpose in accepting the truth [El, Hn, NIC].

2:11 **And because[a] of-this God sends[b] to-them a-working[c] of-delusion[d]**

LEXICON—a. διά (LN 89.26): 'because'. The phrase διὰ τοῦτο is translated 'because of this' [Lns], 'because (they did) this' [SSA], 'for this cause' [KJV], 'for this reason' [Hn, HNTC, ICC; NASB, NIV], 'that is why' [TNT], 'therefore' [WBC; NAB, NEB, NJB, RSV], 'so' [TEV].

b. pres. act. indic. of πέμπω (LN **90.88**): 'to send' [BAGD, Hn, HNTC, ICC, LN, Lns, WBC; all versions except NEB, TNT], 'to put one under' [NEB], 'to cause' [SSA; TNT], 'to cause to experience' [LN].

c. ἐνέργεια (LN 42.3): 'a working' [BAGD, LN, Lns, WBC], 'influence' [BAGD; NASB], 'spirit' [NAB], 'energy' [Hn, ICC], 'power' [HNTC, SSA; NJB], 'power to work' [TEV]. This noun is also translated as an adjective: 'strong' [KJV, RSV], 'powerful' [NIV]; or as a verb: 'to work upon' [NEB], 'to suffer (delusion)' [TNT]. See this word at 2:9.

d. πλάνη (LN 31.8): 'delusion' [BAGD, HNTC, ICC, WBC; KJV, NEB, NIV, RSV, TNT], 'deception' [LN], 'error' [BAGD, Lns; TEV]. This noun is also translated as an adjective which modifies the preceding word: 'deluding' [Hn; NASB], 'perverse' [NAB]; or as a verb: 'to delude' [NJB], 'to be gullible' [SSA]. See this word at 1 Th. 2:3.

QUESTION—What relationship is indicated by διὰ τοῦτο 'because of this'?

This indicates the reason that God sends a working of delusion (2:11) [Alf, Ea, EBC, Hb, Hn, HNTC, ICC, Lns, My, NCBC, NIC, SSA]: because they did not receive the love of the truth, therefore God sends the following.

QUESTION—How are the two nouns related in the genitive construction ἐνέργειαν πλάνης 'a working of delusion'?

1. This means a working that results in delusion [EBC, El, Hn, ICC, NIC, SSA, TH, WBC, Wd; NJB]: God will cause that a power will work in them that causes them to be deluded. Some commentators explain that this is God's power [EBC, SSA]: God, working through his power, will cause them to be deluded. Since they were not willing to receive the truth, God judicially hardens them so that they will believe the falsehood [Hn]. Others explain the power to be more like a moral principle that God has established [Ea, Hb, ICC, NCBC, NIC, WBC, Wd]: they did not love the truth and, as an inevitable judgment, a power operates in them that causes them to be deceived. In this last case, Satan is the author of this deception [WBC].

2. The phrase means a strong delusion [NCBC; KJV, NIV, RSV]: God will send a strong delusion.

3. This means that error works in those people [Alf, Fn, Hb, Lns; NEB]: God will cause that error will work in them so that they will believe the lie.

so-that[a] they believe[b] the falsehood,[c]

LEXICON—a. εἰς (LN 89.57; 89.48): 'so that' [Lns, SSA, WBC; NASB, NIV, NJB, TEV], 'that' [Hn, ICC; KJV], 'to make (them believe)' [HNTC], not explicit [NEB, TNT]. This preposition is also translated as a phrase: 'which leads them to' [NAB], 'to make them' [RSV].

b. aorist act. infin. of πιστεύω (LN 31.35): 'to believe' [BAGD, HNTC, ICC, LN, Lns, SSA, WBC; all versions except NAB, TNT], 'to believe in' [BAGD, Hn], 'to believe to be true' [TNT], 'to give credence to' [BAGD; NAB].

c. ψεῦδος (LN 33.254): 'falsehood' [BAGD, Hn, ICC, LN; NAB], 'lie' [BAGD, LN, Lns, WBC; KJV, NEB, NIV], 'what is false' [HNTC; NASB, NJB, RSV, TEV, TNT], 'what he falsely claims' [SSA]. See this word at 2:9.

QUESTION—What relationship is indicated by εἰς 'so that'?
1. This indicates the purpose of the preceding clause [Alf, Ea, EBC, El, Fn, Hb, Hn, HNTC, ICC, Mn, My, NCBB, TH]: God sends them the working of delusion *in order that* they believe the falsehood. This is called the primary purpose in light of the following verse with its ἵνα purpose clause [Hb, ICC]. It also indicates the contemplated result [Fn, Rb], and the actual result [Hb].
2. This indicates the result of the preceding clause [Lns, SSA, Wd; NAB]: God will send a working of delusion and, *as a result*, they will believe the falsehood. It is to be noted that the man of lawlessness is the one who actually deceives them (2:9–10) [SSA].
3. This explains in what way they will be deceived [NIC]: they will be deluded, *that is*, they will believe the falsehood.

QUESTION—What is the significance of the article in τῷ ψεύδει 'the falsehood'?

This refers to the previous reference to this word in 2:9 [Ea, Rb, SSA, TH]. It refers to the false signs and wonders [Ea, SSA]. It especially refers to the ultimate false claim in 2:4, that he is god [Fn, Hb, SSA], or it refers to the ultimate falsehood that God is not God [WBC]. It contrasts with 'the truth' (2:10) [Ea, Fn, HNTC, ICC, Lns, Mn]. However, some translate without any reference to the article: 'a lie' [KJV], 'a falsehood' [NAB], 'what is false' [HNTC; NASB, NJB, RSV, TEV, TNT].

2:12 **in-order-that[a] may-be-judged[b] all the (ones) not having-believed the truth[c]**

LEXICON—a. ἵνα (LN 89.59; 89.49): 'in order that' [Hn, HNTC, Lns, SSA; NASB], 'that' [WBC; KJV], 'that (finally)' [ICC], 'so that' [NAB, NEB, NIV, NJB, RSV], 'the result is that' [TEV], 'and so' [TNT].
b. aorist pass. subj. of κρίνω (LN 56.20, 56.30): 'to be judged' [BAGD, ICC, Lns, WBC; NASB], 'to stand trial' [LN], 'to be brought to judgment' [NEB], 'to come under judgment' [TNT], 'to be condemned' [BAGD, Hn, HNTC, LN, SSA; NAB, NIV, NJB, RSV, TEV], 'to be damned' [KJV]. In this context, it is implied that the judgment is an adverse one [Alf, El, Fn, Hb, Hn, HNTC, ICC, Lns, Mn, My, NIC, SSA, TH].
c. ἀλήθεια (LN 72.2): 'truth'. See this word at 2:10.

QUESTION—What relationship is indicated by ἵνα 'in order that'?
1. This indicates God's purpose for the preceding verse [Alf, Ea, El, Er, Fn, Hb, Hn, HNTC, ICC, Lns, Mn, My, NCBB, NIC, Rb, SSA, TH, Wd; NASB]: God causes them to believe the falsehood *in order that* they be judged. This is called the ultimate purpose when the preceding clause is

also taken to be a purpose [Alf, Ea, El, Hb, HNTC, ICC, My, NCBC, Rb] and it is contingent on the fulfillment of that purpose [Ea, ICC]: God causes them to be deluded, in order that they might believe the lie, and then be judged.
2. This indicates the result of the preceding verse [EBC, Er; TEV, TNT]: God causes them to believe the falsehood and, *as a result,* they will be judged.

but[a] having-had-pleasure[b] in-unrighteousness.[c]
LEXICON—a. ἀλλά (LN 89.125): 'but' [Hn, HNTC, ICC, Lns, SSA, WBC; all versions except NJB], 'and' [NJB].
  b. aorist act. participle of εὐδοκέω (LN **25.113**; 25.88; 30.97): 'to have pleasure' [KJV, RSV], 'to take pleasure' [BAGD, WBC; NASB, NJB, TEV, TNT], 'to have good pleasure' [Lns], 'to delight' [BAGD, Hn, HNTC; NAB, NIV], 'to gladly choose' [SSA], 'to make a deliberate choice' [NEB], 'to consent' [ICC], 'to enjoy' [LN].
  c. ἀδικία (LN 88.21): 'unrighteousness' [BAGD, Hn, ICC, LN, Lns, WBC; KJV, RSV], 'wickedness' [BAGD, HNTC; NASB, NIV, NJB, TNT], 'what is wicked' [SSA], 'evil doing' [NAB], 'sinfulness' [NEB], 'sin' [TEV]. See this word at 2:10.
QUESTION—What relationship is indicated by ἀλλά 'but'?
This indicates the positive contrast of the preceding negative clause [Hb, HNTC, Lns, NCBC, SSA]: they did not believe the truth, *but* they delighted in unrighteousness. The single article with the two participles indicates that just one class of people is referred to [Hb].

DISCOURSE UNIT: 2:13–3:5 [EGT, Fn; NJB]. The topic is thanksgiving, prayer, and counsel [EGT], encouragement and prayer [Fn], encouragement to stand firm [NJB].

DISCOURSE UNIT: 2:13–17 [Alf, EBC, Er, GNT, Hb, Hn, HNTC, ICC, Lns, My, NCBC, NIC, TH, WBC; NAB, NIV, TEV]. The topic is encouragement [NAB], exhortation to stand firm [My; NIV], assurance of salvation [GNT, HNTC; TEV], the destiny of the Thessalonians [Lns], God's plan for Christians [TH], the contrast of destinies [Hn], thanksgiving and prayer [Hb], thanksgiving and encouragement [NCBC, NIC], thanksgiving, exhortation, and prayer [Alf, Er, ICC, WBC].

DISCOURSE UNIT: 2:13–15 [Mn, NIC, TH]. The topic is thanksgiving [NIC], thanksgiving and exhortation [Mn].

DISCOURSE UNIT: 2:13–14 [EBC, Hb, SSA, WBC, Wd]. The topic is thanksgiving to God for choosing them for salvation.

2:13 Now/But[a] we
LEXICON—a. δέ (LN 89.94; 89.124): 'now' [HNTC, ICC, Lns]; or 'but' [Hn, WBC; KJV, NASB, NEB, NIV, NJB, RSV]; not explicit [SSA; NAB, TEV, TNT].

QUESTION—What relationship is indicated by δέ 'now/but'?
1. This is a particle of transition which indicates the introduction of a new topic with no contrast intended [Hb, HNTC, ICC, Lns, SSA, TH; probably NAB, TEV, TNT]: now we thank God for you. The forefronted 'we' does not contrast Paul and his companions with someone else [HNTC]. 'We' resumes the 'we–you' framework of the letter [SSA], or it emphasizes the strong obligation felt by Paul and his coworkers [Hb, ICC]. One commentator thinks that there is no special emphasis of 'we' since Paul often inserts a personal pronoun when beginning a new section [NCBC].
2. This indicates contrast [Alf, Ea, El, Fn, Hn, My, NCBC, WBC; KJV, NASB, NEB, NIV, NJB, RSV]: but. The contrast is between 'we', Paul and his companions, and 'those who are perishing' (2:10–12) [Alf, El, Fn, My]: but, as for us, we thank God for you. Or, the contrast is between the Thessalonians and those who are perishing [Ea]. Or, the contrast is between the previous topic of the condemnation of the perishing with the new topic of the salvation of God's people [Hn].

we-ought to-thank God always concerning you, brothers
LEXICON—This phrase is the same as the one in 1:3 except that the positions of the verbs are reversed.

having-been-loved[a] by (the) Lord,
LEXICON—a. perf. pass. participle of ἀγαπάω (LN 25.43): 'to be loved' [BAGD, HNTC, LN, SSA; NIV], 'beloved' [Hn, ICC, Lns; KJV, NAB, NASB, NEB, RSV], 'to be dear to' [WBC]. The passive form is also translated actively: '(whom the Lord) loves' [NJB, TEV, TNT]. See this word at 1 Thess. 1:4.
QUESTION—What relationship is indicated by the participial form ἠγαπημένοι 'having been loved'?
This is a description of the Thessalonians [Ea, EBC, El, Fn, Hb, Hn, HNTC, ICC, Lns, NCBC, NIC, SSA, WBC]: brothers who are loved by God. It is appropriate here since it is because God and Christ love people that God chooses them to be saved [EBC, HNTC] and the Lord Jesus is pictured in the preceding context as the judge of evil men [Hb, HNTC].
QUESTION—To whom does 'Lord' refer?
1. It refers to Jesus Christ [Alf, Ea, El, Er, Fn, Hb, HNTC, ICC, Lns, My, NCBC, NIC, Rb, SSA, WBC, Wd].
2. It refers to God [Hn, TH].

because/that[a] God chose[b] you a-firstfruit[c] for[d] salvation[e]
TEXT—Instead of ἀπαρχήν 'a firstfruit', some manuscripts have ἀπ' ἀρχῆς 'from the beginning'. GNT chooses 'a firstfruit' with a C rating, indicating a considerable degree of doubt. 'From the beginning' is chosen by most [Alf, Ea, EBC, El, Er, Fn, Hb, Hn, HNTC, ICC, Lns, My, NCBC, NIC, Rb, SSA, Wd; KJV, NASB, NEB, NIV, NJB, RSV].

LEXICON—a. ὅτι (LN 89.33; 90.21): 'because' [Hn, HNTC, ICC, SSA, WBC; all versions except TEV, TNT], 'for' [TEV, TNT]; or 'that' [Lns].
b. aorist mid. indic. of αἱρέομαι (LN 30.91): 'to choose' [BAGD, Hn, HNTC, ICC, LN, Lns, SSA, WBC; all versions]. The middle voice means that God chose them for himself [Hb, TH].
c. ἀπαρχή (LN 53.23; 61.8): 'firstfruit' [BAGD, WBC; NAB], 'first portion' [LN], 'the first' [LN], 'the first (to be saved)' [TEV], 'the very first' [TNT].
d. εἰς (LN 89.57): 'for' [BAGD, HNTC, WBC; NAB, NASB], 'to' [Hn, ICC; KJV, NIV, NJB, RSV, TEV, TNT], 'unto' [Lns], 'in order that' [SSA], 'to find' [NEB]. See this word at 1 Thess. 5:9.
e. σωτηρία (LN 21.25; 21.26): 'salvation' [BAGD, Hn, HNTC, LN, Lns, WBC; KJV, NAB, NASB, NEB]. This noun is also translated as a verb: 'to be saved' [ICC, SSA; NIV, NJB, RSV, TEV, TNT].

QUESTION—What relationship is indicated by ὅτι 'because/that'?

After the verb 'to thank', the content and the reason are usually the same [SSA] and the one implies the other [Hb]. Some commentators emphasize the reason for thanksgiving [Hb, Hn, HNTC, ICC, NIC, Rb, SSA, WBC, Wd; all versions]: we thank God because he chose you to be saved. Others emphasize the contents of the thanksgiving [Ea, EBC, El, Er, Fn, Lns, My]: we thank God that he chose you to be saved.

QUESTION—What differences do the textual variants make in the structure of the sentence?

1. The choice of the reading ἀπαρχήν 'firstfruit' takes this word as being in apposition to, or as the complement of, ὑμᾶς 'you' [GNT, WBC; NAB, TEV, TNT]: he chose you as/to be firstfruits for salvation. The difficulty of determining in what sense the whole church at Thessalonica can be a firstfruits has been a major reason for many not accepting this reading. Explanations given by those who accept the possibility of the reading 'firstfruits' are the following: the universal church is a firstfruit in the sense that they are the part of that portion of mankind dedicated to God [WBC] or, they were the first to be saved [TH; TEV, TNT], or they were the among the first to be saved in Macedonia, the first believers among them being converted only a few weeks after the time people first believed in Philippi [Mn].

2. The choice of the reading ἀπ' ἀρχῆς 'from the beginning' makes this phrase a temporal circumstance of the verb [Alf, Ea, EBC, El, Er, Fn, Hb, Hn, HNTC, ICC, Lns, My, NCBC, NIC, Rb, SSA, Wd; KJV, NASB, NEB, NIV, NJB, RSV]: he chose you from the beginning for salvation.

    2.1 'The beginning' refers to the beginning of time [HNTC, Lns, NIC, SSA; NEB], or the time of creation [Alf, El, Er, ICC, Lns, NCBC, NIC]. It means from eternity [Ea, EBC, El, Er, Hb, Hn, ICC, Lns, Mn, My, SSA, Wd].

    2.2 It means from the beginning of the preaching of the gospel in Thessalonica [Fn].

QUESTION—What relationship is indicated by εἰς 'for'?

Those who address the question take it to indicate the purpose for which God chose them [Ea, Fn, Hb, Mn, NIC, Rb, SSA]: God chose you *in order that* you be saved.

in[a] sanctification[b] of-Spirit/spirit[c] and faith[d] of-truth,[e]

LEXICON—a. ἐν (LN 89.76; 89.80): 'in' [NAB, NEB], 'through' [Hn, HNTC; KJV, NASB, NIV, RSV], 'by' [ICC, WBC; NJB, TEV, TNT], 'by means of' [SSA], 'in connection with' [Lns].

b. ἁγιασμός (LN 53.44): 'sanctification' [BAGD, Hn, HNTC, Lns, WBC; KJV, NASB, RSV], 'consecration' [BAGD, ICC, LN], 'dedication' [LN], 'holiness' [BAGD; NAB], 'the sanctifying work' [NIV]. This noun is also translated as a verb: 'to make holy' [NJB], 'to make you his holy people' [TEV], 'to consecrate' [NEB, TNT], 'to be set apart for God' [SSA].

c. πνεῦμα (LN 12.18; 30.6; 26.9): 'Spirit' [Hn, HNTC, ICC, LN, SSA, WBC; KJV, NASB, NEB, NIV, NJB, RSV, TEV, TNT]; or 'spirit' [LN, Lns; NAB].

d. πίστις (LN 31.85; 31.88): 'faith' [BAGD, HNTC, ICC, LN, Lns; NASB, NJB, TEV], 'belief' [Hn, WBC; KJV, NIV, RSV], 'fidelity' [NAB]. This noun is also translated as a verb: 'to believe' [SSA; NEB, TNT].

e. ἀλήθεια (LN 72.2): 'truth' [BAGD, Hn, HNTC, ICC, LN, Lns, WBC; all versions], 'the true message' [SSA]. See this word at 2:10 and 2:12.

QUESTION—What relationship is indicated by ἐν 'in'?

1. This indicates the means of salvation [Ea, Er, Hn, HNTC, ICC, My, NCBC, SSA, WBC; KJV, NASB, NIV, NJB, TEV]: to be saved *by means of* sanctification and faith.
2. It indicates the circumstances in which they were saved [Alf, EBC, El, Wd]: to be saved, being sanctified and having faith.
3. It indicates a less precise relationship 'in connection with' [EGT, Fn, Hb, Lns]: to be saved in connection with sanctification and faith.

QUESTION—To what does πνεῦμα 'spirit' refer and how are the event word and the personal word related in the genitive construction ἁγιασμῷ πνεύματος 'sanctification of Spirit/spirit'?

1. This refers to the Holy Spirit and means that sanctification is carried out by the Spirit [Alf, Ea, EBC, El, Er, Hb, Hn, HNTC, Mn, My, NCBC, NIC, Rb, SSA, TH, Wd; NASB, NEB, NIV, NJB, RSV, TEV]: the Spirit sanctifies you.
2. This refers to the individual's spirit and means that sanctification is applied to their spirits [EGT, Fn, Lns; NAB]: your spirits are sanctified.

QUESTION—What is meant by ἁγιασμῷ 'sanctification'?

1. This means the process of becoming holy in character [EGT, Fn, Hb, Hn, HNTC, My, WBC]: by means of the Spirit making you holy in character. It means to be increasingly conformed to Christ's character [Hb, Hn].
2. This means the initial act of being set apart for God [Lns, SSA, TH]: by means of the Spirit setting you apart for God.

3. This means the total consecration of the individual by an act of his will inspired by the Spirit [ICC]: by means of your consecrating yourselves to God under the influence of the Spirit.

QUESTION—How are the event word and attribute related in the genitive construction πίστει ἀληθείας 'faith of truth'?

This means that the truth is the object of their faith [Alf, Ea, EBC, EGT, El, Fn, Hb, HNTC, ICC, Lns, Mn, My, NCBC, NIC, Rb, SSA, WBC; NASB, NEB, NIV, NJB, RSV, TEV, TNT]: your faith in what is true. This refers to the true message in the gospel [HNTC, ICC, Lns, NCBC, NIC, WBC].

2:14 for[a] which also[b] he-called[c] you through[d] the gospel[e] of-us,

TEXT—Some manuscripts omit καί 'also'. GNT puts it in brackets to indicate that its inclusion is doubtful. It is omitted or not translated by most [HNTC, Lns, SSA, WBC; all versions].

LEXICON—a. εἰς (LN 89.57): 'for'. The phrase εἰς ὅ is translated 'for which' [Lns], 'to which' [Hn, HNTC], 'to this' [NIV, NJB, RSV, TEV, TNT], 'to this end' [ICC], 'it was for this' [WBC; NASB, NEB], 'in order that this might happen' [SSA], 'whereunto' [KJV], not explicit [NAB]. See this phrase at 1:11.
  b. καί (LN 89.92; 89.93): 'also' [Hn], 'and' [ICC; NASB], not explicit [HNTC, Lns, SSA, WBC; all versions except NASB].
  c. aorist act. indic. of καλέω (LN **33.312**; 33.307): 'to call' [BAGD, Hn, HNTC, ICC, LN, Lns, WBC; all versions], 'to summon' [BAGD, SSA]. See this word at 1 Thess. 2:12, 4:7, and 5:24.
  d. διά (LN 89.76): 'through' [Hn, WBC; all versions except KJV], 'by' [ICC; KJV], 'by means of' [HNTC, Lns, SSA].
  e. εὐαγγέλιον (LN 33.217): 'gospel' [BAGD, Hn, HNTC, ICC, LN, Lns, WBC; KJV, NASB, NEB, NIV, NJB, RSV], 'good news' [BAGD, LN, SSA; NAB, TEV, TNT]. See this word at 1:8.

QUESTION—What relationship is indicated by εἰς ὅ 'for which'?

This indicates that the preceding phrase 'salvation in sanctification of Spirit and faith of the truth' (2:13) is the purpose of the following verb [EBC, Fn, Hb, Hn, ICC, NCBC, NIC, Rb, SSA, TH, Wd]: in order that you be saved in sanctification and faith, he called you. Some commentators seem to take this to mean a more general relationship, *in reference to* [Alf, Er, HNTC]: God called you to salvation in sanctification and faith. This probably implies that it is the purpose for which he called them.

QUESTION—What relationship is indicated by διά 'through'?

This indicates the means God used to call them [Alf, Ea, EBC, El, Er, Fn, Hb, Hn, HNTC, ICC, Lns, My, NCBC, NIC, Rb, SSA, TH, WBC, Wd; all versions]: God called you *by means of* the gospel. The Gospel contained God's invitation [Ea, EBC, Fn, Hb, ICC] and God applied the gospel message to their hearts [Hn].

QUESTION—How are the noun and pronoun related in the genitive construction τοῦ εὐαγγελίου ἡμῶν 'the gospel of us'?
1. This implies the event of preaching [Alf, Ea, EBC, El, Er, Hn, HNTC, ICC, Lns, My, NCBC, Rb, SSA, WBC, Wd; NAB, TEV]: the gospel which we preach. Some use a more generic term [Fn; NEB, TNT]: the gospel which we brought to you.
2. This implies the event of appropriating [Hb, NIC]: the gospel which we have made our own.

to[a] obtainment[b] of-(the) glory[c] of-the Lord of-us Jesus Christ.
LEXICON—a. εἰς (LN 89.57): 'to' [HNTC, ICC; KJV], 'for' [Lns], 'so that' [NAB, NEB, NJB, RSV, TNT], 'in order that' [SSA], 'that' [WBC; NASB, NIV], 'with a view to' [Hn], not explicit [TEV].
b. περιποίησις (LN 90.74; 57.62): 'obtainment', 'the obtaining' [BAGD, ICC; KJV], 'experience' [LN], 'possession' [LN]. This noun is also translated as a verb: 'to obtain' [Hn, HNTC, Lns, WBC; RSV], 'to achieve' [NAB], 'to gain' [NASB], 'to possess for one's own' [NEB], 'to claim as one's own' [NJB], 'to share' [NIV, TNT], 'to possess one's share' [TEV].
c. δόξα (LN 79.18): 'glory' [BAGD, Hn, HNTC, ICC, LN, Lns, WBC; all versions except NEB], 'splendor' [BAGD, LN; NEB]. This noun is also translated as a verb: 'to be glorified' [SSA].

QUESTION—What relationship is indicated by εἰς 'for'?
This indicates the purpose of the preceding verb [Alf, EBC, Er, Fn, Hb, Hn, HNTC, ICC, Lns, NCBC, SSA, Wd]: he called you *in order that* you obtain glory. Some commentators mention that this is a restatement of the purpose clause preceding the verb: he called you in order that you be saved, that is, he called you in order that you obtain the glory of our Lord. This explains 'for salvation' as being 'for obtaining Christ's glory' [El, Fn, HNTC, ICC, My, Wd]. It is also called the ultimate purpose of the calling [NCBC, Wd], or the goal of salvation [Hb].

QUESTION—How are the event, attribute and person related in the double genitive construction περιποίησιν δόξης τοῦ κυρίου ἡμῶν 'obtainment of the glory of our Lord'?
The Thessalonian believers will do the obtaining, what they obtain is glory, and this glory is what our Lord already possesses [Alf, Ea, El, Hb, Hn, HNTC, ICC, Lns, My, NIC, SSA]: in order that you obtain/acquire the glory which is our Lord's glory. This has various explanations: they will be glorified like the Lord is glorified [SSA], they will share in the glory the Lord has [Alf, Ea, EBC, EGT, Hb, Hn, HNTC, ICC, NIC, TH, WBC; NIV, TEV, TNT]. The glory is the splendor and honor which belong to the Lord [Hb]. It will be fully obtained by believers at the Lord's coming [Hb, HNTC, WBC].

DISCOURSE UNIT: 2:15–17 [Wd]. The topic is an exhortation and prayer.

DISCOURSE UNIT: 2:15 [EBC, Hb, SSA]. The topic is an exhortation to continue believing [EBC, Hb, SSA].

2:15 So then,[a] brothers, stand-firm[b]

LEXICON—a. ἄρα οὖν: 'so then' [BAGD, Hn, HNTC, ICC, WBC; NASB, NIV, RSV, TEV], 'therefore' [SSA; KJV, NAB, TNT], 'then' [NEB, NJB], 'accordingly then' [Lns].

b. pres. act. impera. of στήκω (LN 13.30): 'to stand firm' [BAGD, Hn, HNTC, ICC; all versions except KJV], 'to stand fast' [Lns, WBC; KJV], 'to stand' [LN], 'to be firm' [SSA]. The present tense of this and the following imperative form indicates that these are to be continuing duties [Hb, Hn, HNTC, Lns, NIC, SSA, TH, Wd]. See this word at 1 Thess. 3:8.

QUESTION—In what respect were they to stand firm?

This is a metaphor in which the exact meaning depends upon whether the following command explains this one or is an additional duty. If the following command explains this one, it means that they should remain firm in their belief of the Christian teachings [NCBC, SSA, TH]. If it is different from, or includes more than, the following command, it means that they should stand firm in the Lord (1 Thess. 3:8) [WBC] and they should not be intimidated by opposition or false doctrine [Ea, Er]. It is the positive counterpart to the negative command not to be quickly shaken in 2:2 [Alf, Ea, El, Fn, Hb, HNTC, Lns, My, NIC, SSA, TH].

and/even[a] hold[b] the traditions[c] which you-were-taught[d]

LEXICON—a. καί (LN 89.92): 'and' [Hn, HNTC, ICC, Lns, WBC; KJV, NASB, NEB, NIV, NJB, RSV, TEV], 'that is' [SSA], not explicit [NAB, TNT].

b. pres. act. impera. of κρατέω (LN 13.34): 'to hold' [BAGD, LN, WBC; KJV], 'to hold to' [NASB, NIV, RSV], 'to hold on to' [TEV], 'to hold fast to' [BAGD, HNTC, ICC, Lns; NAB, NEB, TNT], 'to cling to' [Hn], 'to keep' [LN; NJB], 'to continue to believe' [SSA]. The present tense indicates continuing to keep hold [Wd].

c. παράδοσις (LN 33.239): 'traditions' [BAGD, Hn, HNTC, LN, Lns, WBC; KJV, NAB, NASB, NEB, NJB, RSV, TNT], 'teachings' [LN; NIV], 'instructions' [ICC], 'truths' [TEV], 'the body of true teaching' [SSA].

d. aorist pass. indic. of διδάσκω (LN 33.224): 'to be taught' [BAGD, Hn, HNTC, ICC, LN, Lns, WBC; KJV, NASB, RSV], 'to be committed to' [SSA]. The passive form is also translated actively: 'to learn' [NEB], 'to receive' [NAB], 'we passed on to you' [NIV], 'we taught you' [NJB, TEV, TNT].

QUESTION—What relationship is indicated by καί 'and/even'?

1. This indicates a coordinate statement [Ea, EBC, Fn, Hb, Hn, HNTC, ICC, Lns, My, NCBC, WBC; KJV, NASB, NEB, NIV, NJB, RSV, TEV]: stand firm, *and* hold fast to the traditions.

2. This explains the previous clause [HNTC, NCBC, SSA, TH, WBC]: stand firm, *that is*, hold fast to the traditions. It is the specific meaning of the generic statement [SSA], or it indicates one example of standing firm in the Lord [WBC]: stand firm, *for example*, hold fast to the traditions.

QUESTION—What is meant by τὰς παραδόσεις 'the traditions'?

'The traditions' are teachings passed on from teacher to pupil [Er, Fn, Hb, Hn, HNTC, Lns, NCBC, NIC, Rb, SSA, TH; NIV]. Specifically, they are the teachings which Jesus taught to his apostles [Fn, ICC, SSA, WBC], or they were authoritative doctrinal teachings of the apostles [Ea, EBC, Er, Hn, NCBC] which were passed on to others. To hold fast to them means to continue to believe them and to reject false teachings [SSA].

either[a] through[b] word[c] or[a] through[b] a-letter[d] of-us.

LEXICON—a. εἴτε... εἴτε (LN 89.69): 'either... or' [NAB, RSV, TNT], 'whether... or' [Hn, ICC, Lns, WBC; KJV, NASB, NIV, NJB], 'both...and' [HNTC; TEV], '...or' [NEB], '...and' [SSA].

b. διά (LN 89.76): 'through', 'by' [Hn, ICC, WBC; KJV, NAB, NASB, NEB, NIV, NJB, RSV, TNT], 'in' [HNTC; TEV], 'by means of' [Lns, SSA].

c. λόγος (LN 33.98; 33.99): 'word' [BAGD, LN; KJV, NAB, NEB, TNT], 'word of mouth' [WBC; NASB, NIV, NJB, RSV], 'preaching' [TEV], 'speaking' [BAGD, LN, SSA], 'discourse' [Lns], 'oral statements' [HNTC]. This noun is also translated as an adverb without the preposition: 'orally' [Hn, ICC].

d. ἐπιστολή (LN 33.48; 6.63): 'letter' [BAGD, Hn, HNTC, ICC, LN, Lns, SSA; all versions except KJV], 'epistle' [BAGD, WBC; KJV].

QUESTION—What relationship is indicated by διά 'through'?

This indicates the means by which the teachings were taught [Ea, Hb, Lns, SSA]: the teachings taught *by means of* spoken words or/and letters. 'Word' refers to what Paul and his companions taught while they were present in Thessalonica, 'letter' refers to the First Letter to the Thessalonians [Alf, Er, Hb, Hn, HNTC, ICC, Lns, My, NCBC, NIC, Wd].

QUESTION—To what is the genitive ἡμῶν 'of us' to be connected?

1. It is to be connected with both of the preceding nouns [Fn, Hb, HNTC, ICC, Lns, SSA; TEV, probably NAB, NEB, NIV, NJB, RSV, TNT]: you were taught by means of our spoken word or by means of our letter.
2. It is to be connected with the immediately preceding noun [Ea, El, NIC, Rb; KJV, NASB]: by means of speech or by means of our letter.

DISCOURSE UNIT: 2:16–17 [EBC, Hb, Mn, NIC, SSA, TH, WBC]. The topic is prayer for the Thessalonians.

2:16 Now/But[a] **our Lord Jesus Christ himself and God our Father,**

LEXICON—a. δέ (LN 89.94; 89.124): 'now' [Hn, HNTC, ICC, Lns, WBC; KJV, NASB, RSV], 'and' [NEB], not explicit [SSA; NAB, NIV, NJB, TEV, TNT].

QUESTION—What relationship is indicated by δέ 'now/but'?
1. This indicates transition to a new subject [Hb, Hn, HNTC, Lns, SSA, WBC; KJV, NASB, NEB, RSV]: now.
2. This indicates contrast [Ea, EBC, El, Fn, ICC, NIC, TH]: but. The contrast is between the preceding appeal to the Thessalonians and the prayer to God [Ea, EBC, El, ICC, NIC]: we command you to stand firm, but we pray to our Lord and God our Father, who alone can make this possible [ICC]. Or the contrast is between what the Thessalonians are to do and what the Lord Jesus and God are asked to do [TH].

the (one) having-loved[a] us
LEXICON—a. aorist act. participle of ἀγαπάω (LN 25.43; 25.44): 'to love' [BAGD, Hn, HNTC, ICC, Lns, SSA, WBC; KJV, NAB, NASB, NIV, RSV, TEV], 'to show love' [NEB, TNT], 'to give one's love' [NJB]. The aorist tense refers to a certain past event in which he showed his love to us [Alf, Ea, Hb, HNTC, Mn, My, NCBC, NIC, SSA, TH] or when he set his love on us [WBC], or it summarizes all that he has done in loving us [Lns].
QUESTION—To whom does ὁ 'the (one)' refer?
1. This refers to God our Father [Alf, Ea, El, Fn, Hb, Mn, My, NIC, Rb, TH; probably NAB, NJB, TNT]: God who loved us. This interpretation is taken rather hesitantly by some [Alf, Ea, Hb].
2. This refers to both the Lord Jesus Christ and God [EBC, Hn, HNTC, ICC, Lns, NCBC, WBC]: our Lord Jesus Christ and God our Father, who (both) loved us. This agrees with the interpretation in the next verse that the use of the singular verbs 'may he encourage and may he establish you' considers both the Lord Jesus and the Father to be a unity. Some hold that αὐτός 'himself' should be taken to refer to both the Lord Jesus and God the Father [EBC, Lns]: may he, our Lord Jesus Christ and God our Father, who loved us, encourage you.
3. This refers to the Lord Jesus Christ [SSA]: our Lord Jesus Christ (and also God our Father), who loved us. This interpretation is carried on in the next verse to refer the singular verbs to the Lord Jesus.

and having-given[a] eternal[b] encouragement[c] and a-good[d] hope[e] in[f] grace,[g]
LEXICON—a. aorist act. participle of δίδωμι (LN 90.90): 'to give' [BAGD, Hn, HNTC, ICC, Lns, WBC; all versions]. This verb and its object are also translated as a single verb: 'to encourage' [SSA]. The aorist tense refers to a certain past event in which he gave encouragement [TH].
b. αἰώνιος (LN 67.96): 'eternal' [BAGD, HNTC, ICC, LN, Lns, WBC; NAB, NASB, NIV, RSV], 'everlasting' [Hn; KJV], 'lasting' [TNT], 'unfailing' [NEB, TEV], 'ceaseless' [NJB], 'forever' [SSA], 'inexhaustible' [BAGD].
c. παράκλησις (LN 25.150): 'encouragement' [Hn, HNTC, ICC, LN, Lns, WBC; NEB, NIV, NJB, TNT], 'comfort' [BAGD; NASB, RSV], 'consolation' [BAGD; KJV, NAB], 'courage' [TEV].

d. ἀγαθός (LN 65.20; 88.1): 'good' [BAGD, Hn, HNTC, ICC, LN, Lns, WBC; KJV, NASB, NIV, RSV, TNT], 'sure' [NJB], 'firm' [TEV], 'bright' [NEB], not explicit [NAB]. This adjective is also translated as a noun phrase which is the object of the verb form of 'hope': 'good things' [SSA].
e. ἐλπίς (LN 25.59; 25.61): 'hope' [BAGD, Hn, HNTC, ICC, LN, Lns, WBC; all versions]. This noun is also translated as a verb: 'to confidently expect' [SSA].
f. ἐν (LN 89.84; 89.76; 89.26): 'in' [HNTC, Lns; NAB, NEB, TEV, TNT], 'in virtue of' [ICC], 'by' [WBC; NASB, NIV], 'by means of' [SSA], 'through' [KJV, NJB, RSV].
g. χάρις (LN 88.66): 'grace' [BAGD, HNTC, ICC, LN, Lns, WBC; all versions except NAB, TNT], 'kindness' [TNT], 'mercy' [NAB]. The phrase 'in grace' is also translated as an adverb: 'graciously' [Hn]; and as a verb: 'to act graciously' [SSA].

QUESTION—What relationship is indicated by the initial καί 'and'?
1. This is a coordinate conjunction [SSA]: he loved us *and* he also gave us encouragement and hope.
2. This indicates the result of the preceding clause [Alf, Ea, Er, Fn, Hb, HNTC, ICC, Lns, My, NCBC]: he loved us *and therefore* gave us encouragement and hope.

QUESTION—What relationship is indicated by ἐν 'in'?
1. This indicates the manner in which he gave [Alf, El, Hb, Hn]: he graciously gave us encouragement and hope.
2. This indicates the means by which he gave encouragement and hope [ICC, My, NCBC, NIC, SSA, WBC]: who gave us encouragement and hope *by means of* acting in grace.
3. This indicates the reason he gave encouragement and hope [HNTC; probably Lns]: he gave encouragement and hope *because* he is gracious.

QUESTION—What is meant by παράκλησιν αἰωνίαν 'eternal encouragement'?
What he has done for us encourages us forever [El, Fn, Hn, ICC] and it is an encouragement to his people throughout time and eternity [SSA]. Its effects last eternally [Ea, Lns]. Another view is that it is encouragement in respect to eternity [HNTC].

QUESTION—What is meant by ἐλπίδα ἀγαθήν 'a good hope'?
1. 'Good' is the attribute of the object of our hope [Ea, SSA, TH]: he caused us to hope in what is good. These are the good things God will give us [SSA].
2. 'Good' is an attribute of the event of hoping [Ea, Fn, Hb, Hn, ICC, Lns, Mn, WBC]. It means a 'well-founded' hope [Ea, Hb, Hn, ICC], and a hope that is genuine [ICC]. Or, it means that it is beneficial to those who receive it [Fn, Hb, Lns, Mn], it is good to have [Fn].
3. 'Good hope' was a current idiomatic expression used in reference to life after death [HNTC, NCBC].

2:17 may-he-encourage[a] your hearts[b]

LEXICON—a. aorist act. optative of παρακαλέω (LN 25.150): 'to encourage' [BAGD, Hn, HNTC, ICC, LN, Lns, SSA, WBC; NEB, NIV, NJB, TEV, TNT], 'to comfort' [BAGD; KJV, NASB, RSV], 'to console' [LN; NAB].

b. καρδία (LN 26.3): 'hearts' [BAGD, Hn, HNTC, ICC, LN, Lns, WBC; KJV, NAB, NASB, NIV, RSV], 'you' [SSA; NEB, NJB, TEV, TNT].

QUESTION—Why is the singular form of the verb used with the compound subject 'our Lord Jesus Christ himself and God our Father'?

1. Paul thinks of both the Lord Jesus and God our Father as one and therefore used a singular verb to refer to them both as the compound subject [Ea, EBC, Hn, HNTC, ICC, Lns, NCBC, NIC, WBC]: may our Lord Jesus Christ himself and God our Father encourage you. This is similar to the problem and answer in 1 Thess. 3:11.
2. This agrees with the singular 'who' in the preceding verse and refers to God [TH]: may God our Father encourage you.
3. Here the use of the emphatic pronoun αὐτός 'himself' with the Lord Jesus and the use of the full title 'our Lord Jesus Christ' gives prominence to Jesus in this prayer and the singular verbs refer to him [SSA]: may our Lord Jesus Christ himself—and God our Father too—may he encourage you.

and may-he-establish[a] (them/you) in[b] every[c] work[d] and word[e] good.[f]

LEXICON—a. aorist act. optative of στηρίζω (LN 74.19): 'to establish' [BAGD, Lns, WBC; KJV, RSV], 'to strengthen' [BAGD, Hn, HNTC, LN; NAB, NASB, NIV, NJB, TEV, TNT], 'to make more firm' [LN], 'to fortify' [NEB], 'to make one steady' [ICC], 'to cause one to continue to do' [SSA].

b. ἐν (LN 89.5): 'in' [Hn, HNTC, ICC, Lns, WBC; all versions except NAB, TEV], 'for' [NAB], 'to (do and say)' [TEV], not explicit [SSA].

c. πᾶς (LN 59.23; 58.28): 'every' [Hn, HNTC, ICC, Lns, WBC; all versions except TEV], 'every sort of' [SSA]. This adjective is also translated as an adverb modifying the verb form of the nouns: 'always' [TEV].

d. ἔργον (LN 42.11): 'work' [BAGD, Hn, WBC; KJV, NAB, NASB, RSV], 'deed' [BAGD, HNTC, LN, Lns, SSA; NEB, NIV, NJB, TNT], 'act' [LN], 'work you do' [ICC]. This noun is also translated as a verb: 'to do' [TEV].

e. λόγος (LN 33.98; 33.99): 'word' [BAGD, Hn, HNTC, LN, Lns, WBC; all versions except TEV], 'word you utter' [ICC]. This noun is also translated as a verb: 'to say' [TEV], 'to speak' [SSA].

f. ἀγαθός (LN 88.1; 65.20): 'good' [BAGD, Hn, HNTC, ICC, LN, Lns, SSA, WBC; all versions].

QUESTION—What is the implied object of the verb?

1. The implied object is ὑμῶν τὰς καρδίας 'your hearts' as in the preceding clause [Fn, Hb, Hn, HNTC, Lns; NAB, NASB, RSV]: may he establish your hearts.

2. The implied object is ὑμᾶς 'you' [Alf, Ea, El, My, WBC; NEB, NIV, NJB, TEV, TNT]: may he establish you. There is no significant difference in meaning between the two interpretations.

QUESTION—What is meant by 'establishing' them?

This means to bring them to spiritual maturity [Hb]. Or this means that they will firmly grasp the hope [Lns].

QUESTION—What does ἀγαθῷ 'good' modify?

It modifies both of the preceding nouns [Ea, El, Er, Fn, Hb, Hn, HNTC, ICC, Lns, Mn, My, NCBC, SSA, TH, WBC, Wd; all versions]: in every good work and word. 'Good' means beneficial [Hb].

QUESTION—What does παντί 'every' modify?

It modifies both of the following nouns [Alf, Ea, El, Er, Hb, Hn, HNTC, ICC, Mn, My, NCBC, SSA, TH, Wd; all versions]: in every work and every good word.

QUESTION—What does παντί 'every' modify?

1. It modifies both of the preceding nouns [Ea, El, Er, Fn, Hb, Hn, HNTC, ICC, Lns, Mn, My, NCBC, SSA, TH, WBC, Wd; all versions]: in every good work and word. 'Good' means beneficial [Hb].
2. It modifies both of the following nouns [Alf, Ea, El, Er, Hb, Hn, HNTC, ICC, Mn, My, NCBC, SSA, TH, Wd; all versions]: in every work and every good word.

DISCOURSE UNIT 3:1–16 [Mn, Wd]. The topic is consolation and exhortations [Mn], admonition [Wd].

DISCOURSE UNIT: 3:1–5 [Alf, EBC, Er, GNT, HNTC, ICC, My, NCBC, NIC, SSA, TH, WBC; NAB, NIV, TEV]. The topic is further prayers [WBC], a request for prayer [Alf, Er, GNT, My, NCBC; NAB, NIV, TEV], mutual prayers [HNTC], God's faithfulness [NIC]. This is further subdivided 2:1–2, 3–4, 5 [WBC].

DISCOURSE UNIT: 3:1–2 [EBC, Hb, Hn, Mn, NIC, SSA, Wd]. The topic is a request for prayer.

3:1 For-the rest[a] pray,[b] brothers, concerning[c] us,

LEXICON—a. λοιπόν (LN 89.98; 61.14): 'rest', 'furthermore' [LN], 'also' [LN], 'finally' [LN], 'in summary' [LN]. The phrase τὸ λοιπόν is translated 'for the rest' [Hn, WBC; NAB], 'as regards the rest' [Lns], 'as for the other matters' [SSA], 'finally' [BAGD, HNTC, ICC; KJV, NASB, NIV, NJB, RSV, TEV], 'and now' [NEB, TNT]. See this word at 1 Thess. 4:1.

b. pres. mid. (deponent = active) impera. of προσεύχομαι (LN 33.178): 'to pray' [BAGD, Hn, HNTC, ICC, LN, Lns, SSA, WBC; all versions]. Some commentators take the present tense to mean that they are to keep on praying for them [Hb, Hn, HNTC, Lns, NIC, Rb, Wd], while others think that this aspect should not be pressed [NCBC, TH]. See this word at 1 Thess. 5:25.

    c. περί (LN 89.6; 90.39): 'concerning' [BAGD], 'for' [BAGD, Hn, HNTC, ICC, Lns, SSA, WBC; all versions], 'on one's behalf' [My].

QUESTION—What is meant by τὸ λοιπόν 'for the rest'?

Many commentators take it to indicate that the letter is coming to an end [Er, Fn, Hn, HNTC, ICC, WBC]: finally. Some think that Paul intended to end the letter but, after writing this, remembers other matters and adds them [WBC]. Others think that the expression means that the preceding section is coming to an end and this adds a final point before going on to something else [Lns, NCBC]. Others think that this phrase merely introduces the matters that remain to be written [Alf, Ea, EBC, El, Hb, Hn, ICC, My, NCBC, NIC, SSA, TH, WBC].

that[a] the word[b] of-the Lord may-run[c] and be-glorified[d]

LEXICON—a. ἵνα (LN 90.22): 'that' [Hn, HNTC, ICC, Lns, SSA, WBC; all versions].

    b. λόγος (LN 33.260): 'word' [BAGD, Hn, HNTC, ICC, LN, Lns, WBC; KJV, NAB, NASB, NEB, RSV], 'message' [SSA; NIV, NJB, TEV, TNT]. See this word at 1 Thess. 1:8.

    c. pres. act. subj. of τρέχω (LN **28.25**): 'to run' [BAGD, Lns], 'to run its race' [Hn, ICC], 'to make progress' [NAB], 'to spread rapidly/swiftly/quickly' [BAGD, HNTC, LN; NASB, NIV, NJB, TEV, TNT], 'to come to be known quickly' [LN], 'to have free course' [KJV], 'to have a swift course' [NEB], 'to speed on' [WBC; RSV]. This verb is also described: 'more and more people will soon hear' [SSA]. The present tense here and in the following verb may indicate a request for its continual progress [EBC, Fn, Hb, ICC, Lns, Rb, TH; TEV], or it considers the continual stream of people coming to accept the word and be affected by it [ICC].

    d. pres. pass. subj. of δοξάζω (LN 33.357): 'to be glorified' [BAGD, LN, Lns, WBC; KJV, NASB], 'to be praised' [LN], 'to be honored' [NIV], 'to be received with honor' [NJB, TEV, TNT], 'to be hailed' [NAB], 'to triumph' [RSV], 'to be crowned with glory' [Hn, ICC], 'to spread gloriously' [HNTC], 'to have a glorious course' [NEB]. The result of this verb is also made explicit: 'they will believe (this message)' [SSA].

QUESTION—How is this clause related to the request to pray for them?

The prayer for them is not so much for personal matters as for their work as preachers of the gospel [Alf, Ea, Hn, HNTC, ICC, Mn, My, NIC]: pray for us in our work of spreading the gospel, that it will spread rapidly and be glorified.

QUESTION—How are the nouns related in the genitive construction ὁ λόγος τοῦ κυρίου 'the word of the Lord'?

This means the word about the Lord [Hn, SSA]. Some commentators add that it also means that it comes from him [Ea, Hn, My]. It refers to the gospel [Alf, Ea, EBC, EGT, Er, Hb, HNTC, ICC, My, NCBC, TH, WBC], the message that Paul preached [Fn, NIC]. 'Lord' refers to Jesus Christ [Fn, Hb, Hn, ICC, Mn, SSA].

QUESTION—In what sense is the word of the Lord to 'run'?
 1. The message is to be spread rapidly [Alf, EBC, Fn, Hb, HNTC, Lns, Mn, NCBC, NIC, SSA, TH, WBC, Wd; NASB, NEB, NIV, NJB, RSV, TEV, TNT]: pray that the message about the Lord will be spread rapidly. This means that more and more people will hear the message in spite of hindrances [SSA].
 2. The message is to be spread without being hindered from doing so [Hn]: pray that the word of the Lord may not be hindered. This implies that it will spread quickly.
 3. This means both of the above [Ea, El, Er, ICC, My]: pray that the message about the Lord will spread rapidly without being impeded. The Jews would want to hinder it [ICC].
QUESTION—In what sense will the word of the Lord be 'glorified'?
 1. This refers to people giving honor to the word of the Lord [Hb, Mn, My, NCBC, NIC, SSA, TH, WBC, Wd; NIV, NJB, TEV, TNT]: pray that the word may be honored. They will honor it because they see its power in the lives of believers [Hb, NIC], or they will honor it by believing it [NCBC, SSA].
 2. This refers to the word of the Lord displaying its glory [Alf, Ea, Fn, Hn, HNTC, Lns]: pray that the word will show its glory to people. Its glory will be seen by its power to save and change lives [Alf, Fn], or by the very fact that it successfully spreads as people believe it [Ea, HNTC, Lns].
 3. This refers to its triumphal success [EBC, HNTC, ICC; RSV]: pray that the word may triumph.

as[a] (it did/does) indeed/also[b] with you,
LEXICON—a. καθώς (LN 64.14): 'as' [ICC, WBC; KJV, NAB, NJB, RSV, TNT], 'just as' [Hn, HNTC, SSA; NASB, NIV, TEV], 'even as' [Lns], not explicit [NEB].
 b. καί (LN 91.12; 89.93): 'indeed', 'even' [KJV, NAB], 'also' [Lns; NASB], not explicit [Hn, HNTC, ICC, SSA, WBC; NEB, NIV, NJB, RSV, TEV, TNT].
QUESTION—What tense is implied with the supplied verb?
 1. It implies a past tense and concerns the initial success of the word [Alf, Ea, EBC, Er, Hb, Hn, WBC; NAB, NASB, NEB, NIV, NJB, RSV, TEV]: as it did when it *came* to you.
 2. It implies a present tense and concerns a continuation of the word's work [El, HNTC, ICC, NIC, Rb, SSA; KJV, TNT]: as it *continues to do* with you. This includes its present spread in Thessalonica as well as what happened when Paul first brought it to them [El, HNTC, NIC].
QUESTION—What is this clause connected with?
 1. It is connected with the immediately preceding verb [Alf, Ea, My, SSA]: as it was/is glorified among you. The running is only a means to it being glorified [Ea] and running implies more than a single community [TH].

2. It is connected with the two preceding verbs [Er, Fn, Hb, HNTC, ICC, Lns, TH, Wd]: as it ran and was/is glorified among you.
QUESTION: What is meant by καί 'also'?
This reminds them that others have done as they have [Ea, El, Hb].

3:2 and that we-may-be-delivered^a from the perverse^b and evil^c men;

LEXICON—a. aorist pass. subj. of ῥύομαι (LN 21.23): 'to be delivered' [BAGD, HNTC, ICC, LN, WBC; KJV, NAB, NASB, NIV, RSV], 'to be rescued' [BAGD, Hn, LN, Lns, SSA; NEB], 'to be saved' [BAGD; TNT], 'to be preserved' [BAGD; NJB]. The passive voice is also translated actively: '(God) will rescue' [TEV].

b. ἄτοπος (LN 88.111): 'perverse' [HNTC, Lns, SSA, WBC; NASB, TNT], 'unreasonable' [KJV], 'confused' [NAB], 'wrong-headed' [NEB], 'bigoted' [NJB], 'wicked' [NIV, RSV, TEV], 'bad' [LN], 'unrighteous' [Hn, ICC, NIC], 'not fitting' [LN].

c. πονηρός (LN 88.110): 'evil' [BAGD, Hn, ICC, LN, SSA; NAB, NASB, NIV, NJB, RSV, TEV, TNT], 'wicked' [BAGD, HNTC, LN, Lns, WBC; KJV, NEB], 'immoral' [LN].

QUESTION—What is the significance of the aorist tense of the verb and the use of the article in the reference to the perverse and evil men?
This may indicate that a specific time of opposition is referred to [Ea, Hb, Hn, HNTC, NIC, SSA, TH] and also that the Thessalonians already knew about the particular persecutors Paul was referring to [Fn, Hb, HNTC, ICC, NIC, SSA, TH].

because^a not the faith^b of-all.

LEXICON—a. γάρ (LN 89.23): 'because', 'since' [SSA], 'for' [Hn, HNTC, ICC, Lns, WBC; all versions].

b. πίστις (LN 31.102; 31.104): 'faith' [BAGD, Hn, HNTC, LN, Lns, WBC; all versions except TEV], 'Christian faith' [ICC]. This noun is also translated as a verb: 'to believe' [SSA; TEV].

QUESTION—What relationship is indicated by γάρ 'because'?
1. This indicates the reason why there are perverse and evil men [Alf, EBC, El, Er, Hb, Hn, HNTC, ICC, Lns, My, NCBC, Rb, Wd]: pray that we may be delivered from perverse and evil men, and there are such people *because* not all have faith.
2. This indicates the grounds for Paul's request for prayer [SSA]: I ask you to pray that the word will spread and be glorified, *since* not everyone believes the message.
3. It includes both of the above relationships [Ea].

QUESTION—What is the implied verb in this clause?
1. This implies the verb 'to have' [EBC, HNTC, WBC; all versions except TEV]: all do not have faith. Or the reciprocal verb 'to belong to' is used [Lns]: the faith does not belong to all. This is a litotes [EBC, Fn, Hn]: for most oppose the gospel.
2. The verb form of the noun is used [SSA; TEV]: all do not believe.

2 THESSALONIANS 3:2 241

3. This implies the verb 'to be' [Hn, ICC, My, Rb]: faith is not the portion of all the people.

QUESTION—What is the significance of the article in the phrase ἡ πίστις 'the faith'?

1. This refers to the objective body of Christian doctrine [Alf, My]: not all accept/believe the Christian faith/teachings.
2. This refers to the subjective event of believing [Ea, EBC, El, Fn, Hb, Hn, HNTC, ICC, Mn, NCBC, NIC, Rb, SSA, TH, WBC; probably all versions]: not all believe (the gospel). The article refers to the Christian faith, the attitude of acceptance of the gospel [Hb], or it refers to the (true) faith in the gospel [Hn].
3. This includes both of the above interpretations [Lns]: not all have faith in the Faith, not all believe the Christian doctrine.

DISCOURSE UNIT: 3:3–5 [EBC, Hb, Hn, Mn, NIC, SSA, Wd]. The topic is the Lord's strengthening and protection [SSA], the Lord's faithfulness [Mn, NIC, Wd], Paul's prayer for them [EBC].

3:3 But[a] faithful[b] is the Lord,

LEXICON—a. δέ (LN 89.124): 'but' [HNTC, WBC; all versions except NJB], 'yet' [Hn, Lns], 'however' [ICC], not explicit [SSA; NJB].

b. πιστός (LN 31.87): 'faithful' [BAGD, Hn, HNTC, ICC, LN, Lns, WBC; KJV, NASB, NIV, RSV, TEV, TNT], 'trustworthy' [BAGD, LN, SSA]. The phrase 'is faithful' is also translated with another verb: 'to keep faith' [NAB], 'is to be trusted' [NEB], 'you can rely on' [NJB].

QUESTION—What relationship is indicated by δέ 'but'?

This indicates a contrast [Alf, Ea, EBC, El, Er, Fn, Hb, Hn, HNTC, ICC, Lns, Mn, My, NCBC, Rb, TH, WBC; all versions except NJB]: but. The contrast is between the faithless opponents (3:2) and the faithful Lord [Alf, Ea, EBC, Er, Fn, Hb, Hn, ICC, Mn, Rb, TH, WBC].

QUESTION—Who is the Lord?

The 'Lord' is Jesus Christ [Alf, Ea, EBC, El, Fn, Hb, ICC, Lns, My, NCBC, SSA, TH].

QUESTION—In what sense is the Lord faithful?

He fulfils his promises [Hb, NCBC], he does what he has covenanted to do [Hb], and he grants prayers [Hb].

who will-strengthen[a] you

LEXICON—a. fut. act. indic. of στηρίζω (LN 74.19): 'to strengthen' [BAGD, Hn, HNTC, LN; NAB, NASB, NIV, RSV, TEV, TNT], 'to give strength' [NJB], 'to establish' [BAGD, Lns, WBC; KJV], 'to fortify' [NEB], 'to make firm' [ICC], 'to make more firm' [LN], 'to cause one to be steadfast' [SSA]. It will be a continuing action [Hb].

QUESTION—What relationship is implied by the use of the relative clause here?
1. This implies a conclusion to the preceding statement [Hb, Hn, NCBC, SSA]: since the Lord is faithful, *therefore* we know that he will strengthen and guard you.
2. This explains what is meant by the preceding statement [El]: the Lord is faithful, *that is*, he will strengthen and guard you.

QUESTION: In what respect will the Lord strengthen them?
He will give them strength to resist temptations from the evil one [ICC], he will strengthen their wills [TH], he will give them inward stability [Hb, Hn, Lns, Wd], and he will settle them in the faith [NIC].

and will-guard^a from the evil.^b

LEXICON—a. fut. act. indic. of φυλάσσω (LN 37.120): 'to guard' [BAGD, Hn, HNTC, ICC, Lns, WBC; NAB, NEB, NJB, RSV, TNT], 'to guard closely' [LN], 'to protect' [BAGD, SSA; NASB, NIV], 'to keep' [KJV], 'to keep one safe' [TEV]. It will be a continuing protection [Hb].

b. πονηρός (LN 88.110; 12.35): 'evil' [LN, SSA; KJV, RSV, TNT], 'evil' [LN]. With the article it is translated as a substantive: 'the evil one' [BAGD, Hn, ICC, SSA, WBC; NAB, NASB, NEB, NIV, NJB, TEV], 'the wicked one' [HNTC, Lns].

QUESTION—What relationship is indicated by καί 'and'?
1. It is coordinate and indicates a second thing that the Lord will do [Hb, NIC, SSA]: the Lord will strengthen you and will guard you.
2. It indicates the result of the preceding means [ICC]: the Lord will strengthen you and thus guard you.

QUESTION—What is the meaning of the term τοῦ πονηροῦ 'the evil'?
1. This is to be taken as a masculine form and refers to 'the evil person', i.e., Satan [Ea, EBC, El, Er, Fn, Hb, Hn, HNTC, ICC, Lns, Mn, NIC, Rb, WBC, Wd; NAB, NASB, NEB, NIV, NJB, TEV]: he will guard you from the evil one.
2. This is to be taken as a neuter form and refers to evil in a generic sense [Alf, My, TH; KJV, RSV, TNT]: he will guard you from evil.

3:4 And^a we-are-confident^b in^c the Lord about^d you,

LEXICON—a. δέ (LN 89.94): 'and' [WBC; KJV, NASB, RSV, TEV], 'moreover' [Hn, ICC,; TNT], 'now' [Lns], not explicit [HNTC, SSA; NAB, NEB, NIV].

b. perf. act. indic. of πείθω (LN 31.82): 'to be confident' [BAGD, Lns, SSA; NAB, TNT], 'to have confidence' [Hn, HNTC, LN, WBC; KJV, NASB, NIV, NJB, RSV], 'to feel perfect confidence' [NEB], 'to depend on' [LN], 'to have faith' [ICC]. The phrase 'we are confident in the Lord' is translated 'the Lord gives us confidence' [TEV]. The perfect tense indicates an existing state of confidence [HNTC, ICC]. This state began at the time of the conversion of the Thessalonians [HNTC].

c. ἐν (LN 89.26; 89.119): 'in' [Hn, HNTC, Lns, SSA, WBC; all versions except TEV, TNT], 'prompted by (the Lord)' [ICC], 'that (the Lord will not fail us)' [TNT].

d. ἐπί (LN 90.23): 'about' [Hn, HNTC; NEB, RSV], 'concerning' [WBC; NASB], 'regarding' [Lns], 'touching' [KJV], 'in' [ICC, SSA; NJB, TEV], '(where you are) concerned' [TNT], not explicit [NAB, NIV].

QUESTION—Who is the Lord?

'Lord' refers to Jesus Christ [EBC, Fn, Hb, Hn, ICC, My, Wd].

QUESTION—What relationship is indicated by ἐν 'in'?

1. This means that their confidence about what the Thessalonians will do is based on what the Lord will accomplish [Ea, Hb, Mn, My, NIC, WBC; TNT]: we are confident that the Lord will cause you to do the right thing, to go on living in accordance with our commands.
2. This means that their confidence about what the Thessalonians will do is inspired by the Lord who indwells the writers [ICC]: the Lord who indwells us makes us confident that you will live in accordance with our commands.
3. This means that they have confidence about what the Thessalonians will do because of their connection with the Lord [Alf, EBC, El, Hn, HNTC, NCBC, SSA, Wd]: we are confident that you will live in accordance with our commands since we (incl.) are in a spiritual relationship with the Lord. There are some variations in what is involved: we are confident that you will live in accordance with our commands because you believe in the Lord [SSA], or we are confident that you will live in accordance with our commands because you are in union with the Lord (who will perfect what he has begun) [Hn].

that what-things we-command[a] both[b] you-do[c] and you-will-do.[c]

LEXICON—a. pres. act. indic. of παραγγέλλω (LN 33.327): 'to command' [BAGD, Hn, ICC, LN, Lns, SSA; KJV, NASB, NIV, RSV], 'to order' [LN; NEB], 'to enjoin' [NAB], 'to charge' [WBC], 'to instruct' [BAGD, HNTC], 'to tell' [NJB, TEV, TNT].

b. καί (LN 91.12): 'both' [ICC; KJV], 'also' [Lns], not explicit [Hn, HNTC, SSA, WBC; all versions except KJV].

c. pres. and fut. act. indic. of ποιέω (LN 90.45): 'to do' [Hn, HNTC, ICC, LN, Lns, WBC; all versions], 'to obey' [SSA].

QUESTION—What is indicated by the use of the present tense ἃ παραγγέλλομεν 'what we command'?

It refers to the commands given in the letter [Ea, El, Er, Fn, Hb, HNTC, Mn]. Some commentators add that since they are already doing what he commands, this must also include what he commanded previously [NCBC, SSA, TH, WBC], perhaps indicating that he is repeating what he had commanded them as a reminder [NCBC].

3:5 **And/But may the Lord direct^a your hearts^b into^c the love of-God**

LEXICON—a. aorist act. opt. of κατευθύνω (LN **36.1**): 'to direct' [BAGD, Hn, HNTC, Lns, WBC; KJV, NASB, NEB, NIV, RSV, TNT], 'to turn' [NJB], 'to lead' [BAGD, LN; TEV], 'to incline' [ICC], 'to rule' [NAB], 'to cause one to continue (to know)' [SSA].
- b. καρδία (LN 26.3): 'hearts' [BAGD, Hn, HNTC, ICC, LN, Lns, WBC; all versions except TEV], 'you' [SSA; TEV].
- c. εἰς (LN 90.23): 'into' [Lns, WBC; KJV, NASB, NIV], 'towards' [NEB, NJB], 'to' [Hn, HNTC; RSV, TNT], 'in' [NAB], 'into a greater understanding' [TEV], 'to a sense of' [ICC], not explicit [SSA].

QUESTION—What relationship is indicated by δέ 'and/but'?
1. It indicates transition [Lns, WBC]: and/now.
2. It indicates contrast [Ea, El, Fn, Hb, Hn, ICC, NIC]: but. The contrast is between his confidence that they will do what he commands and his knowledge that they need the Lord's help to do so [Ea, Hb, Hn, ICC, NIC].

QUESTION—How are the event word and the person related in the genitive construction τὴν ἀγάπην τοῦ θεοῦ 'the love of God'?
1. God is the actor of the event [EBC, EGT, Er, Fn, Hn, HNTC, ICC, Lns, Mn, Rb, SSA, TH, WBC, Wd]: God loves you.
2. God is the recipient of the event [Alf, Ea, El, My]: you love God.
3. This means both the love that God has for them and their love for God [Hb, NIC]. Their love for God is stimulated by their experiencing God's love for them [Hb, NIC] and this motivates them to obey the commands from God [Hb].
4. This means the quality of the love they are to have [NCBC]: may the Lord direct you to love in the way that he loves. In this context this means that Paul wants them to show God-like love for him by praying for him [NCBC].

QUESTION—What is meant by the Lord directing their hearts into the love of God?
1. 'To direct' means to cause someone to achieve a goal [SSA]: may the Lord cause you to experience more fully God's love for you.
2. 'To direct' means to incline them towards something [EBC, Fn, HNTC, ICC, WBC]: may the Lord incline your hearts to realize and appreciate God's love for you.

and into the steadfastness^a of-Christ.

LEXICON—a. ὑπομονή (LN 25.174): 'steadfastness' [BAGD, HNTC, WBC; NASB, NEB, RSV, TNT], 'constancy' [NAB], 'perseverance' [BAGD; NIV, NJB], 'endurance' [BAGD, Hn, ICC; TEV], 'patience' [BAGD, Lns], 'patient waiting' [KJV]. This noun is also translated as a verbal phrase: 'to continue to be steadfast' [SSA].

QUESTION—How are the attribute and the person related in the genitive construction τὴν ὑπομονὴν τοῦ Χριστοῦ 'the steadfastness of Christ'?
  1. This means the steadfastness displayed by Christ [Alf, Bul (p. 994), Ea, EBC, El, Fn, Hn, Mn, My, NCBC, Rb, SSA, Wd]: may the Lord cause you to be steadfast like Christ was steadfast.
  2. This means the steadfastness imparted by Christ [EGT, ICC, Lns; TEV]: the steadfastness which Christ gives people.
  3. This means both the steadfastness displayed by Christ and the steadfastness he inspires in them [Er, Hb, NIC, WBC].
  4. This means the Thessalonians' patience in waiting for Christ [KJV].

DISCOURSE UNIT: 3:6–16 [EGT, NCBC, SSA, WBC, Wd]. The topic is exhortations [EGT, WBC], commands about the disorderly [Wd], avoidance of the disorderly brothers [SSA], the danger of being idle [NCBC].

DISCOURSE UNIT: 3:6–15 [Alf, EBC, Er, Fn, GNT, Hb, Hn, HNTC, ICC, Mn, My, NIC, TH; NAB, NIV, NJB, TEV]. The topic is how to deal with those who are idle [EBC, Fn, HNTC; NAB], a warning about idleness [GNT; NIV], a warning about idleness and disunity [My; NJB], a warning about disorderliness [Hn], discipline [NIC], how to discipline the disorderly [Hb], the need to work [TEV]. This is further divided: 3:6–10, 11–12, 13–15 [EBC]; 3:6–2, 13–15 [Mn]; 3:6, 7–11, 12, 13, 14, 15 [ICC]; 3:6, 7–10, 11, 12, 13–15 [Hb].

3:6 Now^a we-command^b you, brothers, in the name^c of-the Lord of-us Jesus Christ,

LEXICON—a. δέ (LN 89.94): 'now' [Hn, HNTC, ICC, Lns, WBC; KJV, NASB, RSV], not explicit [SSA; NAB, NEB, NIV, NJB, TEV, TNT].
  b. pres. act. indic. of παραγγέλλω (LN 33.327): 'to command' [BAGD, Hn, ICC, LN, Lns, SSA; KJV, NAB, NASB, NIV, RSV, TEV], 'to order' [LN; TNT], 'to charge' [WBC], 'to urge' [NJB], 'to instruct' [BAGD, HNTC]. This verb is also translated as a phrase: 'these are our orders' [NEB].
  c. ὄνομα (LN 33.126): 'name' [BAGD, Hn, HNTC, ICC, LN, Lns, WBC; all versions]. The phrase 'in the name of' is translated 'with the authority which our Lord Jesus Christ has given us' [SSA].
QUESTION—What relationship is indicated by δέ 'now'?
  This indicates a transition to a new topic [El, Hb, Hn, HNTC, ICC, Lns, TH, WBC; KJV, NASB, RSV]: now.
QUESTION—To whom does ὑμῖν 'you' refer?
  It refers to the majority of church members who need to discipline the disorderly minority [Hb, HNTC, ICC, WBC].
QUESTION—What is meant by ἐν ὀνόματι τοῦ κυρίου Ἰησοῦ Χριστοῦ 'in the name of the Lord Jesus Christ'?
  1. This means that Paul has authority from the Lord to command the church [Ea, Fn, Hb, Hn, HNTC, ICC, Mn, My, NCBC, NIC, Rb, SSA, TH, WBC]: we command you with the authority given us by the Lord Jesus

Christ. The apostles are Christ's representatives [Hb, NCBC, WBC] and what they command is in accordance with Christ's teaching [Hn].
2. This means that what he commands is connected with what Christ revealed [Lns]: we command you according to what was revealed by the Lord Jesus Christ.

you keep-away[a] from every brother walking[b] idly/disorderly[c]

LEXICON—a. pres. mid. infin. of στέλλομαι (LN **34.41**): 'to keep away' [BAGD, ICC, LN; NIV, NJB, RSV, TEV], 'to withdraw' [Lns; KJV], 'to avoid' [NAB], 'to stay away' [Hn], 'to keep aloof' [WBC; NASB], 'to hold aloof' [HNTC; NEB], 'to have nothing to do (with)' [TNT], 'to disassociate oneself' [SSA]. The present tense indicates that they are to make it a practice to keep away from them [Hb].

b. pres. act. participle of περιπατέω (LN 41.11): 'to walk' [ICC, Lns; KJV], 'to live' [BAGD, LN; RSV, TNT], 'to lead a life' [NASB], 'to live a life' [NJB, TEV], 'to conduct oneself' [BAGD, Hn, WBC], 'to behave' [HNTC, LN, SSA]. The negative expression is also translated positively: 'to be (idle)' [NIV], 'to wander (from the straight path)' [NAB], 'to fall into (idle habits)' [NEB]. The present tense indicates that this is to be a persistent practice [Hb].

c. ἀτάκτως (LN **88.247**): 'idly', 'in idleness' [BAGD, ICC; RSV, TNT], 'lazily' [LN], 'as a loafer' [HNTC]; or 'disorderly' [Lns; KJV], 'in a disorderly manner' [BAGD, Hn, SSA, WBC]. This adverb is also translated as an adjective: 'idle' [NIV], 'lazy' [TEV], 'undisciplined' [NJB], 'unruly' [NASB]; or as a noun phrase: 'idle habits' [NEB].

QUESTION—In what sense were they to keep away from such a brother?

This refers to social ostracism [Alf, EBC, Hb, Hn, ICC, NCBC, SSA]. It is intended to indicate disapproval of the brothers' conduct [SSA] and to make it clear that those brothers had separated from the rest [NIC]. It does not refer to excommunication [Alf, Hb, Hn, ICC, Lns, NCBC, SSA, TH, Wd]. Suggestions of what is involved in keeping away are lack of intimate fellowship [Hb, NIC], refusal to supply food [HNTC], exclusion from the love feasts and communion [Fn, Hb, Lns] and from voting and business meetings [Lns].

QUESTION—What is meant by ἀτάκτως 'idly/disorderly'?
1. This refers to idleness [HNTC, LN (88.246), ICC, NCBC, TH; NEB, NIV, RSV, TEV, TNT]: keep away from every brother who lives in an idle manner.
2. This refers to disorderliness [Ea, El, Er, Fn, Hb, Hn, Lns, My, Rb, SSA, WBC; KJV, NASB, NJB]: keep away from every brother who lives in a disorderly manner. This includes idleness, but also refers to its associated evils of depending on others for help and being busybodies [Ea, Hb, Hn, SSA].

and not according-to[a] **the tradition**[b] **which they-received**[c] **from us.**
TEXT—Instead of παρελάβοσαν 'they received', some manuscripts have παρελάβετε 'you (plural) received' and others have παρέλαβον 'he received'. GNT selects 'they received' with a C rating, indicating a considerable degree of doubt. 'They received' is also selected by Alf, Ea, EBC, El, Fn, Hb, HNTC, Lns, My, Rb, and WBC. 'You received' is selected by EGT, Hn, ICC, NCBC, NIC SSA, Wd; NAB, NASB, NEB, NIV, NJB, and RSV. 'He received' is selected only by KJV.
LEXICON—a. κατά (LN 89.8): 'according to' [HNTC, Lns; NASB, NIV], 'in accordance with' [Hn, ICC, WBC; NJB], 'in accord with' [RSV], 'after' [KJV]. The prepositional phrase is also translated as a clause: 'and does not follow' [NAB, NEB, TEV], 'and ignore' [TNT].
b. παράδοσις (LN 33.239): 'tradition' [BAGD, Hn, HNTC, LN, Lns, WBC; all versions except NIV, TEV], 'teaching' [LN; NIV], 'instructions' [ICC; TEV]. The phrase is translated 'not in the manner you were taught by us' [SSA]. See this word at 2:15.
c. aorist act. indic. of παραλαμβάνω (LN 27.13): 'to receive' [BAGD, Hn, HNTC, ICC, Lns, WBC; KJV, NAB, NASB, NEB, NIV, NJB, RSV], 'to be taught' [SSA], 'to learn from someone' [LN], 'to learn about a tradition' [LN]. This is also translated with a reciprocal verb: '(the instructions) we gave (them)' [TEV], 'to pass on' [TNT].

3:7 Because[a]
LEXICON—a. γάρ (LN 89.23): 'because', 'since' [SSA], 'for' [Hn, HNTC, ICC, Lns; KJV, NASB, NIV, RSV], not explicit [WBC; NAB, NEB, NJB, TEV, TNT].
QUESTION—What relationship is indicated by this conjunction?
This indicates the grounds for the preceding command [Ea, El, Er, Hb, Hn, HNTC, ICC, Lns, NCBC, SSA, TH, Wd]: we command you to avoid idle/disorderly brothers *since* you know you ought to behave like we did (by working and supporting ourselves).

you-yourselves know[a] **how**[b] **it-is-necessary**[c] **to-imitate**[d] **us,**
LEXICON—a. perf. act. indic. of οἶδα (LN 28.7): 'to know' [BAGD, Hn, HNTC, ICC, Lns, SSA, WBC; all versions].
b. πῶς (LN 92.16): 'how' [BAGD, Hn, HNTC, ICC, Lns, WBC; all versions except TEV], 'that' [SSA; TEV].
c. pres. act. indic. of δεῖ (LN 71.21): 'it is necessary', 'you ought' [Hn, HNTC, ICC, LN, Lns, SSA; KJV, NAB, NASB, NEB, NIV, RSV], 'you should' [LN; NJB, TEV, TNT], '(our example) should' [WBC].
d. pres. mid. (deponent = active) infin. of μιμέομαι (LN **41.44**): 'to imitate' [BAGD, Hn, HNTC, ICC, Lns, WBC; NAB, RSV, TNT] 'to follow' [BAGD; KJV], 'to follow one's example' [NASB, NIV], 'to copy one's example' [NEB], 'to take one as a model' [NJB], 'to behave like someone behaves' [SSA], 'to do just what another did' [LN; TEV]. The present tense indicates that this should be a continued imitation [Hb].

because/that-is^a we-were not idle^b among^c you,

LEXICON—a. ὅτι (LN 89.33; 91.15): 'because' [Hn, Lns, WBC; NASB], 'for' [HNTC, ICC; KJV]; or 'that is' [SSA]; not explicit [all versions except KJV, NASB].
  b. aorist act. indic. of ἀτακτέω (LN **88.246**): 'to be idle' [BAGD, ICC; NIV, RSV], 'to be idlers' [NEB], 'to live in idleness' [TNT], 'to live as loafers' [HNTC], 'to be lazy' [BAGD, LN; TEV]; or 'to be undisciplined' [NJB], 'to behave disorderly' [KJV], 'to act disorderly' [Lns], 'to live lives of disorder' [NAB], 'to lead disorderly lives' [WBC], 'to conduct oneself in a disorderly manner' [Hn], 'to behave in a disorderly manner' [SSA], 'to act in an undisciplined manner' [NASB]. The area of meaning corresponds to the interpretation take in 3:6.
  c. ἐν (LN 83.9): 'among' [Hn, HNTC, ICC, Lns, SSA, WBC; KJV, NAB, NASB, NEB], 'to be with' [NIV, NJB, RSV, TEV, TNT].

QUESTION—What relationship is indicated by ὅτι 'because/that is'?
  1. This indicates the reason or grounds why they know how to imitate Paul [Ea, ICC, Lns]: you know how you ought to imitate us, *because* (you saw that) we were not idle/disorderly when we were with you.
  2. This indicates the grounds for saying that they ought to imitate Paul [Hb, Hn]: you ought to imitate us, *since* we were not idle/disorderly.
  3. This explains how they behaved [SSA]: you know how you ought to behave like we behaved, *that is,* we were not idle/disorderly when we were with you.

3:8 nor (as) a-gift^a from anyone did-we-eat^b bread,^c

LEXICON—a. δωρεάν (LN **57.85**): 'gift'. This noun in the accusative case is translated 'gratis' [BAGD, Lns], 'as a gift' [BAGD], 'for nothing' [WBC], 'for nought' [KJV], 'without payment' [BAGD, HNTC], 'without paying for it' [Hn, ICC, LN, SSA; NASB, NEB, NIV, NJB, RSV, TEV], 'to depend on' [NAB], 'to be given' [TNT], 'we paid for all' [TNT].
  b. aorist act. indic. of ἐσθίω (LN 23.1): 'to eat' [BAGD, Hn, LN, Lns, SSA, WBC; KJV, NASB, NIV, RSV], 'to accept' [HNTC; NEB, NJB, TEV], 'to receive' [ICC], not explicit [NAB, TNT].
  c. ἄρτος (LN 5.1): 'bread' [BAGD, Hn, Lns, WBC; KJV, NASB, RSV], 'food' [BAGD, LN, SSA; NAB, NIV, NJB, TNT], 'board and lodging' [NEB], 'support' [TEV], 'means of support' [ICC], 'keep' [HNTC].

QUESTION—What is meant by the phrase ἄρτον ἐφάγομεν 'we ate bread'?

Many commentators take this to be an idiom meaning to eat any kind of food [Ea, EBC, HNTC, Mn, My, Rb, SSA, WBC; NAB, NIV, NJB, TNT]: we ate meals. Some take it to have an extended meaning of receiving whatever means of support that was needed [Alf, Fn, Hb, ICC, Lns, My, NCBC, NIC; NEB, TEV]: we received support. This does not mean that they never accepted an invitation to a meal, but that they refused to be dependent on others [Hb, NIC, SSA].

but with toil[a] and labor[b] working[c] night and day,
LEXICON—a. κόπος (LN **42.47**): 'toil' [BAGD, Hn, ICC, Lns; RSV], 'labor' [BAGD, WBC; KJV, NASB], 'hard work' [LN], 'hard labor' [HNTC]. This noun is also translated as a verb: 'to toil' [NEB], 'to labor' [NIV], 'to work' [TEV]. The phrase 'with toil and labor' is also translated as a unit: '(we worked) hard and painfully' [TNT], '(we worked) very hard indeed' [SSA], 'with unsparing energy' [NJB], 'to labor to the point of exhaustion' [NAB].
  b. μόχθος (LN **42.48**): 'labor' [BAGD; RSV], 'toil' [HNTC, LN, WBC], 'travail' [KJV], 'hardship' [BAGD, Hn, ICC, Lns; NASB]. This noun is also translated as a verb: 'to drudge' [NEB], 'to toil' [NIV, TEV].
  c. pres. mid. (deponent = active) participle of ἐργάζομαι (LN 42.41): 'to work' [BAGD, Hn, HNTC, LN, Lns, SSA, WBC; all versions], 'to keep at work' [ICC], 'to labor' [LN], 'we wrought' [KJV]. The present tense indicates a continuing work [Hn, ICC, WBC; NASB, TEV]. See this word at 1 Thess. 4:11.
QUESTION—What is the purpose of using the two nouns κόπῳ 'toil' and μόχθῳ 'labor'?
  See the discussion of this question at 1 Thess. 2:9.
QUESTION—What is implied by placing night before day?
  See the discussion of this question at 1 Thess. 2:9.

in-order-that[a] (we) not burden[b] anyone of-you.
LEXICON—a. πρός (LN 89.60; 89.44): 'in order that' [ICC, SSA], 'in order to' [Hn], 'that' [KJV, RSV, TNT], 'so that' [NASB, NIV], 'so as to' [HNTC, Lns, WBC; NAB, NJB, TEV], 'rather than' [NEB].
  b. aorist act. infin. of ἐπιβαρέω (LN 57.224): 'to burden' [LN; RSV], 'to be a burden' [BAGD, Hn, Lns; NASB, NEB, NIV, NJB, TNT], 'to be a financial burden' [LN], 'to put on someone the burden of maintenance' [ICC], 'to be an expense' [TEV], 'to impose on' [NAB], 'to be chargeable' [KJV], 'to be a charge' [HNTC], 'to become burdensome' [WBC], 'to depend on' [SSA].

3:9 **Not because/that[a] we-do-not-have (the) right,[b]**
LEXICON—a. ὅτι (LN 89.33; 90.21): 'because' [Hn, ICC, SSA, WBC; all versions except NAB], 'that' [BAGD, Lns; NAB], not explicit [HNTC].
  b. ἐξουσία (LN 37.35): 'right' [BAGD, Hn, HNTC, ICC, SSA, WBC; NASB, NEB, NIV, NJB, RSV, TEV, TNT], 'authority' [BAGD, Lns], 'right to control' [LN], 'authority to rule' [LN], 'power' [BAGD; KJV], 'claim' [NAB].
QUESTION—What relationship is indicated by ὅτι 'because'?
  1. This indicates the reason for their actions in the preceding verse [Hb, Hn, NCBC, SSA]: we acted like that, not because we did not have the right to do so, but because we wanted to give you an example to imitate.
  2. This indicates a parenthetical explanation [BAGD, Ea, El, Fn, HNTC, Lns, Mn, My, Rb]: (it is not that we did not have the right to do so, but we

worked in order to give you an example). This qualifies the previous statement to prevent it being misunderstood and misapplied [Ea, El, Mn, My, Rb].

QUESTION—What right is implied?

It is the right to be a burden on them for food or support [Ea, EBC, EGT, El, Er, Fn, Hb, HNTC, ICC, Mn, SSA, TH; NASB, NEB, NIV, NJB, RSV, TEV, TNT], or the right not to work [Ea, NCBC].

but in-order-that[a] we-ourselves might-give an-example[b] to-you in-order-that (you) imitate[c] us.

LEXICON—a. ἵνα (LN 89.59): 'in order that' [Hn, SSA], 'in order to' [Lns; NASB, NIV, NJB], 'to' [HNTC; KJV, NEB, RSV, TEV], 'that' [ICC; NAB], 'so that' [TNT], 'our purpose was' [WBC].

b. τύπος (LN 58.59): 'example' [BAGD, Hn, HNTC, ICC, LN, Lns, SSA, WBC; KJV, NAB, NEB, RSV, TEV], 'model' [BAGD, LN; NASB, NIV, NJB], 'pattern' [BAGD; TNT].

c. pres. mid. (deponent = active) infin. of μιμέομαι (LN 41.44): 'to imitate' [BAGD, Hn, HNTC, ICC, LN, Lns; NAB, NEB, NJB, RSV], 'to follow' [BAGD; KJV, NIV, TEV], 'to follow one's example' [NASB], '(pattern) of behavior' [TNT], 'to behave like' [SSA], 'to do as others do' [LN]. This verb is also translated by the phrase 'to present for imitation' [WBC]. See this word at 3:7.

3:10 Because[a] even/also/and[b] when we-were with you,

LEXICON—a. γάρ (LN 89.23; 91.1): 'because', 'since' [SSA], 'for' [Hn, HNTC, ICC; KJV, NASB, NEB, NIV, RSV], 'indeed' [Lns], not explicit [WBC; NAB, NJB, TEV, TNT].

b. καί (LN 91.12; 89.93; 89.92): 'even' [KJV, NASB, NEB, NIV, RSV], 'indeed' [WBC; NAB, TNT], 'also' [Hn, HNTC, ICC], 'and' [Lns], not explicit [SSA; NJB, TEV].

QUESTION—What relationship is indicated by γάρ 'for'?

This indicates another grounds for the previous command (3:6) [Alf, Ea, El, Fn, Hb, Hn, HNTC, ICC, My, NCBC, SSA]: this we command you *since* this is what we already commanded you when we were with you.

QUESTION—What relationship is indicated by καί 'indeed/also/and'?

1. This is ascensive [Alf, Ea, My, WBC; all versions]: *even/indeed* while we were with you, we gave you the following command.
2. This adds to a previous verse [Alf, Lns, NIC]: not only did we set you an example, we *also* gave you the following command.
3. This adds a second grounds, coordinate with the γάρ in 3:7 [El, Hb, Hn, HNTC, ICC, NCBC]: we command you since you know how you should imitate us, *and also* since we gave the following command.

this we-commanded[a] you,

LEXICON—a. imperf. act. indic. of παραγγέλλω (LN 33.327): 'to command' [BAGD, Hn, ICC, LN, Lns, SSA; KJV], 'to give a command' [RSV], 'to give an order' [BAGD; NASB, TNT], 'to order' [LN], 'to lay down a rule' [NAB, NEB], 'to give a rule' [NIV], 'to give a charge' [WBC], 'to urge' [NJB], 'to instruct' [BAGD, HNTC], 'to tell' [TEV]. The imperfect tense indicates that he commanded them a number of times when he was with them [Ea, Hb, Hn, HNTC, ICC, Lns, NCBC, NIC, SSA, TH; NAB, NASB, TEV].

that if anyone does not want[a] to-work,[b] neither let-him-eat.[c]
LEXICON—a. pres. act. indic. of θέλω (LN 25.1): 'to want' [Hn, LN, Lns], 'would' [KJV, NAB], 'to be willing' [BAGD, HNTC; NASB, NEB, NIV, RSV, TNT]. This verb is also united with the negative: 'to refuse' [ICC, SSA, WBC; NJB, TEV]. The present tense indicates a continuous attitude [NIC].
  b. pres. mid. (deponent = active) infin. of ἐργάζομαι (LN 42.41): 'to work' [BAGD, Hn, HNTC, ICC, LN, Lns, SSA, WBC; all versions], 'to labor' [LN]. See this word at 3:8.
  c. pres. act. impera. of ἐσθίω (LN 23.1): 'to eat' [Hn, HNTC, ICC, LN, Lns, WBC; all versions]. This verb is also translated to show their responsibility: 'you should not feed/support him' [SSA].

3:11 Because[a]
LEXICON—a. γάρ (LN 89.23): 'because', 'since', 'for' [Hn, HNTC, ICC, Lns, WBC; KJV, NASB, RSV], 'because' [NEB, TEV], 'now' [NJB], not explicit [SSA; NAB, NIV, TNT].
QUESTION—What relationship is indicated by this conjunction?
  1. This indicates the third grounds (following the grounds found in 3:7 and 3:10) for the command given in 3:6 [EGT, Er, ICC, SSA]: we command you to avoid those who live idly/disorderly...*since* we hear that some are living idly/disorderly.
  2. This indicates the grounds for mentioning the command in 3:10 [Alf, Ea, EBC, El, My]: we commanded you, 'If any one does not want to work, let him not eat', *since* we hear that some are living idly.
  3. This explains why this subject is discussed [Hb, Hn, Lns, NCBC, TH]: we are concerned about this matter of idleness/disorderliness *since* we hear that some are living idly/disorderly.

we-hear[a] (that) some (are) walking[b] among[c] you idly/disorderly,[d]
LEXICON—a. pres. act. indic. of ἀκούω (LN 33.212): 'to hear' [Hn, HNTC, LN, Lns, WBC; all versions], 'to be informed' [ICC, SSA], 'to receive news' [LN]. The present tense may indicate that they keep hearing reports about this [Hb, ICC, Lns, NIC, SSA], or it may simply be an equivalent of the aorist tense, 'we heard' [HNTC] or of the perfect tense 'we have heard' [EBC, ICC, Mn, NCBC, NIC, SSA].
  b. pres. act. participle of περιπατέω (LN 41.11): 'to walk' [BAGD, ICC, Lns; KJV], 'to be' [NAB, NEB, NIV], 'to lead a life' [NASB], 'to live' [BAGD, LN; RSV, TNT], 'to live a life' [NJB, TEV], 'to conduct oneself'

252   2 THESSALONIANS 3:11

[BAGD, Hn, WBC], 'to behave' [HNTC, LN, SSA]. The present tense points to their habitual conduct [Hb, HNTC] and it was going on at the time of the report [El, Hb]. See this word at 3:6.

c. ἐν (LN 83.9): 'among' [Hn, HNTC, ICC, Lns, WBC; KJV, NASB, NIV, TEV], '(some) of (you)' [SSA; NAB, NEB, NJB, RSV, TNT].

d. ἀτάκτως (LN 88.247): 'idly', 'in idleness' [BAGD, ICC; RSV, TNT], 'lazily' [LN], 'lazy' [TEV], 'as loafers' [HNTC]; or 'disorderly' [Lns; KJV], 'in a disorderly manner' [BAGD, Hn, SSA, WBC], 'unruly' [NAB], 'undisciplined' [NASB], 'without any discipline' [NJB]. The phrase 'walk idly' is translated 'to idle one's time away' [NEB], 'to be idle' [NIV]. See this word at 3:6.

QUESTION—With what is ἐν ὑμῖν 'among you' connected?
  1. It is connected with 'some' and identifies the people walking in this manner: [Hn, HNTC, ICC, NCBC, SSA; all versions except KJV]: some among you are walking idly/disorderly.
  2. It is connected with the verb and indicates where they are so walking [Hb, Lns, WBC; KJV]: some are walking idly/disorderly among you.

QUESTION—What is implied by saying that these people were 'among you'?
  The whole group is addressed, including those who are misbehaving [TH]. It may imply that those who are idle were not really a part of the church [Hb].

nothing[a] working[b] but working-around;[c]

LEXICON—a. μηδείς (LN 92.23): 'nothing' [BAGD, LN; TEV], 'not' [Hn, ICC, SSA, WBC; NAB, NIV, TNT], 'not any' [RSV], 'no' [HNTC; NJB], 'not at all' [Lns; KJV, NASB], not explicit [NEB].

b. pres. mid. (deponent = active) participle of ἐργάζομαι (LN 42.41): 'to work' [BAGD, ICC, LN, Lns, SSA; KJV, TNT], 'to do work' [BAGD, HNTC; NASB, NJB, RSV], 'to labor' [LN], 'to do' [TEV], 'to be busy' [NIV], 'to keep busy' [NAB], 'to be busy workers' [Hn], 'to mind one's business' [NEB], 'to attend to one's own business' [WBC]. The present tense implies working steadily [EBC]. See this word at 3:8, 10.

c. pres. mid. (deponent = active) participle of περιεργάζομαι (LN 88.243): 'to work around', 'to be busybodies' [BAGD, Hn, HNTC, ICC; KJV, NIV, RSV, TNT], 'to act like busybodies' [Lns; NAB, NASB], 'to mind everybody's business' [NEB], 'to interfere with other people's work' [NJB], 'to interfere with what other people are doing' [SSA], 'to meddle in other people's business' [LN; TEV], 'to attend to other people's business' [WBC].

QUESTION—How are the two verbs connected?
  There is a play on words between ἐργαζομένους 'working' and περιεργαζομένους 'working around' [Ea, El, Er, Fn, Hb, Hn, HNTC, ICC, Lns, Mn, My, NCBC, NIC, Rb, SSA, TH, WBC].

3:12 now[a] to-such we-command[b] and exhort[c] in[d] (the) Lord Jesus Christ

TEXT—Instead of ἐν 'in (the Lord Jesus)', some manuscripts have διά 'by'. GNT does not indicate this alternative. Only KJV selects 'by'.

LEXICON—a. δέ (LN 89.94): 'now' [Hn, ICC, Lns; KJV, NASB, RSV], not explicit [HNTC, SSA, WBC; NAB, NEB, NIV, NJB, TEV, TNT].
  b. pres. act. indic. of παραγγέλλω (LN 33.327): 'to command' [BAGD, Hn, ICC, LN, Lns, SSA; KJV, NASB, NIV, RSV, TEV], 'to enjoin' [NAB], 'to order' [LN; TNT], 'to give orders' [BAGD; NEB], 'to charge' [WBC], 'to instruct' [BAGD, HNTC], 'to urge' [NJB]. See this word at 3:4, 6, 10.
  c. pres. act. indic. of παρακαλέω (LN 25.150; 33.168): 'to exhort' [BAGD, ICC, WBC; KJV, NASB, RSV], 'to urge' [BAGD, Hn, SSA; NIV], 'to urge strongly' [NAB], 'to appeal' [BAGD, LN; NEB], 'to request' [HNTC, LN], 'to call on' [NJB], 'to require' [TNT], 'to admonish' [Lns], 'to warn' [TEV], 'to encourage' [LN].
  d. ἐν (LN 89.119): 'in' [Hn, HNTC, Lns, SSA, WBC; NAB, NASB, NIV, NJB, RSV], 'in the name of' [NEB, TEV, TNT], 'prompted by' [ICC].
QUESTION—Why do the verbs παραγγέλλομεν 'we command' and παρακαλοῦμεν 'we exhort' occur together?
  This combination adds emphasis to the command [Ea, SSA, WBC]. Although a command, it is, at the same time, a brotherly exhortation [Hb, Hn, Rb] which adds earnestness to the command [Ea]. Some commentators think that it softens the command [Fn, ICC, NIC, TH], but another denies that it does [Lns].
QUESTION—What relationship is indicated by ἐν 'in'?
  1. This indicates the authority with which they gave the command [ICC, WBC]: we command you with the authority Jesus Christ gives us.
  2. This indicates a close spiritual union [EBC, Hb, Hn, HNTC, NIC, SSA]: we command you on the basis of our union with Jesus Christ. It may refer to the writers' union with the Lord [Hb, Hn], or their mutual relation with the Lord [EBC, HNTC, NIC].

that[a] working[b] with quietness[c] they-may-eat[d] their-own bread.[e]
LEXICON—a. ἵνα (LN 90.22): 'that' [Hn, ICC, Lns, SSA; KJV], 'to' [HNTC, WBC; all versions except KJV].
  b. pres. mid. (deponent = active) participle of ἐργάζομαι (LN 42.41): 'to work' [BAGD, HNTC, ICC, LN, Lns, SSA, WBC; KJV, NAB, NASB, NEB, NJB, TEV], 'to do one's work' [RSV], 'to get on with one's work' [TNT], 'to work for a living' [Hn], 'to labor' [LN], 'to earn' [NIV]. The present tense implies working steadily [EBC, Hb]. See this word at 3:8, 10.
  c. ἡσυχία (LN **88.103; 22.43**): 'quietness' [BAGD, Lns; KJV, RSV], 'tranquility of mind' [ICC]. The phrase 'with quietness' is translated 'quietly' [Hn, HNTC, WBC; NAB, NEB, NJB, TNT], 'in quiet fashion' [NASB], 'to lead orderly lives' [TEV], 'to live quiet lives' [LN], 'to live calmly' [LN], 'to settle down' [SSA; NIV]. See the cognate verb at 1 Thess. 4:11.
  d. pres. act. subj. of ἐσθίω (LN 23.1; **57.190**): 'to eat' [BAGD, Hn, Lns, WBC; KJV, NASB, NIV]. The phrase 'to eat bread' is translated 'to earn

the food they eat' [NAB, NJB], 'to earn their living' [ICC, LN; RSV, TEV, TNT], 'to earn one's keep' [HNTC], 'for their living' [NEB, RSV], 'to support oneself' [SSA]. See this word at 3:8.
- e. ἄρτος (LN 5.1): 'bread' [BAGD, Hn, Lns, WBC; KJV, NASB, NIV], 'food' [LN]. See this word at 3:8.

QUESTION—What relationship is indicated by the participle ἐργαζόμενοι 'working'?

This indicates the means by which they will eat their own bread [Hb, Hn, SSA]: support yourselves *by* working in a quiet manner.

QUESTION—What is the meaning of working μετὰ ἡσυχίας 'with quietness'?
1. This refers to a calm state of mind while working [Alf, Hb, ICC, NIC]: work with a calm mind.
2. This refers to a quiet manner of carrying out their work [El, Hn, HNTC, Lns, Mn, NCBC, WBC; NASB, NIV, TEV]: work in a quiet manner.
3. This involves both their minds and their activity [Ea, My].

DISCOURSE UNIT: 3:13–15 [Hb, Mn]. The topic is exhortations.

3:13 Now/But^a you, brothers,

LEXICON—a. δέ (LN 89.94; 89.124): 'now' [ICC], 'and' [NIV]; or 'but' [Hn, HNTC, Lns, WBC; KJV, NASB, NEB, TEV]; not explicit [NAB, NJB, RSV, TNT].

QUESTION—What relationship is indicated by δέ 'now/but'?
1. This indicates transition to another topic [ICC; NIV]: now.
2. This indicates contrast [Alf, Ea, EGT, El, Er, Fn, Hb, Hn, HNTC, Lns, Mn, NCBC, NIC, Rb, WBC; KJV, NASB, NEB, TEV]: but. The contrast is between the idlers in the preceding paragraph and the Christians now being addressed [Alf, Ea, Er, Hb, Hn, HNTC, NCBC, NIC].

do-not be-weary^a doing-good.^b

LEXICON—a. aorist act. subj. of ἐγκακέω (LN **25.288**): 'to become weary' [BAGD, Hn; KJV, RSV], 'to grow weary' [NAB, NASB], 'to tire' [NEB, NIV], 'to become tired' [BAGD; TEV], 'to grow tired' [ICC], 'to be slack' [HNTC], 'to slacken' [NJB], 'to lose heart' [TNT], 'to become discouraged' [LN, Lns, SSA], 'to give up' [WBC].
- b. pres. act. participle of καλοποιέω (LN **88.5**): 'to do good' [BAGD, LN, WBC; NASB, TEV], 'to do right' [NEB], 'to do what is right' [BAGD, ICC, SSA; NAB, NIV, NJB, TNT], 'in well-doing' [Hn, Lns; KJV, RSV], 'to help' [HNTC].

DISCOURSE UNIT: 3:14–15 [NIC, SSA, WBC]. The topic is relationships with disobedient brothers [SSA], discipline [WBC].

3:14 And^a if anyone does-not obey^b the our word^c through^d the letter,

LEXICON—a. δέ (LN 89.94; 89.124): 'and' [KJV, NASB], 'now' [Hn, HNTC], 'however' [ICC], 'yet' [Lns], 'but' [WBC], not explicit [SSA; all versions except KJV, NASB].

b. pres. act. indic. of ὑπακούω (LN 36.15): 'to obey' [BAGD, Hn, HNTC, ICC, LN, Lns, SSA; all versions except NEB]. The negative 'not to obey' is also translated positively: 'to disobey' [WBC; NEB].
c. λόγος (LN 33.98): 'word' [BAGD, Hn, ICC, LN, Lns, WBC; KJV], 'instruction(s)' [BAGD; NASB, NEB, NIV, TNT], 'injunction' [NAB], 'command' [HNTC], 'message' [TEV], 'what I/we have written' [SSA; NJB], 'what we say' [RSV].
d. διά (LN 90.8; 89.76): 'through', 'by' [KJV], 'conveyed by' [El, Fn, WBC], 'given by' [NEB], 'by means of' [Lns], 'in' [HNTC, SSA; NASB, NIV, NJB, RSV], 'sent in' [TEV], 'given in' [TNT], 'expressed in' [Hn, ICC], 'delivered through' [NAB].

QUESTION—What is implied by τις 'anyone'?
This implies 'any brother among you' [SSA]. The implication is even more specific: 'any brother who will not work' (3:12) [ICC, SSA], or who is disorderly/idle [Hn]. It implies that there may be a few such people [HNTC, ICC].

note[a] this-man, not to associate-with[b] him,

LEXICON—a. pres. mid. impera. of σημειόομαι (LN 29.3): 'to note' [Hn; KJV, RSV], 'to take note of' [HNTC, LN, WBC; NJB, TEV, TNT], 'to take special notice' [BAGD; NASB, NIV], 'to single out' [NAB], 'to publicly identify' [SSA], 'to designate' [ICC], 'to mark' [BAGD, Lns], 'to mark well' [NEB]. The middle voice implies 'note for one's self' [Ea, Fn, Hb, Lns, Mn].
b. pres. mid. (deponent = active) infin. of συναναμίγνυμι (LN 34.1): 'to associate with' [BAGD, HNTC, LN, Lns, SSA, WBC; NASB, NIV], 'to be in the company of' [LN], 'to have company with' [KJV], 'to have dealings with' [NEB], 'to get mixed up with' [Hn], 'to be in intimate association with' [ICC]. The negative 'not to associate with' is also translated positively: 'to be ostracized' [NAB], 'to have nothing to do with' [NJB, RSV, TEV, TNT].

QUESTION—In what way would they note or mark the person?
They would make him known to the congregation [Fn, Hb, Hn, ICC, SSA], perhaps by a public announcement [Fn, ICC, Rb, SSA] or in writing [ICC, Rb]. Or, they would mark that person by avoiding him [El].

in-order-that[a] he-may-be-ashamed;[b]

LEXICON—a. ἵνα (LN 89.59): 'in order that' [Hn, ICC, Lns, SSA, WBC; NIV], 'so that' [HNTC; NASB, NJB, TEV], 'that' [KJV, NAB, RSV], 'until' [NEB], not explicit [TNT].
b. aorist pass. subj. of ἐντρέπω (LN 25.196): 'to become ashamed' [BAGD, Hn, HNTC, LN, Lns, SSA, WBC; KJV, NAB, RSV, TEV], 'to feel ashamed' [NIV], 'to be ashamed of oneself' [NEB, NJB, TNT], 'to be put to shame' [BAGD, ICC; NASB].

QUESTION—What relationship is indicated by ἵνα 'in order that'?
This indicates the purpose of not associating with the disobedient brother [Hb, Hn, HNTC, ICC, Lns, Mn, SSA]: do not associate with him *in order that* he will become ashamed of himself.

3:15 and/but[a] do-not consider[b] as[c] an-enemy,[d]

LEXICON—a. καί (LN 89.92; 91.12): 'and' [Hn, Lns, WBC], 'and so' [ICC]; or 'and yet' [NASB], 'yet' [KJV, NIV], 'but' [NAB, TEV], 'however' [HNTC], 'I do not mean' [NEB, TNT], 'though' [NJB]; not explicit [SSA; RSV].
- b. pres. mid. impera. of ἡγέομαι (LN 31.1): 'to consider' [BAGD, Hn, LN, Lns], 'to count' [ICC, WBC; KJV], 'to treat' [HNTC; NAB, NEB, NJB, TEV, TNT], 'to regard' [BAGD, LN, SSA; NASB, NIV], 'to look on' [RSV]. This verb is in an emphatic position [ICC].
- c. ὡς (LN 64.12): 'as' [HNTC, ICC, WBC; all versions except NAB], 'like' [SSA; NAB], not explicit [Hn, Lns].
- d. ἐχθρός (LN 39.11): 'enemy' [BAGD, Hn, HNTC, ICC, LN, Lns, SSA, WBC; all versions].

QUESTION—What relationship is indicated by καί 'and/but'?
1. This indicates the addition of another instruction [Ea, El, Fn, Hb, Lns, Mn, NIC, WBC]: do not associate with him so that he will be ashamed, *and* consider him not as an enemy but as a brother.
2. This indicates contra-expectation [HNTC, My, TH; KJV, NAB, NASB, NEB, NIV, TEV, TNT]: do not associate with him, *but nevertheless* do not consider him to be an enemy.

but warn[a] as[b] a-brother.

LEXICON—a. pres. act. impera. of νουθετέω (LN 33.424; 33.418): 'to warn' [BAGD, ICC, LN, SSA; NIV, RSV, TEV, TNT], 'to admonish' [BAGD, Hn, HNTC, WBC; KJV, NASB], 'to remonstrate with' [Lns], 'to correct' [NAB, NJB], 'to give friendly advice' [NEB].
- b. ὡς (LN 64.12): 'as' [Hn, HNTC, ICC, Lns, WBC; all versions except NAB], 'as you would' [NAB], 'like' [SSA].

DISCOURSE UNIT: 3:16–18 [EBC, Er, Fn, GNT, Hb, Hn, HNTC, NIC, TH; NAB, NIV, NJB, TEV]. The topic is the conclusion [EBC, Er, Fn, Hb, Lns, NIC], final words [TEV], the benediction [GNT], final prayer and benediction [HNTC; NJB], final greetings [NIV], final blessing and greeting [NAB].

DISCOURSE UNIT: 3:16 [EBC, Hb, ICC, Mn, My, SSA, WBC]. The topic is prayer [ICC, Mn, WBC]. SSA includes the last sentence with the following division.

3:16 Now/But[a] himself[b] the Lord of-the peace[c]

LEXICON—a. δέ (LN 89.94; 89.124): 'now' [Hn, HNTC, ICC, Lns, WBC; KJV, NASB, NIV, RSV], not explicit [SSA; NAB, NEB, NJB, TEV, TNT].

b. αὐτός (LN 92.37; 92.11): 'himself' [HNTC, ICC, SSA, WBC; all versions except NAB], 'he (who is)' [Hn, Lns; NAB]. This word is intensive and emphatic [Hb, NIC]. It adds dignity to the name [El].

c. εἰρήνη (LN 22.42; 25.248): 'peace' [BAGD, Hn, HNTC, ICC, LN, Lns, SSA, WBC; all versions]. See this word in the phrase 'the God of peace' in 1 Thess. 5:23.

QUESTION—What relationship is indicated by δέ 'now/but'?
1. It indicates transition to a new topic [Hn, HNTC, ICC, Lns, WBC; KJV, NASB, NIV, RSV]: now.
2. It indicates contrast between the commands and prayer [Ea, EBC, El]: but.

QUESTION—How are the nouns related in the genitive construction ὁ κύριος τῆς εἰρήνης 'the Lord of peace'?
1. The Lord is the source of peace [Hb, Hn, Mn, My, SSA, TH, Wd; TEV]: the Lord who gives peace.
2. Peace is an attribute of the Lord [Rb]: the Lord who is characterized by peace.

QUESTION—To whom does 'the Lord' here and in the last sentence refer?
'Lord' refers to the Lord Jesus Christ [Alf, Ea, EGT, Er, Fn, Hb, Hn, HNTC, ICC, Lns, Mn, My, NCBC, NIC, Rb, SSA, WBC].

may-he-give[a] to-you the peace[b] through all[c] in every way.[d]

LEXICON—a. aorist act. optative of δίδωμι (LN 90.90): 'to give' [BAGD, Hn, HNTC, ICC, Lns, SSA, WBC; all versions except TNT], 'to cause' [LN], 'to keep in (his peace)' [TNT].

b. εἰρήνη (LN 22.42; 25.248): 'peace' [BAGD, Hn, HNTC, ICC, LN, Lns, SSA, WBC; all versions].

c. πᾶς (LN 67.86; 67.15): 'all'. The phrase διὰ παντός 'through all' is translated: 'at all times' [Hn, Lns; NEB, NIV, NJB, RSV, TEV], 'all the time' [HNTC], 'at every time' [WBC], 'always' [SSA; KJV], 'continually' [ICC; NASB], '(give) continued (peace)' [NAB]. This phrase is also combined with the following phrase: 'whatever befalls' [TNT].

d. τρόπος (LN 89.83): 'way' [LN], 'manner' [LN]. The phrase ἐν παντὶ τρόπῳ 'in every way' is translated 'in every way' [BAGD, WBC; NIV, NJB, TEV], 'in all ways' [Hn, Lns; NEB, RSV], 'in every circumstance' [HNTC, ICC; NASB], 'in every situation' [SSA], 'in every possible way' [NAB], 'by all means' [KJV].

QUESTION—What is the significance of the article in the phrase τῆς εἰρήνης 'the peace'?

The article refers to the reference to peace in the preceding phrase [Lns]. It means *his* peace [Lns, WBC]. It means the well-known peace which comes from Christ [Hb].

The Lord (be) with^a all of-you.

LEXICON—a. μετά (LN 89.108): 'with' [Lns]. This is also translated with the implied verb: 'be with' [Hn, HNTC, ICC, WBC; all versions], 'to continue to be present with' [SSA].

QUESTION—In what way does he want the Lord to be with them?

This means that he wants the Lord to be present with them [Er, NIC, SSA], and since the Lord already is present, it is implied that he asks that the Lord will continue to be present with them [SSA]. Other commentators think that this indicates the means by which the preceding prayer for peace will be accomplished [Hb, Lns, NIC]: may the Lord give you peace by being present with you. The Lord's presence implies the influence, guidance, and power that is brought by his presence [Ea]. The realization of the Lord's promised presence should cause the believers to yield to the Lord's will so that his peace will be shown in their lives [Er].

DISCOURSE UNIT: 3:17–18 [Alf, EBC, EGT, Mn, My, NCBC, WBC, Wd]. The topic is the closing of the letter.

DISCOURSE UNIT: 3:17 [Hb, ICC]. The topic is the final greeting.

3:17 **(Here is) the greeting^a by-my hand^b of-Paul,**

LEXICON—a. ἀσπασμός (LN 33.20): 'greeting' [BAGD, Hn, HNTC, ICC, LN, WBC; NAB, NASB, NEB, NIV, NJB, RSV], 'greetings' [TEV, TNT], 'salutation' [Lns; KJV]. This noun is also translated as a verb: 'to greet' [SSA].

b. χείρ (LN 8.30): 'hand' [BAGD, Hn, HNTC, ICC, LN, Lns, WBC; all versions except TNT], 'handwriting' [BAGD; TNT]. This is also translated with a phrase: 'I am writing myself' [SSA].

QUESTION—What is implied by the reference to his hand?

This implies that up to this point the letter was dictated to someone else who did the writing [Alf, Ea, EBC, EGT, Er, Fn, Hb, Hn, HNTC, Lns, My, NCBC, NIC, Rb, WBC, Wd].

which is a-sign^a in every letter:

LEXICON—a. σημεῖον (LN 33.477): 'sign' [BAGD, HNTC, LN, Lns], 'mark' [RSV], 'distinguishing mark' [BAGD; NASB, NIV], 'mark of genuineness' [BAGD; NJB], 'token' [BAGD, WBC; KJV], 'token of genuineness' [Hn, ICC], 'signature' [NAB, TNT], 'the way I sign' [TEV]. This is also translated as a verbal phrase: 'this authenticates' [NEB], 'that you may know' [SSA].

QUESTION—What is the fact that he wrote the greeting personally a sign of?

It is a sign that the letter is really from Paul [Ea, El, Hb, Hn, HNTC, ICC, NCBC, NIC, Rb, SSA, WBC, Wd; NEB, NJB].

QUESTION—Why did he need a sign

There was the danger of receiving a letter falsely claiming to be from him (2:2) [Alf, Ea, EBC, Hb, Hn, Lns, Mn, NIC, SSA, WBC]. The unruly would not be able to assert that this letter was not from Paul [Hn, ICC].

thus^a I-write.^b

LEXICON—a. οὕτως (LN 61.10; 61.9): 'thus', 'so' [Hn, Lns; KJV], 'this/it is the way' [HNTC, ICC, SSA; NASB, RSV], 'this is how' [WBC; NEB, NIV, TEV], 'this is' [NJB], 'according to (my usual practice)' [TNT], not explicit [NAB].

    b. pres. act. indic. of γράφω (LN 33.61): 'to write' [BAGD, Hn, HNTC, ICC, LN, Lns, SSA, WBC; all versions except NJB], 'writing' [NJB].

QUESTION—What does οὕτως 'thus' refer to?

This adds a comment about his style of handwriting [Ea, Hb, HNTC, ICC, Mn, My, NIC, SSA]. Some commentators think that his handwriting is assumed to be known [ICC, NCBC, NIC]. Others think that his handwriting was not known and this informs them of its appearance [My].

DISCOURSE UNIT: 3:18 [Hb, ICC]. The topic is blessing.

3:18 The grace^a of-the Lord of-us Jesus Christ (be) with^b all of-you.

TEXT—Some manuscripts end this verse with ἀμήν 'amen'. GNT omits this word with a C rating, indicating a considerable degree of doubt in doing so. It is included only by KJV.

LEXICON—a. χάρις (LN 88.66): 'grace' [BAGD, Hn, HNTC, ICC, LN, Lns, WBC; all versions]. This noun is also translated as a verb: 'to act graciously' [SSA]. See this word at 1 Thess. 5:28.

    b. μετά (LN 90.60): 'with' [Lns]. This is also translated with the implied verb: 'be with' [Hn, HNTC, ICC, Lns, WBC; all versions].

www.ingramcontent.com/pod-product-compliance
Lightning Source LLC
Chambersburg PA
CBHW070246230426
43664CB00014B/2414